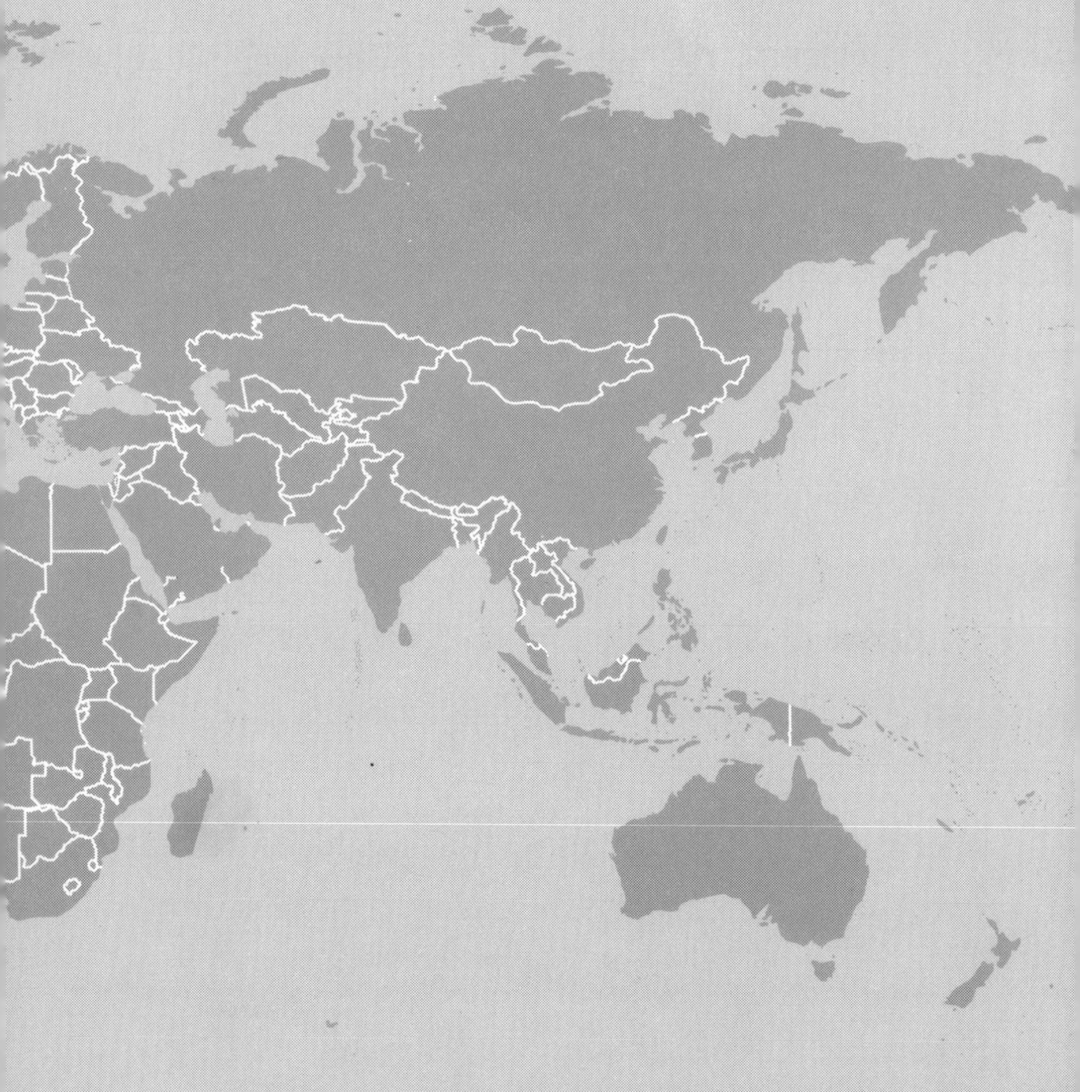

Mexico
a country study

Federal Research Division
Library of Congress
Edited by
Tim L. Merrill and
Ramón Miró
Research Completed
June 1996

On the cover: A giant stone warrior from the Toltec temple of Tlahuizcalpantecuhtli in Tula

Fourth Edition, First Printing, 1997.

Library of Congress Cataloging-in-Publication Data

Mexico : a country study / Federal Research Division, Library of Congress ; edited by Tim L. Merrill and Ramón Miró. — 4th ed.

    p. cm. — (Area handbook series, ISSN 1057–5294) (DA Pam ; 550–79)

    "Supersedes the 1985 edition of Mexico : a country study, edited by James D. Rudolph."—T.p. verso.

    "Research completed June 1996."

    Includes bibliographical references (pp. 353–381) and index.

    ISBN 0–8444-0855–7 (hardcover : alk. paper)

    1. Mexico. I. Merrill, Tim, 1949– . II. Miró, Ramón, 1968– . III. Library of Congress. Federal Research Division. IV. Series. V. Series: DA Pam ; 550–79.

F1208.M5828 1997   97–13481

972—DC21   CIP

Headquarters, Department of the Army
DA Pam 550–79

For sale by the Superintendent of Documents, U.S. Government Printing Office
Washington, D.C. 20402

Foreword

This volume is one in a continuing series of books prepared by the Federal Research Division of the Library of Congress under the Country Studies/Area Handbook Program sponsored by the Department of the Army. The last two pages of this book list the other published studies.

Most books in the series deal with a particular foreign country, describing and analyzing its political, economic, social, and national security systems and institutions, and examining the interrelationships of those systems and the ways they are shaped by historical and cultural factors. Each study is written by a multidisciplinary team of social scientists. The authors seek to provide a basic understanding of the observed society, striving for a dynamic rather than a static portrayal. Particular attention is devoted to the people who make up the society, their origins, dominant beliefs and values, their common interests and the issues on which they are divided, the nature and extent of their involvement with national institutions, and their attitudes toward each other and toward their social system and political order.

The books represent the analysis of the authors and should not be construed as an expression of an official United States government position, policy, or decision. The authors have sought to adhere to accepted standards of scholarly objectivity. Corrections, additions, and suggestions for changes from readers will be welcomed for use in future editions.

Louis R. Mortimer
Chief
Federal Research Division
Library of Congress
Washington, DC 20540–4840

Acknowledgments

The authors would like to acknowledge the contributions of Elizabeth de Lima-Dantas, Robert S. North, Jorge P. Osterling, Craig H. Robinson, and Phyllis Greene Walker, who wrote the 1985 edition of *Mexico: A Country Study*. The present volume incorporates portions of their work.

The authors are grateful to individuals in various government agencies and private institutions who gave of their time, research materials, and expertise in the production of this book. None of these individuals is, however, in any way responsible for the work of the authors.

The authors also would like to thank those people on the staff of the Federal Research Division who contributed directly to the preparation of the manuscript. They include Sandra W. Meditz, who reviewed drafts, provided valuable advice on all aspects of production, and conducted liaison with the sponsoring agency; Marilyn L. Majeska, who managed editing and production; Andrea T. Merrill, who edited figures and tables; Janie L. Gilchrist and Izella Watson, who did word processing and initial typesetting; and Stephen C. Cranton and Janie L. Gilchrist, who prepared the camera-ready copy. In addition, thanks go to Christopher R. Conte and Ayo I. Mseka, who edited chapters; Beverly Wolpert, who performed the final prepublication editorial review; and Sandi Schroeder, who compiled the index.

Thanks also go to David P. Cabitto of the Federal Research Division, who provided valuable graphics support and prepared the maps with the assistance of Maryland Mapping and Graphics. Special thanks go to Wayne Horne, who designed the cover, and to Gustavo Mendoza, who designed the illustrations for each title page. Finally, the authors acknowledge the generosity of the individuals and the public and private agencies who allowed their photographs to be used in this study.

Contents

Richard Haggerty

List of Figures

Preface

Like its predecessor, this study is an attempt to examine objectively and concisely the dominant historical, social, economic, political, and military aspects of contemporary Mexico. Sources of information included scholarly books, journals, monographs, official reports of governments and international organizations, and numerous periodicals. Chapter bibliographies appear at the end of the book; brief comments on sources recommended for further reading appear at the end of each chapter. To the extent possible, place-names follow the system adopted by the United States Board on Geographic Names. Measurements are given in the metric system; a conversion table is provided to assist readers unfamiliar with metric measurements (see table 1, Appendix A). A glossary is also included.

Although there are numerous variations, Spanish surnames for men and unmarried women usually consist of two parts: the patrilineal name followed by the matrilineal. In the instance of Luis Echeverría Álvarez, for example, Echeverría is his father's name; Álvarez, his mother's maiden name. In informal use, the matrilineal name is often dropped. When a woman marries, she generally drops her matrilineal name and replaces it with her husband's patrilineal name preceded by a "de." Thus, when Cristina García Rodríguez marries Antonio Pérez Cevallos, she becomes Cristina García de Pérez. In informal use, a married woman's patrilineal name is dropped (Cristina Pérez is the informal usage). Some individuals use only the patrilineal name in formal as well as informal use. The patrilineal for men and unmarried women and the husband's patrilineal for married women are used for indexing and bibliographic purposes.

The body of the text reflects information available as of May 1996. Certain other portions of the text, however, have been updated. The Introduction discusses significant events that have occurred since the completion of research; the Country Profile and Glossary include updated information as available; several figures and tables are based on information in more recently published sources; and the Bibliography lists recent sources thought to be particularly helpful to the reader.

Table A. Chronology of Important Events

Period	Description
PRE-COLUMBIAN	
ca. 10,000 B.C.	First hunters and gatherers reach area of present-day Mexico.
ca. 1500 B.C.	Villages appear, and inhabitants produce clay products.
ca. 200 B.C.–A.D. 100	Monte Albán civilization in southern Mexico.
ca. A.D. 1–650	Teotihuacán civilization in central Mexico.
ca. A.D. 600–900	Classic Mayan civilization in the Yucatan peninsula.
early 1300s	Aztec arrive in the Valley of Mexico.
1376	First Aztec king crowned.
1502–20	Reign of Moctezuma II (Montezuma).
COLONIAL	
1519–21	Hernán Cortés and about 700 men conquer the Aztec Empire.
early sixteenth century	Colonial administration established. European settlers pour into colony seeking wealth. Native population decimated by disease and harsh labor practices.
late sixteenth century	Ranching and industry grow, and mining expands.
seventeenth century	Colony stagnates. Society becomes stratified along racial and social lines.
eighteenth century	Reforms by new Bourbon monarchs in Spain revitalize colony. Immigration increases, and economy and trade expand.
late eighteenth century	Pressure for independence builds, especially among criollos.
1808–13	French occupation of Spain throws colonies into political turmoil.
1810	Grito de Dolores (Cry of Dolores)—Miguel Hidalgo y Costilla's call for independence—on September 16.
1811	Hidalgo executed. Independence movement led by José María Morelos y Pavón.
1815–20	Morelos executed. Independence movement degenerates into sporadic guerrilla fighting. Vicente Guerrero most important guerrilla leader.
EARLY INDEPENDENCE	
1821	Colonization grant given to Moses Austin to settle Texas. Plan of Iguala proclaims Mexican independence. Augustín de Iturbide and Spanish envoy sign Treaty of Córdoba recognizing Mexico's independence; treaty not honored by Spanish government, however.
1822	Army of the Three Guarantees occupies Mexico City under Iturbide's command. Iturbide becomes emperor of Mexico as Agustín I. Iturbide deposed, and republic proclaimed by Antonio López de Santa Anna Pérez de Lebrón.
1823	Guadelupe Victoria becomes first Mexican president.
1824	Federal republican government is established under new constitution. Guerrero becomes president.

Table A. (Continued) Chronology of Important Events

Period	Description
1828	Santa Anna repels Spain's attempt to regain control of Mexico. Guerrero abolishes slavery as means of discouraging migration of United States southerners to Texas.
1830	Political disturbances. Rebellion drives Guerrero from presidency. Immigration to Texas from United States prohibited but not enforced.
1833–34	Santa Anna elected president in 1833. Dictatorship established in 1834. End of first liberal reforms. Tithes abolished.
1835–36	Texas pioneers seek independence from Mexico in 1835, achieving it in March 1836. Santa Anna defeated and forced to recognize independence of Texas. Spain and Vatican recognize Mexican republic in 1836.
1837	Anastasio Bustamante becomes president, initiating a process of centralization.
1841	Conservative rebellion against Bustamante. Santa Anna's dictatorship.
1842	Santa Anna retires to his hacienda and leaves government to Nicolás Bravo.
1843	Santa Anna chosen as president of Mexico.
1844	Santa Anna forced into exile.
1845	Santa Anna returns to Mexico. Annexation of Texas by United States.
1846	Mexico severs diplomatic relations with United States. Beginning of Mexican-American War.
1848	Treaty of Guadalupe Hidalgo ends Mexican-American War. Texan independence confirmed. United States annexes territories of Upper California and New Mexico.
1853	Santa Anna returns to Mexico and becomes president. Sells additional territory to United States under Gadsden Purchase.
1854	Triumph of Plan of Ayutla under leadership of Benito Juárez.
1855	Santa Anna resigns in August. Juárez Law ends *fueros* (privileges) enjoyed by military and clergy.
1857	Constitution of 1857 promulgated.
1858–61	War of the Reform between conservatives/clericalists and liberals engulfs country in three years of bitter struggle. After liberal victory, Juárez promulgates Reform Laws, establishing nationalization of ecclesiastical properties without compensation, as well as suppression of religious orders.
1861	Moratorium on foreign debt payments. Tripartite agreement for intervention signed by Britain, France, and Spain.
FRENCH INTERVENTION	
1862	French forces march on capital but suffer defeat at Puebla.

Period	Description
1863	French enter Puebla, then Mexico City. Juárez forced to abandon the city.
1864	Ferdinand Maximilian Joseph's reign as Maximilian I begins. He confirms Reform Laws, except for those that refer to indigenous communities.
1866	French troops depart.
1867	Juárez offensive takes place. Maximilian surrenders at Querétaro and is executed. Juárez moves his government to Mexico City and becomes president.
RESTORATION AND PORFIRIATO	
1872	Death of Juárez. Sebastián Lerdo de Tejada inaugurated president.
1873	Reform Laws incorporated into Mexican constitution confirming separation of church and state.
1876	José de la Cruz Porfirio Díaz leads rebellion on platform of "no reelection" and starts his presidential career, which lasts for thirty-four years (except 1880–84), of "order and progress." Finances, trade, industry, and mining sector modernized. Political ideology based on positivism.
1880	United States railroad companies receive favorable concessions; railroad boom.
1880–84	Presidency of Manuel González.
1884	Mining code reformed. Subsoil ownership given to landowners. Reelection of Díaz.
1888	Constitution changed to allow Díaz to succeed himself.
1904	Constitution changed to allow for six-year presidential term.
1906	Proclamation against Díaz issued by the liberals in St. Louis, Missouri.
1908	Díaz states his intention of not seeking reelection in interview. Francisco I. Madero publishes *The Presidential Succession of 1910*.
REVOLUTION	
1910	Mexico's 100 years of independence celebrated. Seventh reelection of Díaz. Madero's Plan of San Luis Potosí. Rebellion breaks out in north and in Puebla.
1911	Rebellion spreads throughout Mexico. After attack on Ciudad Juárez, Díaz resigns. Madero returns in triumph to Mexico City and is elected to presidency. Emiliano Zapata publishes Plan of Ayala demanding quick reforms.
1912	Pascual Orozco rebels against Madero. Victoriano Huerta's troops crush rebellion. Huerta exiled to France. Zapata and Francisco "Pancho" Villa enter Mexico City. Venustiano Carranza establishes constitutional government at Veracruz.
1913	Madero overthrown by coup d'état staged by Felix Díaz and Huerta. Madero assassinated. Carranza, Villa, and Álvaro Obregón lead northern rebellion

Table A. (Continued) Chronology of Important Events

Period	Description
	while Zapata remains in charge of southern rebel forces. Huerta deposed and Congress dissolved.
1914	United States troops land at Veracruz. Huerta defeated and forced into exile.
1915	Obregón turns against Villa. Villa continues to fight and raids United States border towns for next five years. Carranza recognized by United States as chief of government forces.
1916	General John J. "Blackjack" Pershing's punitive expedition pursues Villa and provokes bitterness between Mexico and United States.
1917	Constitution of 1917 promulgated. Carranza elected president.
POST-REVOLUTION	
1920	Obregón rebels. Carranza dies. Obregón elected president.
1923	United States recognizes Obregón government.
1924	Plutarco Elías Calles elected president.
1926	Anticlerical policies spark Cristero Rebellion.
1927	Constitution of 1917 amended to extend presidential term to six years.
1928	Calles succeeded by Obregón, who is assassinated before taking office. Calles, who is to remain political strongman through 1935, chooses Emilio Portes Gil as president.
1929	Cristero Rebellion suppressed. Founding of official political party—National Revolutionary Party (Partido Nacional Revolucionario—PNR). Pascual Ortiz Rubio elected president of country, but Calles remains as recognized political boss.
1930	Portes Gil succeeded by Ortiz Rubio as president.
1932	Ortiz Rubio resigns; Abelardo Rodríguez chosen to complete term.
1934–40	Lázaro Cárdenas presidency. Forced exile of Calles (1936). Cárdenas begins socialist policies. Agrarian reform establishes *ejidos* (see Glossary) and collectivization. Official party renamed Party of the Mexican Revolution (Partido de la Revolución Mexicana—PRM); includes representatives from all sectors of society. Nationalization of oil industry in 1938.
MODERN	
1940–46	Manuel Ávila Camacho presidency. Mexico joins Allies in declaring war on Axis powers. PRM reorganized to provide wider representation and renamed Institutional Revolutionary Party (Partido Revolucionario Institucional—PRI). *Bracero* (migrant Mexican worker) agreement established between Mexico and United States.
1946–52	Miguel Alemán Valdés presidency. Industrialization, public works, and creation of a new campus for the National Autonomous University of Mexico (Universidad Nacional Autónoma de México—UNAM).

Period	Description
	Urban growth at expense of agrarian improvements. Per capita agricultural production reaches prerevolutionary levels. Inter-American Treaty of Reciprocal Assistance signed in 1947.
1952–58	Adolfo Ruiz Cortines presidency. Women's suffrage extended to national level. Beginning of political stability through appointment of PRI candidates to presidency.
1958–64	Adolfo López Mateos presidency. Increased foreign investments in Mexico and control of economy by foreign (mainly United States) interests. Land redistribution policies and increased agricultural production. Greater participation of minority parties in political process.
1964–70	Gustavo Díaz Ordaz presidency. Termination of *bracero* program. Foreign firms operate in Mexico on grand scale. Student unrest leads to Tlatelolco Massacre in 1968.
1970–76	Luis Echeverría Álvarez presidency. Emphasis by Mexico on participation in Third World policies against imperialism and foreign economic control. Oil boom in Chiapas and Tabasco. Economic difficulties.
1976–82	José López Portillo y Pacheco presidency. Mexico becomes world's fourth largest producer of oil and also one of world's leading debtor countries. Political reform, leading to increase of minority party representation in Chamber of Deputies by proportional representation system. Foreign debt and inflation soar. Government corruption rampant.
1982–88	Miguel de la Madrid Hurtado presidency. Economy contracts, and standard of living falls. Foreign debt renegotiated. Government adopts economic austerity measures.
1988–94	Carlos Salinas de Gortari presidency. Continuation of austerity policies leads to upturn in economy. Government takes steps to control corruption. Free-trade measures introduced. Mexico joins North American Free Trade Agreement (NAFTA). Measures taken to open governorships to opposition parties. Guerrilla group, Zapatista Army of National Liberation (Ejército Zapatista de Liberación Nacional—EZLN) appears in Chiapas. PRI nominee for next *sexenio*, Donald Luis Colosio Murrieta, assassinated.
1994–	Ernesto Zedillo Ponce de León presidency. Devaluation of new peso leads to investor panic and near-economic collapse; massive foreign intervention required to stabilize situation. Military action against Zapatistas results in stalemate. Former President Salinas leaves country in disgrace amid charges of corruption and possible involvement in series of assassinations.

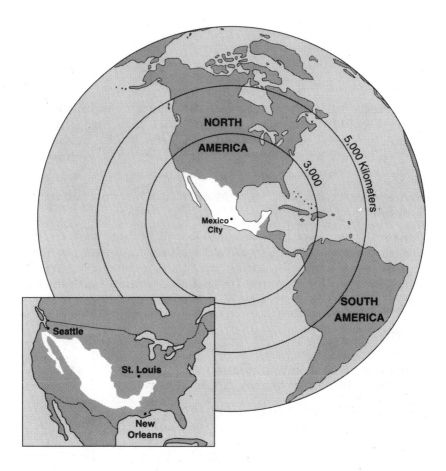

Country

Formal Name: United Mexican States (Estados Unidos Mexicanos).

Short Form: Mexico.

Term for Citizen(s): Mexican(s).

Capital: Mexico City (called México or Ciudad de México in country).

Date of Independence: September 16, 1810 (from Spain).

National Holidays: May 5, commemorating the victory over the

French at the Battle of Puebla; September 16, Independence Day.

Geography

Size: 1,972,550 square kilometers—third largest nation in Latin America (after Brazil and Argentina).

Topography: Various massive mountain ranges including Sierra Madre Occidental in west, Sierra Madre Oriental in east, Cordillera Neovolcánica in center, and Sierra Madre del Sur in south; lowlands largely along coasts and in Yucatan Peninsula. Interior of country high plateau. Frequent seismic activity.

Drainage: Few navigable rivers. Most rivers short and run from mountain ranges to coast.

Climate: Great variations owing to considerable north-south extension and variations in altitude. Most of country has two seasons: wet (June–September) and dry (October–April). Generally low rainfall in interior and north. Abundant rainfall along east coast, in south, and in Yucatan Peninsula.

Society

Population: Estimated population of 94.8 million persons in mid-1996. Annual rate of growth 1.96 percent.

Language: Spanish official language, spoken by nearly all. About 8 percent of population speaks an indigenous language; most of these people speak Spanish as second language. Knowledge of English increasing rapidly, especially among business people, the middle class, returned emigrants, and the young.

Ethnic Groups: Predominantly mestizo society (60 percent); 30 percent indigenous; 9 percent European; 1 percent other.

Education and Literacy: Secretariat of Public Education has overall responsibility for all levels of education system. Compulsory education to age sixteen; public education free. Government distributes free textbooks and workbooks to all primary schools. Official literacy rate in 1990 was 88 percent.

Health and Welfare: Health care personnel and facilities generally concentrated in urban areas; care in rural areas confined to understaffed clinics operated mostly by medical graduate students. Life expectancy in 1996 estimated at seventy-three years. Infant mortality twenty-six per 1,000 live births. Leading causes of death infections, parasitic diseases, and respiratory and circulatory system failures.

Religion: About 90 percent of population Roman Catholic, according to 1990 census. Protestants (about 6 percent) ranked second. Number of Protestants has increased dramatically since 1960s, especially in southern states.

Economy

Overview: From a colonial economy based largely on mining, especially silver, in the twentieth century, the economy has diversified to include strong agriculture, petroleum, and industry sectors. Strong growth from 1940–80 interrupted by series of economic crises, caused in part by massive overborrowing. 1980s marked by inflation and lowering standard of living. Austerity measures and introduction of free-market policies led to a period of growth from 1990–94. Membership in North American Free Trade Agreement (NAFTA) in 1993 led to hopes of continued economic growth. However, growing trade deficit and overvalued exchange rate in 1994 financed by sale of short-term bonds and foreign-exchange reserves. Series of political shocks and devaluation of new peso in late 1994 caused investor panic. Inflation soared, and massive foreign intervention was required to stabilize situation. Although overall economy remains fundamentally strong, lack of confidence makes short-term prospects for strong growth unlikely.

Gross Domestic Product (GDP): Estimated at US$370 billion in 1994; approximately US$4,100 per capita.

Currency and Exchange Rate: Relatively stable throughout most of twentieth century, the peso (Mex$) began to depreciate rapidly during economic crisis of 1980s. In January 1993, peso replaced by new peso (NMex$) at rate of NMex$1 = Mex$1,000. Exchange rate in January 1993, US$1 = NMex$3.1; rate in April 1997, US$1 = NMex$7.9.

Agriculture: Contributed 8.1 percent of GDP in 1994. Main crops for domestic consumption corn, beans, wheat, and rice. Leading agricultural exports coffee, cotton, vegetables, fruit, livestock, and tobacco.

Industry: Mining, manufacturing, and construction contributed 28 percent of GDP in 1994. Industrialization increased rapidly after 1940. By 1990 large and diversified industrial base located largely in industrial triangle of Mexico City, Monterrey, and Guadalajara. Most industrial goods produced, including automobiles, consumer goods, steel, and petrochemicals. World's sixth largest producer of petroleum and major producer of nonfuel minerals.

Energy: More than 120 billion kilowatt-hours produced in 1993, about 75 percent from thermal (mostly oil-burning) plants, 20 percent from hydroelectric, and the rest from nuclear or geothermal plants. One nuclear plant with two reactors at Laguna Verde in Veracruz State. Huge petroleum deposits discovered in Gulf of Mexico in 1970s. In 1995 sixth-largest producer of oil and had eighth-largest proven reserves.

Exports: US$60.8 billion in 1994. Manufactured exports include processed food products, textiles, chemicals, machinery, and steel. Other important export items are metals and minerals, livestock, fish, and agricultural products. Major exports to United States are petroleum, automotive engines, silver, shrimp, coffee, and winter vegetables.

Imports: US$79.4 billion in 1994. Main imports are metal-working machines, steel-mill products, agricultural machines, chemicals, and capital goods. Leading imports from United States include motor vehicle parts, automatic data processing parts, aircraft repair parts, car parts for assembly, and paper and paperboard.

Debt: Massive foreign debt. Buoyed by discovery of large petroleum reserves, government borrowed heavily in 1970s. When severe recession hit in 1982, government declared moratorium on debt payments, precipitating international economic crisis. Austerity measures and renegotiation of the debt eased crisis, but in 1995 debt stood at US$158.2 billion.

Balance of Payments: Large trade deficits from 1989 to 1993 pushed current account deeply into deficit. Dramatic improvement in trade balance in 1994 and 1995, however, nearly eliminated deficit. Heavy international borrowing allowed international reserves to rise to US$15.7 billion at end of 1995.

Fiscal Year: Calendar year.

Transportation and Telecommunications

Roads: Extensive system of roads linking all areas. More than 240,000 kilometers of roads, of which 85,000 paved (more than 3,100 kilometers expressway). Heaviest concentration in central Mexico. Many roads in poor condition as result of lack of maintenance and heavy truck traffic.

Railroads: More than 20,000 kilometers. Standard gauge, largely government-owned. System concentrated in north and central areas. Numerous connections to United States railroads; system largely used for freight and in need of modernization. Extensive, heavily used subway system in Mexico City; smaller subway in Guadalajara.

Ports: No good natural harbors. On east coast, Veracruz is principal port for cargo; Tampico, Coatzacoalcos, and Progreso handle petroleum. Guaymas, Mazatlán, and Manzanillo are principal ports on Pacific.

Air Transport: Adequate system of airlines and airports. More than 1,500 airstrips in 1994, of which 202 had permanent-surface runways. Principal international airport in Mexico City; other international airports in Monterrey, Guadalajara, Mérida, and Cancún. Aéromexico is main domestic airline.

Telecommunications: Highly developed system undergoing expansion and privatization. Long-distance telephone calls go via mix of microwave and domestic satellite links with 120 ground stations. International calls via five satellite ground stations and microwave links to United States. Demand still exceeds supply for new telephones in homes, but situation improving. More than 600 mediumwave amplitude modulation (AM) stations, privately owned. Twenty-two shortwave AM stations. Almost 300 television stations, most organized into two national networks.

Government and Politics

Government: Constitution of 1917 in force in 1997. Formally a federal republic, although federal government dominates governments of thirty-one states and Federal District. Central government power concentrated in president, who directs activities of numerous agencies and state-owned business enterprises. Bicameral legislature (128-member Senate and

500-member Chamber of Deputies) relatively weak. Federal judiciary headed by Supreme Court of Justice. State governments headed by elected governors; all states have unicameral legislatures; state courts subordinate to federal courts. Federal District governed by mayor (*regente*) indirectly elected by legislative body of the Federal District beginning in 1996; more than 2,000 local governments headed by elected municipal presidents and municipal councils.

Politics: Authoritarian system governed by president, who cannot be reelected to another six-year term. Major political organization Institutional Revolutionary Party (Partido Revolucionario Institucional—PRI), which incorporates peasant groups, labor unions, and many middle-class organizations within its ranks. Many opposition parties have had limited electoral success; largest is the conservative Party of National Action (Partido de Acción Nacional—PAN). Direct elections at regular intervals; rule of no reelection applies to most offices. Election by majority vote, except for 200 seats in Chamber of Deputies reserved for opposition parties chosen by proportional representation. Extensive participation by interest groups and labor unions in government and PRI affairs.

Foreign Relations: Major attention devoted to United States. Trade and immigration along shared border subjects of continuing negotiations. Foreign policy traditionally based on international law; nonintervention the major principle. Widely active in hemispheric affairs, including good relations with Cuba.

International Agreements and Memberships: Party to Inter-American Treaty of Reciprocal Assistance (Rio Treaty). Membership in international organizations includes Organization of American States and its specialized agencies, United Nations and its specialized agencies, Latin American Alliance for Economic Development, and Latin American Economic System. Joined NAFTA in 1993.

National Security

Armed Forces: Total strength in 1996 about 175,000 active-duty personnel. Army, 130,000; air force, 8,000; and navy (including naval aviation and marines), 37,000. Approximately 60,000 conscripts, selected by lottery. Reserve force of 300,000.

Women serving in armed forces have same legal rights and duties as men but in practice not eligible to serve in combat positions, be admitted to service academies, or be promoted beyond rank equivalent of major general in United States armed forces.

Military Units: Two government ministries responsible for national defense: Secretariat of National Defense and Secretariat of the Navy. Country divided into nine military regions with thirty-six military zones. Each military zone usually assigned at least two infantry battalions composed of some 300 troops each; some zones also assigned cavalry regiments (now motorized) or one of three artillery battalions. Personnel assigned to air force also within command structure of Secretariat of National Defense, distributed among air base installations throughout country. Principal air base, Military Air Base Number 1, located at Santa Lucía in state of México. Personnel under command of Secretariat of the Navy assigned to one of seventeen naval installations located in each coastal state.

Equipment: Under modernization program begun in 1970s, armed forces began to replace aging World War II-vintage equipment. Attention also given to development of domestic military industry. Mexican navy benefited significantly in terms of new vessels—most domestically built. Plans for additional acquisitions from abroad constrained by country's economic problems.

Police: Various federal, state, and local police provide internal security. Senior law enforcement organization is Federal Judicial Police, controlled by attorney general, with nationwide jurisdiction. More than 3,000 members in 1996. Each state and the Federal District has its own force, as do most municipalities. Low pay and corruption remain serious problems at all levels. Protection and Transit Directorate—known as "Traffic Police"—major Mexico City police force; in 1996 employed some 29,000 personnel.

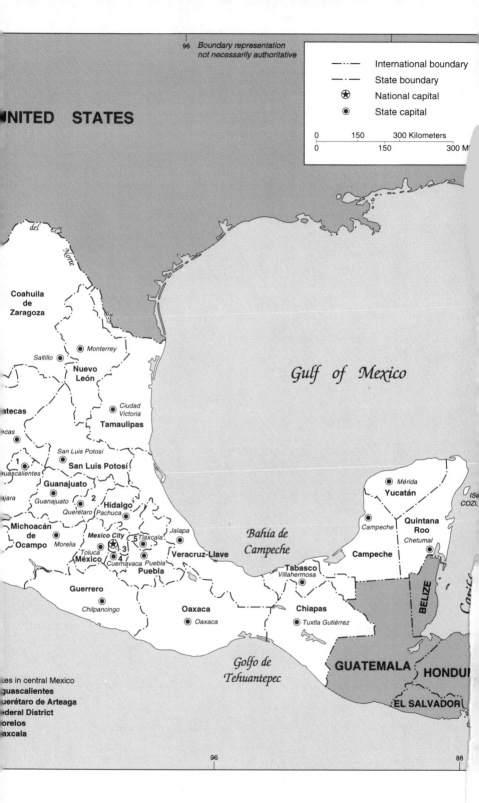

Boundary representation
not necessarily authoritative

——··— International boundary
——·— State boundary
⊛ National capital
◉ State capital

0	150	300 Kilometers
0	150	300 M

NITED STATES

del

Norte

**Coahuila
de
Zaragoza**

◉ Monterrey
Saltillo ◉
**Nuevo
León**

Gulf of Mexico

◉ Ciudad
Victoria
Tamaulipas

atecas
cas
◉

San Luis Potosí
◉ **San Luis Potosí**

1 ◉
uascalientes

Guanajuato
ajara
Guanajuato ◉ 2
Querétaro **Hidalgo**
Pachuca ◉

**Michoacán
de
Ocampo** ◉ Morelia
Toluca
México

Mexico City ⊛ 5 Tlaxcala ◉
Cuernavaca 4 Puebla ◉
Puebla

Jalapa ◉

Veracruz-Llave

*Bahía de
Campeche*

◉ Mérida
Yucatán

*ISI
COZ*

◉
Campeche
**Quintana
Roo**
Chetumal
◉

Campeche

Tabasco
Villahermosa
◉

BELIZE

Car

Guerrero
Chilpancingo
◉

Oaxaca
◉ Oaxaca

Chiapas
◉ Tuxtla Gutiérrez

GUATEMALA **HONDU**

*Golfo de
Tehuantepec*

EL SALVADOR

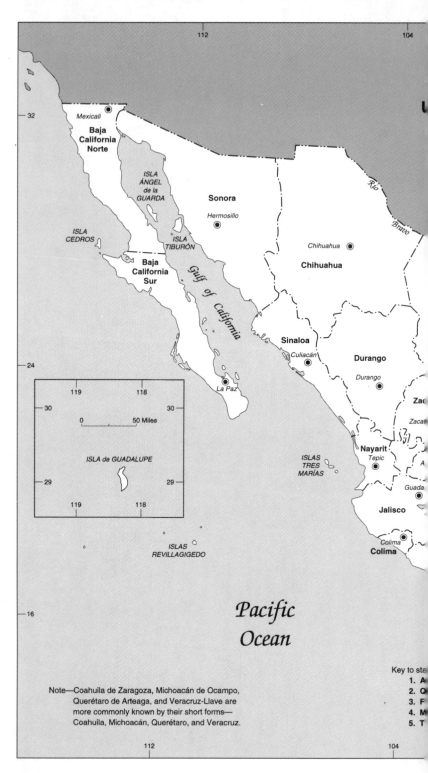

Note—Coahuila de Zaragoza, Michoacán de Ocampo, Querétaro de Arteaga, and Veracruz-Llave are more commonly known by their short forms—Coahuila, Michoacán, Querétaro, and Veracruz.

Figure 1. Administrative Divisions, 1996

Introduction

CULTURALLY, POLITICALLY, AND ECONOMICALLY, Mexico is a nation undergoing rapid change. Past characterizations of the country as rural, undemocratic, and protectionist have been replaced in the last decades of the twentieth century by descriptions that refer to Mexico as urban, opening to democracy, and market-oriented. For a country composed mostly of peasants before the Revolution (1910–20), Mexico has undergone broad and rapid urbanization; Mexico City has emerged as one of the world's largest cities at the end of the twentieth century. Throughout most of its history, Mexico has been ruled by strongmen or a one-party system; in 1997 pressures for an open democracy are greater than ever. Under the presidencies of Carlos Salinas de Gortari (1988–94) and Ernesto Zedillo Ponce de León (1994–), the economy, long one of the most protectionist and statist of the nonsocialist countries, dramatically about-faced, embracing open-market policies and free-trade links with the United States and countries throughout the Americas.

Mexico's history is long. Although the timing of the arrival of the first inhabitants to the Americas has been a point of major controversy among archaeologists, recent archaeological findings indicate that tribes from northeast Asia walked across what is now the Bering Straits perhaps as early as 35,000 years ago. Finding abundant wildlife these peoples gradually moved south, populating the entire Americas over the next several thousand years.

In the area of present-day Mexico, the earliest settlers found a rugged and varied topography with only limited areas suited for human habitation. Viewed from space, modern Mexico roughly resembles a cornucopia, wide at the top but narrowing and curving to the east as it stretches southward. At the southern tip of the "cornucopia," the rectangular Yucatan Peninsula, described by some as a thumb, extends northward into the Caribbean Sea. Another discongruous piece of land, the Baja California Peninsula, is a long sliver of land offshore and paralleling the northwest coast.

The land itself is characterized by a roughly Y-shaped series of mountain ranges. The two forks of the Y are rugged ranges that parallel the northern parts of the Pacific and Gulf of Mexico coasts. The base of the Y is a spine of mountains, with occasional breaks, that extends from central Mexico into Guatemala on the south. The center of the Y is a knot of active volcanoes in the center of the country, just south of Mexico City. Between the two northern ranges lies a high arid plateau, and the small coastal plains outside these mountain ranges are tropical rain forests. The Yucatan Peninsula is a flat humid jungle, and the Baja California Peninsula is a desert with yet another low mountain range running down its center.

Although most of the land has warm temperatures year round, lack of rainfall and rugged terrain were obstacles for the early inhabitants. Only the narrow coastal plains, the Yucatan Peninsula, and a few valleys in the southern area of the central plateau or in the volcanic central regions receive reliable rainfall for crops. Despite these constrictions, evidence indicates that between 7000 B.C. and 2000 B.C., corn had been domesticated, and agricultural villages had sprung up. By 1500 B.C., the Olmec, the first of a string of civilizations in Middle America, flourished.

The next three millennia would see a series of civilizations, each built on some of the advancements and traditions of its predecessors. After the Olmec in what is now called the Classic Period (0–A.D. 700), the Teotihuacán, Veracruz, and Monte Albán cultures built large ceremonial cities in south-central and eastern Mexico. From A.D. 700 to A.D. 900 in the Yucatan, the classic phase of the Maya civilization, considered by most archaeologists to be the most advanced pre-Columbian civilization in the Americas, was at its zenith. After A.D. 900, the center of power and culture shifted to the Valley of Mexico, site of present-day Mexico City, with the development of the Toltec and finally the Aztec empires.

The destruction of the Aztec Empire by the Spanish conquistadors in 1519 was one of the most decisive events in Mexican history. Aided by superior firepower and technology, and carrying deadly diseases for which the native inhabitants had no immunity, a band of several hundred European soldiers of fortune overran an empire of millions of inhabitants. In one of history's greatest epic stories, one which still reverberates in the Mexican psyche of today, a great civilization was virtually wiped out and replaced by an alien culture and political system. The Aztec capital of Tenochtitlán was leveled, and atop the ruins the Spanish built Mexico City, capital of half of their vast colonial empire in the New World.

Fueled by its rich silver mines, a new colonial society emerged stratified by race and wealth. The upper echelon was European, in the middle were people of mixed European-indigenous heritage, and at the bottom were the descendants of the native peoples who had survived the European onslaught of the 1500s. The Roman Catholic Church was omnipresent in all aspects of society, religion, and education. The colony was ruled by a viceroy appointed by the king of Spain.

Troubled by turmoil in Europe and influenced by the liberal ideas of French and American philosophers and the French and American revolutions, voices in Mexico began agitating for independence in the late 1700s and early 1800s. The formal break began with a proclamation by Father Miguel Hidalgo on September 16, 1810. The struggle for independence was long and fitful, however, and freedom from Spain was not finally realized until 1821.

Despite hopes that independence would bring political and economic change for the nation's masses, in reality the only change was in the country's ruler. For the next several decades, various strongmen held power. A disastrous war in 1848 resulted in the country ceding more than half its territory to the United States. A civil war in the late 1850s set the stage for a brief democratic interlude under President Benito Juárez, a French occupation and the establishment of an empire under Maximilian I, and finally the beginning of a dictatorship in 1871 under Porfirio Díaz that would last four decades.

Historians' view of the Porfiriato, as the dictatorship of Porfirio Díaz is called, is a schizophrenic one. On the one hand, the dictator opened the country to development, building a modern system of railroads, roads, factories, and schools. On the other hand (and this is the view stressed in Mexico's version of its history), the wealth generated by this period of political stability and increased trade was concentrated in a small upper class while the condition of the lower classes degenerated. Indigenous traditions or associations were totally rejected while European fashion and mores were slavishly imitated.

In 1910 the pent-up resentment of the lower classes coincided with the political disaffection of middle-class intellectuals, producing the series of violent political convulsions known as the Mexican Revolution. Rebel groups sprang up across the nation, and Díaz resigned. Instead of uniting, however, the rebel groups soon turned on each other. Various men, supported by one of the rebel factions or remnants of the former central government, held the presidency in rapid succession as fighting swept back and forth over the country. Although they disagreed over who should run the country, the leaders of the Revolution were united in their calls for social justice, land reform, and a new sense of nationalism based on Mexico's indigenous heritage. When the fighting finally ended in 1920, the ideals that they evoked defined the new Mexican nation that emerged.

The constitution of 1917, still in effect, established the present-day framework of Mexican politics. A strong president with a six-year term, a relatively weak legislature dominated by the party of the Revolution, and a nominally independent judiciary were all established. The Roman Catholic Church was stripped of most of its properties and formal power. Much of the land was taken from large landowners and organized into *ejidos* (see Glossary), or communes, for peasants to work. Heavily influenced by foreign liberal and leftist ideas and born of a popular revolution against oppression, the constitution had a decided revolutionary cast. The National Revolutionary Party (Partido Nacional Revolucionario—PNR) was formed in 1929 to successfully carry out the constitution's goals (the party later added the adjective "institutional" to indicate the consolidation of the redistribution phase of the revolutionary program—Partido Revolucionario Institucional—PRI).

The extent to which post-revolutionary administrations have implemented revolutionary ideals has been a benchmark by which Mexican historians have generally judged these administrations. Administrations in the 1920s and 1930s adhered to these goals more faithfully, the most significant act during these years being the nationalization of the petroleum industry. Post-1940 governments, however, seemed more concerned with political stability and economic growth than with land reform or new social programs.

The Revolution also had a profound effect on the role of the military. Formerly one of the largest and most influential players in Mexican politics, the armed forces were reduced in size after 1920 and their role redefined as one of guaranteeing domestic political stability. Quelling social unrest and eliminating guerrilla activity became their primary duties. As "servants of the people," units were more likely to be involved in development-oriented civic action than in training to defend the country from foreign intervention.

The Revolution added another irritant in the frequently stormy relations between the governments of Mexico and the United States. Long at odds over a variety of issues—including Mexican bitterness over territory lost in the Mexican War of 1848 and political and military interventions by the United States in Mexican affairs—the United States was alarmed by the leftist tone of revolutionary rhetoric and Mexico's friendliness with socialist governments and revolutionary movements worldwide. Often fueled by unspoken prejudices and stereo-types on both sides, friction between the two countries some-times resulted in chilly relations and bitter denunciations by politicians. Not until the end of the twentieth century, when the two countries realized how economically interdependent they had become, did the rhetoric cool and genuine attempts at cooperation and understanding each other's political posi-tion occur.

Economic growth was probably the most significant legacy of the PRI in the mid-twentieth century. From 1940 to 1980, growth was rapid and sustained. The nation's vast mineral wealth was exploited. Petroleum reserves, estimated to be among the largest in the world, were used by the government to develop new petrochemical industries. Agriculture diversi-fied and expanded, and government planners gave particular emphasis to the development of new crops for export. The industrial sector accounted for an ever larger share of the economy, and *maquiladoras* (see Glossary), or assembly plants along the United States border, grew exponentially. By 1980 Mexico was the world's fifteenth largest industrial nation.

Although the numbers of Mexicans who could be classified as middle class rose, the benefits of economic growth were not shared by all of Mexico's citizens. The stark inequality that had characterized Mexico at the turn of the century was not signifi-cantly ameliorated by the processes of modernization that began in the 1940s. Despite the economy's rapid growth rate in the post-World War II period, an even faster rate of population growth meant that the economy could not produce sufficient jobs for the many millions of young people entering the work-force every year. The exhaustion of the land available for redis-tribution in the 1950s also created conditions of severe rural unemployment. Beginning in the 1950s, rural-to-urban migra-tion began to change the face of Mexico from a predominantly rural to an urban society. The search for work often resulted in displaced workers living in worse conditions than before. The population of Mexico City, for example, swelled to 15 million in the 1990s, with millions living in miserable slums on hillsides or on marginal land on the outskirts of the city. Statistics on standard of living indices showed improvement in some urban areas and throughout the north, but few improvements in the south, where Mexico's population tended to be more rural and more heavily mestizo or indigenous.

The PRI's legacy of political stability and economic growth generated little enthusiasm or gratitude among the Mexican people. In fact, the opposite occurred, as the rise of an urban middle class produced pressures for political reform during the 1980s. Either by legal or fraudulent means, the PRI consistently won every election at the state and national levels, ceding only the occasional municipality to the conservative National Action Party (Partido de Acción Nacional—PAN) or to government-financed "satellite" parties. Widespread corruption only heightened cynicism. Corruption became synonymous with all government dealings, from the presidency to daily life, where most Mexicans had to bribe petty government officials to obtain basic public services. The PRI, the party of revolutionary change in the early years of the century, was now seen as the primary obstacle to reform.

Beginning in the mid-1980s, the PRI's overwhelming dominance over the political system began to decline. The massive earthquake that struck Mexico City in 1985 underscored the corruption and ineptitude of the authorities, who were slow to provide relief to the hundreds of thousands made homeless by the natural catastrophe. Spurred by government inaction, hundreds of nongovernmental civic associations arose in the aftermath of the Mexico City earthquake. In addition to providing resources for community self-help, many of these new organizations became a nucleus for opposition political activity during the latter 1980s.

The national elections of 1988 were a turning point in twentieth-century Mexican politics. For the first time in its six decades of continuous rule, the PRI's presidential candidate faced a formidable challenger in the person of Cuauhtémoc Cárdenas, a former PRI leader who had defected from the party because of its emerging free-market stance and its authoritarian practices. Ironically, Cárdenas was the son of one of the PRI's greatest national heros, President Lázaro Cárdenas (1934–40). During the late 1930s and early 1940s, the elder Cárdenas had assured his place in the annals of Mexican history by reviving the country's moribund land reform and by taking the unprecedented step of nationalizing the foreign-owned oil companies in Mexico.

After an intense campaign that was bitterly fought by both sides, the PRI's candidate, Carlos Salinas de Gortari, was declared the winner. The election results, which were delayed by a week because of a mysterious breakdown of the electoral computer system, were immediately contested by Cárdenas and his supporters. The Cárdenas camp alleged that the PRI had caused the computer malfunction and had systematically destroyed thousands of ballots to produce a last-minute victory for its candidate. Despite the left's protests, Salinas was sworn in as president in December 1988. The ensuing *sexenio* (as Mexico's six-year presidential term is commonly known) would be characterized by the most dramatic transition in Mexico's political economy since the 1910 Revolution.

As he began his presidential term, Salinas appeared to most Mexicans as an obscure but competent figure chosen from among several contenders within the cabinet of outgoing President Miguel de la Madrid Hurtado (1982–88). Salinas, however, faced a storm of opposition protests and bitter divisions within his own party. Moreover, for the first time in its history, the PRI held less than a two-thirds majority in the national Congress, a fact that would necessitate cooperation with the congressional opposition in order to pass the broad constitutional reforms needed to liberalize the economy.

The newly elected president was hard-pressed in the first months of his term to show that he could provide the strong leadership expected of a Mexican head of state. Salinas was quick to assert his authority, however. Within weeks of taking office, he ordered the army to arrest the corrupt leader of the powerful oil-workers union, who had been a vocal opponent of Salinas's candidacy. Throughout his term, Salinas repeatedly used his extensive powers to remove PRI officials, including several state governors who resisted his reform efforts or whose fraudulent election victories were too controversial to ignore.

Despite his stated commitment to democratization, President Salinas significantly augmented the already formidable powers of the executive branch. To push a series of sweeping economic reforms through the political system, Salinas concentrated broad policy-making authority in a technocratic elite committed to market economics, trade liberalization, and rapprochement with the United States. By the early 1990s, the Salinas administration's priorities had become clear. Political reform would be encouraged, but primary emphasis would be placed on the economic aspects of modernization.

Building on the policies of President de la Madrid, the Salinas administration carried out a comprehensive structural transformation of the Mexican economy. Salinas's domestic macroeconomic policies put into practice a package of market-oriented reforms endorsed by the United States and international financial organizations; these reforms collectively became known as the "Washington consensus." The three pillars of Mexico's structural adjustment program were the privatization of the country's vast network of parastatals, the liberalization of its foreign trade, and the modernization of its financial system.

It was through its comprehensive economic program, rather than its political reforms, that the Salinas administration left a lasting impact on Mexico. By the time Salinas entered office, Mexico had already dramatically reversed its foreign trade practices by acceding to the General Agreement on Tariffs and Trade (GATT—as of January 1995 became known as the World Trade Organization) in August 1986. As a result of its accession to GATT, Mexico unilaterally lowered its average tariff level from 100 percent ad valorem to a structure with a top rate of 20 percent. At the same time, it reduced or eliminated many non-tariff barriers such as import licenses and quotas, the combined effect of which had been to close the Mexican market to most foreign imports for more than fifty years.

The Salinas administration expanded the process of structural adjustment begun by its predecessor. A key element of the government's structural adjustment program was the privatization of Mexico's vast network of parastatal industries. Between 1986 and 1994, the government privatized more than 700 state-owned companies, including all eighteen government-owned commercial banks, the national telephone company, a national television network, airlines, movie theaters, several sugar- and food-processing plants, several large copper mines, steel production facilities, and the maritime port system. The sale of state-owned companies generated US$22 billion in government revenues, the majority of which was used to reduce the massive foreign debt and to finance new infrastructure and social expenditures.

In addition to the sale of state companies, the government also undertook a major overhaul of its Byzantine financial and regulatory systems. The Salinas administration oversaw the privatization of the domestic commercial banks and the passage of a new national Law of Banking and Credit that thoroughly modernized domestic banking. Opportunities for foreign investment, which had been severely restricted since the Revolution, were expanded considerably under the 1993 Foreign Investment Law. For the first time since the Revolution, foreigners were allowed to own commercial and residential property directly, rather than through a Mexican intermediary. New commercial and securities market regulations encouraged a massive influx of foreign direct and portfolio investment during the early 1990s. The most visible consequence of increased foreign investment was the explosive growth of the in-bond (tariff and tax-free) *maquiladora* manufacturing plants along the Mexico-United States border. Additionally, after 1993 the capitalization of the Mexican stock market soared, as a new generation of foreign (mainly United States) investors sought the higher returns afforded by emerging markets such as Mexico's.

The dramatic restructuring and austerity measures of the Salinas years produced a positive turnaround in Mexico's macroeconomic performance, although they did not produce the sustained high growth rates which many had hoped for. Annual inflation fell from 159 percent in 1987 to 6.7 percent during the first three quarters of 1994. Concurrently, the average annual economic growth rate between 1988 and 1994 was a modest 2.6 percent. Unemployment and underemployment remained high, especially in the countryside, fueling record levels of legal and illegal migration to the United States. Moreover, the new prosperity was unevenly distributed, being largely concentrated in the north and among a minority of relatively well-educated, urban professionals and white-collar workers.

Perhaps the single most important catalyst for the transformation of Mexican economic policy was the Salinas administration's ambitious goal of participating as a full partner in the emerging North American free-trade zone begun by Canada and the United States in the early 1990s. President Salinas and his advisers viewed Mexico's integration into the world trading system as the only viable basis for their country's future long-term growth. Bowing to geographic reality, Salinas discarded decades of protectionist and nationalistic practices by past Mexican governments to forge a close and lasting economic and political partnership with the United States. The objective was nothing less than Mexico's full incorporation into the emerging North American financial and trading bloc. In 1991 Mexico began negotiations with Canada and the United States on the terms of a trilateral free-trade treaty, the North American Free Trade Agreement (NAFTA).

NAFTA became the cornerstone of Mexico's reform efforts and the ultimate test of its recognition as a new entrant in the community of modern nations. In preparation for Mexico's accession to NAFTA, the Salinas administration redoubled its efforts to open its markets and to increase the competitiveness of its domestic economy. Mexico also became more receptive to United States concerns on a range of bilateral issues, including narcotics trafficking and illegal immigration. In response to international pressure, the Mexican government improved its human rights practices and made the electoral process more transparent. In the weeks preceding the vote on ratification of NAFTA by the United States Congress, Mexico and the United States negotiated a series of side agreements on environmental protection that helped assure the entry into force of the treaty on January 1, 1994.

The ratification of NAFTA boosted international confidence in the Mexican economy, spurring an influx of foreign capital and fueling predictions of an imminent economic boom. National opinion polls showed President Salinas's popularity to be at an all-time high, and the PRI was preparing to pass the mantle of the presidency to Salinas's handpicked successor, Luis Donaldo Colosio Murrieta, in the August 1994 presidential election.

The triumphant mood in Mexico City was dashed on January 1, 1994, the day NAFTA entered into force, when a heretofore unknown insurgent group, the Zapatista Army of National Liberation (Ejército Zapatista de Liberación Nacional—EZLN), briefly took over four municipalities in the southern state of Chiapas. The Zapatistas, as members of the EZLN came to be known, consisted of several hundred indigenous people from the Chiapas highlands as well as a leadership and support network of white, university-educated Marxists and former guerrillas. The Zapatistas justified their armed movement and their violent takeover of the Chiapas municipalities as gestures of protest against the market-oriented economic policies of the Salinas administration, including NAFTA. These policies were blamed for the worsening living conditions of Mexico's rural poor. Additionally, the Zapatistas decried the state's historical discrimination and neglect of Mexico's indigenous communities and the authoritarian practices of the ruling PRI. The Chiapas rebellion galvanized the Mexican left and created a heightened awareness of the difficult circumstances of many of Mexico's indigenous people. It also provoked a strong military reaction and shattered the image of stability that the Salinas administration had tried to project to the world.

An even greater setback to Mexico's stability occurred on March 22, 1994, when PRI presidential candidate Colosio was assassinated at a campaign rally in the northern city of Tijuana. The Colosio murder was the first major instance of political violence against a high-level PRI official since the assassination of President Álvaro Obregón in the 1920s. Following initial reports that a lone gunman was responsible for the killing, additional evidence pointed to a conspiracy involving at least half a dozen security personnel believed to be linked to a local drug cartel.

Colosio was replaced on the PRI presidential ticket by his campaign manager and former education secretary, Ernesto Zedillo Ponce de León. The PRI once again faced a competitive election, with the main opposition challenge coming this time from the conservative PAN. Unlike the election of Salinas in 1988, the 1994 presidential election was judged by domestic and international observers to be relatively free and fair. During the months preceding the vote, the PRI had agreed to several major reforms of the electoral process, including antifraud measures such as transparent ballot boxes, photo-identification cards for voters, and the inclusion of a larger number of non-PRI seats in the National Electoral Commission. Zedillo won the election with a plurality of the vote, thus extending the PRI's dubious record as the world's longest-ruling political party (surpassing even the Communist Party of the former Soviet Union). Although Zedillo was elected to the presidency by a slimmer margin than Salinas, the results of what was probably the cleanest presidential election in modern Mexican history were accepted as legitimate by most observers and opposition groups.

The salutary effect of the August elections was not destined to endure, however. In September, another high-level PRI official, José Francisco Ruiz Massieu, was assassinated on a Mexico City street. Widespread speculation that an interfactional war was taking place within the PRI was supported by evidence linking a fugitive PRI congressman to the second killing. The scandal broadened shortly after the Zedillo administration took office, when evidence was uncovered linking former president Salinas's brother, Raúl, to the Ruiz Massieu murder.

The first month of the Zedillo administration coincided with a dramatic financial crisis that dealt a severe setback to Mexico's economic recovery efforts. The crisis was rooted in Mexico's accumulation of a dangerously high current-account deficit throughout 1994. To finance increased government spending, the Mexican government had floated a large number of short-term, high-yield bonds known as *tesebonos*. As the successive political shocks of 1994 drove capital from the Mexican stock and bond markets, and as interest rates rose in the United States, the Mexican government became increasingly dependent on short-term, high-yield instruments to attract scarce capital.

Following the Ruiz Massieu assassination, Mexican investors withdrew large amounts of capital from the Mexican market. This situation made it impossible for the government to pay dividends on a series of *tesebonos* that were scheduled to mature in December. Despite its untenable financial situation, the government dismissed the possibility of a devaluation of the new peso (for value of the new peso—see Glossary), but subsequently reversed itself in late December. The devaluation and the disclosure of Mexico's short-term liquidity crisis set off a run on the new peso and caused the Mexican stock market to lose half its value. The crash of the Mexican stock market reverberated throughout Latin America and other developing countries.

The consequences of the currency crisis in Mexico were severe. Consumer interest rates shot up to an average of 80 percent, making it impossible for many borrowers to pay interest on their loans or to make credit-card payments. Mexico's expanding commercial sector was devastated, as thousands of businesses were forced into bankruptcy or were required to lay off much of their workforce. The devaluation of the currency pushed annual inflation from 6 percent to nearly 50 percent, imposing a severe burden on consumers and pushing millions of people below the poverty line.

In January 1995, the United States provided assistance to Mexico in the form of a US$20 billion emergency debt relief package. The concession by the United States government of an emergency loan to Mexico was highly controversial in both countries. To assuage congressional opposition to the loan package, the administration of United States President William J. Clinton took the unprecedented step of requiring the Mexican government to commit its revenues from the national oil company as collateral.

As Mexico's economy stabilized in the wake of the financial crisis, a series of bizarre political events unfolded in the opening months of 1995. In the aftermath of the financial crisis, a rare public feud developed between former president Salinas and the Zedillo administration, with each side blaming the other for mishandling the crisis. Hailed as a modernizer just a few months before, Salinas had become the main target of public blame for the near-collapse of the financial system. Salinas's reputation suffered a further blow in connection with his brother Raúl's reported role in the José Francisco Ruiz Massieu assassination. Shortly after being cleared as a suspect by the attorney general's office, Salinas quietly left Mexico for apparent exile in Ireland.

Charges of high-level corruption, bribery, and the role of drug money in the assassination of government officials continued to grow. Despite convictions for the 1994 murder of PRI official José Francisco Ruiz Massieu, the motives behind the killing remained unanswered. Questions about the assassination increased when, in November 1994, Mario Ruiz Massieu, Mexico's assistant attorney general, younger brother of José Francisco Ruiz Massieu and the official in charge of the murder investigation, abruptly resigned, claiming that high-ranking PRI officials were thwarting his investigation efforts. When the investigation resumed with a new prosecutor in charge, Raúl Salinas de Gotari, brother of the former president, was arrested and charged with hiring a hit man to murder José Francisco Ruiz Massieu. It was widely assumed that pressure from high government officials to ignore Salinas's involvement was the reason for Mario Ruiz Massieu's resignation.

On March 2, 1995, Mario Ruiz Massieu was arrested at Newark International Airport before boarding a plan for Spain and charged by United States customs officials with failing to declare US$46,000. He was placed under house arrest, and proceedings for deportation began. Investigations of Mario Ruiz Massieu's finances revealed a US$9 million bank account in Houston. United States federal prosecutors charged that the money had come from Mexican drug traffickers, and a civil trial to seize the money began in February 1997. Despite claims from Mario Ruiz Massieu that the money was obtained legally, documents and witnesses in the civil trial claimed that the money had come from payoffs from drug traffickers to avoid prosecution. The case began to be called the "Mexican Watergate" as the Mexico City newspapers *El Proceso* and *La Jornada* published documents from the trial that also implicated former president Salinas and his brother Raúl in drug trafficking. Other stories implied that payoffs from drug traffickers might have played a role in the José Francisco Ruiz Massieu killing and in Mario Ruiz Massieu's resignation from the investigation.

As the Mario Ruiz Massieu investigation and trial continued, another drug-related scandal broke. On February 18, General Jesús Gutiérrez Rebollo, newly appointed head of the National Institute to Combat Drugs, was fired and arrested. While Gutiérrez Rebollo aggressively prosecuted several Mexican drug cartels in his ten weeks in office, he allegedly protected the Ciudad Juárez drug cartel leader, Amado Carillo Fuentes. Known as the "lord of the skies," Carillo Fuentes used a fleet of Boeing 747s to ferry cocaine from Colombia to Mexico and then to the United States. The revelations of bribery and involvement in drug trafficking were particularly embarrassing to the Mexican military, long considered the one institution in Mexico largely untouched by corruption. That assumption was again challenged when, in March 1997, Brigadier General Alfredo Navarro Lara was arrested and accused of trafficking, bribery, and criminal conspiracy in a protection scheme involving a Tijuana-based drug cartel.

In an effort to clean up the scandal-ridden National Institute to Combat Drugs, Attorney General Jorge Madrazo Cuéllar named Mariano Federico Herrán Salvatti as the institute's new head. Herrán had previously served as the top prosecutor in Mexico City, and underwent extensive background checks and drug and lie detector tests before being offered the position. All employees of the institute were given drug tests, and, in another embarrassment, the attorney general's office reported that 424 tested positive, about half of those for cocaine use. In his swearing in, Herrán reported that his greatest challenge would be "recovering the confidence lost and damaged by corruption, impunity, and the irresponsible actions of many bad public servants over many years."

The scandals surrounding the Colosio and Ruiz Massieu assassinations underscored a growing problem of corruption of Mexican political and law enforcement institutions and coincided with a surge in criminal activity in much of the country. By the mid-1990s, local drug mafias with connections to Colombian drug cartels posed a serious challenge to state authority in several remote areas of Mexico. With their control over enormous sums of money, manpower, and real estate, the cartels were able to evade prosecution through a combination of innovation and outright bribery of local officials and law enforcement agencies. In some cases, entire local and state law enforcement agencies had been effectively neutralized through the payment of bribes and the placement of local drug cartel informants in police units. These measures allowed the cartels to establish relatively secure transshipment corridors for United States-bound drugs. Mexican authorities reported that drug traffickers had even resorted to buying and retrofitting old airliners to carry cocaine from South America to the Mexico-United States border region.

Organized crime not only represented a direct challenge to the rule of law but also was indirectly responsible for undermining democratic institutions. Evidence gathered from the Colosio and Ruiz Massieu murder investigations suggested that the drug cartels may have formed alliances with some of the informal political networks within the PRI. Reports in the Mexican media of corruption by public officials and law enforcement agencies eroded the public's confidence in Mexico's political institutions and created a climate of severe cynicism and mistrust of all politicians.

The erosion of public confidence in government agencies was reinforced by the apparent inability of police to stem a growing tide of criminal behavior in Mexico City and other large urban areas. By the mid-1990s, the problem of rising organized and common crime—a problem that Mexico shared with several other countries undergoing simultaneous democratic reform and economic austerity—had become a paramount public concern.

Responding to domestic and international pressure to fight crime and reduce official corruption, during the first weeks of his administration President Zedillo outlined a plan for the overhaul of the justice system and the professionalization of police agencies. To demonstrate his resolve to solve the 1994 assassination cases, Zedillo took the unusual step of appointing as attorney general a well-respected member of the opposition PAN.

President Zedillo's reform efforts were derailed by the financial crisis and by the continuation of guerrilla activity in Chiapas and, subsequently, in the states of Guerrero and Oaxaca. In April 1995, Zedillo ordered a major military offensive against the Zapatistas and their urban command structure. The operation managed to disrupt the Zapatistas' urban support network, but failed to capture the guerrillas' eccentric field commander and spokesman, Subcommander Marcos.

The government's war against narcotrafficking, as well as its counterinsurgency efforts in Chiapas and Guerrero, raised the military's profile in Mexico's civilian-dominated political system. The military, whose role since the 1940s has been largely confined to civic action and disaster-relief activities, despite some instances of corruption, was increasingly being called upon to replace unreliable police agencies in the interdiction of narcotics shipments. The army's indefinite deployment in Chiapas and Guerrero, which also represented a significant expansion of its mission, prompted some observers to warn of a growing political role for the military in the Mexican political system.

By early 1997, the Mexican economy had stabilized and the political system was continuing its gradual transition toward increased representativeness and responsiveness. Throughout 1996 the opposition PAN won a number of important municipal and gubernatorial elections. The left did not fare as well as the right, having failed to regain the momentum it had acquired during the late 1980s. The opposition victories in 1996 set the stage for strong challenges to the PRI in the 1997 midterm congressional elections, the first balloting for the key post of mayor of Mexico City in the summer of 1997, and the 2000 presidential race.

In the medium term, Mexico faces the continuing challenge of carrying through its political and economic reforms in the face of further potential setbacks. A major challenge facing Mexico is that of restoring healthy economic growth and improving domestic productivity and national competitiveness in global markets. Mexico's participation in NAFTA provides strong incentives and opportunities to increase the competitiveness of the Mexican economy. One of the key problems will be to continue opening the economy while minimizing the potentially destabilizing human costs of economic dislocation, particularly of rural communities that have been threatened in the short run by freer trade.

Another key problem facing Mexico into the twenty-first century will be that of promoting balanced development among the country's diverse regions. Data from the 1990 national census show a declining but still significant gap in basic quality-of-life and educational indicators between the relatively prosperous north and the less developed south and southwest. Once sustained growth is restored, Mexico will be challenged to overcome the wide regional disparities that threaten to create, in effect, two Mexicos.

Finally, Mexico appears to be undergoing a fundamental transformation of its political culture. The corporatist patterns of political participation that were promoted by the PRI during its sixty-year period of undisputed rule are being replaced by more liberal forms of civic association. Recent electoral reforms and opposition victories at the state and local levels suggest that Mexico is in transition from a one-party authoritarian system to a multiparty democracy. During the first half of his term, President Zedillo took significant steps to weaken the historically strong link between the PRI and the state. The reform process is threatened, however, by the growing problem of crime and the penetration of the state by criminal organizations. One of the principal political challenges facing President Zedillo and his successors will be that of fashioning a robust response to crime that does not resort to authoritarian methods that could reverse the reform process.

March 24, 1997   Tim Merrill and Ramón Miró

Chapter 1. Historical Setting

The conquest of Tenochtitlán, adapted from two paintings by Diego Rivera

MEXICO'S MANY ARCHAEOLOGICAL treasures, its architectural wealth, and its diverse population provide physical clues to a past that has given rise to stories of migration, settlement, conquest, and nation-building. The cultural heritage of the Aztec, the Maya, and other advanced civilizations, seen in the ruins of their temples and in their artifacts, bears witness to the achievements of the early inhabitants of Mesoamerica (see Glossary). Following a pattern that spans the pre-Columbian era to modern times, new civilizations have been built on the ruins of the old. In this ongoing process of cultural superimposition, many elements of the past have endured, despite occasional efforts to root out traditional practices and native identities. A major change came with the Spanish conquest. The conquest caused a traumatic break in the ebb and flow of native kingdoms and led to a single, albeit stratified, society that was neither wholly native nor European, but mestizo.

The conquistadors unified the populations of the former Mesoamerican kingdoms under the rule of a militaristic and theocratic Spanish monarchy. After early attempts by the conquerors and their descendants to establish a decentralized feudal society, central aristocratic authority prevailed. Throughout the colonial period, a distinctly "Mexican" national identity was emerging among the mestizo and creole inhabitants of New Spain. By the early nineteenth century, Spain's mercantilist trade policies and its discrimination against native-born Mexicans in colonial business and administrative affairs fostered widespread resentment and a desire for greater autonomy. The geopolitical crisis of the Napoleonic wars and the influence of Enlightenment ideas provoked a sudden break with Madrid in 1810.

In the aftermath of independence, Mexico suffered a prolonged tumultuous period of factionalism and foreign intervention. Riven by bitter disputes between conservatives and liberals and governed by a series of military strongmen, the country languished in political turmoil while it lost half of its territory to an expanding United States. Stability, when it was finally achieved at the close of the nineteenth century, was imposed by the modernizing but politically repressive regime of José de la Cruz Porfirio Díaz.

Throughout most of the nineteenth century, Mexico's population was denied opportunities for individual prosperity and fair and equal treatment before the law. In a country that remained predominantly rural until the 1950s, landlessness and rural unemployment had become endemic. The suppression of civil liberties and the excessive concentration of wealth during the Porfiriato (the name given to the years of the Porfirio Díaz dictatorship, 1876–1910) polarized Mexican society and eventually led to the bitter and destructive factional wars collectively known as the Mexican Revolution. After nearly a decade of devastating warfare, the combatants came together in the town of Querétaro in 1917 to draft a grand compromise that would incorporate the ideals of the diverse revolutionary factions.

The constitution of 1917 gave Mexicans the legal and ideological framework on which to base national development: equality before the law, national self-determination, and a state-mediated balance between private property rights and social welfare objectives. In the decades that followed, different Mexican administrations would alternatively promote redistribution or economic growth, depending on a variety of circumstances.

By the late twentieth century, the burgeoning Mexican state could no longer assure the Revolution's promise of growth with equity. After decades of semiauthoritarian rule by the dominant Institutional Revolutionary Party (Partido Revolucionario Institucional—PRI), corruption and excessive clientelism had overshadowed the ideal of equality before the law. Poverty, although lessened, continued to beset half of the population. The debt crisis of the early 1980s marked the end of Mexico's protectionist, state-centered economic model and set the stage for far-reaching trade and financial liberalization and systematic privatization of key industries. By the early 1990s, Mexico's economy was thoroughly integrated into the global market, and a renascent civil society was exercising increasing autonomy from Mexico's corporatist political institutions. Mexico thus approached the end of the twentieth century in a state of profound transition (see fig. 1).

Preconquest Mexico

Despite Mexico's rich pre-Columbian history, following the Spanish conquest in 1519, the country's new rulers made a concerted attempt to erase all things related to indigenous cultures. Conquerors and missionaries felt divinely inspired to

4

"civilize and evangelize" the native peoples of the New World. The attempts to Europeanize and Christianize Mexico led to the devaluation of much of the indigenous culture for the next 400 years.

This situation was finally reversed in the 1920s during what has become known as the cultural phase of the Revolution, when a conscious effort was undertaken to search for a national cultural identity known as *mexicanidad* ("Mexican-ness"). The search for this new national consciousness resulted in a renewed appreciation of the advanced civilizations encountered by the Spanish in 1519. Since the 1920s, extensive scholarship has been devoted to native Mexican values and the cultural expressions of those indigenous values in contemporary society.

Ancient Mexico

The first humans in the Americas were descendants of northeast Asian nomads who took part in a series of migrations across the Bering Strait perhaps as early as 30,000 B.C. Archaeological evidence testifies to the presence of early hunters and gatherers in Mexico around 10,000 to 8000 B.C. During the next few thousand years, humans domesticated indigenous plants, such as corn, squash, and beans. With a constant food supply assured, people became permanent settlers. Leisure time became available and was used for developing technical and cultural skills. Villages appeared as the number of people and food supplies increased. By 1500 B.C., the early inhabitants were producing handmade clay figurines and sophisticated clayware.

Between 200 B.C. and A.D. 900, Mesoamerica was the scene of highly developed civilizations. Archaeologists have designated this Classic Period as the Golden Age of Mexico. This era was a time when the arts and sciences reached their apex, when a writing system developed, and when a sophisticated mathematical system permitted the accurate recording of time. Religion was polytheistic, revering the forces of nature in the gods of rain, water, the sun, and the moon. The most important deity was Quetzalcóatl, the feathered serpent and the essence of life, from whom all knowledge derived. Metals came into use only by the end of the period, but despite this handicap, impressive architectural structures in the pyramids at Teotihuacán near Mexico City, the Pyramid of the Niches at El Tajín in the state of Veracruz, and the Temple of the Sun at Palenque in present-day Chiapas were built and survive to this day.

These civilizations produced pottery, statuary, and ornate buildings, despite their being supported by a simple agricultural economy based on the cultivation of a few staples. Social stratification produced a ruling class of priests and intellectuals who oversaw the labor and social affairs of the peasant majority.

The three most important Classic sites were Teotihuacán (in central Mexico), Monte Albán (to the south in the state of Oaxaca), and the Mayan complexes (in the states of Chiapas, Tabasco, Campeche, Yucatán, and Quintana Roo, as well as in the nearby countries of Honduras, Guatemala, and Belize). The fall of Teotihuacán around A.D. 650 effectively transferred the center of power from central Mexico to the Mayan city states of the Yucatan Peninsula. The lowland Mayan culture flourished from A.D. 600 to A.D. 900 when it abruptly declined. The exact causes of this rapid fall remain unknown, but archaeologists speculate that it might have been because of one or a combination of factors: bad harvests, plague, drought, ecological problems from overpopulation, or pressure from more warlike neighbors. Whatever the factors may have been, they provided the groundwork for the next phase, the Post-Classic period, which would be a radical change from the Classic.

The main characteristic of the Post-Classic period was a sudden surge of militarism. The population underwent great turmoil and numerous migrations; people moved everywhere and anywhere they could find allies to fight their common enemies. Wars ceased to be waged for territorial expansion and became a means for exacting tribute and for capturing prisoners to be sacrificed to the gods. For the first time, architecture centered on defense and fortification. Numerous civilizations rose and fell during this period, including the Toltec in central Mexico and the Zapotec and Mixtec in southern Mexico.

The Aztec

Throughout its long history of human habitation, the Valley of Mexico drew people from Mesoamerica who were attracted by its abundant sources of water, easy communication, and plentiful game and vegetation. The valley was a corridor through which many migrating groups passed and sometimes settled. During the pre-Columbian era, the valley was in con-

Pyramids at Teotihuacán
Ceremonial temple at Palenque
Courtesy Arturo Salinas

stant turmoil except when central authority and political hegemony existed.

The last nomadic arrivals in the valley were the Mexica, more commonly known as the Aztec. Although recent linguistic and archaeological work suggests the Aztec may have come from northwest Mexico, their origins are obscure. According to legend, the Aztec came from Aztlán, a mythical place to the north of the Valley of Mexico around A.D. 1100. They were said to have made their way to the valley guided by the chirps of their sun and war god Huitzilopichtli (meaning "hummingbird on the left"). The inhabitants of the valley viewed the new arrivals with suspicion and tried to prevent their settlement. After much wandering and a few wars, in the early 1300s, the Aztec reached the marshy islands in Lago de Texcoco (site of present-day Mexico City), where they saw an eagle perching on a cactus tree and holding a snake in its beak (an image reproduced on the modern Mexican flag). According to Aztec legend, this was a sign indicating where they should build their new capital city. Tenochtitlán was eventually built on an island in Lago de Texcoco and gradually became an important center in the area. Drinking water came from Chapultepec hill on the mainland, and causeways connected the island to the shores of the lake. The Aztec established a monarchy in 1376, naming Acamapichtli as their first king. By the early sixteenth century, Aztec domination reached into most of central and southern Mexico (with the exception of the Mayan areas in the southeast).

Before the settlement at Tenochtitlán, Aztec society was quite simple in its organization and was composed of peasants, warriors, and priest-rulers. Afterward, and with a much larger population, there was an increasing division of labor and a more complex social structure. The emperor was selected according to merit from among the ruling dynasty. The nobility was composed of the high priests, the military, and political leaders. The merchant class lived apart in the city and had its own courts, guilds, and gods. Commoners, the largest segment of society, were farmers, artisans, and lower-level civil servants. The lowest rung of society was composed of conquered peoples brought to Tenochtitlán as slaves.

The political structure of the Aztec empire was based on a loose coalition of city-states under the fiscal control of Tenochtitlán. The main objective of Aztec expansion was to exact tribute from conquered peoples. Tributes were in kind; cocoa, cotton, corn, feathers, precious metals and stones, shells, and jaguar skins were among those sent. The towns also had the obligation to provide soldiers and slaves and to recognize Aztec supremacy and the supremacy of the Aztec god Huitzilopichtli. Otherwise, towns were basically free to conduct their internal affairs, and Aztec hegemony was never fully consolidated—a fact that eventually became a major element in the fall of the empire.

The Spanish Conquest

Lured by stories of the riches of the Aztec, a Spanish adventurer, Hernán (sometimes referred to as Fernando or Hernando) Cortés, assembled a fleet of eleven ships, ammunition, and over 700 men and in 1519 set sail from Cuba to Mexico. The party landed near present-day Veracruz in eastern Mexico and started its march inland. Superior firepower, resentment against the Aztec by conquered tribes in eastern Mexico, and considerable luck all aided the Spanish in their conquest of the Aztec. The Aztec and their allies had never seen horses or guns, the Spanish had interpreters who could speak Spanish, Maya, and Náhuatl (the Aztec language), and perhaps what was most important, Cortés unwittingly had the advantage of the legend of Quetzalcóatl, in which the Aztec are said to have believed that a white god would arrive in ships from the east in 1519 and destroy the native civilizations.

Unwilling to confront the mysterious arrival whom he considered a god, the Aztec emperor, Moctezuma II (anglicized as Montezuma), initially welcomed the Spanish party to the capital in November 1519. Montezuma soon was arrested, and the Spanish took control of Tenochtitlán. The Aztec chieftains staged a revolt, however, and the Spanish were forced to retreat to the east. The Spanish recruited new troops while a smallpox epidemic raged through Tenochtitlán, killing much of the population, possibly including Montezuma. By the summer of 1521, the Spanish were ready to assault the city. The battle raged for three weeks, with the superior firepower of the Spanish eventually proving decisive. The last emperor, Cuauhtémoc, was captured and killed. In the nineteenth century, the legend of Cuauhtémoc would be revived, and the last Aztec emperor would be considered a symbol of honor and courage, the first Mexican national hero.

New Spain

After the fall of Tenochtitlán, the Spaniards' task was to settle and expand the new domains on the mainland of North and Central America that became known as New Spain. Cortés dispatched several expeditions to survey the areas beyond the Valley of Mexico and to establish political control over the land and its inhabitants. Once released from the central political control of Tenochtitlán, most towns surrendered to Cortés's men. As a symbol of political continuity, the capital of the new colony was to be built squarely atop the ruins of Tenochtitlán and was renamed Mexico after the Mexica tribe.

Encomiendas

The conquest of the Aztec empire required an enormous effort and a tremendous sacrifice by Cortés's army, and after their victory, the soldiers demanded what they had come for: prestige and wealth. The spoils from the city largely had been lost; Cortés had to resort to some other strategy to provide for his men. The conquistador had already surveyed all Aztec records related to tributes and tributary towns, and on the basis of this information, he decided to distribute grants of people and land among his men. This practice had already been tried in the Caribbean, and Cortés himself had received *encomiendas,* grants of land and people, in Hispaniola in 1509 and in Cuba in 1511. Granting *encomiendas* became an institution throughout New Spain to ensure subordination of the conquered populations and the use of their labor by the Spanish colonizers, as well as a means to reward Spanish subjects for services rendered to the crown.

The *encomienda* was a Spanish institution of Roman origin, and in the New World, the Spanish government established a series of rights and obligations between the *encomendero* (grantee) and the people under his care. The indigenous people were required to provide tribute and free labor to the *encomendero,* who was responsible for their welfare, their assimilation into Spanish culture, and their Christianization. Political and social stratification among the *encomenderos* was easily achieved by the simple fact that there were communities of different sizes. The larger the grant, the larger the amount of tribute and labor available, and thus the greater the potential wealth and prestige of the assignment. In reality, the native population was accustomed to a similar organization of tributary towns under the Aztec. In time, the *encomenderos* became the New World version of Spanish feudal lords. This new source of political power came to worry the Spanish authorities because of the dangers of a local nobility capable of contending peninsular authority.

Although disease and hardship decimated the indigenous population, increasing numbers of Spaniards arrived with great expectations of new wealth. Along with this flow of Europeans came the African slaves, who were directed to the central areas of New Spain. In 1549 the Spanish government ended yearlong labor obligations, as well as payment of tribute. To compensate for this loss, the crown instituted a new system of forced labor allotments (*repartimientos*) of forty-five days a year, for which every person was to be paid in wages. The *repartimiento* became a source of abuse by employers who would pay wages in advance and then obligate workers indefinitely as repayment.

In the late seventeenth and early eighteenth centuries, royal control of the granting of *encomiendas* became more strict. On November 13, 1717, a royal decree abolished *encomiendas*, an act that was confirmed by other decrees in 1720 and 1721. However, in the most remote areas, *encomiendas* were often kept throughout the colonial period in complete defiance of the royal decree in order to populate these regions.

Colonial Administration

The first royal judicial body established in New Spain in 1527 was the *audiencia* of Mexico City. The *audiencia* consisted of four judges, who also held executive and legislative powers. The crown, however, was aware of the need to create a post that would carry the weight of royal authority beyond local allegiances. In 1535 control of the bureaucracy was handed over to Antonio de Mendoza, who was named the first viceroy of New Spain (1535–50). His duties were extensive but excluded judicial matters entrusted to the *audiencia*.

Viceregal power was characterized by a certain amount of independence from royal control, mainly because of distance and difficult communications with the mother country. Viceroys were notorious for applying orders with discretion, using the maxim "I obey but do not comply." In addition, viceroys and *audiencias* were in conflict most of the time, with the latter not responsible to the viceroy but reporting directly to the crown.

By the end of the seventeenth century, the Viceroyalty of New Spain reached from New Mexico to Panama and included the Caribbean islands and the Philippines. In the most distant areas, local *audiencias* enjoyed greater autonomy, and viceregal authority was merely nominal. After the sixteenth-century expansion of power, the seventeenth century was marked by a decline in central authority, even though the administrative structure transplanted to the New World remained intact.

Socioeconomic Structures

The philosophy of mercantilism was the force behind all overseas ventures by European colonial powers. This set of ideas emphasized that the most important function of colonial possessions was to enrich the mother country. This accumulation of wealth was largely accomplished by the levy of the *quinto* (royal fifth) on all colonial production. Trade duties protected manufacturers and merchants in Spain from competition in the colonies and placed strict restrictions on the colonial economies. Mexico was required to supply raw materials to Spain, which would then produce finished goods to be sold at a profit to the colonies.

From the mid-sixteenth century on, some land grants were provided to Europeans willing to farm the land and raise livestock in underpopulated areas. The European acquisition of land often encroached upon native villages. Displacement and fear of forced labor in the early seventeenth century led entire villages to flee to larger towns, mining camps, or haciendas, where the displaced persons hired themselves out as artisans, servants, peons, or laborers. Although originally kept apart in separate "republics," close contact of all sorts with the Spaniards was responsible for the indigenous peoples' acculturation. The mestizos, who would later play the dominant role in Mexican society and history, could trace their origins to this period of intense assimilation of the two cultures (see Ethnicity and Language, ch. 2).

Agricultural production was directed to internal markets, while exports consisted mainly of precious metals and animal hides. During the initial phase of the colonial period, gold had been collected from the Aztec treasures and from some mining operations. However, silver soon became the dominant colonial product, followed by the red dye cochineal, and by the late sixteenth century, silver accounted for 80 percent of all exports from New Spain. Exploration and the search for mines led the

Spaniards to the north, far beyond the Aztec empire. The rich mines of Zacatecas, Real del Monte, Pachuca, and Guanajuato in north-central Mexico were discovered between 1546 and 1552. Silver production continued into the seventeenth century, and it employed most available labor.

During the sixteenth century, a dual economy developed in New Spain: the hacienda economy in the Valley of Mexico and the south and the frontier economy of the silver mines to the north. By the mid-seventeenth century, however, silver production collapsed when mercury, necessary to the refining process, was diverted to the silver mines of Potosí (in present-day Bolivia). The seventeenth-century mining crisis led to widespread bankruptcy among miners and hacendados (hacienda owners) and also had a negative effect on transatlantic trade. However, the financial crisis did promote the production of crude manufactures and food for domestic consumption by the growing population of New Spain.

Colonial society was stratified by race and wealth although these were not hard and fast distinctions. The three main groups were whites (European- and American-born), *castas* (mestizos), and native peoples; each had specific rights or privileges (*fueros*) and obligations in colonial society. The major *fuero* was the right of an individual to be tried by his or her peers. The church, the military, the bureaucracy, and the merchants enjoyed their set of *fueros.* Membership in the upper classes was open to whites only, particularly *peninsulares*, whites who were born in Spain and moved to the colonies. Criollos (American-born whites, also known as creoles) tended to marry *peninsulares* for reasons of upward social mobility. Nevertheless, many examples exist of race changes after birth.

The lower classes were a mixture of poor whites, *castas*, and native peoples who worked in the same occupations as whites or *castas* but who had different rights and obligations. Indigenous groups were protected from the Inquisition (the Roman Catholic court designed to combat heresy), paid head taxes, and could not own property as individuals but were the primary beneficiaries of social services in health and education. Mestizos were under the same obligations as whites but were not considered for most of the jobs in the Spanish administration. These jobs were held only by *peninsulares*. Poor whites and mestizos often competed with native people for the same jobs. The only unifying force in a society that was divided by race and privilege was the Roman Catholic Church. The clergy provided education and social services to the rich and the destitute alike, and clergy also functioned as a buffer in social conflicts.

The Road to Independence

The beginning of the eighteenth century in Spain coincided with the crowning of Spain's first Bourbon king. Under the Habsburgs, Spain had been ruined by wars abroad and conflicts at home. The new Bourbon administration that assumed power in 1707 was determined to effect structural changes in Spain's government and the economy to centralize power in the monarch. The colonies also received increased attention, mainly in terms of their defense and the reorganization of their economies.

The Bourbon Reforms

During the reign of the third Bourbon king of Spain, Charles III (1759–88), the Bourbons introduced important reforms at home and in the colonies. To modernize Mexico, higher taxes and more direct military control seemed to be necessary; to effect these changes, the government reorganized the political structure of New Spain into twelve *intendencias*, each headed by an *intendente* under a single commandant general in Mexico City, who was independent of the viceroy and reported directly to the king.

The economic reforms were directed primarily at the mining and trade sectors. Miners were given *fueros* and were allowed to organize themselves into a guild. Commerce was liberalized by allowing most Spanish ports to trade with the colonies, thus destroying the old monopoly held by the merchants of the Spanish port of Cádiz.

The Bourbon reforms changed the character of New Spain by revising governmental and economic structures. The reforms also prompted renewed migration of Spaniards to the colonies to occupy newly created government and military positions. At the same time, commerce, both legal and illegal, was growing, and independent merchants were also welcomed. The new monied classes of miners and merchants were the real promoters of the successes of the reforms enacted by the Bourbons.

Early Discontent: Criollos and Clergy

Economic expansion and a certain degree of political relaxation in the 1700s gave rise to greater expectations of autonomy by the colonists, especially after the republican revolutions in the United States (1776), France (1789), and Haiti (1804). Social stratification in New Spain, marked by discrepancies between the rich and the poor and between criollos and *peninsulares*, however, worked to prevent the necessary social cohesion for a revolutionary undertaking, even though the tensions for a revolution continued to build. *Peninsulares* from all walks of life believed themselves superior to their American-born counterparts. In reaction to such discrimination, criollos showed pride in things that pertained to Mexico. Criollos considered themselves subjects of the Spanish crown, however, and also abided by the doctrines of the Roman Catholic Church. More important, criollos did not want an egalitarian society—privileges were fine as long as they benefited from them.

In Europe, Napoleon Bonaparte invaded the Iberian Peninsula in 1808. When French troops entered Madrid, the Habsburg king, Charles IV, abdicated, and Napoleon named his brother Joseph Bonaparte as the new king. Many Spanish patriots in unoccupied parts of Spain declared Ferdinand VII, son of Charles IV, as the new monarch. When the news of Charles IV's abdication reached New Spain, considerable turmoil arose over the question of whether Ferdinand VII or Joseph was the legitimate ruler of the colony. Hoping to be named king of a newly independent country, Viceroy José de Iturrigaray supported the criollos of New Spain when they proposed a junta to govern the colony. *Peninsulares* realized the danger of such an association between criollos and the administration and thus orchestrated a coup d'état in 1808 to defend their privileges and standing in colonial society. After the coup, Iturrigaray was replaced by a senile puppet Spaniard, Pedro Garibay, much to the despair of the criollos.

Wars of Independence, 1810–21

The eleven-year period of civil war that marked the Mexican wars of independence was largely a byproduct of the crisis and breakdown of Spanish royal political authority throughout the American colonies. A successful independence movement in the United States had demonstrated the feasibility of a republican alternative to the European crown. For most politically articulate criollos, however, a strong cultural affinity with the mother country, a preference for stability and continuity, and alienation from Mexico's native and poor mestizo populations were significant disincentives to a radical break with the established order. Dissatisfaction with *peninsular* administrative practices and anti-criollo discrimination at many levels of the colonial government and society were important foci of discontent, but beyond small pockets of radical conspirators, these grievances had not yet spawned a pronounced wave of proindependence criollo sentiment at the beginning of the nineteenth century.

The French occupation of Spain and the overthrow of the Iturrigaray junta created a vacuum of legitimacy, as it was no longer clear that the ad hoc *peninsular* administration represented any authority or interests other than its own. A revolt would no longer necessarily be a challenge to the paternal crown and the faith that it ostensibly defended, but would instead shake off the rule of the increasingly despised *gachupines*, as the *peninsulares* were derisively called. It was in this context that a radical criollo parish priest, Miguel Hidalgo y Costilla, was able to lead the first truly widespread insurrection for Mexican independence.

Hidalgo and Morelos

Soon after being named parish priest in the small town of Dolores, Hidalgo began to promote the establishment of various small manufacturing concerns. He realized the need for diversification of industrial activities in an area that had the mines of Guanajuato as its major business. At the same time, during his seven years at Dolores, Hidalgo promoted discussion groups at his house, where Indians, mestizos, criollos, and *peninsulares* were welcomed. The themes of these discussions were current events, to which Hidalgo added his own input of social and economic concerns. The independence movement was born out of these informal discussions and was directed against Spanish domination of political and economic life in New Spain. December 8, 1810, was set for the beginning of the uprising.

The plans were disclosed to the central government, and the conspirators were alerted that orders had been sent for their arrest. Pressed by this new development, on September 16, 1810, Hidalgo decided to strike out for independence without delay (this date is celebrated as Mexico's independence day). The church bells summoned the people, and Hidalgo asked them to join him against the Spanish government and the *peninsulares* in the famous Grito de Dolores (Cry of Dolores):

"Long live Our Lady of Guadalupe! Death to bad government! Death to the *gachupines!*" The crowd responded enthusiastically, and soon an angry mob was marching toward the regional capital of Guanajuato. The miners of Guanajuato joined with the native workers of Dolores in the massacre of all *peninsulares* who resisted them, including the local *intendente.*

From Guanajuato, the independence forces marched on to Mexico City after having captured Zacatecas, San Luis Potosí, and Valladolid. On October 30, 1810, they encountered resistance at Monte de las Cruces and, despite a rebel victory, lost momentum and did not take Mexico City. After a few more victories, the revolutionary forces moved north toward Texas. In March of the following year, the insurgents were ambushed and taken prisoner in Monclova (in the present-day state of Coahuila). Hidalgo was tried as a priest by the Holy Office of the Inquisition and found guilty of heresy and treason. He was later condemned to death. On July 31, 1811, Hidalgo was executed by firing squad. His body was mutilated, and his head was displayed in Guanajuato as a warning to other would- be insurgents.

After the death of Hidalgo, José María Morelos Pavón assumed the leadership of the revolutionary movement. Morelos took charge of the political and military aspects of the insurrection and further planned a strategic move to encircle Mexico City and to cut communications to the coastal areas. In June 1813, Morelos convoked a national congress of representatives from all of the provinces, which met at Chilpancingo in the present-day state of Guerrero to discuss the future of Mexico as an independent nation. The major points included in the document prepared by the congress were popular sovereignty, universal male suffrage, the adoption of Roman Catholicism as the official religion, abolition of slavery and forced labor, an end to government monopolies, and an end to corporal punishment. Despite initial successes by Morelos's forces, however, the colonial authorities broke the siege of Mexico City after six months, captured positions in the surrounding areas, and finally invaded Chilpancingo. In 1815 Morelos was captured and met the same fate as Hidalgo.

From 1815 to 1821, most of the fighting by those seeking independence from Spain was done by isolated guerrilla bands. Out of these bands rose two men, Guadalupe Victoria (whose real name was Manuel Félix Fernández) in Puebla and Vicente Guerrero in Oaxaca, both of whom were able to command allegiance and respect from their followers. The Spanish viceroy, however, felt the situation was under control and issued a general pardon to every rebel who would lay down his arms.

After ten years of civil war and the death of two of its founders, by early 1820 the independence movement was stalemated and close to collapse. The rebels faced stiff Spanish military resistance and the apathy of many of the most influential criollos. The violent excesses and populist zeal of Hidalgo's and Morelos's irregular armies had reinforced many criollos' fears of race and class warfare, ensuring their grudging acquiescence to conservative Spanish rule until a less bloody path to independence could be found. It was at this juncture that the machinations of a conservative military caudillo coinciding with a successful liberal rebellion in Spain, made possible a radical realignment of the proindependence forces.

Iturbide and the Plan of Iguala

In what was supposed to be the final government campaign against the insurgents, in December 1820, Viceroy Juan Ruiz de Apodaca sent a force led by a royalist criollo officer, Augustín de Iturbide, to defeat Guerrero's army in Oaxaca. Iturbide, a native of Valladolid, had gained renown for the zeal with which he persecuted Hidalgo's and Morelos's rebels during the early independence struggle. A favorite of the Mexican church hierarchy, Iturbide was the personification of conservative criollo values, devoutly religious, and committed to the defense of property rights and social privileges; he was also disgruntled at his lack of promotion and wealth.

Iturbide's assignment to the Oaxaca expedition coincided with a successful military coup in Spain against the new monarchy of Ferdinand VII. The coup leaders, who had been assembled as an expeditionary force to suppress the American independence movements, compelled a reluctant Ferdinand to sign the liberal Spanish constitution of 1812. When news of the liberal charter reached Mexico, Iturbide saw in it both a threat to the status quo and an opportunity for the criollos to gain control of Mexico. Ironically, independence was finally achieved when conservative forces in the colonies chose to rise up against a temporarily liberal regime in the mother country. After an initial clash with Guerrero's forces, Iturbide switched allegiances and invited the rebel leader to meet and discuss principles of a renewed independence struggle.

While stationed in the town of Iguala, Iturbide proclaimed three principles, or "guarantees," for Mexican independence from Spain: Mexico would be an independent monarchy governed by a transplanted King Ferdinand or some other conservative European prince, criollos and *peninsulares* would henceforth enjoy equal rights and privileges, and the Roman Catholic Church would retain its privileges and religious monopoly. After convincing his troops to accept the principles, which were promulgated on February 24, 1821, as the Plan of Iguala, Iturbide persuaded Guerrero to join his forces in support of the new conservative manifestation of the independence movement. A new army, the Army of the Three Guarantees, was then placed under Iturbide's command to enforce the Plan of Iguala. The plan was so broadly based that it pleased both patriots and loyalists. The goal of independence and the protection of Roman Catholicism brought together all factions.

Iturbide's army was joined by rebel forces from all over Mexico. When the rebels' victory became certain, the viceroy resigned. On September 27, 1821, representatives of the Spanish crown and Iturbide signed the Treaty of Córdoba, which recognized Mexican independence under the terms of the Plan of Iguala. Iturbide, a former royalist who had become the paladin for Mexican independence, included a special clause in the treaty that left open the possibility for a criollo monarch to be appointed by a Mexican congress if no suitable member of the European royalty would accept the Mexican crown.

Empire and Early Republic, 1821–55

The Abortive Empire, 1821–23

According to the Plan of Iguala, a provisional government was set up while an independent congress deliberated on the future of the nation. Congress was able to agree on two major issues: to cut the size of the Army of the Three Guarantees and to determine the eligibility of officials for the planned regency that eventually would replace the provisional government. As congress deliberated, Iturbide realized that power was slipping from his hands and decided to stage a dramatic demonstration on his behalf. On the evening of May 18, 1822, his troops were ordered to march through Mexico City in support of their commander. The demonstration by the Army of the Three Guarantees was joined by other soldiers and by the populace as it proceeded toward Iturbide's residence. "Long live Agustín I, Emperor of Mexico!" was the acclamation, at which Iturbide pretended surprise. The following day, congress named Iturbide as the constitutional emperor of Mexico. The arrangements for the coronation were pretentious but still in accord with Iturbide's understanding of the Mexican ethos. Iturbide recalled the importance of the monarchy in maintaining stability and control during the colonial period, and he decided to take full advantage of tradition.

The new empire faced serious economic problems. After the wars, the public coffers were empty, and the bureaucracy had grown. Modest tax adjustments were tried, but the results were meager. In congress, discontented factions sharply criticized the government, and Iturbide's recourse was to dissolve the legislative branch and to have all opposition delegates arrested in August 1822. In Veracruz, the commander of the garrison, Antonio López de Santa Anna Pérez de Lebrón, rose against Iturbide and proclaimed a republic on December 1, 1822. Santa Anna was quickly joined by other revolutionaries— including a disenchanted Vicente Guerrero, Nicolás Bravo, and Guadalupe Victoria. Together, they drew up the Plan of Casa Mata on February 1, 1823. By midmonth, Iturbide, realizing the failure of his efforts, abdicated the throne. Rebel forces encountered no opposition when they arrived in Mexico City. In July the United Provinces of Central America (consisting of Spanish-speaking Central America except for present-day Panama), which had been forcibly incorporated into the empire by Iturbide, declared their independence. (The province of Chiapas, belonging to the Captaincy General of Guatemala, opted to remain a part of Mexico.) The experience of an empire had failed, and the idea of a monarchical system for Mexico would be dismissed for four decades. Iturbide's excesses had worked to the benefit of the republicans.

The Federalist Republic, 1824–36

After the fall of the empire, a provisional government was installed consisting of Bravo, Victoria, and Pedro Celestino Negrete. Delegates were elected to the Constitutional Congress that entered into session on November 27, 1823. The congress had two major factions: the federalists, who feared control from a conservative Mexico City and were supported by liberal criollos and mestizos; and the more conservative centralists, who preferred the rule of tradition and drew their allegiance from the clergy, conservative criollos, the landowners, and the military.

Although the federalist forces largely prevailed in writing the new constitution, the centralists won three major concessions. The constitution of 1824, which was strongly influenced by the United States constitution and Mexico's legislative relationship with Spain since 1810, established the United Mexican States (Estados Unidos Mexicanos) as a federal republic composed of nineteen states and four territories (see Constitutional History, ch. 4). Power was distributed among executive, legislative, and judicial branches of government. Legislative power was wielded by the Senate and the Chamber of Deputies, while executive power was exercised by a president and a vice president elected by the state legislatures for four-year terms. In spite of the liberal outlook of the constitution, certain traditional privileges were maintained: Roman Catholicism remained the official religion, the *fueros* were retained by the military and clergy, and in national emergencies the president could exercise unlimited powers.

During the administration of Mexico's first president, Guadalupe Victoria, economic conditions worsened as government expenditures soared beyond revenues. Declining economic conditions convinced the criollos that there was more behind the economic decline than bad management by *peninsulares*. One of the government's major burdens was the assumption of all debts contracted during the late colonial period and the empire, a substantial sum. The government's ability to service the debt was severely constrained by the costs of maintaining a 50,000-strong standing army and the insufficiency of revenues generated by tariffs, taxes, and government monopolies. To cover the shortfall, Victoria accepted two large loans on stiff terms from British merchant houses. The British had supported independence movements in Spanish colonies and saw the loans as an opportunity to further displace Spain as the New World's dominant mercantile power.

Mexico's financial crisis was overshadowed in 1827 by a conservative rebellion led by Vice President Bravo. The revolt was quickly suppressed by generals Santa Anna and Guerrero, but political tensions remained high as the presidential elections of 1828 approached. The September 1828 elections pitted General Guerrero as the liberal candidate for the federalists against conservative Manuel Gómez Pedraza, who had served as secretary of war in Victoria's bipartisan cabinet. The voting results from the state legislatures showed Gómez Pedraza to be the winner in ten of the nineteen states, but the liberals refused to turn over the government, claiming that Gómez Pedraza had used his authority over the army to pressure the states into voting in his favor. A period of confusion ensued as two rival governments and their respective military factions battled over the presidential succession. The liberals finally emerged victorious after Gómez Pedraza abandoned the presidential palace under sustained pressure from rebels commanded by Santa Anna and Lorenzo de Zavala.

President Guerrero took power over a liberal government shrouded in questionable legality and dependent upon the loyalty of the military. Immediately upon assuming office, Guerrero experienced his first major crisis when the Spanish attempted to retake Mexico. A Spanish force of 3,000 soldiers under the command of General Isidro Barradas landed at Tampico in July 1829. Guerrero sent Santa Anna to dislodge the Spanish force in August, but the Mexican general could not launch an effective assault and instead dug in for a siege. Cut off from supplies and weakened by disease, the Spanish surrendered to the Mexicans in October. In the aftermath of the Spanish withdrawal, Santa Anna was widely hailed as the savior of the republic.

With the Spanish threat gone, Guerrero enacted several liberal reforms, including the abolition of slavery in September 1829. His forceful style of governing, made possible by his retention of emergency presidential powers obtained during the Spanish invasion, gave the conservatives renewed cause to rebel. In early 1830, the conservative vice president, Anastasio Bustamante, led a successful military-backed revolt against Guerrero and installed himself as Mexico's third president. While attempting to flee the country in January 1831, Guerrero was captured and executed by government soldiers on Bustamante's orders. Bustamante's conservative government was highly unpopular and repressive. In early 1832, Santa Anna denounced Bustamante in Veracruz, occupied the city, and appropriated its custom revenues. Santa Anna's defiance spurred additional revolts throughout the states, leading to the eventual collapse of the conservative government and the return of the liberals.

The highly popular Santa Anna was elected president under the liberal banner in early 1833. Instead of assuming office, however, he withdrew into semiretirement and delegated the presidency to his vice president, Valentín Gómez Farías. The liberal Gómez Farías government was strongly reformist, to the detriment of traditional church and military privileges. Among its reforms, the new administration decreed that payment of tithes would no longer be compulsory, and it transferred to the nation the right to make ecclesiastical appointments. In addition, Gómez Farías reduced the size of the army and eliminated its *fueros*.

Gómez Farías's far-reaching reforms drew a characteristically strong response from conservative elites, the army, and the church hierarchy. Under the banner of *religión y fueros*, the inevitable conservative backlash gained strength throughout the winter of 1833. In April 1834, Santa Anna abandoned the liberal cause and deposed Gómez Farías. The renowned general promptly dismissed congress and assumed dictatorial powers, bringing an end to liberal rule under the federal republic.

Centralism and the Caudillo State, 1836–55

In the two decades after the 1834 collapse of the federal republic, Santa Anna dominated Mexico's politics. Between 1833 and 1855, the caudillo occupied the presidency eleven times, completing none of his terms and frequently leaving the government in the hands of weak caretaker administrations. During this period, Mexico went to war on three separate occasions and lost half of its territory through sale or military defeat. Fiscal insufficiency kept Mexico constantly on the verge of bankruptcy and foreign military intervention.

Santa Anna repeatedly rose to the presidency, only to be cast out in the wake of scandals and military defeats. Invariably, he returned—even from exile—to lead the republic once more into military glory or out of insolvency. Santa Anna's bravery, energy, and organizational abilities were often matched by his vanity, cruelty, and opportunism. His feats of heroism in victorious battle, his bold interventions in the political life of the country, and his countless shifts from one side of the political spectrum to the other responded to the insecurities of Mexican nationalists and the vacillations of the republic's fractious political class.

The Constitution of 1836

Upon assuming dictatorial powers, Santa Anna promptly annulled Gómez Farías's reforms and abolished the constitution of 1824. The authoritarian principles that underlay Santa

Anna's rule were subsequently codified in the constitution of 1836, also known as the Siete Leyes (Seven Laws). Under the constitution of 1836, Mexico became a centralist regime in which power was concentrated in the president and his immediate subordinates. The states of the former federal republic were refashioned as military districts administered by regional caudillos appointed by the president, and property qualifications were decreed for congressional officeholders and voters.

The nationalist and authoritarian style of the new centralist regime soon brought it into conflict with the loosely governed lands of Mexico's northern frontier. Santa Anna's efforts to exert central authority over the English-speaking settlements in the northern state of Coahuila-Tejas eventually collided with the growing assertiveness of the frontier population that described itself as Texan.

The Loss of Texas

Texas (known as Tejas) had been part of New Spain since the early colonial period. In 1821 in an effort to colonize and populate Texas, the Spanish commander in Monterrey granted a concession to a United States pioneer, Moses Austin, to settle the area under the Roman Catholic faith. Land could be acquired for a nominal charge of US$0.25 per hectare, and soon colonists from the United States started to pour into the area. By 1835 they outnumbered the Mexicans, four to one. Texas had no autonomous government and was politically attached to the state of Coahuila. Most Mexicans began to fear the incursions by North Americans and the possibility of losing Texas to the United States. Restrictions were placed on the future immigration of colonists from the United States, and slavery was abolished in 1829 in the hope of discouraging United States southerners from moving into the area.

Santa Anna's move to bring Texas under the political domination of Mexico City pushed the Texans to secede from Mexico on November 7, 1835, and to declare their independence in March 1836. In 1835 Santa Anna marched north in the direction of San Antonio with an army of 3,000 men. He reached San Antonio in March 1836 and learned that about 150 armed Texans had taken refuge at an old Franciscan mission, called the Alamo. He laid siege to the mission for several days before the final attack on March 6, 1836. The Mexican force took the mission the next day, killing all but five of the defenders in battle (the five prisoners were later executed). On

March 23, the Texan town of Goliad was surrounded by Mexican forces, who compelled the Texan commander in charge to surrender. On express orders from Santa Anna, 365 prisoners were executed. The events at the Alamo and at Goliad stirred strong anti-Mexican sentiment in the United States. Volunteer fighters poured into Texas to stage a decisive blow against Santa Anna. The Mexican commander in chief and his army were ambushed and roundly defeated near the San Jacinto River by a force commanded by Sam Houston on April 21. Santa Anna, who had fled the scene of the battle, was captured by the Texans two days later.

While under custody of the Texans, Santa Anna signed two treaties with the Texas government: one ended hostilities by pledging the withdrawal of Mexican troops to positions south of the Río Bravo del Norte (Rio Grande), and the other, a secret treaty, recognized Texan independence from Mexico.

The Mexican-American War

After Texas attained its independence, the idea of its incorporation into the United States gained support both in Texas and in the United States Congress. Definitive action on the measure was delayed for several years, however, because of the divisive issue of admitting another slave state into the United States and the likely prospect that annexation would provoke a war with Mexico. In early 1845, the United States Congress passed a resolution in favor of the annexation of Texas, which prompted Mexico to sever diplomatic relations with the United States. The Mexican congress had never ratified Santa Anna's secret treaty with the Texans, and to underscore its opposition to Texas's independence, the Mexican congress passed a law that retroactively annulled any treaties signed by a Mexican negotiator while in captivity.

Further aggravating the dispute was the fact that the Texans had issued a dubious territorial claim that expanded the republic's southern and western boundary from the previously accepted Nueces River to the Río Bravo del Norte. By claiming all of the land up to the headwaters of the Río Bravo del Norte, the Texans more than doubled the size of their republic to include parts of present-day New Mexico, Colorado, Oklahoma, Kansas, and all of present-day western Texas.

Shortly after Texas was admitted to the Union as the twenty-eighth state, President James K. Polk dispatched a special envoy, John Slidell, to Mexico City to settle the Texas boundary dispute and to arrange the purchase of California. The Mexican president, José Joaquín Herrera, had been willing to recognize an independent Texas but was under intense domestic pressure to reject United States annexation and Texas's expanded territorial claim. As a result, he refused to meet Slidell and began reinforcing Mexican army units along the Río Bravo del Norte.

Hostilities between Mexico and the United States began on April 25, 1846, when several United States soldiers were killed in a cavalry skirmish with Mexican forces in the disputed territory. Shortly after the two sides declared war, Santa Anna was recalled from exile in Cuba to once again lead Mexican troops against a foreign invasion.

The United States Army attacked on three fronts: one column, under General Stephen W. Kearney, occupied California and New Mexico; another column, under General Zachary Taylor, entered northern Mexico; and a third detachment, commanded by General Winfield Scott, landed at Veracruz and marched to Mexico City. California and New Mexico fell with little bloodshed. Northern Mexico was the scene of fierce battles between Taylor and Santa Anna's armies at Buena Vista. Santa Anna initially struck hard at the outnumbered United States forces, but he later abandoned the battle and returned to Mexico City, prematurely claiming victory.

The heaviest fighting was done by Scott's Army of Occupation, which landed at Veracruz on March 9, 1847. Rather than attempt to occupy the city outright, Scott positioned his forces west of it, cutting off Veracruz's supply line from the capital. After several days of heavy naval bombardment that killed hundreds of civilians, Veracruz surrendered on March 27, 1847.

In Mexico City, the situation was chaotic. President once again, Santa Anna denounced both congress and his own subordinates in the executive branch for their lack of resolve in preparing the defense of the capital. They, in turn, denounced him for his failures in battle. On August 20, 1847, the Army of Occupation asked for the surrender of Mexico City, but the battle continued until September 13, 1847, when the last bastion of Mexican resistance fell during the famous Battle of Chapultepec. During the battle, young cadets from the Mexican military academy, the Niños Héroes (or "boy heroes") leapt to their deaths rather than surrender. The United States victory marked the end of the war and the beginning of negotiations for peace.

Treaty of Guadalupe Hidalgo

According to the terms of the Treaty of Guadalupe Hidalgo of February 2, 1848, the boundary between Mexico and the United States was established at the Río Bravo del Norte. Mexico was then required to relinquish its territories of New Mexico and Upper California (the present-day states of California, Nevada, Utah, and parts of Arizona, New Mexico, Colorado, and Wyoming) and to accept Texas's incorporation into the United States. As compensation, the United States agreed to pay US$15 million for the territories and to assume more than US$3 million in claims from private citizens of these areas against the Mexican government. Mexico lost more than one-half of its territory as a result of the war with the United States. The territorial losses and the brief but traumatic occupation of Mexico City by United States troops engendered a deep-seated mistrust of the United States that still resonates in Mexican popular culture. Anti-United States nationalist sentiment was a major intellectual current in the Mexican Revolution and continues to manifest itself in some aspects of Mexican society (see Foreign Relations, ch. 4).

Santa Anna's last political venture resulted in the sale of more Mexican territory. In what is known in the United States as the Gadsden Purchase, ratified by the United States Congress in 1854, Santa Anna sold 77,692 square kilometers of land in southern New Mexico and Arizona for US$10 million (see fig. 2). This additional loss of territory alienated a large, reform-minded group of young Mexicans, who then conspired to oust Santa Anna.

Reform and French Intervention, 1855–67

The Revolution of Ayutla and the Reform Laws

The Mexican reform movement was inspired by the liberal political philosophies of European intellectuals, such as Jean-Jacques Rousseau, John Stuart Mill, and Pierre Joseph Proudhon. Their views were adopted by a group of Mexican intellectuals who shared a strong commitment to moralize Mexican politics. The most outstanding member of the group was Benito Juárez, a Zapotec lawyer and politician. Juárez and his cohorts went into exile in Louisiana, where they drew up the Plan of Ayutla in 1854 for the overthrow of Santa Anna. As the plan gained broad-based support, the conspirators began to

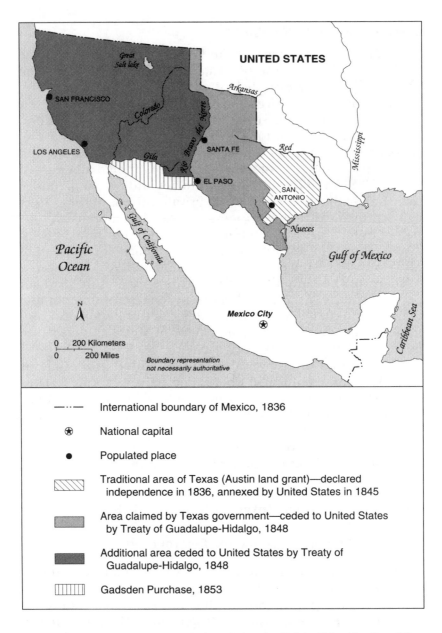

International boundary of Mexico, 1836

National capital

Populated place

Traditional area of Texas (Austin land grant)—declared independence in 1836, annexed by United States in 1845

Area claimed by Texas government—ceded to United States by Treaty of Guadalupe-Hidalgo, 1848

Additional area ceded to United States by Treaty of Guadalupe-Hidalgo, 1848

Gadsden Purchase, 1853

Source: Based on information from Cathryn L. Lombardi, John V. Lombardi, and K. Lynn Stoner, *Latin American History: A Teaching Atlas*, Madison, Wisconsin, 1983, 50, 53.

Figure 2. Mexican Territorial Losses to the United States, 1836–53

return to Mexico. In August 1855, in response to growing opposition, Santa Anna resigned for the last time.

A provisional government was installed under Juan Ruiz de Álvarez and the intellectuals of Ayutla; the ensuing period of liberal rule came to be known as the Reform. The Reform was touted as a Mexican version of the French Revolution. Several laws, known collectively as the Reform Laws, abolished the *fueros*, curtailed ecclesiastical property holdings, introduced a civil registry, and prohibited the church from charging exorbitant fees for administering the sacraments.

The Reform Laws polarized Mexican society along pro- and anticlerical lines at a time when delegates were preparing the constitution of 1857, as provided for in the Plan of Ayutla. The new constitution was derived from that of 1824, but it reflected a more liberal vision of society through its incorporation of the Reform Laws. It reaffirmed the abolition of slavery, secularized education, and guaranteed basic civil liberties for all Mexicans. Both the Reform Laws and the constitution, however, divided the political classes and set the stage for a civil war.

Civil War and the French Intervention

The civil war, commonly known as the War of the Reform, that engulfed Mexico between 1858 and 1861 brought to light the underlying conflicts that had been present in Mexican society since independence. The conservative faction launched the Plan of Tacubaya and, with the support of the military and the clergy, dissolved congress and arrested Juárez. Juárez escaped and established a "government in exile" in Querétaro (the liberals later moved their capital to Veracruz). The initial military advantage was held by the conservatives, who were better armed and had plentiful supplies, but by 1860 the situation was reversed. The final battle took place just before Christmas 1860. The victorious liberal army entered Mexico City on January 1, 1861.

In March 1861, Juárez won the presidential election, but the war left the treasury depleted. Trade was stagnant, and foreign creditors were demanding full repayment of Mexican debts. Juárez proceeded to declare a moratorium on all foreign debt repayments. In October 1861, Spain, Britain, and France decided to launch a joint occupation of the Mexican Gulf coast to force repayment. In December troops from the three nations landed at Veracruz and began deliberations. Because the representatives of the three nations could not agree on the means to enforce the collection of the debt, Britain and Spain recalled their armies. Spurred by dreams of reestablishing an empire in the New World, the French remained and, with the support of Mexican conservatives, embarked on an occupation of Mexico.

In Puebla, the French troops encountered strong resistance led by one of Juárez's trusted men, General Ignacio Zaragoza, who defeated the foreigners on May 5, 1862 (May 5 is celebrated today as one of Mexico's two national holidays). The following May, Puebla was surrounded once again by French troops, who laid siege to the city for two months until it surrendered. The fall of Puebla meant easy access to Mexico City, and Juárez decided to evacuate the capital after receiving approval from congress.

The French encountered no resistance to their occupation of Mexico City. In June 1863, a provisional government was chosen, and in October a delegation of Mexican conservatives invited Ferdinand Maximilian Joseph von Habsburg of Austria to accept the Mexican crown, all according to the plans of French emperor Napoleon III. Maximilian was a well-intentioned monarch who accepted the crown believing that this act responded to the desire of a majority of Mexicans. Before departing for Mexico, Maximilian signed an agreement with Napoleon III, under which Maximilian assumed the debts incurred for the upkeep of the French army in Mexico. On June 12, 1864, the Emperor Maximilian I and his Belgian wife, Marie Charlotte Amélie Léopoldine, now called Empress Carlota, arrived in Mexico City. The republican government under Juárez retreated to the far north.

Maximilian, schooled in the European liberal tradition, was a strong supporter of Mexican nationalism. He soon found resistance from all quarters of the political spectrum, however. The conservatives expected the emperor to act against the Reform Laws, but Maximilian refused to revoke them. Mexican liberals appealed for military assistance from the United States on the basis of the French violation of the 1823 Monroe Doctrine, but the United States was involved in its own civil war. The end of the Civil War in the United States in 1865, however, prompted a more assertive foreign policy toward Mexico and released manpower and arms that were directed to help Juárez in his fight against the French. In Europe, France was increasingly threatened by a belligerent Prussia. By November 1866, Napoleon III began recalling his troops stationed in Mexico.

Conservative forces switched sides and began supporting the Mexican liberals. United republican forces resumed their campaign on February 19, 1867, and on May 15, Maximilian surrendered. He was tried and, on Juárez's orders, was executed on June 19.

The Restoration, 1867–76

The liberal republicans under Juárez's leadership consolidated the victory of the principles of the constitution of 1857. The Restoration, as the period from 1867 to 1876 is called, was marked by peace and tolerance toward the conservatives. Juárez returned to Mexico City on July 15, 1867, called for presidential elections, and presented himself as a candidate. By the end of the year, he was victorious.

The economy and the education system were vitally important to Juarez's new administration. Economic development was based on the improvement of communications, the exploitation of the country's natural resources, and the revamping of the mining sector through favorable tax guidelines. Seeking to reduce banditry and to attract investment capital, Juárez strengthened the *rurales,* the Rural Defense Force (Guardia Rural) responsible for the security of roads and land cargo, and placed it under the Ministry of Interior. The improvement of communications began with the completion in 1873 of the railroad that linked Mexico City with Veracruz, a Mexican venture that had been started in the 1850s. In the area of education, a complete reorganization was directed by a commission headed by the prominent physician and positivist intellectual, Gabino Barreda. He devised a school curriculum that concentrated on mathematics and the physical sciences. For the first time, education became mandatory. Despite new schools, the liberal aspiration for literacy and schools open to all remained an unfulfilled goal, as in most nineteenth-century rural societies.

At the end of his term in 1871, Juárez decided to seek reelection. His opponents were José de la Cruz Porfirio Díaz and Sebastián Lerdo de Tejada, whose candidacies divided the liberal faction and resulted in none of the candidates receiving a majority of the votes. With no clear winner, it was up to congress to choose among the three candidates or to reelect the incumbent president. The congress chose Juárez. Díaz invoked the principle of "no reelection" in the constitution of 1857 and staged a revolt in November 1871. On July 18, 1872, amidst the Díaz rebellion, Juárez died of a heart attack.

New elections were called in 1872, and Lerdo won the presidency. His administration was characterized by a continuous effort to bring peace to the country, and he intervened militarily in the countryside whenever it was necessary. Lerdo maintained the emphasis on communications through new railroad and telegraph lines. In education, he directed his energies to the construction of new schools and the enrollment of more students. When the time came for electing a new president, Lerdo showed interest in another four-year term. Díaz rose in rebellion a second time in March 1876, again defending the "no reelection" principle. Lerdo went into exile in the United States, and on November 21, 1876, Díaz occupied Mexico City. A political mastermind, surrounded by capable advisers, he held power directly or indirectly for the next thirty-four years. The period known as the "Porfiriato" (the period of Porfirio Díaz's rule) had begun.

The Porfiriato, 1876–1910

Propitious economic conditions did not greet Porfirio Díaz upon his rise to power in 1876. Mexico remained saddled with a huge foreign debt and an empty treasury. An army of bureaucrats was owed back wages, the country had a poor international credit rating, and persistent current account deficits caused serious balance of payments problems. Investment, whether foreign or domestic, was scarce, and the mining industry had yet to recover from the revolutionary wars. The relatively few mines in operation in 1876 were exploited haphazardly, and extraction and smelting techniques were archaic. Only a few miles of rail had been laid, transportation and communications were rudimentary, and dock facilities were dilapidated and unsafe. Endemic rural violence further hindered commerce.

During his first four years in office, Díaz began to tackle economic backwardness. He first decreed stiff measures against contraband moving across the United States border. Smugglers and bandits crossed the border from both sides, but Díaz would not permit United States troops to enter Mexico in search of them. Instead, he enlarged the Mexican border patrol. In 1877 Díaz agreed to honor US$4 million in claims by United States citizens against Mexico.

*José de la Cruz Porfirio Díaz,
president, 1876–80, 1884–1911
Courtesy New York Public Library*

In 1880 at the end of his term and despite his followers' wishes, Díaz left office. The next president, Manuel González, continued Diaz's modernization program. Telegraph lines began to operate, and railroad construction was kept apace. In an attempt to meet his foreign debt obligations, González withheld the salaries of government officials, a move that led to a harsh campaign against the president.

During González's tenure, Díaz gathered a large following that restored him to office in 1884. Mexican positivism, embodied in the slogan "order and progress," was the backbone of the modernization scheme supported by the *científicos*, intellectual followers of Barreda. Led by José Ives Limantour, who served as adviser to Díaz, the *científicos* developed a plan for economic recovery that was to be carried out through the next twenty-seven years of the Porfiriato.

Porfirian Modernization

Diaz's strategy of export-oriented growth led to Mexico's rapid integration into the world economy. The modernization program was based on exploitation of the country's natural resources, using cheap domestic labor and foreign capital and technology for export production.

Foreign capital fueled dynamic growth, and an expanding rail network promoted export agriculture, manufacturing, and mining. Agriculture and livestock export products expanded to include cattle and cattle hides, coffee, cotton, henequen, sugar, vanilla, and chicle. Railroads allowed the exploitation of new land in the north for cotton cultivation and enabled Mexico to double its cotton production between 1887 and 1910.

The Díaz regime encouraged manufacturing through export incentives, high protective tariffs on foreign manufactured products, low transportation costs, and abolition of the transactions tax on business. The number of industrial enterprises—most of them heavily backed by United States, French, German, and British investors—grew rapidly, and the volume of manufactured goods doubled between 1877 and 1910.

The railroads also contributed to the revival of mining because they provided the only feasible means of transporting huge amounts of ore. Legal reforms in 1884 lowered taxes on mining and allowed foreign ownership of subsoil resources, spurring a large increase in United States and European investment in Mexican mines.

Society under the Porfiriato

Ironically, Mexico's economic success during the Porfiriato had negative social consequences. Although the economy grew at an average annual rate of 2.6 percent, real income per capita had recovered only to pre-1821 levels by 1911. After 1900 unemployment increased as mechanization displaced artisans faster than unskilled workers were absorbed into new productive enterprises. Additionally, real and financial assets were increasingly concentrated in the hands of a few local and foreign investors.

The rural peasantry bore most of the cost of modernization. Government seizure of private and communal land increased the landless rural population and led to further concentration of land ownership. Taking advantage of an 1883 land law intended to encourage foreign investment, by 1888 land companies had obtained possession of more than 27.5 million hectares of rural land. By 1894 these companies controlled one-fifth of Mexico's total territory. By 1910 most villages had lost their *ejidos* (communal land holdings—see Glossary), a few hundred wealthy families held some 54.3 million hectares of the country's most productive land, and more than half of all rural Mexicans worked on these families' huge haciendas.

The modernization program was also brought about at the expense of personal and political freedom. Díaz made certain that "order" was maintained at all costs for the sake of "progress." Force was used whenever necessary to neutralize opponents of the regime. Freedom of the press was nonexistent. The army and the *rurales* became the forces of repression for the maintenance of the Porfirian peace during the Porfiriato. Mock elections were held at all levels of government, while Díaz appointed his loyal friends as political bosses. Despite the modernization, Mexico remained a predominantly poor and rural country, and class stratification became entrenched.

The wealth that flowed into urban areas during the Porfiriato fostered the growth of an urban middle class of white-collar workers, artisans, and entrepreneurs. The middle class had little use for anything Mexican, but instead identified strongly with the European manners and tastes adopted by the urban upper class. The emulation of Europe was especially evident in the arts and in architecture, to the detriment of indigenous forms of cultural expression. The identification of the urban middle class with the European values promoted by Díaz further aggravated the schism between urban and rural Mexico.

The Revolution, 1910–20

The Early Phase

In the political arena, the Porfiriato was marked by the systematic violation of the principles of the constitution of 1857. Díaz courted foreign interests, allowed the clergy again to become openly influential in temporal matters, and gave the army a free hand to violate guaranteed civil liberties while opponents of the regime were either coopted or sent to jail.

Meanwhile, liberal writers and journalists began to challenge the regime. These attacks became more coordinated with the organization of liberal clubs and a liberal convention at San Luis Potosí in 1900 and 1901 that defended the principles of the constitution of 1857. For the next two years, liberal congresses were held, but the persecution of representatives led many liberals to seek asylum in the United States. The exiles (especially the Flores Magón brothers, Juan Saraia, Antonio I. Villareal, and Librado Rivera) issued a liberal proclamation on July 1, 1906, from St. Louis, Missouri, that called for the overthrow of Díaz. They then started a publication, *Redención,* to set forth their ideas. The program presented in the proclamation of St. Louis introduced new concepts in education, labor relations, land distribution, and agricultural credit. These ideas reached Mexico through issues of *Redención* smuggled across the border.

In 1908 an unexpected development brought hope of political change to the anti-Díaz political opposition. In an interview with a United States reporter, Díaz stated that he would not seek reelection in 1910. Liberals and dissident intellectuals immediately seized the opportunity and nominated Francisco I. Madero, the scion of a wealthy family in Coahuila, to run in the upcoming election. In June 1910, relying on harsh measures, including the imprisonment of thousands of opposition activists, Díaz was reelected. Madero, himself imprisoned, was released from jail and went into exile in the United States.

Díaz began preparing a joint celebration—the one-hundredth anniversary of Mexican independence and his eightieth birthday—in September 1910. Mexico City went through a full refurbishing. Buildings were dedicated, monuments were unveiled, and numerous balls and celebrations were attended by the entire diplomatic corps. The streets of the capital were cleared of refuse and undesirables in order to present foreigners with a positive picture of the society created by the Porfiriato.

In October 1910, Madero drafted the Plan of San Luis Potosí, which called for the people to rise on November 20 to demand the restoration of the democratic principles of the constitution of 1857 and the replacement of Díaz with a provisional government. Although it was mainly a political document with scant reference to redressing Mexico's many social ills, the Plan of San Luis Potosí was enthusiastically received among the widespread, but uncoordinated movements that were already on the verge of rebellion against their respective state governments. Copies of the plan, which Madero had drafted in St. Louis, soon reached Mexico and were widely distributed. On the appointed day, Madero and a small band of rebels crossed into Mexico, but finding no rebel armies with which to rendezvous, they soon turned back.

By January 1911, however, a large-scale insurrection had broken out in the northern state of Chihuahua, led by Pascual Orozco, a local merchant, and Francisco "Pancho" Villa. Madero, who had declared himself provisional president in the Plan of San Luis Potosí, returned to Mexico to lead the nascent

Francisco "Pancho" Villa,
revolutionary leader, 1911–17,
with a group of fighters
Courtesy Library of Congress

Emiliano Zapata,
revolutionary leader, 1911–17
Courtesy New York Public Library

revolution. The successes of the rebel bands in Chihuahua sparked similar uprisings throughout the country. As early as 1909 in Morelos, the peasant leader, Emiliano Zapata, had recruited thousands of hacienda laborers and landless peasants to attack the haciendas and reclaim lost lands.

In April Díaz sent finance minister Limantour to negotiate an armistice with the northern rebels, who were besieging Ciudad Juárez. When Limantour refused to negotiate Díaz's resignation, Villa and Orozco renewed their attack on Ciudad Juárez and captured the town. By May several state capitals had been lost to the rebels, and mobs filled the streets of Mexico City shouting for Díaz to resign. On May 25, 1911, the eighty-year-old dictator submitted his resignation to congress and turned power over to a provisional government. The following day Díaz quietly sailed for exile in France.

Madero's Government

Madero assumed the presidency in November 1911. The new administration faced insurmountable problems. The fall of Díaz raised popular expectations of far-reaching social reforms, especially land reform. Zapata had come to Mexico City to claim hacienda land for the peasants of Morelos, which to him was the only acceptable result of the overthrow of the Díaz regime. Instead, Madero ordered Zapata to disband his troops, and reluctantly Zapata acceded to Madero's request. The interim government did not think Zapata was demobilizing fast enough, however, and sent federal troops to disarm the revolutionaries by force. Even though Madero was not responsible for this action, Zapata withdrew his support for Madero. Madero soon realized that to the liberals, the Revolution meant political change, but to the revolutionary fighters it meant radical social and economic transformations that Madero would not be able to fulfill. Madero dealt with the labor and land tenure problems politically through the National Agrarian Commission and the Department of Labor. However, the only tangible change was that labor groups felt free to organize. They were also allowed to publish the newspaper *Luz*. Labor unrest continued, despite the government's attempts to control strikes. Madero's democratic administration was failing its staunchest supporters, and rebellions began to surface.

In November the Zapatista faction revolted under the principles of the Plan of Ayala, which asked for restoration of privately owned lands to rural villages. The armed revolt spread through the states of Morelos, Guerrero, Tlaxcala, Puebla, México, and even into Mexico City. By 1912 the Zapatista forces had caused severe damage to railroad and telegraph lines and had won several battles against federal troops.

Revolutionaries from other areas began to challenge the new government, and an offensive was launched in March 1912 by Orozco, who accused Madero of abandoning the principles of the Plan of San Luis Potosí. Orozco was defeated, however, by Victoriano Huerta, the unscrupulous commander of the federal forces. Meanwhile, Félix Díaz (Porfirio's nephew) was assembling an army in Veracruz to march against Madero, but Madero was able to order his arrest andbring him to Mexico City.

Félix Díaz and other counterrevolutionaries plotted a military coup from inside prison and proceeded to take the National Palace on February 8, 1913. With the aid of loyal troops under Huerta, Madero initially resisted the Díaz forces, but street fighting and chaos overtook the city. On February 18, Huerta, seeing an opportunity to seize power, joined the coup against Madero and had both the president and Vice President José María Pino Suárez arrested.

Huerta's decision to change sides was made with the knowledge and assistance of United States ambassador Henry Lane Wilson in what became known as the Pact of the Embassy. Huerta extracted resignations from both Madero and Pino Suárez and had himself appointed secretary of interior, which made him the heir to the presidency, according to the provisions of the constitution of 1857. That same evening, Huerta was sworn in as president, and on February 21, Madero and Pino Suárez were assassinated while being transferred to the penitentiary in Mexico City.

The Huerta Dictatorship

Opposition to Huerta began to emerge once he assumed power. Venustiano Carranza in Coahuila, Villa in Chihuahua, and Álvaro Obregón in Sonora formed a front against the dictator under the Plan of Guadalupe, issued in March 1913. Zapata preferred to maintain his troops' independence from the northern coalition, but remained in revolt against Huerta. The latter responded by increasing the size of the military by forced conscription. Federal forces terrorized the countryside and looted villages, and political assassinations became a trademark of Huerta's rule. The country faced other problems. The federal treasury was empty, and each faction began issuing its own currency. Huerta's government had not been recognized by the United States, which considered him a usurper of the previously elected government. Seeking a return to constitutional rule, the administration of President Woodrow Wilson channeled aid indirectly to the northern coalition.

By early 1914, Huerta was clearly losing on all fronts, but there was one specific event that precipitated his resignation. When United States sailors were arrested at Veracruz for trespassing on dock facilities, the commander of the United States naval forces off Tampico demanded ceremonial salutes of the United States flag by Mexican personnel. When the United States demands were not met, United States troops occupied Veracruz. Indignation brought about a series of reprisals against United States citizens and their flag throughout Mexico. In the face of growing disorder, Huerta resigned on July 8, 1914.

The Constitution of 1917

After the fall of Huerta, Carranza, chief of the northern coalition, invited all revolutionary leaders to a military conference at Aguascalientes to determine the future course of Mexico. A split developed almost immediately: on one side were Carranza, Obregón, and supporters of the plans of San Luis Potosí and Guadalupe; on the other side were Zapata, Villa, and the supporters of the Plan of Ayala. The convention chose Eulalio Gutiérrez, who had the support of the Villistas and the Zapatistas, as provisional president, while Carranza, with Obregón's support, established a dissident government in Veracruz. The country went through another period of civil war and anarchy in which four governments claimed to represent the will of the people: Carranza in Veracruz, Obregón in Mexico City (after Gutiérrez had left the city and established his headquarters in Nuevo León), Roque González Garza (supported by the Zapatistas), and Villa in Guanajuato. Later that year, Carranza emerged as the victorious commander of the revolutionary forces. His government was soon recognized by the United States, and his troops were supplied by munitions abandoned when United States forces left Veracruz.

United States support for Carranza prompted an aggressive reaction from Villa. After 1916 Villa frequently raided United States border towns and then retreated to Mexico. United

States General John J. "Blackjack" Pershing's troops crossed the border in pursuit of Villa several times during 1917. Despite Villa's "victories" over Pershing, the true victor was Carranza. To consolidate his power further and to institutionalize the Revolution, he called for a meeting at Querétaro, where the constitutionalists drew up a new supreme law for Mexico. The Congress of Querétaro met for the first time on December 1, 1916. In commemoration of that event, the inauguration of all Mexican constitutional presidents has taken place on December 1.

Carranza presented his draft of a constitution to the congress. The draft was similar in many ways to the constitution of 1857, but gave extensive powers to the executive. The final version of the constitution of 1917, however, gave additional rights to the Mexican people. It was the fruit of the Revolution—an expression of popular will that guaranteed civil liberties, no presidential succession, and protection from foreign and domestic exploitation to all Mexicans (see Constitutional History, ch. 4).

Carranza's Presidency

After formally accepting the constitution of 1917, Carranza won the presidential election and was sworn into office on May 1, 1917. Conditions in Mexico were again close to chaos: the economy had deteriorated during the years of civil war, communications had been seriously disrupted, and shortages had led to rampant inflation. Land and labor remained the basic issues for the Mexican people, but Carranza chose to overlook the constitutional provisions dealing with these issues and returned lands expropriated during the Revolution. Despite the president's opposition, public enthusiasm for the labor provisions of Article 123 led to the creation in 1918 of the Regional Confederation of Mexican Workers (Confederación Regional de Obreros Mexicanos—CROM), which would unify and lead the labor movement in the years ahead. Meanwhile, Mexico took advantage of United States involvement overseas in World War I, its attention and troops distant from any further intervention in Mexico.

In 1918 parts of the country still saw military action; the fighting was particularly fierce in Morelos. The Zapatistas in that area, who had very specific grievances, wanted more than a constitution. In March 1919, Zapata sent an open letter to Carranza, hoping by this means to bring the Zapatistas' demands before the whole population. Zapata expected that Carranza, once confronted by public pressure, would be willing to address the Zapatistas' grievances. Carranza's response was very different, however. Jesús M. Guajardo, a colonel in the federal army, was contracted to deceive Zapata by offering allegiance to the revolutionaries. Zapata's cautious acceptance of Guajardo's protests of loyalty led to a meeting on April 10, 1919, in Zapata's territory. As Zapata entered the meeting area, Guajardo's men appeared ready to fire a salute in his honor but instead they fired point-blank, killing the peasant leader and thereby eliminating the last significant military opposition.

In 1920 just as Carranza was about to nominate a loyal subordinate, Ignacio Bonilla, to serve as a puppet president, Adolfo de la Huerta and Plutarco Elías Calles rose in opposition. Under the Plan of Agua Prieta, they raised a constitutionalist army of northerners and marched to Mexico City. Carranza fled the capital and was assassinated in May while on the road to exile. De la Huerta served briefly as provisional president, but was replaced in November 1920 by Obregón, who was elected to a four-year term. Shortly thereafter, Villa accepted a peace offer from the federal government.

The Constructive Phase, 1920–40

The Obregón Presidency, 1920–24

The four years of Obregón's presidency (1920–24) were dedicated to beginning to realize the objectives of the constitution of 1917. The military phase of the Revolution was over, and the new administration began to build the bases for the next stage of the revolutionary process of reconstruction.

Obregón's choice for secretary of education was José Vasconcelos, a distinguished lawyer and professor who had rejected the elitist positivism of the *científicos*. Vasconcelos adapted the curricula of rural schools to Mexican reality by teaching students basic skills in reading, writing, mathematics, history, and geography. Seeking to integrate indigenous peoples into Mexican society through education, Vasconcelos dispatched hundreds of teachers to remote villages. Between 1920 and 1924, more than 1,000 rural schools and more than 2,000 public libraries were established. Vasconcelos also believed in instructing through images, and for that purpose he commissioned works by Mexican muralists—foremost among them Diego

Rivera—to decorate public buildings while depicting important events in Mexican history and the ideals of the Revolution.

Obregón's agrarian policies proved more traditional. He believed that the Mexican economy could not afford to forego productivity for the sake of radical agrarian reform. Consequently, redistribution of land proceeded slowly. During his administration, Obregón redistributed 1.2 million hectares to landless peasants, a fraction of the eligible land. Obregón was careful in handling Article 27 of the constitution, which restricted land ownership by foreigners, because of fear of intervention by the United States. Despite Obregón's moderation, United States oil companies launched a campaign against the Mexican government, fearing possible implementation of Article 27. A joint Mexican-United States commission agreed to meet on Bucarelli Street in Mexico City in 1923. Under the terms of the commission agreements, known as the Bucarelli Agreements, Mexico upheld the principle of "positive acts." Mexico agreed that if a foreign enterprise improved the land (in the case of oil, by installing oil drilling equipment), the company's holdings would not be nationalized. The United States fulfilled its part of the agreement by recognizing the Mexican government.

When the time came for the next presidential nomination, Obregón's choice was his secretary of interior, Plutarco Elías Calles. The nomination met with strong opposition from landowners, who feared Calles's radical reputation. Obregón succeeded in imposing his candidate because Calles had the support of labor unions and Mexican nationalists. Overall, Obregón's government disappointed the more radical revolutionary factions, as well as conservative interests, such as the military, wealthy landowners, and the Roman Catholic Church, but it brought Mexico a welcome degree of political stability.

The Calles Presidency, 1924–28

Calles was perhaps Mexico's strongest political figure since the Díaz dictatorship. Calles began seriously to implement agrarian reform by distributing some 3.2 million hectares of land during his term, in addition to developing agricultural credit and irrigation. Labor was still organized into one national union, CROM, run by Calles's crony Luis Morones, even though independent unions were emerging. Public education facilities continued to expand, and Calles's administration built another 2,000 schools.

A major crisis developed, however, between the government and the Roman Catholic Church. In 1926 the archbishop of Mexico City, José Mora y del Río, made public his view that Roman Catholics could not follow the religious provisions of the constitution of 1917. In defiance of the declaration by the archbishop, Calles decided to implement fully several of the constitutional provisions: religious processions were prohibited; the church's educational establishments, convents, and monasteries were closed; foreign priests and nuns were deported; and priests were required to register with the government before receiving permission to perform their religious duties. The church reacted by going on strike on July 31, 1926, and during the three years that followed, no sacraments were administered. Bloody revolts broke out in the states of Michoacán, Puebla, Oaxaca, Zacatecas, Jalisco, and Nayarit. To the call of "Viva Cristo Rey" (Long live Christ the King), bands of militant Roman Catholics, known as Cristeros, attacked government officials and facilities and burned public schools. The government responded with overwhelming force, using the army and its own partisan bands of Red Shirts to fight the Cristeros. The fighting was vicious, with both sides engaging in indiscriminate acts of terrorism against civilians and widespread destruction of property. By 1929 the revolt had been largely contained, and the Cristeros were compelled to lay down their arms and accept most of the government's terms.

The Maximato

In defiance of the "no-reelection" principle that had been one of the key political legacies of the Revolution, Calles supported Obregón's bid to recapture the presidency in 1928. Beginning with the 1928 election, the presidential term was increased from four to six years (*sexenio*). Thereafter, the *sexenio* formed the basis for regular and orderly political succession. Obregón won the election but was assassinated by a religious fanatic before taking office on July 17, 1928. Seeking to ensure political stability, Calles opted not to violate the "no-reelection" principle and instead chose one of his supporters, Emilio Portes Gil, as interim president (December 1928 to February 1930) until new elections could be held.

During the next six years (a period known as the Maximato), Calles exercised behind-the-scenes control over Mexican politics through the actions of three presidents who were essentially his puppets. By 1929 Calles's political machine had found institutional expression as the National Revolutionary Party (Partido Nacional Revolucionario—PNR). Unlike previous parties, which existed only in name during electoral campaigns and dissolved immediately thereafter, the PNR was designed to be a permanent organization run exclusively by Calles as *jefe máximo* (supreme leader), through which he acted as de facto president. Henceforth, the "official" party of the revolutionary regime served as the dominant political organization in the country and the primary dispenser of official patronage.

In the special election of 1929, called to select a figurehead to serve out the remaining four years of Obregón's term, Calles chose Pascual Ortiz Rubio as the PNR candidate. Ortiz Rubio was opposed by José Vasconcelos, who decried Calles's thinly veiled authoritarian rule and the growing corruption of the older revolutionary generation. Relying on ballot stuffing and other forms of electoral fraud, Ortiz Rubio defeated Vasconcelos with 99.9 percent of the vote. Ortiz Rubio's presidency would be short-lived, however. Having demonstrated excessive independence from Calles once in office, the president was summarily removed by the "supreme leader" in September 1932 and replaced with a more compliant figure, Abelardo Rodríguez.

The last two years of the Maximato under the presidency of Rodríguez witnessed a steady rightward drift of the revolutionary regime. Deciding that the country could not forego agricultural productivity for the sake of equity, Calles ordered a near halt to further land redistribution. Organized labor, which was seen as overly sympathetic to bolshevism and not loyal enough to the PNR, was disavowed and suppressed. By the early 1930s, the government was persecuting the Mexican Communist Party and allowing fascist organizations to terrorize Mexico's small Jewish population.

As the election for the 1934–40 presidential *sexenio* approached, Calles came under increasing pressure from the left wing of the PNR to pursue with more vigor the social welfare provisions of the constitution of 1917. Seeking to avoid a party split, Calles mollified his party's left wing by nominating Lázaro Cárdenas, a popular state governor, to succeed Rodríguez. Cárdenas had participated in the revolutionary conflict as a constitutionalist military officer, achieving the rank of brigadier general. While governor of his home state of Michoacán, Cárdenas gained recognition for his support of public education and his good relationship with organized labor and peasant organizations. Cárdenas's modest efforts at land reform at the state level earned him a reputation as a populist. Calles, although wary of Cárdenas, nevertheless expected the new president to fall into line much as his three predecessors had done.

Cardenismo and the Revolution Rekindled, 1934–40

Cárdenas immediately showed his independence by becoming the first Mexican president to campaign for office. Once in office, he began his *sexenio* by adopting several popular measures. He reduced his presidential salary and decided not to move into the national palace, he ordered a resumption of land reform on an unprecedented scale, and he expressed tacit support for a wave of urban strikes. Calles followed these developments with unease, and soon sought to undermine the new president's authority. A definitive break occurred between Calles and Cárdenas when the new president fired many of Calles's followers in the federal bureaucracy and closed down a network of gambling houses owned by Calles's associates. It became apparent that Calles had underestimated Cárdenas's commitment to reform and his political skills. Calles's open opposition to Cárdenas finally earned the former leader forced exile to the United States in 1936. Conservatives from San Luis Potosí staged a rebellion in protest, but the military remained loyal to the president and brought the revolt under control.

Land reform was one of Cárdenas's major accomplishments. In the course of six years, he distributed almost 18 million hectares—more than twice as much land as all of his predecessors combined—to two-thirds of the Mexican peasantry through the system of communal farms or *ejidos* (see Land Tenure, ch. 3). Even though agriculture suffered an initial setback because of the loss of economies of scale and a lack of resources and credit, the redistribution proved tremendously popular with the majority of the Mexican people and earned Cárdenas a special place in Mexican history.

Church relations also improved during Cárdenas's presidency. Key was the intervention of Luis María Martínez, archbishop of Mexico. Martínez encouraged Roman Catholics to be more sensitive to the social and economic welfare of society, even though national education continued to be secular and had become socialist in its emphasis. The labor movement also received Cárdenas's attention. The president supported Vicente Lombardo Toledano, a Marxist who reorganized labor

Lázaro Cárdenas, president,
1934–40
Courtesy Library of Congress

into the Confederation of Mexican Workers (Confederación de Trabajadores Mexicanos—CTM). The old CROM had become corrupt through the years, and the CTM became the new, quasi-official representative of Mexican workers, developing programs and pushing for improvement of working conditions and minimum wage schedules (see Organized Labor, ch. 4).

Cárdenas also reorganized the official Mexican party, the PNR, to broaden its political base. The party was renamed the Party of the Mexican Revolution (Partido de la Revolución Mexicana—PRM), and membership expanded to include representatives of four corporately defined "sectors" of Mexican society: labor, agrarian, military, and popular. The agrarian sector consisted of peasants and rural laborers, and the popular sector included the small but growing middle class, civil servants, and small-scale merchants.

Cárdenas's boldest act was his expropriation in March 1938 of all foreign oil operations on Mexican territory. In response to a strike by oil workers seeking higher wages, the government intervened on their behalf, demanding that the mostly United States-owned companies share more of their technical and managerial expertise with Mexican nationals. When the companies failed to comply with the worker-training demand, Cárdenas issued his sweeping expropriation of all foreign oil operations. Compensation was based on the underreported "book" value of the properties. The expropriation, which Cárdenas considered a natural outcome of the constitutional claim to national ownership of all subsoil resources, temporarily disrupted commerce between Mexico and the United States. Nationalization, however, won Cárdenas widespread praise both within Mexico and throughout Latin America, where nationalist sentiment against foreign commercial interests ran high.

In November 1941, on the eve of United States entry into World War II, Mexico and the United States finally settled their differences over the expropriated properties. Although it was a significant political victory for Cárdenas, the oil expropriation cost Mexico dearly in terms of capital flight and foreign investment. For nearly twenty years, the new national petroleum company, Mexican Petroleum (Petróleos Mexicanos—Pemex) suffered from inadequate technical expertise and outdated equipment.

By the end of his term in 1940, Cárdenas had dramatically transformed the Mexican political system. Continuing the legacy of executive predominance begun by Calles, Cárdenas further augmented presidential power by subordinating the entire apparatus of the official party under the chief executive. In addition, Cárdenas expanded the role of the state in Mexican society, establishing patron-client relationships among various state agencies and the corporately defined interest groups. The "institutionalization" of the Revolution resulted in a situation in which the state became the sole mediator among competing interest groups and the final arbiter of political disputes.

From Revolution to Governance, 1940–82

Ávila Camacho's Wartime Presidency, 1940–46

Cárdenas's nomination of Manuel Ávila Camacho, a relatively unknown career military officer, as the PRM candidate for the presidency in 1940 surprised many Mexicans. Numerous party members were aware of Ávila Camacho's conservative tendencies. Moreover, in contrast to the anticlerical position held by most Mexican politicians since the Revolution, during the presidential campaign Ávila Camacho had stated that he was a believer and a Roman Catholic. The new president took office on December 1, 1940, and, as expected, did not push for enforcement of the most populist articles of the constitution.

Land reform was slowed down, and its emphasis shifted from reconstituting *ejidos* to promoting private ownership of land.

The conservative bent of the new administration was especially evident in the administration's attitude toward labor. Fidel Velásquez, a more conservative labor leader, replaced Lombardo Toledano as head of the CTM. The government withdrew much of its support for organized labor, and controls were placed on the rights of strikers. By 1942 the CTM had lost textile and building industry workers, who felt alienated from the new leadership. Although the Ávila Camacho administration created the Mexican Institute of Social Security (Instituto Mexicano del Seguro Social—IMSS), the program initially benefited only a small portion of the labor force.

Changes were also apparent in education as the Ávila Camacho administration introduced new education programs. Greater emphasis was placed on private schools, and the government started a campaign that encouraged each literate citizen to teach another person to read and write. Launched with much fanfare, the impact of the campaign was short-lived, however.

Ávila Camacho's administration witnessed the expansion of World War II in Europe. Exercising its independence from the United States, Mexico initially attempted to remain neutral after the United States entered the war in December 1941. However, when two Mexican tankers were sunk by German submarines in May 1942, Mexico declared war on Germany. The declaration received full support from congress and most of the Mexican population. On September 16, 1942, several former presidents held an unprecedented meeting at the National Palace for a public display of solidarity in the face of war. Those present included former presidents de la Huerta, Calles, Portes Gil, Ortiz Rubio, Rodríguez, and Cárdenas. A comprehensive national security policy was developed to counter Axis espionage against Mexico and to defend Mexican oil fields and military industries. Mexico participated in the war effort mainly as a supplier of labor and raw materials for the United States, although a Mexican fighter squadron fought and sustained casualties in the Pacific theater.

In 1942 the Mexican and United States governments negotiated a program to enlist migrant Mexican workers (*braceros*) to assist in harvesting United States crops. The program was initially intended to supplement the depleted rural labor force in the United States, who had been displaced by the war effort.

The *bracero* program, which continued into the 1960s, subsequently lured hundreds of thousands of Mexican laborers with and without legal documentation to seek employment across the border.

By early 1946, the PRM's political power base included new groups in Mexican society. The party now had representatives of the business and industrial communities within its popular sector. As a sign that the official party viewed the transitional phase of the Revolution as ended, officials decided to rename the party the Institutional Revolutionary Party (Partido Revolucionario Institucional—PRI). The same January 1946 convention nominated Miguel Alemán Valdés to be the PRI candidate for the presidential term of 1946–52.

The Alemán *Sexenio,* 1946–52

The Alemán presidency marked a turning point in contemporary Mexican politics. With the election of Alemán (a lawyer by profession), the torch was passed to a new generation of civilian politicians who had not participated in the military campaigns of the Revolution. The age of the generals in Mexican politics was over. Henceforth, the military assumed a low profile, surrendering many of its institutional prerogatives to a civilian-dominated PRI.

Alemán's presidency was also noteworthy because it represented the consolidation in power of a PRI faction that was more probusiness and less nationalistic than the Cárdenas wing of the party. One of Alemán's first acts as president was to reaffirm amicable postwar relations between Mexico and the United States. In a symbolic gesture of rapprochement, United States President Harry S Truman and President Alemán visited each other's countries. On September 2, 1947, Mexico was among the signatories of the Inter-American Treaty of Reciprocal Assistance (Rio Treaty), which outlined a system of mutual defense on the part of Western Hemisphere nations against outside aggression.

The Alemán administration attempted to promote industrialization and economic growth by embarking on an extensive program of infrastructure improvements. Major flood control and irrigation projects were built in northern Mexico, greatly expanding the opportunities for large-scale agribusiness. The exploitation of cheap hydroelectric power and the expansion of the national road network were undertaken to help spur heavy industry and tourism. By the end of Alemán's *sexenio* in

1952, Mexico had four times as many kilometers of paved roads (roughly 16,000 kilometers) as in 1946. Another legacy of the Alemán era was the completion in 1952 of a new campus—in what was then suburban Mexico City—for the flagship of the Mexican university system, the National Autonomous University of Mexico (Universidad Nacional Autónoma de México—UNAM).

Alemán was viewed as much less sympathetic than his immediate predecessors to the demands of labor and the rural populations of central and southern Mexico. To promote growth without generating high inflation, the government acted through the PRI-affiliated unions to suppress the wage demands of labor. The government also began a new strategy of "stabilizing development." The new program was based on promoting industrialization through import substitution (see Glossary), heavy subsidies of industry, and maintaining low inflation by suppressing real wages.

Further straying from the ideals of the Revolution, Alemán's administration became noted for its tolerance of official corruption. The government's growing involvement in the economy provided ample opportunities for kickbacks and other forms of illicit enrichment, and several senior government officials became wealthy while in office. The scale of official venality was enough to spark a public outcry and protests from within the PRI. To restore popular faith in the ruling party, Alemán nominated Adolfo Ruiz Cortines, a former governor of Veracruz, minister of interior, and a man noted for his impeccable character, to succeed him in 1952.

The Ruiz Cortines *Sexenio,* 1952–58

Despite his friendship with Alemán, Ruiz Cortines set out to eliminate the corruption and graft that had tainted the previous administration. In his inaugural speech on December 1, 1952, Ruiz Cortines promised to require complete honesty from officials in his government and asked that they make public their financial assets. He later fired several officials on charges of corruption.

The economy continued to grow with government support. The government, for example, devalued the peso (Mex$— for value, see Glossary), a move that helped to encourage investors from abroad. Ruiz Cortines did not promote a new construction boom but rather channeled money into public health programs. The IMSS, under the directorship of Antonio Ortiz

Mena, was expanded to provide medical services at hospitals and clinics throughout the country, and a more comprehensive system of benefits for eligible workers and their families was created.

By the end of Ruiz Cortines's *sexenio* in 1958, three consecutive administrations had pursued probusiness policies that departed significantly from the agrarian populism practiced by Cárdenas. Import-substitution industrialization had generated rapid growth in urban areas, while land reform was scaled back and redefined to emphasize individual private farming. Meanwhile, Mexico's population more than doubled in less than thirty years, from 16 million in the mid-1930s to 34 million in 1960. The resulting population pressure, as well as the concentration of services and new jobs in urban areas, encouraged massive urban migration—most notably in and around Mexico City. The proliferation of urban shantytowns in the capital's outskirts became a growing symbol of the imbalance between urban and rural development in postwar Mexico.

With wartime calls for unity and austerity now well past, the Cárdenas faction of the PRI reemerged as a powerful force acting on behalf of the party's core agrarian and labor constituencies. Former President Cárdenas (who continued to wield considerable influence in national politics) persuaded the party to nominate one of his followers, Adolfo López Mateos, as the PRI candidate for the 1958 presidential election.

López Mateos and the Return to Revolutionary Policies, 1958–64

The election of López Mateos to the presidency in August 1958 restored to power the PRI faction that had historically emphasized nationalism and redistribution of land. As in past elections, the PRI won handily over the conservative candidate of the opposition National Action Party (Partido de Acción Nacional—PAN) with an overwhelming 90 percent of the vote. Although the PRI regularly engaged in vote buying and fraud at the state and local levels, presidential races were not credibly contested by the opposition, and little interference was required to keep the official party in office. Although the 1958 election was the first in which women were able to vote for the president, the enfranchisement of women did not significantly affect the outcome of the presidential race.

López Mateos was widely viewed as the political heir of Cárdenas, whose nationalism and social welfare programs had left a lasting impact on Mexican political culture. After nearly two decades of urban bias in government policy, López Mateos took tentative steps to redress the imbalance between urban and rural Mexico. His administration distributed more than 12 million hectares of land to *ejidos* and family farmers and made available new land for small-scale cultivation in southern Mexico. In addition, the IMSS program was introduced into rural areas, and major public health campaigns were launched to reduce tuberculosis, poliomyelitis, and malaria.

Whereas the government regained much of the support of agrarian interests, López Mateos's relations with organized labor were strained. As Ruiz Cortínes's labor minister, López Mateos had gained a reputation for fairness and competence in the settlement of labor disputes. As president, however, he opposed the growing radicalization and militancy among elements of organized labor and acted forcefully to put down several major strikes. Reflecting a growing ideological polarization of national politics, the government imprisoned several prominent communists, including the famed muralist David Alfaro Siqueiros. Relations between labor and the government eased somewhat in 1962, when López Mateos revived a constitutional provision that called for labor to share in the profits of large firms.

Following Cárdenas's example, López Mateos restored a strongly nationalist tone to Mexican foreign policy, albeit not with the fervor that had characterized his populist predecessor. In 1960 the government began to buy foreign utility concessions (as opposed to expropriating them, as Cárdenas had done). Some of the larger companies bought were Electric Industries (Impulsora de Empresas Eléctricas) (from the American and Foreign Power Company of the United States), Mexican Light and Power Company (from a Belgian firm), and Mexican Electric Company (Industria Eléctrica Mexicana) (from the United States-based California Power Company). The film industry, previously owned by United States firms, was also brought under Mexican control. Mexican nationalism was most evident in its response to United States-led efforts to isolate the communist regime of Fidel Castro Ruz in Cuba. Alone among the members of the Organization of American States (OAS), Mexico refused to break diplomatic relations with Cuba or to observe the hemispheric embargo of the island approved at the OAS's Punta del Este Conference in 1962 (see Foreign Relations, ch. 4).

Authoritarianism Unveiled, 1964–70

By choosing his minister of interior, Gustavo Díaz Ordaz, to succeed him, López Mateos yielded to growing concerns within the PRI about maintaining internal order and spurring economic growth. As government minister, Díaz Ordaz had been responsible for some very controversial policy decisions, including the arrest of Siqueiros, the violent suppression of several strikes, and the annulment of local elections in Baja California Sur, in which the PAN had received most of the votes.

Business interests once again received priority, and students and labor were kept under control so as not to disrupt economic growth. Antigovernment protests reached unprecedented proportions, however, in the demonstrations of the summer of 1968, just prior to the Summer Olympic Games that were to be held in Mexico City in October. From July through October, academic life in the city and throughout Mexico was halted as students rioted. The antigovernment demonstrations were ignited by student grievances, but many discontented sectors of society joined the students.

As the Olympic Games approached, the PRI and Díaz Ordaz were preparing the country to show foreign visitors that Mexico was politically stable and economically sound. Student unrest grew louder and more violent, however. Student demands included freedom for all political prisoners, dismissal of the police chief, disbanding of the antiriot police, guarantees of university autonomy, and the repeal of the "law of social dissolution" (regulating the punishment of acts of subversion, treason, and disorder). Luis Echeverría Álvarez, the new interior minister, agreed to discuss the issues with the students but changed his mind when they demanded that the meeting be televised. The students, their demands unmet, escalated the scale and frequency of their protests. In late August, they convened the largest antigovernment demonstration to date, rallying an estimated 500,000 protesters in the main plaza of the capital. Seeking to bring a halt to the demonstrations, Díaz Ordaz ordered the army to take control of UNAM and to arrest the student movement leaders.

To show that they had not been silenced, the students called for another rally at the Plaza of the Three Cultures in Mexico City's Tlatelolco district. On October 2, 1968, a crowd of about 5,000 convened on the plaza in defiance of the government crackdown. Armed military units and tanks arrived on the scene and surrounded the demonstrators, while military helicopters hovered menacingly overhead. The helicopters began to agitate the crowd by dropping flares into the densely packed gathering. Shortly thereafter, shots rang out (according to some accounts, the shooting was started by the military, while others claim the first shots were fired at soldiers by antigovernment snipers in the surrounding buildings). The panicked crowd suddenly surged toward the military cordon, which reacted by shooting and bayoneting indiscriminately into the crowd. Estimates of the number of people killed ranged from several dozen to more than 400. Despite the violence, the Olympic Games proceeded on schedule. However, the Tlatelolco massacre had a profound and lasting negative effect on the PRI's public image. The authoritarian aspects of the political system had been starkly brought to the surface.

Reconciliation and Redistribution, 1970–76

Despite the groundswell of urban protest unleashed against the government, the PRI candidate easily won the 1970 presidential election. The new president, Echeverría, was expected to continue his predecessor's policies. Contrary to expectations, however, once in office Echeverría swung the ideological pendulum of the regime back to the left. The government embarked on an ambitious public relations campaign to regain the loyalty of leftist intellectuals and the young. To solidify the support of its core labor and agrarian constituencies, the PRI also launched a barrage of social welfare programs.

Echeverría was determined to coopt the dissatisfied elements of the middle class that had become radicalized during the 1960s. Government patronage became an important mechanism of rapprochement. Thousands of intellectuals and young leftists were given posts in the government's bloated bureaucracy, and prominent student leaders were brought into the president's cabinet. To attract support from the young— who now represented a majority of the population—Echeverría lowered the voting age to eighteen, and the ages for election to the Senate and Chamber of Deputies to thirty and twenty-one, respectively. In addition, he freed most of the demonstrators arrested during the raid on UNAM and the Tlatelolco massacre.

Despite his aversion to domestic communist movements, Echeverría became a champion of leftist causes in Latin America. He was a strong advocate of the proposed "new international economic order" to redistribute power and wealth more equitably between the industrialized countries and the developing world. Demonstrating his independence from the United States, Echeverría became only the second Latin American head of state to visit Castro's Cuba. In 1974 he warmly received Hortensia Allende, widow of leftist Chilean president Salvador Allende Gossens, as a political refugee from Chile's right-wing military dictatorship.

In domestic economic affairs, the Echeverría administration ended the policies of stabilizing development that had been pursued since the early 1950s. Echeverría abandoned Mexico's commitment to growth with low inflation and undertook instead to stimulate the economy and redistribute wealth through massive public-spending programs. The new policy of "shared development" was premised on heavy state investment in the economy and the promotion of consumption and social welfare for the middle and lower classes.

The focus of Echeverría's social welfare policies was the Mexican countryside. Despite ample evidence that the *ejidos* were less efficient than private farming, Echeverría resumed the redistribution of land to *ejidos* and expanded credit subsidies to cooperative agriculture. The government also pursued an extensive program of rural development that increased the number of schools and health clinics in rural communities. By refusing to defend rural property owners from squatters, the Echeverría government encouraged a wave of land invasions that reduced land pressure in the countryside but seriously undermined investor confidence.

In addition to providing broad subsidies for agriculture, the government embarked on several costly infrastructure projects, such as the US$1 billion Lázaro Cárdenas-Las Truchas Steel Plant (Sicartsa) steel complex in Michoacán state. State subsidies to stimulate private and parastatal (see Glossary) investment grew from 16 billion pesos (US$1.2 billion) in 1970 to 428 billion pesos (US$18.6 billion) by 1980. Although this type of spending generated high economic growth throughout the 1970s, much of the money was either wasted in unnecessary and inefficient projects or lost to corruption. The government relied heavily on deficit spending to finance its domestic programs, incurring heavy debt obligations with foreign creditors to make up the shortfall in public revenues.

Under Echeverría, the historically uneasy relationship between the PRI and the national business community took a sharp turn for the worse. Echeverría's antibusiness rhetoric and the government's interference in the economy deterred new foreign and domestic investment. Although the government avoided full-scale expropriations, it increased the state's role in the economy by buying out private shareholders and assuming control of hundreds of domestic enterprises. By the end of Echeverría's term, the government owned significant shares in more than 1,000 corporations nationwide.

Despite warning signs of a looming financial crisis, deficit spending continued unabated throughout Echeverría's *sexenio*. The public sector's foreign debt rose by 450 percent to US$19.6 billion in six years, while the peso was allowed to become overvalued. By the end of his *sexenio*, Echeverría was facing the consequences of his administration's unrestrained spending. In August 1976, mounting currency speculation, large-scale capital flight, and lack of confidence in Mexico's ability to meet its debt repayment schedule forced the government to devalue the peso for the first time since 1954. The outgoing president bequeathed to his successor, José López Portillo y Pacheco, an economy in recession and burdened by severe structural imbalances. The only bright spot in an otherwise bleak economic picture was the discovery in the mid-1970s of vast reserves of oil under the Bahía de Campeche and in the states of Chiapas and Tabasco.

Recovery and Relapse, 1976–82

President López Portillo was inaugurated on December 1, 1976, amid a political and economic crisis inherited from the previous administration. A rising foreign debt and inflation rate, a 55 percent currency devaluation, and a general climate of economic uncertainty that had spurred capital flight plagued the economy. The new administration also faced a general lack of confidence in government institutions. Unexpected help arrived as a result of the confirmation of the large oil reserves. The Mexican government chose to follow a policy of increasing oil production only gradually to prevent an inflationary spiral that would disrupt economic recovery. Nevertheless, by 1981 Mexico had become the fourth largest producer of oil in the world, its production having tripled between 1976 and 1982. While production increased, so did the price per barrel of crude oil.

The immense revenues generated by oil exports during the administration of López Portillo gave Mexico a greater degree of confidence in international affairs, particularly in its ever important relations with the United States. The government, for example, refused to participate in the United States-led boycott of the 1980 Summer Olympic Games in Moscow. When the two countries could not agree on the price of natural gas, Mexico flared its excess resources rather than sell to the United States below its asking price. Also in defiance of United States wishes, Mexico recognized the Farabundo Martí National Liberation Front rebels in El Salvador as a representative political force. These steps occurred although the United States remained Mexico's major oil customer and its major source of investment capital (see Petroleum, ch. 3; Foreign Relations, ch. 4).

As in so many developing countries, oil did not solve all of Mexico's problems, however. The oil industry grew rapidly but could not employ the ever-increasing ranks of the unskilled. Oil made Mexico a rich nation in which a majority of the people continued to live in poverty. Foreign banks and the international lending agencies, seeing Mexico as a secure investment with abundant energy resources, flooded the country with loans that kept the peso overvalued.

"The Crisis" Begins, 1982

Although its effects rippled through every aspect of national life, the roots of what came to be known simply as "the crisis" were exclusively economic. The roots of the crisis lay in the oil boom of the late 1970s. Oil prices rose sharply at a time when oil exploration in Mexico was at a peak. The nation found itself awash in petrodollars. Its infrastructure, barely adequate before the boom, was overwhelmed by the influx of imported goods that followed Mexico's rising foreign exchange reserves and the overvalued peso. López Portillo promised "to transform nonrenewable resources into renewable wealth." In other words, he vowed to invest substantial amounts of the new oil revenue in areas and projects that would establish sustainable economic growth. This promise went unfulfilled.

Government spending did increase substantially following the oil boom. Little, if any, of the new spending, however, qualified as productive investment. Food subsidies, long a political necessity in Mexico, accounted for the largest single portion of the new spending. Although impossible to quantify, many accounts agree that the level of graft and corruption skyrocketed. The new money fueled a level of inflation never before seen in modern Mexico; the inflation rate eventually surpassed

100 percent annually. The López Portillo administration chose to ignore warning signs of inflation and opted instead to increase spending.

The macroeconomic trends that preceded the crisis also displayed warning signs that went unheeded. Oil income rose from 1979 to 1980. Oil exports began to crowd out other exports; the petroleum sector accounted for 45 percent of total exports in 1979, but dominated exports with 65.4 percent of the total in the second quarter of 1980. Like so many other developing nations, Mexico became a single-commodity exporter. With almost 50 billion barrels in proven reserves serving as collateral, Mexico also became a major international borrower. Significant foreign borrowing began under President Echeverría, but it soared under López Portillo. Foreign banks proved just as shortsighted as the Mexican government, approving large loans in the belief that oil revenue expansion would continue over the terms of the loans, assuring repayment. Hydrocarbon earnings for the period from 1977 to 1982, US$48 billion, were almost matched by public-sector external borrowing over the same period, which totaled US$40 billion. By 1982 almost 45 percent of export earnings went to service the country's external debt.

Living standards had already begun to decline when the oil glut hit in 1981. Although the economy grew by an average of 6 percent per year from 1977 to 1979, purchasing power over that period dropped by 6.5 percent. By mid-1981, overproduction had softened the international oil market considerably. In July the government announced that it needed to borrow US$1.2 billion to compensate for lost oil revenue. The month before, Pemex had reduced its sales price for crude oil on the international market by US$4 per barrel. Continued high import levels and the drop in oil exports had boosted Mexico's current account deficit to US$10 billion. This uncertain situation—high external debt, stagnant exports, and a devalued currency as of February 1982—prompted investors to pull their money out of Mexico and seek safer havens abroad. This action, in turn, led López Portillo to nationalize the banks in September 1982 in an effort to staunch wounds that were largely of his own making.

López Portillo left office in 1982 a discredited figure, in no small part because the press publicized accounts of his luxurious lifestyle. The Mexican public, long-suffering and pragmatic in political matters, found López Portillo's calls for "sacrifice" and austerity unacceptable when contrasted with his own life-style.

To the Brink and Back, 1982–88

The de la Madrid *Sexenio,* 1982–88

When he took office in December 1982, Miguel de la Madrid Hurtado faced domestic conditions arguably more serious than those confronting any postrevolutionary president. The foreign debt had reached new heights, the gross national product (GNP— see Glossary) was contracting rather than growing, inflation had hit 100 percent annually, and the peso had lost 40 percent of its value. Moreover, and perhaps most critical, the Mexican people had begun to question and criticize the system of one-party rule that had caused this situation. Abroad, commentators (including United States president Ronald W. Reagan) speculated as to the potential for revolutionary upheaval in what had been considered a stable, if not democratic, southern neighbor. Some Mexicans shared this concern. The government and most in the PRI, de la Madrid included, believed that they could continue to hold power by keeping the people well fed and reversing economic trends.

Hand-picked by López Portillo, de la Madrid inherited the former president's economic mismanagement and that of several of his predecessors. Lack of fiscal restraint, encouraged by a sudden flood of oil wealth, lay at the root of the crisis. Overprinting of the peso cheapened the currency, fed inflation, and exacerbated rather than cured the economic sins that prompted it. And corruption, the traditional parasite of economic vitality in Mexico, made its contribution to the crash.

Although weak compared with earlier presidents, de la Madrid still wielded formidable power in both the economic and political arenas. The day of his inauguration, he recognized the nation's "emergency situation" by instituting a sweeping program of economic austerity measures. The ten-point program included federal budget cuts, new taxes, price increases on some previously subsidized items, postponement of many scheduled public works projects, increases in some interest rates, and the relaxation of foreign- exchange controls enacted during the waning days of the López Portillo administration. Aside from its anticipated adverse impact on the standard of living, many Mexicans resented the program for other reasons. Nationalists saw the measures as inspired and all but imposed by the International Monetary Fund (IMF—see Glossary), which reportedly had taken a hard line in debt talks with the government. Others resented the austerity edicts because they believed that the government and the PRI had brought the nation to the brink of ruin, but that the people would have to bear the burden of official incompetence.

The sudden reversal of a long trend of steady economic growth in Mexico threw the political system into turmoil, undermined the authority of the PRI, and raised the already high levels of popular skepticism. Economic austerity exacerbated the elitist aspect of the populist authoritarian system that developed after the Revolution. Conditions such as inflation, devaluation, and the withdrawal of subsidies hit the poor hardest. The wealthy found ways to insulate themselves from such developments; as a result, the rich grew richer. This was true both within the private sector and among the bureaucracy. In addition to the schism between the poor and the rich, the crisis and its impact on the PRI's authority sharpened the long-standing dichotomy between central and southern Mexico and the north. The immediate political beneficiary of the crisis was the PAN, a conservative, probusiness party with its roots in the northern border states.

To counteract the ferment, the government decided to allow some opening of the political system—enough to provide a safety valve for public discontent—but not enough to threaten the PRI's control, a balance difficult to attain. The first volley in the campaign against the PRI and its policies came with the elections of July 3, 1983. Although the PRI took a large majority of municipal and state legislative races in five northern states, the PAN captured an unprecedented nine mayoralties and registered gains in all five state legislatures.

In addition to the economic and political arenas, de la Madrid sought to exert influence in the area of ethics. Early in his administration, the president announced a program of "moral renewal." Despite its high-minded rhetoric, the program never enacted major legislation to discourage corrupt practices. One exception was a new rule that eliminated government subcontracting, a device that union leaders often used to earn kickbacks from contractors. In addition to instituting this new rule, the moral renewal campaign chose to make examples of a handful of corrupt officials, including former Pemex director Jorge Díaz Serrano and former Mexico City police chief Arturo Durazo Moreno, both of whom served prison sentences for illegal personal gain.

The United States and the Crisis in Mexico

Historically, United States relations with Mexico have followed a reactive pattern of neglect, activism, and intervention. The crisis of the 1980s, which appeared to threaten the long-standing stability of Mexico, triggered a new period of activist attention to its southern neighbor by the United States. The prospect of an economically overextended Mexico defaulting on US$100 billion in foreign loans caused alarm in Washington and throughout the industrialized world. The possibility of resulting political upheaval was particularly worrying to the United States. As a result, other lesser issues between the two countries—migration, drugs, environmental concerns, investment, and trade—received increased attention.

United States president Reagan, a former governor of California, brought to the White House an appreciation of the importance of the relationship between the two countries. Reagan met with President López Portillo in Ciudad Juárez on January 5, 1981, becoming the first United States president-elect to visit Mexico. One of the topics that the two leaders discussed in Ciudad Juárez was the political crisis in Central America, where the leftist Sandinista National Liberation Front (Frente Sandinista de Liberación Nacional—FSLN), also known as Sandinistas (see Glossary), held power in Nicaragua and supported guerrilla movements in El Salvador and Guatemala. López Portillo reportedly cautioned Reagan, a conservative who had strongly condemned the Nicaraguan government, regarding United States intervention in the region. At this time, Mexico considered Central America, particularly Guatemala, to lie within its geopolitical sphere of influence. Mexican policy, since the victory of the FSLN in 1979, had sought to provide an alternative to United States, Cuban, or Soviet influence on the isthmus. This Mexican strategy, however, eventually failed because Cuban influence on the Nicaraguan Sandinistas was rooted in years of clandestine support for the revolutionary cause.

The United States, however, rejected Mexico's conciliatory approach to Central American affairs in favor of military support to friendly governments, such as those in El Salvador and Honduras, and the even more controversial policy of backing anti-Sandinista guerrilla forces. After the economic crisis of

1982, Mexico lost much of its influence in Central America. Mexican governments, in turn, also became more guarded in their criticism of United States policy in order to assure Washington's support in financial forums such as the World Bank (see Glossary) and the IMF.

Although the two nations did not always agree on the best strategy for dealing with Mexico's burgeoning foreign debt, the United States government continued to work with the Mexicans and support efforts to buoy the Mexican economy and reschedule the debt. Washington announced the first of several debt relief agreements in August 1982. Under the terms of the agreement, the United States purchased ahead of schedule some US$600 million in Mexican crude oil for its strategic oil reserve; the United States treasury also provided US$1 billion in guarantees for new commercial bank loans to Mexico. Privately, United States officials reportedly pressured commercial banks to postpone a US$10 billion principal payment that fell due that same month.

A bank advisory group representing 530 foreign creditors reached an accord with Mexico in late August 1984. The rescheduling agreement allowed Mexico to repay its foreign debt over a term of fourteen years at interest rates lower than those originally contracted. United States Federal Reserve Board Chairman Paul A. Volcker, among others, had pushed for the interest rate reduction, in part as recognition of Mexico's having instituted difficult austerity measures and needing some fiscal relief in order to restore economic growth.

Other concerns meanwhile strained the Mexican-United States relationship. Perhaps the most dramatic was drug trafficking. The consumption of cocaine rose steadily in the United States during the late 1970s and early 1980s, becoming a major law enforcement and public health problem. Mexico has never been a major producer of cocaine. Geography, however, made Mexico a conduit for the transshipment of cocaine hydrochloride from South America to the United States. Difficult terrain; sparse population in many rural areas; an adequate infrastructure for transporting goods by land, sea, and air; and the relative ease of bribing both local and federal officials all lured drug traffickers to use Mexico as a conduit.

Eventually, an isolated incident came to symbolize Mexican drug corruption and the friction between the two nations on the issue of drug trafficking. The United States Drug Enforcement Administration (DEA) maintained a comparatively large presence in Mexico. One of its resident offices operated out of the consulate in Guadalajara. In March 1985, Mexican authorities unearthed the body of DEA special agent Enrique Camarena on a ranch in Michoacán state, some 100 kilometers from Guadalajara. Mexican drug traffickers, reports later revealed, had tortured Camarena to death, perhaps in retaliation for his discovery of a major marijuana cultivation operation. Initial protest from the United States government brought little or no response from Mexican officials. As a result, the United States Customs Service closed nine lesser points of entry from Mexico to the United States and began searching every vehicle that passed northward. The resultant traffic backups, complaints, and economic losses infuriated the Mexican government. Mexicans claimed that the appearance of their inaction stemmed from misperceptions of the Mexican legal system, not from efforts to protect drug traffickers.

Despite the eventual arrest of a key suspect in the Camarena murder, relations between the United States and Mexico on the drug issue followed a rocky course. On April 14 and 15, 1985, United States Attorney General Edwin Meese III met with his Mexican counterpart, Sergio García Ramírez. The two agreed to closer monitoring of the two nations' joint counter-drug programs. The Camarena case, however, continued to cast a pall over these efforts. Leaked information from the United States Department of State and from law enforcement agencies indicated that Mexican authorities had made only token efforts against drug production and trafficking. According to Department of State figures, by the end of 1985, Mexico was the largest exporter of marijuana and heroin to the United States. Efforts at eradicating these crops had failed abysmally, and output in 1985 exceeded 1984 levels.

As controversy continued over Mexican drug policy, United States politics forced another bilateral issue to the fore. The United States had made sporadic efforts over the years to exert greater control over its porous southern border. Mexican and Central American illegal immigrants crossed the border almost at will to seek low-paid jobs. Organized labor, among others, urged the United States Congress to act. This pressure, based on the belief that illegal aliens took large numbers of jobs that United States citizens might otherwise fill, gave impetus to the Simpson-Rodino bill of 1986. The bill's two major provisions constituted a carrot and a stick for illegal immigrants. The carrot came in the form of an amnesty for all undocumented residents who could prove continuous residence in the United States since January 1, 1982. The stick imposed legal sanctions on employers of illegal aliens, an unprecedented attempt to deter migrants indirectly by denying them employment.

The Simpson-Rodino bill, which became law as the United States Immigration Reform and Control Act of 1986, represented the most serious effort to date to reduce illegal Mexican immigration. Northern migration had provided an economic safety valve from the Mexican economy's chronic inability to produce sufficient employment. Many Mexicans resented the timing of this new law, which came in the midst of severe economic distress in Mexico and relative prosperity in the United States. Although the level of migration dropped immediately after passage of the law, joblessness and poverty eventually drove the number of illegal migrants up again.

Despite the irritants of drug trafficking and migration, the United States concern for stability in Mexico led both countries to continue the search for a solution to Mexico's crushing debt burden. By the end of 1987, the United States government publicly recognized that Mexico could not "grow its way out" of the debt merely by stretching out payments and investing more borrowed funds. Acknowledging that some portion of the debt would never be repaid, the Department of the Treasury offered to issue zero-coupon bonds that would allow Mexico to buy back its debt at a discount (see 1982 Crisis and Recovery, ch. 3). Although not a panacea, the plan represented a new approach to the debt problem, one that helped to improve Mexican public opinion of the United States.

Economic Hardship

While the Mexican government, with assistance from the United States, struggled to improve its status in the world financial community, conditions at home remained unsettled. After the GNP contracted by 5 percent in 1983, Mexican optimism surged briefly in 1984, when the economy posted a 3.5 percent growth rate. The next year hope faded as the economy contracted by 1 percent.

A major natural disaster in 1985 further depressed the economic situation. In mid-September, central Mexico experienced two major earthquakes. Between 5,000 and 10,000 people died as a result, and some 300,000 lost their homes. The cost of relief and reconstruction placed a heavy burden on an already struggling nation. The de la Madrid administration successfully cited the earthquakes as negotiating points in its efforts to obtain better terms from its creditors.

In the political arena, initial optimism also gave way to disillusionment. The liberalization that appeared to have begun in 1983 ended by 1984. The ruling PRI easily swept municipal elections in the northern cities of Mexicali and Tijuana, in Coahuila and Sinaloa states, and in the city of Puebla. Despite public protests alleging widespread fraud, the results stood. The PRI easily maintained its majority in congress, but some party leaders were concerned that of the combined vote in five large cities—Mexico City, Guadalajara, Nezahualcóyotl, Monterrey, and Ciudad Juárez—the PRI polled less than 45 percent. The vote in the northern cities could be seen to reflect the traditional regional schism, but the poor showing in the capital area and Guadalajara signaled a growing alienation from the PRI, particularly among the middle class.

Moreover, the persistent fall in oil prices and continuing high levels of foreign debt service forced a new round of austerity measures. De la Madrid effected an additional US$465 million in federal budget cuts by reducing subsidies and government investments, selling more than 200 state-owned parastatals, and placing a partial freeze on federal hiring. As the president announced these new belt-tightening measures, he could also point to some significant achievements. Inflation, which had exceeded 100 percent in 1982, had declined to 60 percent annually. The public-sector deficit had also decreased from 13.6 percent of gross domestic product (GDP—see Glossary) to 6.9 percent. Although these figures fell short of the goals prescribed by the IMF, they represented progress.

De la Madrid did not exaggerate the importance of these positive economic indicators. In his 1986 State of the Nation address, he declared that "our austerity effort is permanent" and vowed again not to deviate from his economic course. Just months before, his administration had reached a precedent-setting agreement with the IMF in which the amount of new loans to Mexico would be tied to fluctuations in the world price of crude oil. But the crisis was far from over.

Carlos Salinas de Gortari: Economic Liberalization, Political Indecision

The Passing of the Torch, 1987–88

The year 1987 in Mexico was the last full year of de la

Madrid's presidential term. In both economic and political terms, de la Madrid's last months in office proved tumultuous. Economically, the administration's failure to restore sustainable growth rates produced a new flare-up. On November 18, 1987, the government recognized the overvalue of the peso and announced that the national currency would be allowed to float on the free exchange market. The free float produced an overnight devaluation of 18 percent; devaluation in turn reignited inflation, which jumped to 144 percent on an annual basis. To avoid an economic disaster, de la Madrid mandated the Economic Solidarity Pact among government, business, and labor to control both prices and wages. Although the government had always exercised immense influence over the economy, wage and price controls of this scope were unheard of. Their implementation by a president who had made sincere but ineffective efforts to liberalize the economy demonstrated both de la Madrid's frustration and his determination to avoid personal blame for the intractable crisis.

The man who inherited this unenviable legacy was a forty-year-old economist with wide experience in the Mexican bureaucracy. Carlos Salinas de Gortari was de la Madrid's minister of budget and planning when the president decided that Salinas was best qualified to assume the helm of state. The selection of Salinas appeared calculated to signal the continuation of de la Madrid's austere economic policies, which were largely shaped by Salinas. A Harvard-educated Ph.D., Salinas was a *técnico*, a competent technocrat with little or no grassroots political experience. Technically, he was highly qualified to deal with the nation's problems. Politically, however, he had to define himself on the campaign trail.

Although throughout his administration de la Madrid had publicly vowed to promote political reform, this promise was not realized. De la Madrid's failure to open up the political system to genuine competition dashed the expectations of Mexicans both within and outside the ruling party. As a result some disaffected PRI members chose to establish the Democratic Current (Corriente Democrático—CD) within the party in October 1986.

The CD leaders were Porfirio Muñoz Ledo, a former chairman of the PRI, and Cuauhtémoc Cárdenas, former governor of Michoacán state and son of president Cárdenas. The primary issue binding the faction members together was the exclusionary nature of party-nominating procedures. They particularly condemned the practice of the *dedazo,* whereby the sitting president chooses his successor, who is then declared the party's candidate by acclamation. In addition, CD members and their sympathizers also objected to de la Madrid's austere economic policies on nationalistic grounds. The president, they believed, had mortgaged the national patrimony to foreigners. Such policies, these dissidents claimed, resulted from the noncompetitive nomination of *técnico* presidents who had no feeling for the plight of the average Mexican.

The CD did not find a receptive audience for its message within the PRI. At the party's national assembly in March 1987, party president Jorge de la Vega condemned the CD, recommending that those who could not abide by the party's rules should resign. Months later, the PRI leadership formally "condemned, rejected, and denounced" Muñoz and Cárdenas, rendering them persona non grata within their own party.

Ostracized by his former party members, Cárdenas declared himself an independent candidate for president on July 3, 1987. Backed by a coalition of leftist parties that eventually dubbed itself the National Democratic Front (Frente Democrático Nacional—FDN), Cárdenas advocated a "return to the original principles of the Mexican Revolution." The candidate's familial heritage infused this message with legitimacy and had considerable emotional appeal for the Mexican voter. Nationalistic policy prescriptions, such as repudiation of the foreign debt and the redistribution of oil exports away from the United States, appealed to the poor, whose lives had clearly not improved under de la Madrid's administration. Like most Mexicans, Cárdenas was mestizo. The prospect of rule by someone other than an elite, light-skinned *técnico* further added to Cárdenas's appeal.

Many in the PRI recognized the threat posed by Cárdenas's candidacy. In response, the party leadership attempted to make it appear that the presidential nominating process had been made more pluralistic. On August 14, 1987, de la Vega announced a list of six candidates for the nomination, including Salinas, but not Cárdenas. The convention formally nominated Salinas on October 4, 1987. Salinas began his campaign having to defend unpopular policies against a popular rival at a time when his party's solidarity and influence were in question. Despite Salinas's pronouncements mandating electoral probity, the July 1988 elections appeared to most observers to be fraudulent. The most serious incidents were the deaths of two key aides to Cárdenas, Xavier Ovando and Román Gil, which were never adequately explained.

Post-election reports by outside observers and voter interviews indicated that much of the rural vote experienced some degree of tampering; the FDN and the PAN had insufficient observers to monitor such elections. After much delay, the election commission declared Salinas the winner on July 13, 1988. The surprise was the total number of votes for the victor— 50.36 percent. The low total, which itself spoke of manipulation, demonstrated the people's disaffection with the PRI.

President Salinas

The 1988 election did not end Salinas's struggle to succeed his mentor, de la Madrid. Cárdenas rejected the Electoral Commission's results, which showed him with 31.1 percent of the national vote. On July 17, 1988, Cárdenas addressed a rally of some 200,000 in Mexico City, in an effort to force a recount. Eventually, along with the PAN candidate Manuel Clouthier, the two opposition candidates united to demand that the elections be nullified and an interim president appointed.

On August 15, 1988, the National Congress, sitting as the electoral college, met to ratify the presidential vote. Cárdenas filed criminal charges against Minister of Interior Manuel Bartlett Díaz, who also served as head of the Federal Electoral Commission. Despite an August 15 rally by the FDN and the PAN, nationwide protests never materialized; the electoral college ratified Salinas's victory as expected.

Meanwhile, during his final months in office, de la Madrid sought to maintain the economy on an even keel for his successor. On August 15, 1988, the government extended the wage and price freeze through November 30, the end of de la Madrid's term. The freeze had done what had been expected— it had reduced inflation from 15.5 percent in January to 1 percent in August. To ease the burden somewhat on the poor, the administration also eliminated a 6 percent value-added tax on basic foodstuffs and medicine and decreed a 30 percent tax cut for low-income workers. The exchange rate of the peso to the dollar remained fixed at the 2,270-to-1 level established in December 1987.

On October 17, 1988, the United States government announced a US$3.5 billion loan to Mexico to help ease the revenue shortfall resulting from the continued drop in oil prices. The loan was considered a bridge loan to tide Mexico over until it could reach agreement with the IMF and the World Bank. Many observers considered the United States action to have been prompted more by political concerns than economic ones. From 1982 to 1988, real income in Mexico had fallen by 40 percent; inflation had reached almost 160 percent annually, privatization efforts had eliminated thousands of jobs that had not yet been replaced by the private sector, and the economy had contracted more than it had grown. In late April 1988, candidate Salinas visited the United States to sound out both United States presidential candidates George H.W. Bush and Michael Dukakis and to visit with members of the United States Congress, interest groups, the press, academics, and influential Mexican-Americans. Even before his election, it was clear that Salinas set great store on productive relations with Mexico's northern neighbor. The October loan may have been one result of his efforts.

Salinas took office on December 1, 1988. In preinaugural interviews, he promised the "political, economic, and cultural modernization" of Mexico and an improvement in Mexico's standing abroad. During the inaugural ceremony, Cárdenas's supporters walked out in protest; PAN members protested silently throughout. In his speech, Salinas stressed the importance of a sound economy to the nation's future. The debt, he claimed, was the primary problem in this regard. He urged further renegotiation, "no longer to pay, but to return to growth." Salinas, however, had no intention of reneging on any portion of the debt. The new president also promised further political reform.

Salinas made the economy his first priority. On December 12, 1988, he ended the wage, price, and exchange-rate freeze instituted under de la Madrid. In its place, the new president advocated price restraint, a modest wage increase, and a scheduled devaluation averaging one peso per day against the dollar. Salinas endorsed de la Madrid's efforts for Mexico's entry into the General Agreement on Tariffs and Trade (GATT), although imports had risen and foreign reserves had dwindled since membership had first been proposed. Salinas privately held that Mexico must open and integrate itself more extensively into the world economy in order to progress and meet the employment needs of a burgeoning young population. Over the short term, however, he admitted that 1989 would be a "year of transition," with little overall economic growth.

Initially, Salinas hoped to diversify Mexico's markets by expanding trade with the industrialized nations of Europe and perhaps with Japan. A state tour of Europe and other contacts, however, convinced him that this hope was illusory. Geography, history, infrastructure, investment, financial ties, and other factors made the United States the arbiter of Mexican economic progress, whether President Salinas liked it or not. Accordingly, Salinas began to develop a notion that he had first proposed to United States president-elect Bush in late November 1988. The Mexican president-elect suggested the establishment of free trade between the two nations, as a natural extension of bilateral agreements already negotiated in such areas as steel, textiles, and automobiles. Bush had promised to take the suggestion under advisement.

In several ways, Salinas followed the pattern established by his predecessor. He wasted little time in moving against potential political enemies in his own moral renewal campaign. Where de la Madrid had moved quietly, however, Salinas acted more dramatically. The corrupt leader of the oil workers union, Joaquín Hernández Galicia (also known as La Quina), surrendered after a gunfight with federal police at union headquarters (see Petroleum, ch. 3). Subsequently, authorities took into custody broker Eduardo Leorreta, a PRI member and former fundraiser for the party, on charges of tax fraud.

With his political flanks covered, and having included both *técnicos* and oldtime PRI members (disparagingly nicknamed "dinosaurs") among his cabinet, Salinas felt secure enough to begin his program of economic liberalization and reform. In May 1989, he ended previous restrictions on foreign ownership of business in Mexico and opened to foreign investment some previously restricted areas. The president also promised to simplify the bureaucratic process that often had deterred investors in the past. The new administration also continued the process of privatization begun under de la Madrid. The major casualty of this process was Altos Hornos de México, a state-owned steel mill in Monclova, where 1,740 workers lost their jobs under a foreign-financed modernization program begun in June 1989. The previous administration had closed outright the Fundidora Monterrey, another steel mill, in 1986, putting almost 13,000 out of work.

In laying the groundwork for economic liberalization, the government announced in July 1989 that it had reached another accord with its foreign creditors after four months of negotiations. Under the so-called Brady Plan, an approach advocated by United States Secretary of the Treasury Nicholas F. Brady to reduce Mexico's debt principal, the IMF agreed to provide US$3.5 billion over three years, US$1 billion of which was designed to assure Mexico's bank payments. In addition, the World Bank was to provide US$6 billion over three years for economic development and guarantees. The government of Japan also provided US$2.05 billion in debt reduction loans. Foreign creditor banks received three options: to make new loans to Mexico, to reduce the principal by writing off some percentage of their loans, or to cut the interest rates they charged on Mexican loans. The net effect of the terms was to reduce Mexico's foreign debt payments by US$8 billion per year.

The debt agreement behind him, Salinas began to make good on his promise of political reform. In the balloting of July 1989, the PRI conceded the governorship of Baja California Norte to the candidate of the PAN. This was a historic event, the first time that the PRI had admitted the loss of a state election. At the same time, however, the PRI took a firm stand in Cárdenas's home state of Michoacán, where the ruling party claimed to have won eleven of eighteen seats in the state legislature. Cárdenas's party, now known as the Democratic Revolutionary Party (Partido Revolucionario Democrático—PRD), protested that its candidates had taken fifteen of the eighteen seats. The PRI, they claimed, had stuffed ballot boxes.

Allegations of voting fraud aside, the United States government, led by President Bush, was very supportive of Salinas and his efforts, particularly in the economic arena. Salinas's original suggestion of a free-trade agreement received serious consideration in Washington. Eventually, after the debt reduction agreement and liberalization efforts in such areas as foreign investment and privatization, United States officials felt that a free-trade accord was a logical next step in opening the Mexican economy and incorporating it into a North American trading bloc. Accordingly, on June 11, 1990, the two governments agreed in principle to negotiate a "comprehensive free-trade agreement" that would eliminate not only tariff barriers, but also "import quotas, licenses, and technical barriers" to the free flow of goods, services, and capital between the two nations. As negotiations progressed, the treaty would become known as the North American Free Trade Agreement (NAFTA) (see Trade Agreements, ch. 3). The agreement fit logically into Salinas's vision of a modernizing Mexico, at least in an economic sense. In 1992 NAFTA was approved by the legislatures of Mexico, the United States, and Canada to take effect on January 1, 1994.

With the president's support, congress passed modest political reforms during the last half of Salinas's term. In 1992 constitutional restrictions on the Roman Catholic Church were repealed (see Church-State Relations, ch. 2). The following year, congress passed a package of electoral reforms, including limits on campaign financing, expansion of the Senate to allow a third minority-party senator from each state, and increased proportional representation in the Chamber of Deputies (see The Salinas Presidency: Reform and Retrenchment, ch. 4).

As in previous *sexenios*, the last year of the Salinas administration was a time of crisis. On January 1, 1994, the Zapatista Army of National Liberation (Ejército Zapatista de Liberación Nacional—EZLN), a heretofore unknown group, suddenly overran several towns in Chiapas (see National Security Concerns, ch. 5). The overwhelming military response forced the rebels into the mountains, but the rebels' demands for reform reminded the country that recent economic improvements had failed to reach many in the lower classes or in the impoverished south.

Political uncertainty increased during 1994. In March Luis Donaldo Colosio Murrieta, the PRI presidential candidate, was assassinated while campaigning in Tijuana. Several investigations failed to produce a motive or the existence of a conspiracy. Rumors circulated, however, that the assassination was drug-related or the action of old-line PRI members opposed to political reform. Anxious to divorce itself from a reputation of fraud, the PRI quickly nominated reform-minded Ernesto Zedillo Ponce de León as its presidential candidate. Zedillo had been Salinas's secretary of budget and secretary of education and was widely perceived as someone who would continue Salinas's policies.

With all eyes focused on the presidential campaign and the uprising in Chiapas, few noticed the worsening economy in 1994. A rising deficit in the current account made the economy increasingly vulnerable to shifts in external capital flow. Although statistics showed a healthy rise in exports, most of the exports were goods from the border-zone *maquiladora* (see Glossary) industries, with little overall benefit to the Mexican economy or Mexican workers. In addition, rising interest rates in the United States diverted much-needed capital from the developing world. The government was reluctant to take stringent economic measures in an election year, however, and instead issued short-term, dollar-denominated bonds to finance government spending.

The election results of August 21, 1994, contained no surprises. The PRI candidate, Zedillo, won the presidency with 49 percent of the vote. The PAN took 26 percent of the total, the major candidate on the left garnered 16 percent, and six minor parties accounted for the rest. Despite some irregularities, international observers declared that the election was generally honest, and Zedillo was inaugurated on December 1, 1994.

With the election over, attention turned to the economy. Most economists felt that the currency was overvalued, and a devaluation was widely anticipated. When a devaluation was announced on December 20, however, the result was unexpected. Investors panicked, and large amounts of capital were pulled out of Mexico or converted to dollars. Government measures to stem the exodus of funds only exacerbated the problem. Government debt rose sharply, and inflation and interest rates soared. Only large-scale international intervention stopped the downward spiral.

President Salinas had hoped that his free-market economic policies and political reforms would bring sustained economic growth and increased democratization. The realities of the last years of the twentieth century differed, however. The Mexican economy suffered one of its worst downturns since the Great Depression of the 1930s. The PRI's lessening grip on power led not to stability but to an era of increased political and social turmoil. As so often in Mexico's past, in the late 1990s democracy and prosperity remained only tantalizing goals.

*   *   *

An enormous wealth of historical literature exists on Mexico. Both Mexican and foreign historians have produced analyses of the developments leading to the country's position in contemporary Latin America. The most useful standard histories of Mexico are Henry Bamford Parkes's *A History of Mexico*, Charles C. Cumberland's *Mexico: The Struggle for Modernity*, Frank Tannenbaum's *Mexico: The Struggle for Peace and Bread*, and Jan S. Bazant's *A Concise History of Mexico*. Although now slightly dated, the most complete and best researched general historical analysis available in English is Michael C. Meyer and William L. Sherman's *The Course of Mexican History*, a comprehensive book that presents Mexican history from preconquest times to the inauguration of President de la Madrid in 1982.

For the study of pre-Columbian peoples and their origins, Eric R. Wolf's *Sons of the Shaking Earth* and Michael D. Coe's *Mexico* are extremely useful. The Aztec traditions and belief system are also well researched and artfully presented in José López Portillo's *Quetzalcóatl*. The classic work of Bernal Díaz del Castillo, *The Discovery and Conquest of Mexico, 1517–1521*, remains one of the best sources of information about the arrival of the Spaniards in Mexico and the victory over the Aztec.

For the colonial period, useful studies are Clarence Henry Haring's *The Spanish Empire in America*, Charles Gibson's *Spain in America*, François Chevalier's *Land and Society in Colonial Mexico*, William B. Taylor's *Landlord and Peasant in Colonial Oaxaca*, and James Lockhart and Stuart B. Schwartz's *Early Latin America*. The struggle for independence and the Mexican Revolution are the best researched subjects. Aside from the general works already cited, useful sources include W. Dirk Raat's *Mexico: From Independence to Revolution, 1810–1910*, Victor Alba's *The Mexicans: The Making of a Nation*, Jesús Romero Flores's *La revolución mexicana (anales históricos, 1910–1974)*, John Womack Jr.'s classic *Zapata and the Mexican Revolution*, and many more.

For the modern period, the following sources are helpful: Thomas G. Sanders's *Mexico in the 70s*, Howard F. Cline's *Mexico: Revolution to Evolution, 1940–1960*, Fernando Benítez's *Lázaro Cárdenas y la revolución mexicana* (three volumes), Frank R. Brandenburg's *The Making of Modern Mexico*, Jaime Castrejón Díaz's *La república imperial en los 80s*, Kenneth F. Johnson's *Mexican Democracy*, Dan Hofstadter's *Mexico, 1946–73*, and the articles published in the *Mexican Forum*. (For further information and complete citations, see Bibliography.)

Chapter 2. The Society and Its Environment

A representation of a Mexican mother and children from a painting by David Álfaro Siqueiros

it turns east along the nineteenth parallel to the central portion of the state of Veracruz. The region is distinguished by considerable seismic activity and contains Mexico's highest volcanic peaks. This range contains three peaks exceeding 5,000 meters: Pico de Orizaba (Citlaltépetl)—the third highest mountain in North America—and Popocatépetl and Iztaccíhuatl near Mexico City. The Cordillera Neovolcánica is regarded as the geological dividing line between North America and Central America.

Several important mountain ranges dominate the landscape of southern and southeastern Mexico. The Sierra Madre del Sur extends 1,200 kilometers along Mexico's southern coast from the southwestern part of the Cordillera Neovolcánica to the nearly flat isthmus of Tehuantepec. Mountains in this range average 2,000 meters in elevation. The range averages 100 kilometers in width, but widens to 150 kilometers in the state of Oaxaca. The narrow southwest coastal plain extends from the Sierra Madre del Sur to the Pacific Ocean. The Sierra Madre de Oaxaca begins at Pico de Orizaba and extends in a southeasterly direction for 300 kilometers until reaching the isthmus of Tehuantepec. Peaks in the Sierra Madre de Oaxaca average 2,500 meters in elevation, with some peaks exceeding 3,000 meters. South of the isthmus of Tehuantepec, the Sierra Madre de Chiapas runs 280 kilometers along the Pacific Coast from the Oaxaca-Chiapas border to Mexico's border with Guatemala. Although average elevation is only 1,500 meters, one peak—Volcán de Tacuma—exceeds 4,000 meters in elevation. Finally, the Meseta Central de Chiapas extends 250 kilometers through the central part of Chiapas to Guatemala. The average height of peaks of the Meseta Central de Chiapas is 2,000 meters. The Chiapas central valley separates the Meseta Central de Chiapas and the Sierra Madre de Chiapas.

Mexico has nearly 150 rivers, two-thirds of which empty into the Pacific Ocean and the remainder of which flow into the Gulf of Mexico or the Caribbean Sea. Despite this apparent abundance of water, water volume is unevenly distributed throughout the country. Indeed, five rivers—the Usumacinta, Grijalva, Papaloapán, Coatzacoalcos, and Pánuco—account for 52 percent of Mexico's average annual volume of surface water. All five rivers flow into the Gulf of Mexico; only the Río Pánuco is outside southeastern Mexico, which contains approximately 15 percent of national territory and 12 percent of the national population. In contrast, northern and central Mexico, with 47

The Sierra Madre Oriental starts at the Big Bend region of the Texas-Mexico border and continues 1,350 kilometers until reaching Cofre de Perote, one of the major peaks of the Cordillera Neovolcánica. As is the case with the Sierra Madre Occidental, the Sierra Madre Oriental comes progressively closer to the coastline as it approaches its southern terminus, reaching to within seventy-five kilometers of the Gulf of Mexico. The northeast coastal plain extends from the eastern slope of the Sierra Madre Oriental to the Gulf of Mexico. The median elevation of the Sierra Madre Oriental is 2,200 meters, with some peaks at 3,000 meters.

The Mexican altiplano, stretching from the United States border to the Cordillera Neovolcánica, occupies the vast expanse of land between the eastern and western sierra madres. A low east-west range divides the altiplano into northern and southern sections. These two sections, previously called the Mesa del Norte and Mesa Central, are now regarded by geographers as sections of one altiplano. The northern altiplano averages 1,100 meters in elevation and continues south from the Río Bravo del Norte through the states of Zacatecas and San Luis Potosí. Various narrow, isolated ridges cross the plateaus of the northern altiplano. Numerous depressions dot the region, the largest of which is the Bolsón de Mapimí. The southern altiplano is higher than its northern counterpart, averaging 2,000 meters in elevation. The southern altiplano contains numerous valleys originally formed by ancient lakes. Several of Mexico's most prominent cities, including Mexico City and Guadalajara, are located in the valleys of the southern altiplano.

One other significant mountain range, the California system, cuts across the landscape of the northern half of Mexico. A southern extension of the California coastal ranges that parallel California's coast, the Mexican portion of the California system extends from the United States border to the southern tip of the Baja Peninsula, a distance of 1,430 kilometers. Peaks in the California system range in altitude from 2,200 meters in the north to only 250 meters near La Paz in the south. Narrow lowlands are found on the Pacific Ocean and the Gulf of California sides of the mountains.

The Cordillera Neovolcánica is a belt 900 kilometers long and 130 kilometers wide, extending from the Pacific Ocean to the Gulf of Mexico. The Cordillera Neovolcánica begins at the Río Grande de Santiago and continues south to Colima, where

meter border with the United States. The meandering Río Bravo del Norte (known as the Rio Grande in the United States) defines the border from Ciudad Juárez east to the Gulf of Mexico. A series of natural and artificial markers delineate the United States-Mexican border west from Ciudad Juárez to the Pacific Ocean. On its south, Mexico shares an 871-kilometer border with Guatemala and a 251-kilometer border with Belize. Mexico has a 10,143-kilometer coastline, of which 7,338 kilometers face the Pacific Ocean and the Gulf of California, and the remaining 2,805 kilometers front the Gulf of Mexico and the Caribbean Sea. Mexico's exclusive economic zone (EEZ), which extends 200 nautical miles off each coast, covers approximately 2.7 million square kilometers. The landmass of Mexico dramatically narrows as it moves in a southeasterly direction from the United States border and then abruptly curves northward before ending in the 500-kilometer-long Yucatan Peninsula. Indeed, the capital of Yucatán State, Mérida, is farther north than Mexico City or Guadalajara.

Topography and Drainage

Two prominent mountain ranges—the Sierra Madre Occidental and the Sierra Madre Oriental—define northern Mexico. Both are extensions of ranges found in the United States. The Sierra Madre Occidental on the west is a continuation of California's Sierra Nevada (with a break in southeastern California and extreme northern Mexico), and the Sierra Madre Oriental on the east is a southward extension of the Rocky Mountains of New Mexico and Texas. Between these two ranges lies the Mexican altiplano (high plain), a southern continuation of the Great Basin and high deserts that spread over much of the western United States.

Beginning approximately fifty kilometers from the United States border, the Sierra Madre Occidental extends 1,250 kilometers south to the Río Santiago, where it merges with the Cordillera Neovolcánica range that runs east-west across central Mexico. The Sierra Madre Occidental lies approximately 300 kilometers inland from the west coast of Mexico at its northern end but approaches to within fifty kilometers of the coast near the Cordillera Neovolcánica. The northwest coastal plain is the name given the lowland area between the Sierra Madre Occidental and the Gulf of California. The Sierra Madre Occidental averages 2,250 meters in elevation, with peaks reaching 3,000 meters.

PROFOUND CHANGES OCCURRED IN Mexican society during the second half of the twentieth century. A sharp decline in mortality levels, coupled with fertility rates that remained relatively high until the mid-1970s, produced a massive population increase. Indeed, the 1990 census total of approximately 81 million Mexicans was more than triple the figure recorded forty years earlier. Mexico's stagnant agricultural sector could not absorb the millions of additional workers, triggering a steady migration to the cities. As a result, Mexico shifted from a predominantly rural to a heavily urban society. Because of the lack of available housing, migrants generally clustered on the periphery of Mexico City and other major urban centers. The local infrastructure often could not keep pace with such growth, resulting in serious environmental concerns.

Despite the massive problems caused by the rapid population shift, successive Mexican governments could point to notable accomplishments in improving the quality of life of their citizens. In the years after World War II, the percentage of deaths caused by infectious, parasitic, and respiratory illnesses fell dramatically. Both the number and percentage of Mexicans with access to basic services such as running water and electricity grew substantially. Literacy and educational levels continued to climb.

The benefits of modernization were not equally distributed, however. Residents of southern Mexico consistently trailed the rest of the country in "quality-of-life" indicators. Urban workers in the informal sector of the economy did not have access to the same level of health care as their counterparts in the formal sector and did not qualify for retirement or pension payments. Income distribution had become increasingly skewed in favor of the wealthiest sectors of society. Mexican policy makers thus faced the difficult challenge of ensuring economic growth while also confronting the persistence of poverty.

Physical Setting

Mexico's total area covers 1,972,550 square kilometers, including approximately 6,000 square kilometers of islands in the Pacific Ocean, Gulf of Mexico, Caribbean Sea, and Gulf of California (see fig. 3). On its north, Mexico shares a 3,326-kilo-

Pico de Orizaba in eastern Mexico
Courtesy Embassy of Mexico, Washington
Typical cactus and scrub vegetation in north-central Mexico
Courtesy Inter-American Development Bank

percent of the national area and almost 60 percent of Mexico's population, have less than 10 percent of the country's water resources.

Seismic Activity

Situated atop three of the large tectonic plates that constitute the earth's surface, Mexico is one of the most seismologically active regions on earth. The motion of these plates causes earthquakes and volcanic activity.

Most of the Mexican landmass rests on the westward moving North American plate. The Pacific Ocean floor off southern Mexico, however, is being carried northeast by the underlying motion of the Cocos plate. Ocean floor material is relatively dense; when it strikes the lighter granite of the Mexican landmass, the ocean floor is forced under the landmass, creating the deep Middle American trench that lies off Mexico's southern coast. The westward moving land atop the North American plate is slowed and crumpled where it meets the Cocos plate, creating the mountain ranges of southern Mexico. The subduction of the Cocos plate accounts for the frequency of earthquakes near Mexico's southern coast. As the rocks constituting the ocean floor are forced down, they melt, and the molten material is forced up through weaknesses in the surface rock, creating the volcanoes in the Cordillera Neovolcánica across central Mexico.

Areas off Mexico's coastline on the Gulf of California, including the Baja California Peninsula, are riding northwestward on the Pacific plate. Rather than one plate subducting, the Pacific and North American plates grind past each other, creating a slip fault that is the southern extension of the San Andreas fault in California. Motion along this fault in the past pulled Baja California away from the coast, creating the Gulf of California. Continued motion along this fault is the source of earthquakes in western Mexico.

Mexico has a long history of destructive earthquakes and volcanic eruptions. In September 1985, an earthquake measuring 8.1 on the Richter scale and centered in the subduction zone off Acapulco killed more than 4,000 people in Mexico City, more than 300 kilometers away. Volcán de Colima, south of Guadalajara, erupted in 1994, and El Chichón, in southern Mexico, underwent a violent eruption in 1983. Paricutín in northwest Mexico began as puffs of smoke in a cornfield in 1943; a decade later the volcano was 2,700 meters high.

Although dormant for decades, Popocatépetl and Ixtaccíhuatl ("smoking warrior" and "white lady," respectively, in Náhuatl) occasionally send out puffs of smoke clearly visible in Mexico City, a reminder to the capital's inhabitants that volcanic activity is near. Popocatépetl showed renewed activity in 1995 and 1996, forcing the evacuation of several nearby villages and causing concern by seismologists and government officials about the effect that a large-scale eruption might have on the heavily populated region nearby.

Climate

The Tropic of Cancer effectively divides the country into temperate and tropical zones. Land north of the twenty-fourth parallel experiences cooler temperatures during the winter months. South of the twenty-fourth parallel, temperatures are fairly constant year round and vary solely as a function of elevation.

Areas south of the twentieth-fourth parallel with elevations up to 1,000 meters (the southern parts of both coastal plains as well as the Yucatan Peninsula), have a yearly median temperature between 24°C and 28°C. Temperatures here remain high throughout the year, with only a 5°C difference between winter and summer median temperatures. Although low-lying areas north of the twentieth-fourth parallel are hot and humid during the summer, they generally have lower yearly temperature averages (from 20°C to 24°C) because of more moderate conditions during the winter.

Between 1,000 and 2,000 meters, one encounters yearly average temperatures between 16°C and 20°C. Towns and cities at this elevation south of the twenty-fourth parallel have relatively constant, pleasant temperatures throughout the year, whereas more northerly locations experience sizeable seasonal variations. Above 2,000 meters, temperatures drop as low as an average yearly range between 8°C and 12°C in the Cordillera Neovolcánica. At 2,300 meters, Mexico City has a yearly median temperature of 15°C with pleasant summers and mild winters. Average daily highs and lows for May, the warmest month, are 26°C and 12°C, and average daily highs and lows for January, the coldest month, are 19°C and 6°C.

Rainfall varies widely both by location and season. Arid or semiarid conditions are encountered in the Baja Peninsula, the northwestern state of Sonora, the northern altiplano, and significant portions of the southern altiplano. Rainfall in these regions averages between 300 and 600 millimeters per year. Average rainfall totals are between 600 and 1,000 millimeters in most of the year in most of the major populated areas of the southern altiplano, including Mexico City and Guadalajara. Low-lying areas along the Gulf of Mexico receive in excess of 1,000 millimeters of rainfall in an average year, with the wettest region being the southeastern state of Tabasco, which typically receives approximately 2,000 millimeters of rainfall on an annual basis. Parts of the northern altiplano and high peaks in the Sierra Madre Occidental and the Sierra Madre Oriental occasionally receive significant snowfalls.

Mexico has pronounced wet and dry seasons. Most of the country experiences a rainy season from June to mid-October and significantly less rain during the remainder of the year. February and July generally are the driest and wettest months, respectively. Mexico City, for example, receives an average of only 5 millimeters of rain during February but more than 160 millimeters in July. Coastal areas, especially those along the Gulf of Mexico, experience the largest amounts of rain in September. Tabasco typically records more than 300 millimeters of rain during that month. A small coastal area of northwestern coastal Mexico around Tijuana has a Mediterranean climate with considerable coastal fog and a rainy season that occurs in winter.

Mexico lies squarely within the hurricane belt, and all regions of both coasts are susceptible to these storms from June through November. Hurricanes on the Pacific coast are less frequent and often less violent than those affecting Mexico's eastern coastline. Several hurricanes per year strike the Caribbean and Gulf of Mexico coastline, however, and these storms bring high winds, heavy rain, extensive damage, and occasional loss of life. Hurricane Hugo passed directly over Cancún in September 1989, with winds in excess of 200 kilometers per hour producing major damage to hotels in the resort area. In September 1988, Hurricane Gilbert struck northeast Mexico. Flooding from the heavy rain in that storm killed dozens in the Monterrey area and caused extensive damage to livestock and vegetable crops.

Environmental Conditions

Mexico faces significant environmental challenges affecting almost every section of the country. Vast expanses of southern and southeastern tropical forests have been denuded for cattle-raising and agriculture. For example, tropical forests covered almost half of the state of Tabasco in 1940 but less than 10 percent by the late 1980s. During the same period, pastureland increased from 20 to 60 percent of the state's total area. Analysts reported similar conditions in other tropical sections of Mexico. Deforestation has contributed to serious levels of soil erosion nationwide. In 1985 the government classified almost 17 percent of all land as totally eroded, 31 percent in an accelerated state of erosion, and 38 percent demonstrating signs of incipient erosion.

Soil destruction is particularly pronounced in the north and northwest, with more than 60 percent of land considered in a total or accelerated state of erosion. Fragile because of its semi-arid and arid character, the soil of the region has become increasingly damaged through excessive cattle-raising and irrigation with waters containing high levels of salinity. The result is a mounting problem of desertification throughout the region.

Mexico's vast coastline faces a different, but no less difficult, series of environmental problems. For example, inadequately regulated petroleum exploitation in the Coatzacoalcos-Minatitlán zone in the Gulf of Mexico has caused serious damage to the waters and fisheries of Río Coatzacoalcos. The deadly explosion that racked a working-class neighborhood in Guadalajara in April 1992 serves as an appropriate symbol of environmental damage in Mexico. More than 1,000 barrels of gasoline seeped from a corroded Mexican Petroleum (Petróleos Mexicanos—Pemex) pipeline into the municipal sewer system, where it combined with gases and industrial residuals to produce a massive explosion that killed 190 persons and injured nearly 1,500 others.

Mexico City confronts authorities with perhaps their most daunting environmental challenge. Geography and extreme population levels have combined to produce one of the world's most polluted urban areas. Mexico City sits in a valley surrounded on three sides by mountains, which serve to trap contaminants produced by the metropolitan area's 15 million residents. One government study in the late 1980s determined that nearly 5 million tons of contaminants were emitted annually in the atmosphere, a tenfold increase over the previous decade. Carbons and hydrocarbons from the region's more than 3 million vehicles account for approximately 80 percent of these contaminants, with another 15 percent, primarily of sulfur and nitrogen, coming from industrial plants. During the dry winter months, untreated fecal matter also becomes airborne. The resulting dangerous mix is responsible for a wide range of respiratory illnesses. One study of twelve urban areas worldwide in the mid-1980s concluded that the residents of Mexico City had the highest levels of lead and cadmium in their blood. The volume of pollutants from Mexico City has damaged the surrounding ecosystem as well. For example, wastewater from Mexico City that flows north and is used for irrigation in the state of Hidalgo has been linked to congenital birth defects and high levels of gastrointestinal diseases in that state.

Beginning in the mid-1980s, the government enacted numerous antipollution policies in Mexico City with varied degrees of success. Measures such as vehicle emissions inspections, the introduction of unleaded gasoline, and the installation of catalytic converters on new vehicles helped reduce pollution generated by trucks and buses. In contrast, one of the government's most prominent actions, the No Driving Day program, may have inadvertently contributed to higher pollution levels. Under the program, metropolitan area residents were prohibited from driving their vehicles one day each work week based on the last number of their license plate. However, those with the resources to do so purchased additional automobiles to use on the day their principal vehicle was prohibited from driving, thus adding to the region's vehicle stock. Thermal inversions reached such dangerous levels at various times in the mid-1990s that the government declared pollution emergencies, necessitating sharp temporary cutbacks in vehicle use and industrial production.

Population

The eleventh annual census, conducted in 1990, reported a total Mexican population of 81,250,000. This figure represented a 2.3 percent per annum growth rate from the 1980 census and indicated successful government efforts at slowing down the level of population increase. The government reported that the population stood at 91,158,000 at the end of 1995, a 1.8 percent increase over the previous year. Assuming that this most recent level of growth were maintained through the rest of the 1990s, Mexico's population would stand at approximately 100 million persons in the year 2000. A return to the higher 1980 to 1990 growth rate, however, would result in a population total of approximately 102 million persons by the year 2000.

The pace of migration to the United States increased markedly during the 1980s. One analyst, Rodolfo Corona Vázquez, estimated that 4.4 million Mexicans resided outside the country (almost all in the United States) in 1990, roughly double the estimated number in 1980. Corona Vázquez also noted a changing pattern of emigration since the 1960s. Seven contiguous states in north central Mexico—Jalisco, Michoacán, Guanajuato, Zacatecas, Durango, San Luis Potosí, and Aguascalientes—accounted for approximately 70 percent of all emigrants in 1960, but only 42 percent in 1990. New important sources of emigration included Chihuahua in the northeast, the Federal District (the administrative unit that includes Mexico City), and the southernmost state of Oaxaca.

Notable variations exist in the country's population density (see fig. 4). Four states, three of them in the arid northwest, had fewer than ten persons per square kilometer in 1990, and another thirteen states, mostly in the north, had density levels between ten and fifty persons per square kilometer. By contrast, two states clustered near the capital had densities in excess of 200 persons per square kilometer. The rate in Mexico City itself was approximately 5,500 persons per square kilometer (see table 2, Appendix).

The state of Mexico and the Federal District accounted for over 22 percent of the national population in 1990. The state of Mexico's spectacular population growth (the state alone accounted for more than 12 percent of national totals) reflected the expansion of the Mexico City metropolitan area. Almost 69 percent of the state of Mexico's population resided in the twenty-seven municipalities that, together with the Federal District, comprise the Mexico City metropolitan area. More than 40 percent of state residents lived in four working-class municipalities—Nezahualcóyotl, Ecatepec, Naucalpán, and Tlalnepantla—that serve as bedroom communities for Mexico City.

During the course of its history, Mexico has experienced dramatic shifts in population. Demographers estimate that the country's population at the time of the Spanish conquest in the early 1500s was approximately 20 million. By 1600, however, barely 1 million remained—the result of deadly European diseases and brutal treatment of the indigenous inhabitants by the Spanish colonizers (see New Spain, ch. 1). At the onset of the

Mexican Revolution in 1910, Mexico's population stood at approximately 15 million persons. Not until 1940 did Mexico reach the population level it had in 1519.

Although the population growth between 1910 and 1940 appeared relatively modest in absolute numbers, the seeds were sown for a spectacular increase over the next thirty years. Because of advances in preventive medicine and the gradual control of diseases such as yellow fever, the crude death rate declined from 33.2 per 1,000 inhabitants in the period 1905 to 1910 to 23.4 in 1940 (see table 3, Appendix). As sanitation conditions improved in post-World War II Mexico, the crude death rate dropped sharply to 10.1 by 1970. At the same time, however, fertility rates (the number of children the average woman would bear from fifteen to forty-nine years of age) remained relatively stable. Because of the stable fertility rate and declining death rate, the population increased by 2.7 percent per annum between 1940 and 1950, by 3.1 percent per annum between 1950 and 1960, and by 3.4 percent per annum between 1960 and 1970. By 1970 Mexico's population stood at approximately 48.2 million persons, almost two and one-half times its pre-World War II number. Demographers in 1970 ominously forecast that the population would reach 125 million persons by the year 2000.

Shortly after assuming the presidency in 1976, José López Portillo y Pacheco (1976–82) adopted an aggressive national family planning program. This effort paid immediate dividends by reducing Mexico's fertility rate from 5.4 in 1976 to 4.6 in 1979. The family planning initiative produced a fundamental change in attitudes that continued and accelerated into the 1990s. Indeed, the government reported that the fertility rate had declined to 2.9 in 1993. This lower fertility rate produced a slightly older average population in 1990, compared with two decades earlier. In 1970, 46.2 percent of all Mexicans were younger than fifteen years of age, and 56.7 percent were under twenty years of age. By 1990, these numbers had dropped to 38.3 and 50.6 percent, respectively (see fig. 5).

Ethnicity and Language

Ethnicity is an important yet highly imprecise concept in contemporary Mexico. Students of Mexican society, as well as Mexicans themselves, identify two broad ethnic groups based on cultural rather than racial differences: mestizos and Indians. Each group has a distinct cultural viewpoint and perceives

Source: Based on information from Mexico, National Institute of Statistics, Geograp
de población y vivienda, 1990, Aguascalientes, 1992, 13.

Figure 4. Population Density by State, 1990

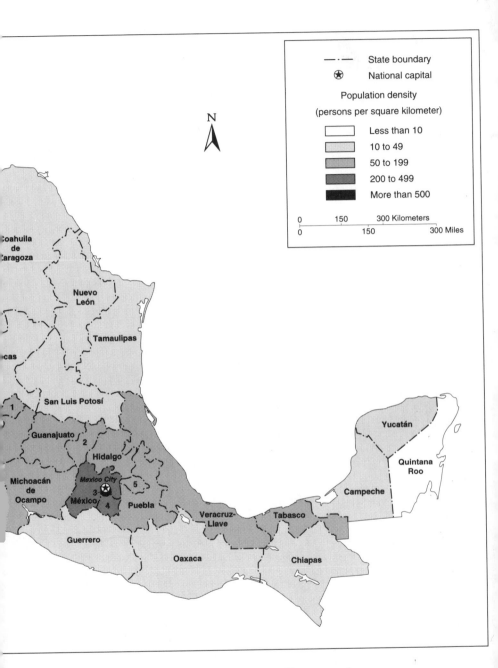

itself as different from the other. At the same time, however, group allegiances may change, making measurement of ethnic composition problematic at best.

Originally racial designators, the terms *mestizo* and *Indian* have lost almost all of their previous racial connotation and are now used entirely to designate cultural groups. Historically, the term *mestizo* described someone with mixed European and indigenous heritage. Mestizos occupied a middle social stratum between whites and pure-blooded indigenous people (see Socieconomic Structures, ch. 1). Whites themselves were divided into *criollo* (those born in the New World) and *peninsular* (those born in Spain) subgroups. In contemporary usage, however, the word *mestizo* refers to anyone who has adopted Mexican Hispanic culture. Seen in this cultural context, both those with a solely European background and those with a mixed European-indigenous background are automatically referred to as mestizos. *Mestizo*, then, has become a synonym for culturally Mexican, much as *ladino* is used in many Latin American countries for those who are culturally Hispanic. Members of indigenous groups also may be called (and may call themselves) mestizos if they have the dominant Hispanic societal cultural values.

If an indigenous person can become a mestizo, who, then, is an Indian? Anthropologist Alan Sandstorm lists minimum criteria that compose a definition of Indian ethnicity. According to Sandstorm, an Indian is someone who identifies himself as such; chooses to use an indigenous language in daily speech; remains actively involved in village communal affairs; participates in religious ceremonies rooted in native American traditions; and attempts to achieve a harmony with, rather than control over, the social and natural worlds. Should one or more criteria become absent over time, the individual probably has begun the transition to becoming a mestizo.

Although mestizos and Indians may both reside in rural areas and have relatively comparable levels of income, they maintain different lives. Such differences can lead to highly negative perceptions about each other. Mestizos often contend that Indians are too unmotivated and constrained by tradition to deal appropriately with the demands of modern society. Indians, in turn, frequently complain that mestizos are aggressive, impatient, and disrespectful toward nature.

Given the cultural use of the terms, it would be unrealistic to expect Mexican census officials to count the number of mesti-

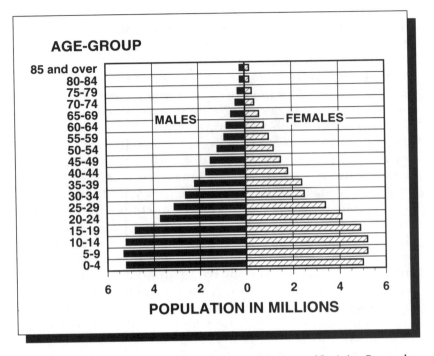

Source: Based on information from Mexico, National Institute of Statistics, Geography, and Informatics, *Mexico Today,* Aguascalientes, 1992, 25.

Figure 5. Population by Age and Gender, 1990

zos and Indians based on racial criteria. However, in measuring how many people speak an indigenous language, the census at least serves to identify a minimum number of racially unmixed Indians. In 1990, 7.5 percent of the Mexican population, or approximately 5.3 million people five years of age and over, spoke an Indian language. Of that total, approximately 79 percent knew Spanish as well and thus were at least potential cultural converts to the mestizo world.

Enormous statewide differences exist in familiarity with indigenous languages (see fig. 6). Roughly speaking, familiarity with indigenous languages increases from north to south. The latest census showed that almost no native speakers lived in a band of eight contiguous states stretching from Coahuila in the northeast to Jalisco and Colima along the north-central Pacific coast. Speakers of indigenous languages constituted less than 5 percent of the population in states in the far northwest and along a central belt of states from Michoacán in the west to

Tlaxcala in the east. The percentage climbed to between 10 and 20 percent in another contiguous grouping of states from San Luis Potosí to Guerrero, to 26 percent in Oaxaca, to 32 and 39 percent, respectively, in Quintana Roo and Chiapas, and to 44 percent in Yucatán. Only 63 percent of users of indigenous languages in Chiapas also knew Spanish.

Specialists have identified twelve distinct Mexican linguistic families, more than forty subgroups, and more than ninety individual languages. Nearly 23 percent of all native speakers speak Náhuatl, the language of the Aztec people and the only indigenous language found in fifteen states. Other major indigenous languages include Maya (spoken by approximately 14 percent of all Indians and primarily used in the southeast from the Yucatan Peninsula to Chiapas); Zapotec (spoken by approximately 7 percent of all Indians and largely used in the eastern part of Oaxaca); Mixtec (also spoken by approximately 7 percent of all Indians and primarily found in Oaxaca and Guerrero); Otomí (spoken by approximately 5 percent of all Indians and used in central Mexico, especially the states of México, Hidalgo, and Querétaro); Tzeltal (spoken by nearly 5 percent of all Indians and used in Chiapas); and Tzotzil (spoken by roughly 4 percent of the Indian population and also used in Chiapas). With twelve different Indian languages, Oaxaca has the nation's most diverse linguistic pattern.

Census data reveal that Indians remain the most marginalized sector of Mexican society. More than 40 percent of the Indian population fifteen years of age and older was illiterate in 1990, roughly three times the national rate. Thirty percent of Indian children between six and fourteen years of age did not attend school. Indians also had significantly higher morbidity and mortality rates associated with infectious and parasitic illness, higher levels of nutritional deficiencies, and less access to such basic services as indoor plumbing, piped water, and electricity.

Income Distribution

In the mid-1990s, Mexico had a highly inequitable distribution of income, a pattern that, according to government statistics, became particularly skewed during the economic crisis of the 1980s. The country's continuing inability to create sufficient employment opportunities for its labor force has produced high levels of unemployment and underemployment and has required aggressive survival strategies among Mexico's

97

poor. Such strategies include sending more family members, even children, into the labor market and reducing consumption of basic commodities.

The 1990 census reported a total national workforce of 24.3 million people. Although population growth slowed to around 2 percent per annum in the early and mid-1990s, analysts estimated that the workforce expanded by up to 4 percent per annum over the same period. Workforce expansion is expected to remain at these rates through the late 1990s, as those born during the peak fertility years of 1970–76 come of age. Thus, Mexico will need approximately 1 million new jobs each year through the remainder of the 1990s to provide work for persons entering the job market. During the early 1990s, however, net job growth was believed to have been less than 500,000 per annum.

Approximately 10 percent of all Mexicans can be characterized as belonging to the upper- and upper-middle-income sectors, consisting of the nation's business executives and government leaders. Upper-income Mexicans are both highly urbanized and well educated. Government surveys of household income revealed that these groups absorbed an increasing share of wealth during the 1980s. The top 10 percent of the population accounted for 33 percent of all income in 1984 and 38 percent in 1992.

The middle sector comprises approximately 30 percent of the nation. Like its upper-income counterparts, this sector is largely urban and has educational levels superior to the national average. It consists of professionals, mid-level government and private-sector employees, office workers, shopkeepers, and other nonmanual workers. The middle-sector share of overall income declined from 39 percent in 1984 to 36 percent in 1992. Inflation seriously eroded the purchasing power of the middle class during that period, causing many to modify their buying habits and to withdraw from private education and health care systems.

The remaining 60 percent of Mexicans make up the lower sector, itself a heterogeneous group of industrial workers, informal-sector employees, and peasants. Of these, industrial workers have the most favored situation, reflecting both their higher wage scale and membership in the health care system and retirement or disability programs of the Mexican Institute of Social Security (Instituto Mexicano del Seguro Social— IMSS) (see Health and Social Security, this ch.). However,

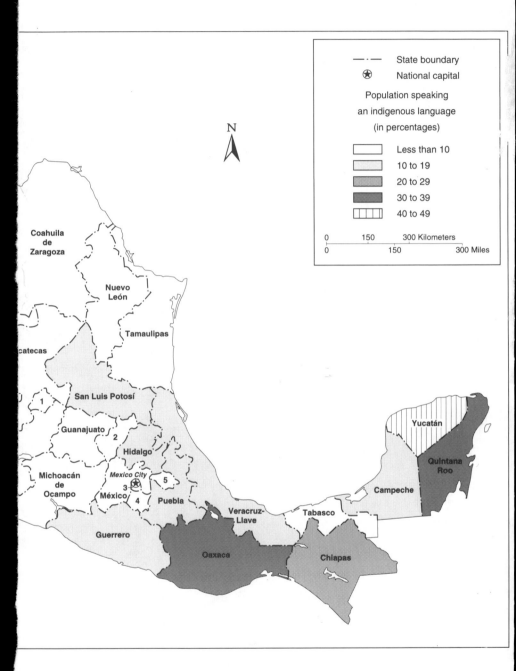

phy, and Informatics, *Estados Unidos Mexicanos: Resumen general. XI censo general de*

genous Languages by State, 1990

Key to states in central Mexico
1. **Aguascalientes**
2. **Querétaro de Arteaga**
3. **Federal District**
4. **Morelos**
5. **Tlaxcala**

Source: Based on information from Mexico, National Institute of Statistics, Geogr;
población y vivienda, 1990, Aguascalientes, 1992, 42–55.

Figure 6. Population (Five Years of Age and Older) Speaking Indi

industrial workers also experienced a decline in purchasing power and share of national income during the 1980s. Overall, the bottom 60 percent of the population saw its share of total income fall from 29 percent in 1984 to 26 percent in 1992.

Analysts estimate that the informal sector of the economy represents from 30 to 40 percent of the urban workforce in the mid-1990s. Informal-sector workers are self-employed or work in small firms (during 1993, businesses with one to five employees accounted for 42 percent of the urban workforce). They face considerable job instability, and, unlike those in the formal sector, are effectively excluded from IMSS benefits. The informal sector includes street vendors, domestic servants, pieceworkers in small establishments, and most construction workers.

During the early 1990s, Mexico reported unemployment rates of between 3 and 4 percent. These rates, based on surveys of conditions in Mexico's three dozen largest cities, excluded those who had ceased looking for work over the previous two months, as well as those working only a few hours per week. A much more accurate government measure of unemployment and underemployment includes both the unemployed and those who work less than thirty-five hours per week. This level of urban partial employment and unemployment stood at around 20 percent during the early 1990s. The government does not measure rural unemployment or underemployment, where rates are regarded by analysts as significantly higher than those found in urban Mexico.

According to government statistics, the vast majority of urban workers in the early 1990s earned less than US$15 per day. Minimum wage rates vary according to region and are adjusted every January to account for inflation. If inflation rates are high, labor groups can ask the regulatory committee, the Tripartite National Minimum Wage Commission, to consider an additional raise during the year. In December 1995 in Mexico City, the daily minimum wage stood at 20.15 new pesos, or US$2.70 (for value of new peso—see Glossary). In 1993 the government reported that 10 percent of workers earned less than the minimum wage, 34.7 percent made between one and two times the minimum wage, and 36.5 percent received between two and five times the minimum wage.

Government surveys of household income in 1984 and 1989 revealed a worsening pattern of income distribution. As noted by economist Rodolfo de la Torre, the poorest 30 percent of the population had only 9 percent of total national income in 1984, a figure that had dropped to 8.1 percent in the 1989 survey. The poorest half saw its share of income drop from 20.8 percent in 1984 to 18.8 percent in 1989. The middle 30 percent of the population controlled 29.7 percent of the total income in 1984 but only 27 percent in 1989. In contrast, the wealthiest 20 percent received 49.5 percent of all income in 1984 and 53.6 percent in 1989. Income for the top 10 percent alone increased from 32.8 percent in 1984 to 37.9 percent five years later.

Throughout 1995 Mexico experienced a sharp economic contraction. Observers estimated that approximately 1 million jobs were lost during this period. Official unemployment rates skyrocketed to more than 6 percent for the year. Interest rates also rose sharply in the wake of several currency devaluations. Millions of Mexicans with adjustable-rate mortgages or substantial credit-card debt were particularly hard hit. Analysts suggested that the events of 1995 may have contributed to a further skewing of income distribution, with the wealthiest Mexicans more able to weather the economic storm because their capital often resided abroad.

Structure of Society

Social Indicators

In the early 1990s, Mexico reported substantial improvement in overall living conditions compared with the previous twenty years. The 1990 census demonstrated expanded access to basic public services such as running water and indoor plumbing. It also revealed, however, that Mexicans had not shared equally in these improvements, with southern Mexico consistently lagging behind the rest of the nation in quality-of-life indicators. In addition, rural living conditions countrywide paled in comparison to those found in urban areas.

According to the 1990 census, 79.4 percent of all Mexican households had access to running water, a notable improvement from the 61 percent and 70.3 percent rates recorded in 1970 and 1980, respectively. Significantly, however, access to running water did not necessarily mean indoor plumbing. Indeed, a household whose residents obtained water from a piped system elsewhere on the property or from a public faucet were considered to have access to running water. In addition, the census did not measure the quality or quantity of piped water. Many lower-class communities had access only to untreated running water, and even that for only a portion of each day.

Even using the broad definition of access to running water, wide variations emerged. Four states in southern Mexico— Chiapas, Oaxaca, Guerrero, and Tabasco—reported access levels below the 1970 national average. Access to running water was especially low in rural communities. Only 48.1 percent of all communal farming communities or *ejidos* (see Glossary) nationwide reported access in 1988, with levels below 30 percent for *ejidos* in Veracruz and Yucatán, and below 40 percent for *ejidos* in Chiapas, San Luis Potosí, Tabasco, and Tamaulipas (see Rural Society, this ch.).

Similar variations also were evident in a number of other social indicators. Nationally, 63.6 percent of all households had indoor plumbing in 1990, as compared with 41.4 percent and 50.7 percent in 1970 and 1980, respectively. However, indoor plumbing rates ranged from more than 90 percent in Mexico City to less than 40 percent in Oaxaca and Chiapas. National household access to electricity climbed from 58.9 percent in 1970 to 74.4 percent in 1980 and to 87.5 percent in 1990. Yet although Aguascalientes, Nuevo León, and Mexico City reported rates exceeding 95 percent in 1990, less than 70 percent of all Chiapas households had electricity. Only 68.3 percent of all *ejido* communities had electricity in 1988, with rates below 60 percent for *ejidos* in Chiapas, San Luis Potosí, Veracruz, and Yucatán, and below 50 percent for *ejidos* in Chihuahua.

Finally, 19.5 percent of all households had dirt flooring in 1990, a notable improvement from the 41.1 percent average in 1970 and the 25.8 percent average in 1980. Again, however, jurisdictions reported enormous disparities. Although Mexico City and five northern states—Aguascalientes, Baja California, Coahuila, Chihuahua, and Nuevo León—had levels below 10 percent, more than 40 percent of all households in the southern states of Chiapas and Guerrero and more than 50 percent of all households in Oaxaca had dirt floors.

Social Spending

Analysts have offered widely varied assessments of the magnitude of poverty in Mexico. The United Nations Economic Commission for Latin America and the Caribbean estimated in 1989 that 39 percent of all Mexican households were in poverty, including 14 percent in extreme poverty (indigence). The National Solidarity Program (Programa Nacional de Solidaridad—Pronasol) reported that 51 percent of the population in 1987 fell below the poverty line, of which 21 percent were extremely poor. Mexican author Julieta Campos asserted that approximately 60 percent of all Mexicans in 1988 were poor, including 25 percent indigent.

Despite these numerical differences, analysts generally agree on basic trends and characteristics. First, poverty levels declined in the 1960s and 1970s but escalated in the wake of the economic crisis that began in 1982 and continued for most of that decade. For example, Pronasol estimated that poverty levels declined from 76 percent in 1960 to 54 percent in 1977 and to 45 percent in 1981 before substantially increasing over the next six years. Second, indigence has its roots in the rampant economic problems of the countryside. Economist Santiago Levy estimated that approximately three-quarters of all rural residents in the late 1980s were extremely poor. In addition, the urban poor often have migrated from the countryside in search of opportunities for themselves and their families. Third, the indigent often suffer from nutritional deficiencies and other health maladies that contribute to lower life expectancy than the population as a whole. Finally, those in extreme poverty have larger families; children are expected to work to help support the household.

Mexican governments over the years have introduced numerous antipoverty initiatives, with varying degrees of success. In 1977 the López Portillo administration established the General Coordination of the National Plan for Depressed Zones and Marginal Groups (Coordinación General del Plan Nacional de Zonas Deprimidas y Grupos Marginales—Coplamar). An umbrella organization, Coplamar developed linkages with numerous existing government agencies for improvements in health care, education, and other basic infrastructure. For example, approximately 2,000 rural health clinics were built under the auspices of IMSS-Coplamar. The National Company of Popular Subsistence (Compañía Nacional de Subsistencias Populares—Conasupo)-Coplamar established thousands of stores that sold basic products to low-income families at subsidized prices. Although many of its programs were reduced or eliminated after 1982, Coplamar contributed to a noteworthy, although temporary, reduction in poverty.

*Modern apartment complex in
Mexico City
Courtesy Arturo Salinas*

*Substandard housing on outskirts of
Mexico City
Courtesy Arturo Salinas*

In his November 1993 State of the Nation address, President Salinas announced that government spending on social projects had risen 85 percent in real terms between 1989 and 1993. Spending for education rose 90 percent; for health, 79 percent; and for environment, urban development, and distribution of drinking water, 65 percent. Much of that social spending was channeled through Pronasol, an umbrella organization established by Salinas in December 1988 to promote improved health, education, nutrition, housing, employment, infrastructure, and other productive projects to benefit those living in extreme poverty.

Salinas claimed that Pronasol marked a departure from previous policies of broad subsidies, high levels of unfocused government spending, and heavy state intervention in the economy. According to Denise Dresser, it advanced President Salinas's goal of adapting the state's traditional social role to the straitened economic conditions of the late 1980s and early 1990s by replacing general subsidies with strategic, targeted intervention. Salinas designed Pronasol to achieve the dual objectives of making social spending more cost-effective and fostering greater community involvement and initiative in local development projects. The main themes of Pronasol included grassroots participation and minimum bureaucracy (both of which are essential for project success) and the promise of immediate results. The federal government provided financing and raw materials for improving basic community services, although community members were required to conceive the projects and perform the work.

Approximately 250,000 grassroots Pronasol committees designed projects in collaboration with government staff to address community needs. They mobilized and organized community members, evaluated proposed public works, and supervised implementation. The government disbursed funds to the committees to finance the public works projects or to complement regional development programs, which fell within three strategic areas: social services, production, and regional development. Committees obtained matching funds from state and municipal governments in order to qualify for Pronasol funds. This match served to multiply the economic scale and the potential positive impact of the program.

Pronasol's social service aspect, Solidarity for Social Well-being (Solidaridad para el Bienestar Social), contained a wide range of programs that included education, health care, water, sewerage, and electrification projects; urbanization improvements; and low-income housing. Over a six-year span, Pronasol created some 80,000 new classrooms and workshops and renovated 120,000 schools; awarded scholarships to keep nearly 1.2 million indigent children in primary schools; established more than 300 hospitals, 4,000 health centers, and some 1,000 rural medical units; provided piped water access for approximately 16 million people; and provided materials to repair or reinforce 500,000 low-income homes and build nearly 200,000 new homes. Solidarity for Production (Solidaridad para la Producción) provided loans to approximately 1 million peasants who did not qualify for government or private credits, established 2,000 low-income credit unions, and supported some 250,000 low-income coffee producers (80 percent of them Indians) and nearly 400,000 agricultural day laborers (*jornaleros*). Solidarity for Regional Development (Solidaridad para el Desarrollo Regional) funded the construction or renovation of 200,000 kilometers of roads and more than 100,000 municipal improvement projects.

Despite these achievements, critics contended that Pronasol was merely a politicized repackaging of traditional welfare and public works projects that ameliorated but did not address the root causes of poverty in Mexico. In the view of these critics, Pronasol's raison d'être was to enable Salinas and his supporters to build new political linkages with autonomous low-income interest groups, thereby revitalizing the Institutional Revolutionary Party (Partido Revolucionario Institucional—PRI) for future elections. Despite Pronasol's stated purpose, critics also maintained that resources often did not reach those in extreme poverty. In 1995 President Ernesto Zedillo restructured Pronasol as the Alliance for Well-being (Alianca para el Bienestar), strengthening the resource allocation roles of states and municipalities and reducing those of the presidency.

Urban Society

At the beginning of the twentieth century, only 10.5 percent of the national population lived in localities with more than 15,000 residents. A slow but steady increase of such urban communities occurred over the next four decades, accounting for 20 percent of the country's total population in 1940. They climbed rapidly to 27.9 percent in 1950, 36.5 percent in 1960, 44.7 percent in 1970, 51.8 percent in 1980, and 57.4 percent in

1990. An estimated 71 percent of all Mexicans lived in communities of at least 2,500 residents in 1990.

Three cities—Mexico City, Guadalajara, and Monterrey—dominated the urban landscape in the mid-1990s. Their metropolitan areas accounted for about one-fourth of the nation's population and more than 40 percent of the total urban population. Nonetheless, the highest growth rates between 1970 and 1990 occurred in cities containing populations ranging from 100,000 to 1 million. Roughly 23 percent of the nation resided in Mexico's fifty-six mid-level cities in 1990.

With 15 million residents reported in the 1990 census, the Mexico City metropolitan area alone contained 18.5 percent of the total national population. However, the metropolitan area expanded only 5.8 percent from 1980 to 1990, far below the 2.3 percent per annum national population growth rate over the same period. The population of Mexico City itself declined from 9.2 million in 1980 to 8.2 million in 1990, a 10.9 percent reduction. This decline probably reflected both dislocations experienced by low-income, center-city residents following the 1985 earthquake and contracting employment opportunities during the economic crisis of the 1980s. However, one analyst, Alfonso X. Iracheta Cenecorta, contends that Mexico City should be viewed not as a single metropolitan area but rather as an emerging megalopolis also incorporating the cities and surrounding environs of Puebla, Toluca, and Cuernavaca. Seen from this perspective, the region continued to grow during the 1980s, and included slightly more than 17 million people in 1990.

To relieve the strains of rapid growth on Mexico's largest cities, the Salinas administration encouraged businesses and government agencies to move their operations from the major metropolitan areas to mid-level cities. During the 1980s, mid-level cities experienced the nation's highest growth rates. Several cities in northern Mexico, especially along the border with the United States, were particularly dynamic during this period. They included Torreón, Tijuana, Mexicali, Matamoros, and Ciudad Juárez. Other rapidly expanding cities included Cuernavaca and Jalapa near the capital, and Tampico and Coatzacoalcos on the Gulf of Mexico coast.

The dramatic growth of cities over the past forty years has seriously taxed the nation's ability to build urban infrastructure, especially housing. Adequate and affordable housing emerged as a paramount concern of low-income residents after

1940. Prior to that time, most urban poor lived in center-city rental units. Real estate investors frequently converted deteriorating colonial structures into *vecindades* (sing., *vecindad*). A *vecindad* typically consists of a large number of rented rooms constructed around an interior open area. Residents share kitchen and bathroom facilities, often of marginal quality. Following institution of rent control by the government during World War II, investors often abandoned the *vecindad* market, depleting an already poor housing stock.

Government efforts to address the urban housing shortfall after World War II generally proved inadequate. During the 1950s and 1960s, the government financed some housing units in major metropolitan areas, the largest of which—the Nonoalco-Tlatelolco housing complex in northern Mexico City—contained nearly 12,000 units.

However, public employees were the principal beneficiaries of government housing programs. During the administration of Luis Echeverría Álvarez (1970–76), the government took a more active role in fostering formal- and informal-sector housing. Three funds were established in 1972: the Institute of the National Housing Fund for Workers (Instituto del Fondo Nacional de la Vivienda para los Trabajadores—Infonavit); the Housing Fund of the Institute of Social Security and Services for State Workers (Fondo para la Vivienda del Instituto de Servicios y Seguridad Social de los Trabajadores del Estado—Fovissste); and the National Institute for Community Development (Instituto Nacional para el Desarrollo de la Comunidad—Indeco). These funds were designed to meet the needs of private-sector formal workers, state employees, and informal-sector workers, respectively. Of the three funds, Infonavit was the most extensive, with nearly 900,000 units financed over a twenty-year period. Still, demand far exceeded supply and a lottery system was used to determine occupancy. In addition, most workers could not afford the monthly payments required.

For the majority of the urban lower class, so-called self-help housing has emerged as the only viable option. A self-help housing community typically begins with the purchase by investors of large tracts of contiguous land on the periphery of urban areas. In some cases, these transactions involve illegal purchases of *ejido* properties of dubious agricultural worth. Whether *ejido* or not, however, the tracts usually consist of marginal lands ill-suited for middle- and upper-class residential developments or for industrial purposes. Investors subdivide the land into numerous lots and sell them to low-income families, who then build modest brick structures, often with only single large rooms. Ostensibly, investors cannot sell lots until they have installed water and sewer lines, paved streets, and completed other basic infrastructure. Frequently, however, investors do little more than mark the lots for sale. Because a large land tract may contain thousands of potential lots, investors often realize enormous profits.

Nezahualcóyotl, Mexico's quintessential self-help housing community, burst onto the national scene during the 1960s. During the late 1950s, a group of investors purchased more than sixty square kilometers of land east of Mexico City in an area in the state of México just outside the Federal District. The land in question, a dried lakebed, flooded during the rainy season and was prone to dust storms during the dry season. Nonetheless, investors created 160,000 low-income housing lots. By 1970 Nezahualcóyotl contained nearly 700,000 residents, but there were few public services.

Local governments have varied widely in the degree of support extended to self-help housing developments. Although the Federal District blocked most self-help housing after the early 1950s, the neighboring state of México actively encouraged the development of communities such as Nezahualcóyotl, in effect serving as a safety valve for Mexico City. Likewise, Guadalajara generally has endorsed such development as an appropriate response to the housing needs of the urban poor. By contrast, Monterrey and a number of other cities in northern Mexico have opposed self-help communities, a decision that has sparked frequent squatter invasions of *ejido* land. Local authorities sometimes have used force to dislodge the invaders, but often have tacitly allowed the new communities to remain.

Despite obvious problems, self-help housing has addressed numerous important and cross-cutting social issues. These communities substantially increase the housing stock available to low-income urban residents. As sociologists Alan Gilbert and Peter Ward have observed, without self-help construction, the government either would have to expend many more resources on housing projects or raise wages to enable the poor to compete in the formal housing market. By forcing people to build their own homes, the government has been able to preserve funds to underwrite industrial development. Self-help housing also allows lower-income residents to become owners rather than renters. And as self-help communities mature and resi-

Rush-hour traffic in Mexico City
Courtesy Inter-American Development Bank
Street scene in downtown Guadalajara
Courtesy Rodolfo García

dents add to initial structures, renters (typically poorer, younger, and more recently arrived in the city than owners) have housing options other than *vecindades*.

Even including self-help construction, however, Mexico faced a severe housing crisis in the mid-1990s. The Zedillo administration reported in 1995 that more than 25 percent of the 17.8 million houses needed to be repaired or replaced. Because two-thirds of the population are under thirty years of age, analysts project sharp increases in demand for new housing over the next two decades.

Rural Society

Nearly eighty years after enactment, agrarian reform remains at once one of the Mexican Revolution's most impressive accomplishments and enduring failures. At the onset of the revolution, huge haciendas controlled almost all agricultural land. By 1991 agrarian reform beneficiaries (and their heirs) held about half of all national land. More than 3.5 million campesinos live and work in nearly 30,000 communities formed as a direct result of various agrarian reform initiatives. At the same time, however, most campesinos hold marginal *parcelas* (individual plots) that cannot meet the subsistence needs of their families. These campesinos, as well as those with no land at all, have to work periodically for large landowners or agribusinesses, migrate seasonally to the United States, or take a variety of other actions to survive.

The Agrarian Reform Act of 1915 and the constitution of 1917 laid the groundwork for dramatic changes in Mexico's land tenure system. These documents established that the nation retained ultimate control over privately held land, which could be expropriated and redistributed in the public interest to campesinos.

The *ejido*, or communally farmed plot, emerged as the uniquely Mexican form of redistributing large landholdings. Under this arrangement, a group of villagers could petition the government to seize private properties that exceeded certain specified sizes—initially 150 hectares for irrigated land and 200 hectares for rain-fed holdings. Assuming a favorable review of the petition, the government then expropriated the property and created an *ejido*. The state retained title to the land but granted the villagers, now known as *ejidatarios*, the right to farm the land, either in a collective manner or through the designation of individual *parcelas*. *Ejidatarios* could not sell or mortgage their land but could pass usufruct rights to their heirs. *Ejidatarios* had to work their land regularly in order to maintain rights over it. In cases where villagers established that they had collectively farmed the land in question before its eventual consolidation into a hacienda, the government created an agrarian community (*comunidad agraria*). *Comuneros* (members of agrarian communities), who lived primarily in southern Mexico, had largely the same rights and responsibilities as *ejidatarios*.

Mexican administrations have varied widely in the importance accorded to the *ejido*. During the 1920s and early 1930s, policy makers typically viewed the *ejido* as a transitional system that would lead to small private farms nationwide. For example, President Plutarco Elías Calles (1924–28) described the *ejido* as a school from which *ejidatarios* eventually would graduate as private farmers. Given this perspective, policy makers encouraged *ejidos* to divide their lands into individual *parcelas*. In contrast, President Lázaro Cárdenas (1934–40) saw the *ejido* as an essential and permanent component of agricultural development, and he encouraged a collectivist organizational structure to maximize resources. During his six-year term, Cárdenas expropriated nearly 18 million hectares of privately owned land for redistribution as *ejidos*, more than double the total amount recorded since the revolution ended. The *ejido* share of total cultivable land increased from roughly 13 percent in 1930 to approximately 47 percent in 1940.

During the next three decades, the government favored large-scale commercial agriculture at the expense of the *ejido*. Federally funded irrigation projects in the states of Sonora and Sinaloa and in the agriculturally important Bajío region of Guanajuato and northern Michoacán were designed to enable large landowners to compete in the United States agricultural market. The government also narrowed the definition of private properties eligible for expropriation.

Upon assuming the presidency in 1970, Luis Echeverría Álvarez shifted government priorities back to the *ejido*. Espousing the same philosophy as Cárdenas three decades before, Echeverría felt that the *ejido* would play a leading role in meeting domestic food demand. Echeverría increased *ejido* holdings by some 17 million hectares, including the expropriation of rich irrigated lands in Sonora. Collectivized *ejidos* received preferential access to credit and farm equipment through government agencies such as the National Bank of Rural Credit (Banco Nacional de Crédito Rural—Banrural).

The Echeverría administration marked the last significant redistribution of landholdings. Echeverría's successor, López Portillo, distributed only about 1.8 million hectares to *ejidos.* Yet like Echeverría, López Portillo sought to channel government resources to *ejidos.* Following the discovery of vast petroleum reserves along Mexico's southeastern coast, López Portillo used oil profits to establish the Mexican Food System (Sistema Alimentario Mexicano—SAM), which sought to ensure national self-sufficiency in basic staples, such as corn and beans. López Portillo encouraged *ejidos* to play a major role in this effort and channeled petrodollars to agencies offering credit to *ejidatarios.* For many *ejidatarios,* however, credit merely generated increased debt and dependence on government bureaucracies without significantly improving their overall conditions. In the wake of the debt crisis that began in 1982, the administration of Miguel de la Madrid Hurtado (1982–88) abolished the SAM and cut agricultural funding by two-thirds.

Despite collectivist efforts of Echeverría and, to a much lesser extent, López Portillo, a national survey released at the beginning of the Salinas presidency revealed that approximately 88 percent of *ejidatarios* and *comuneros* farmed individual *parcelas.* (Government statistics did not differentiate between *ejidos* and agrarian communities.) The survey also indicated a notable differentiation between the 16 percent of *ejidos* and agrarian communities that had irrigated fields and the remainder that did not. The former reported significantly higher percentages in the use of improved seeds, pesticides, and fertilizers, as well as access to technical assistance. Sixty-five percent of all *ejidatarios* and *comuneros* indicated that they grew corn as their principal crop.

Mexico's post-1940 population explosion produced a continual subdivision of most *parcelas,* resulting in holdings that were below subsistence level. According to the 1981 agricultural census, nearly 31 percent of all *ejidatarios* held *parcelas* of two hectares or less, far below the amount of land required to support a family. Another 27 percent maintained holdings ranging from two to five hectares, with 38 percent farming *parcelas* of between five and twenty *hectares.* Less than 3 percent of *ejidatarios* held individual plots of between twenty and fifty hectares.

Data from the 1981 agricultural census on private landholding patterns revealed an even more stratified picture. Nearly 40 percent of all private (non-*ejido*) farmers held plots of two hectares or less, with an additional 17 percent working plots of between two and five hectares. Together, these two groups had only 2 percent of the privately owned land area. In contrast, 2 percent of all landholders controlled nearly 63 percent of the privately owned land. Holdings exceeding 2,500 hectares were particularly in evidence in the north (especially in Chihuahua and Sonora) and in Chiapas.

With plots too small to support even a modest standard of living, farming has become a secondary source of income for most campesinos. Many worked as day laborers for large land-holders. The 1981 agricultural census recorded approximately 3 million farm laborers, 60 percent of them temporary. *Ejidatarios*, in effect, form a cheap and available labor pool for commercial agriculture. These sectors are further linked through the illegal before 1992 but nevertheless widespread practice of renting *ejido* land. Although the government maintains no statistics on this activity, some observers estimate that up to half of the irrigated *ejido* lands in Sonora and Sinaloa and up to half of such holdings in the Bajío region of Guanajuato and southern Michoacán are rented. Regular migration to the United States also is an essential survival strategy for many campesinos, with remittances allowing many families to remain in the countryside. Many young campesinos spend the bulk of the year working in the United States, returning to their plots only during the planting and harvesting seasons. An unknown number of campesinos in isolated communities in southern and western Mexico also engage in narcotics trafficking.

In the 1970s, sociologist Rodolfo Stavenhagen and other scholars suggested that the *ejidatarios* were among Mexico's poorest and most exploited rural workers. Their productivity was low because of the poor quality of their land, the lack of timely technical assistance, and the unavailability of low-cost agricultural inputs. Yet the government's official policy historically has been to keep agricultural prices low in an effort to subsidize the urban population.

Ejidatarios remain highly dependent on the bureaucratic channels of both the state and the ruling PRI). All *ejidatarios* are automatically members of the peasant sector of the PRI; but owing to their lack of political experience, they become easily manipulated by professional "peasant" leaders in Mexico City, who are usually of middle-class backgrounds. Many *ejidatarios* look to the state as a modern *patrón* (traditional paternalistic landlord) who has the power to control prices, credit opportunities, and access to farm machinery and water rights and who must be continuously courted and reminded of their pressing needs.

Confronted with the dysfunctional character of much of Mexican agriculture, the government in 1992 radically changed the *ejido* land tenure system, codifying some existing actions that were illegal but widely practiced and introducing several new features. Under the new law, an *ejido* can award its members individual titles to the land, not merely usufruct rights to their *parcelas*. *Ejidatarios* can, in turn, choose to rent, sell, or mortgage their properties. *Ejidatarios* do not need to work their lands to maintain ownership over them. They also may enter into partnerships with private entrepreneurs. The law also effectively ends the redistribution of land through government decree. Finally, the processing and resolution of land disputes are decentralized.

The government's perspective is that these new measures provide *ejidatarios* with more realistic and sensible options. A winnowing effect is anticipated, as some inefficient and marginal producers sell their properties to more efficient farmers. With property to mortgage, the more entrepreneurial *ejidatarios* have collateral that can be used to obtain private-sector credit. By removing the prospect of widespread government-directed land redistribution, owners will be more likely to invest resources to increase agricultural production. Government critics fear, however, that the revisions will increase landlessness and poverty among *ejidatarios* and solidify inequitable patterns of land distribution in states such as Chiapas.

As part of its overall agricultural program, the Salinas administration attempted to restructure Banrural as a more efficient and streamlined organization, limiting its scope to serving those *ejidatarios* with production capabilities. To assist more marginal producers in dealing with the agricultural transformation, Salinas established the Procampo program in 1993 as part of the Pronasol initiative. Procampo provided direct payments to farmers based on the size of their holdings. In 1995 President Zedillo shifted Procampo's operation to the newly created Alliance for the Countryside (Alianza para el Campo) and extended it for a fifteen-year period.

Interpersonal Relations

Interpersonal relations are more important in the functioning of Mexican society than impersonal, bureaucratic norms and regulations. *Parentela* (extended family) members, *compa-*

dres (godparents), *cuates* (very close buddies), and friends expect from one another various degrees of loyalty, material and spiritual assistance, emotional support, physical protection, and even flexibility in the enforcement of laws, norms, and regulations.

Primary ties are structured through blood descent, which is traced equally through the father's and mother's side. Every person is, therefore, a member of two family lines. The person's name, which often includes the matrilineal after the patrilineal, represents this arrangement.

One's *parentela* usually includes all the descendants of a great-grandparent or of a grandparent on both the father's and the mother's sides. Thus, it is fairly common for a person to claim having a dozen or more "uncles" and "aunts" and several dozen cousins. However, this same person can easily identify the several degrees of the specific type of relationships that exist within the family.

The Mexican household—that is, those family members who dwell under the same roof—differs from the North American household. Mexican households can include the parents' nuclear family as well as that of a married son or daughter and their young children. Living arrangements vary among the different kinds of households. In most cases in which two or more nuclear families share the same roof, each nuclear family keeps its separate budget and, often, a separate kitchen. After a few years of living with their parents, married children who opt for this arrangement often set up independent households. Other household members can include out-of-town relatives, fellow townsmen, and *arrimados* (literally "the leaned-on," that is, renters or "permanent guests").

Family membership presupposes an inalienable bond among first-, second-, third-, and fourth-generation relatives, a bond that is accompanied by a corresponding set of rights and obligations. Family members are expected to display affection openly and reciprocally, as well as provide each other material and moral support. The traditional family has the power to enforce these virtues through the exercise of pressure over its members and through a series of actions usually performed by its elder members. These include social pressure, manipulation, and gossip.

Despite the dramatic changes that have occurred in Mexican society since 1940, the family remains the most important social institution. Indeed, the economic crisis of the 1980s may have enhanced its role as the place to turn when in need. A national opinion poll conducted in 1982 by the Center for Educational Studies confirmed the centrality of the Mexican family. The majority of those surveyed identified the family as the institution where they felt most secure and confident. Most viewed the family as the essential safety net providing help and protection. Economic survival often requires several family members to enter the workforce and pool their incomes. As noted previously, remittances from one or more children working in the United States allow many families to continue living in rural areas.

The critical role of the Mexican family was also confirmed in a 1995 national survey sponsored by the Institute of Social Research of the National Autonomous University of Mexico (Universidad Nacional Autónoma de México—UNAM). Respondents associated the family with such positive terms as love, household, children, and well-being. Respondents also identified rejection by one's family as a worse occurrence than injustice and abuse of authority, poverty, and work conflicts.

Although Mexicans generally hold their families in high esteem, such may not be the case with those outside the family web. Eighty percent of those interviewed by the Center for Educational Studies agreed that one should be cautious in relations outside the family. The center's analysts linked this low level of confidence and trust with a distinction most Mexicans made between their own moral codes and those of others. In general, Mexicans feel that they adhere to a much higher moral standard than do their neighbors. Thus, for example, 80 percent of those interviewed believed it important to honor one's parents. However, when asked if others felt the same way, only three out of ten agreed. As a result of the focus on one's family for trust and help, fewer than half of those surveyed reported membership in civic or social organizations.

Attitudes towards non-family members may be evolving, however, as Mexicans increasingly endorse the tenets of a modern and open society. The UNAM researchers found considerable evidence that Mexicans had become tolerant of others and supportive of cultural differences. Such attitudes are particularly prevalent among Mexican youth and those with higher educational and income levels.

For many families, however, *compadrazgo*, or the system of godparenting, offers a way to expand their support structure. A family initiates this ritual kinship network by inviting a man

Faces of Mexico
Courtesy Inter-American Development Bank

and woman to serve as godparents for a child. Through *compadrazgo*, the child's parents and godparents—now known as *compadres* (literally "co-fathers") and *comadres* ("co-mothers")— enter into a complex relationship of rights and obligations. Often, the relationship cuts across social classes. When in need, a family often turns to its children's godparents for assistance. For instance, an employer is expected to look first to his or her children's godparents when hiring additional workers. In exchange, the *compadrazgo* demands intense loyalty to the employer from the worker hired by that means.

"Permanent" social relations also are built through *cuatismo* among men and comparable associations of women. *Cuate* (from the Náhuatl word meaning twin brother) is used throughout Mexico to describe a special male friend or group of friends with whom one spends considerable leisure time and who can be trusted with intimate information. *Cuate* groups can include up to ten members who share common interests, who are bound by intense friendship and personal relations, and who commit themselves to assisting each other in case of need.

Role of Women

Beginning in the 1970s and over the next two decades, dramatic changes occurred in the role of women in the Mexican economy. In 1990 women represented 31 percent of the economically active population, double the percentage recorded twenty years earlier. The demographics of women in the workforce also changed during this period. In 1980 the typical female worker was under twenty-five years of age. Her participation in the workforce was usually transitional and would end following marriage or childbirth. After the 1970s, however, an emerging feminist movement made it more acceptable for educated Mexican women to pursue careers. In addition, the economic crisis of the 1980s required many married women to return to the job market to help supplement their husbands' income. About 70 percent of women workers in the mid-1990s were employed in the tertiary sector of the economy, usually at wages below those of men.

The growing presence of women in the workforce contributed to some changes in social attitudes, despite the prevalence of other more traditional attitudes. The UNAM 1995 national opinion survey, for example, found a growing acceptance that men and women should share in family responsibilities.

Approximately half of all respondents agreed that husbands and wives should jointly handle child-care duties and perform housekeeping chores. However, such views were strongly related to income and educational level. Low income and minimally educated respondents regarded household tasks as women's work. The UNAM responses correlated with the findings of Mercedes González de la Rocha, whose research focused on working-class households in Guadalajara. González de la Rocha reported that the members of these households held traditional norms and values regarding the roles of men and women. In addition, these women were often subjected to control, domination, and violence by men.

Observers noted that women generally were held to a stricter sexual code of conduct than men. Sexual activity outside of marriage was regarded as immoral for "decent" women but acceptable for men.

Religion

The 1980s and early 1990s witnessed a notable shift in religious affiliation and in church-state relations in Mexico. Although Mexico remains predominantly Roman Catholic, evangelical churches have dramatically expanded their membership. Motivated in part by the evangelical challenge, the leadership of the Roman Catholic Church has sought greater visibility, speaking out on sensitive public issues and ignoring constitutional bans on clerical involvement in politics. These actions ultimately led in 1992 to dramatic constitutional changes and a resumption of diplomatic relations with the Vatican.

The Roman Catholic share of the population declined steadily during the period from 1970 to 1990. In 1970, 96.2 percent of the population five years of age and older identified itself as Roman Catholic. That dropped to 92.6 percent of the population in the 1980 census and to 89.7 percent in 1990. The 1990 census revealed significant regional variations in numbers of Roman Catholics. Roman Catholics represented more than 95 percent of all Mexicans in a band of central-western states extending from Zacatecas to Michoacán. In contrast, the least Roman Catholic presence was found in the southeastern states of Chiapas, Campeche, Tabasco, and Quintana Roo.

Dozens of evangelical denominations have engaged in strong recruitment efforts since 1970. Protestant or "evangelical" affiliation—the terminology used by Mexican census officials—surged from 1.8 percent in 1970 to 3.3 percent in 1980 and to 4.9 percent in 1990. Traditional Protestant denominations, including Lutherans, Methodists, and Presbyterians, have had a small urban presence dating from the late 1800s. However, the Protestant membership explosion during the 1970–90 period was led by congregations affiliated with churches such as the Assemblies of God, the Seventh Day Adventists, the Church of Jesus Christ of Latter Day Saints (Mor mons), and Jehovah's Witnesses. For example, the Mormons reported that membership surged from 248,000 in 1980 to 617,000 in 1990 and increased further to 688,000 by 1993.

Protestant or evangelical growth was especially strong in southeastern Mexico. In 1990 Protestants or evangelicals composed 16 percent of the population in Chiapas, 15 percent in Tabasco, 14 percent in Campeche, and 12 percent in Quintana Roo. Yet a significant evangelical presence also has appeared in several other areas, including the states of Veracruz and México, where more than 20 percent of all Protestants or evangelicals live.

Church-State Relations

The Roman Catholic Church's role in Mexican history goes back to 1519. When Hernán Cortés, the Spanish conqueror of New Spain, landed on the coast of Mexico, he was accompanied by Roman Catholic clergy. All new Spanish territories were to be conquered in the name of the cross as well as the crown. Since those early days, the Roman Catholic Church has always been present, playing different roles, some of which have led to violent confrontations.

The history of the relationship between church and state following independence involves a series of efforts on the part of the government to curtail the church's influence. Nineteenth-century liberals, trained in the law and influenced by the French Revolution, were anticlerical. Liberals, who also were federalist and favored free competition, were highly concerned that the Roman Catholic Church, by owning between one-quarter and one-half of the land and by controlling most schools, hospitals, and charitable institutions, was practically a state within the Mexican state.

Between 1833 and the early 1840s, the Mexican government produced various pieces of legislation to limit the power of the church. In 1833 the government adopted several anticlerical measures, including one providing for the secularization of

Metropolitan Cathedral in downtown Mexico City
Courtesy Arturo Salinas

education and another declaring that the payment of the ecclesiastical tithe was not a civil obligation.

The first major confrontation between the church and the state occurred during the presidency of Benito Juárez (1855–72). The 1855 Juárez Law drastically reduced traditional ecclesiastical privileges. On March 11, 1857, a new constitution was adopted that denied all ecclesiastical entities the right to own real estate and abolished most remaining ecclesiastical privileges. On July 12, 1857, Juárez confiscated all church properties, suppressed all religious orders, and empowered the state governors to designate what buildings could be used for religious services. Mexico's first religious civil war was fought between 1857 and 1860 in reaction to the legislation (see Civil War and the French Intervention, ch. 1).

The constitution of 1917 highlighted and institutionalized many of the nineteenth-century secular reforms. The new constitution included at least five articles that affected all religious groups, regardless of denomination. These articles, which remained in effect until 1992, appeared to preclude any national role for the Roman Catholic Church. Article 3 forbade churches from participating in primary and secondary education. Article 5 prohibited the establishment of religious orders. Article 24 mandated that all religious ceremonies occur within church buildings. Article 27 gave the state ownership of all church buildings.

Article 130 contained the most extensive restrictions on the Roman Catholic Church. The article stated that the Roman Catholic Church lacks legal status; ecclesiastical marriages have no legal standing; state legislatures can determine the maximum number of clergy operating within their boundaries; and operation of church buildings requires explicit government authorization. Among the most contentious provisions of Article 130 was Section 9: "Neither in public nor private assembly, nor in acts of worship or religious propaganda shall the ministers of the religions ever have the right to criticize the basic laws of the country, of the authorities in particular or of the government in general; they shall have neither an active nor passive vote, nor the right to associate for political purposes."

Beginning in 1926 and continuing until the late 1930s, various federal and state administrations strenuously enforced these constitutional edicts and related laws. Their actions paved the way for the second Mexican religious war, the bloody Cristero Rebellion of 1926–29 in western Mexico (see The Calles Presidency, 1924–28, ch. 1). During this period, the governor of Sonora ordered all churches closed, officials in the state of Tabasco required priests to marry if they were to officiate at mass, and the Chihuahua government allowed only one priest to minister to the entire statewide Roman Catholic population.

Church-state conflict officially ended with the administration of Manuel Ávila Camacho (1940–46). With the notable exception of Article 130, Section 9, the government tacitly offered nonenforcement of key constitutional provisions in exchange for the Roman Catholic Church's cooperation in achieving social peace. Over the next four decades, enforcement of Article 130, Section 9, served the interests of both the government and the Roman Catholic Church. The constitutional restriction on ecclesiastical political participation enabled the state to limit the activities of a powerful competitor. It also permitted the Roman Catholic Church to sidestep controversial political issues and to concentrate on rebuilding its ecclesiastical structure and presence throughout the country.

By the early 1980s, however, this unspoken consensus supporting the legal status quo had eroded. The Roman Catholic Church regarded the constitution's anticlerical provisions, especially those governing ecclesiastical political activity, as anachronistic. It demanded the right to play a much more visible role in national affairs. At the same time, the church became increasingly outspoken in its criticism of government corruption. The Mexican bishops' Global Pastoral Plan for 1980–1982, for example, contained a highly critical assessment of the Mexican political system. According to the Roman Catholic hierarchy, democracy existed only in theory in Mexico. The ruling PRI monopolized power, producing apathy and frustration among citizens and judicial corruption. The principal worker and peasant unions were subject to political control. Peasants and Indians constituted an exploited, marginalized mass barely living at a subsistence level and subject to continual repression. During the mid-1980s, the bishops of Chihuahua and Ciudad Juárez assumed prominent roles in denouncing electoral fraud in northern Mexico. In the south, the bishops of San Cristóbal de las Casas and Tehuantepec frequently accused the government of human rights violations.

The Roman Catholic Church hierarchy has emphasized that its renewed interest in political affairs does not equate with church involvement in party activities. According to the Mexican episcopate, priests should be above all political parties and may not become political leaders. However, the church hierarchy also argues that priests have a moral responsibility to denounce actions that violate Christian morality.

The Salinas administration's 1991 proposal to remove all constitutional restrictions on the Roman Catholic Church, recommendations approved by the legislature the following year, allowed for a more realistic church-state relationship. At the same time, however, tensions remained in the relationship, particularly in southern Mexico in general and in Chiapas in particular. Local government and PRI officials and ranchers accused the Bishop of San Cristóbal de las Casas of having supported the rebellion that began in Chiapas in 1994, a charge that the bishop denied. Federal soldiers repeatedly searched diocesan churches in their pursuit of the rebels. The government also expelled foreign clergy who were accused of inciting violence and land seizures. In addition, the Vatican accused the San Cristóbal prelate of theological and pastoral distortions and named a coadjutor (successor) bishop for the diocese in the mid-1990s. For their part, the rebels insisted that the bishop continue to serve as mediator in their negotiations with the federal government.

Popular Beliefs

Mexican Catholicism is extremely varied in practice. It ranges from those who support traditional folk religious practices, usually in isolated rural communities, to those who adhere to the highly intellectualized theology of liberation, and from charismatic renewal prayer groups to the conservative Opus Dei movement. Lay groups with different goals, purposes, and political orientations are well known and common in contemporary Mexico. The largest and best known include Mexican Catholic Action, Knights of Columbus, Christian Study Courses, Christian Family Movement, and a wide range of university students' and workers' organizations.

The Virgin of Guadalupe has long been a symbol enshrining the major aspirations of Mexican society. According to Roman Catholic belief, in December 1531, the Virgin Mary appeared on three occasions to a Christian Indian woodcutter named Juan Diego on the hill of Tepeyac, six kilometers north of Mexico City's main plaza. She spoke to him in the Náhuatl language and identified herself by the name of Guadalupe. The Virgin commanded Juan Diego to seek out Bishop Juan de Zumárraga and to inform him of her desire to have a church built in her honor on that spot. After two unsuccessful visits to the bishop's house, Juan Diego returned to Tepeyac and was ordered by the Virgin to pick up some roses, carry them on his cloak, and attempt to make a third visit to the skeptical bishop. Once in the bishop's office, Juan Diego unfolded his cloak to present the roses, and an image of a mestizo Virgin had been miraculously imprinted upon it. Bishop Zumárraga acknowledged the miracle, and a shrine was built on the site of the appearances.

Today, two neighboring basilicas of Our Lady of Guadalupe are at the foot of Tepeyac hill. The first basilica, which was dedicated in 1709 but now is closed to services, accommodated 2,000 worshipers; the new ultramodern basilica, inaugurated in October 1976, accommodates up to 20,000 people. Juan Diego's original cloak with the mestizo Virgin image imprinted on it hangs above the altar of the new basilica.

According to anthropologist Eric R. Wolf, the Guadalupe symbol links family, politics, and religion; the colonial past and the independent present; and the Indian and the Mexican. It reflects the salient social relationships of Mexican life and embodies the emotions they generate. It is, ultimately, a way of talking about Mexico. Wolf's views are shared by Harvey L. Johnson of the University of Houston. For him, worship of the brown-skinned Virgin has resulted in the reconciliation of two opposing worlds, in the fusion of two religions, two traditions, and cultures. Devotion to Our Lady of Guadalupe remains strong even as other aspects of Mexican society have changed. The UNAM national opinion poll found, for example, that nine out of ten Mexicans continued to ask intercessions from the Virgin or a saint.

Education

Despite impressive gains in enrollment levels over the previous forty years, significant interrelated problems plague the Mexican education system in the early 1990s. Many primary- and secondary-school-age students, especially in rural areas, fail to complete their education programs. Instructional quality, as measured by student test scores, remains low. Although operation of all nonuniversity education was given to the states in 1993, the system continues to be overly centralized and subject to bureaucratic encumbrances. In addition, students are often poorly prepared to meet the challenges of a global economy.

Approximately 27 million students attended school at all levels during the 1995–96 instructional year, more than an eightfold increase from the enrollment total recorded in 1950. The length of compulsory education was raised from six to nine years in 1992, but in practice this new law is largely ignored. Approximately 54 percent of all students attend a six-year primary-school program that, together with preschool, special education, and secondary school, constitute the basic education system. Children in nursery school or kindergarten accounted for 12 percent of matriculation at all levels in 1995–96. As the Mexican population gradually aged during the 1980s, the primary-school share of matriculation at all levels declined from 70 percent in 1980 and was projected to continue to fall through the year 2000 (see Population, this ch.; table 4, Appendix). Upon successful completion of primary school, students enter a three-year secondary-school program, or vocational-education program. Approximately 19 percent of all students in 1995–96 were in secondary school. Those gradu-

127

ating from secondary school can pursue mid-level education, either through a three-year college preparatory program—the *bachillerato*—or advanced technical training; this encompassed 10 percent of all students in 1995–96. Higher education consists of four-year college and university education—the *licenciatura*—and postgraduate training. Approximately 5 percent of all students in 1995–96 were in postsecondary institutions.

Higher education consists of three types: universities, technological colleges, and teacher-training institutes. There are private and public institutions of all three types, but public institutions are more numerous and usually larger, with over 80 percent of students attending public universities and colleges. Each state has at least one public university, often having campuses in different cities. The largest public university, the National Autonomous University of Mexico (Universidad Nacional Autónoma de México—UNAM) in Mexico City, has more than 100,000 students. Over ninety technological institutes had about 17 percent of the total higher education population in 1994. Teacher-training institutes are separate from general universities and generally offer a four-year curriculum. Universities in fourteen states offer postgraduate courses, and in 1991 over 28,000 students were enrolled in master's degree programs and 1,250 in doctoral studies. Most students pursuing graduate work, however, do so outside Mexico.

Students' access and retention remain critical concerns for educators. The government reported in 1989 that each year, 300,000 children who should be in first grade do not attend. An additional 880,000 students drop out of primary school annually, 500,000 of them in the first three grades. Nationally, in 1989 only 55 percent of students successfully completed their primary education, and graduation rates were only 10 percent in many rural areas. However, the government reported that in 1995 the national graduation rate reached 62 percent.

Approximately 15,000 schools—20 percent of the total—did not offer all six primary grades in 1989. In that year, 22 percent of all primary schools had only one teacher. The government could meet only 10 percent of potential demand for special education. Thirty percent of all secondary-school enrollers failed to complete the three-year curriculum. As a result, government education officials estimated that 20.2 million Mexicans had not completed primary education and another 16 million had not finished secondary school.

Source: Based on information from Mexico, National Institute of Statistics, Geogra
población y vivienda, 1990, Aguascalientes, 1992, 103–7.

Figure 7. Literacy Level (Fifteen Years of Age and Older) by State,

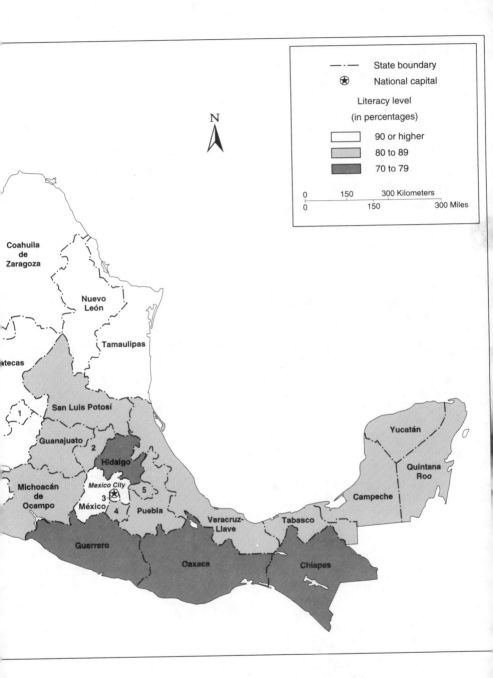

Legend

- —·—·— State boundary
- ⊛ National capital

Literacy level
(in percentages)

- 90 or higher
- 80 to 89
- 70 to 79

```
0        150        300 Kilometers
0        150        300 Miles
```

N

Coahuila de Zaragoza

Nuevo León

Tamaulipas

atecas

San Luis Potosí

1

Guanajuato

2

Hidalgo

Michoacán de Ocampo

Mexico City

México

3

4

5

Puebla

Guerrero

Oaxaca

Veracruz-Llave

Tabasco

Chiapas

Yucatán

Quintana Roo

Campeche

ohy and Informatics, *Estados Unidos Mexicanos: Resumen general. XI censo general de*

The disparity in educational opportunity is reflected in national literacy levels (see fig. 7). According to the 1990 census, 86.8 percent of all Mexicans fifteen years of age and older indicated that they could read and write. Two states in northern Mexico—Baja California and Nuevo León—reported literacy rates exceeding 95 percent, and several other northern states and Mexico City indicated levels between 90 and 95 percent. In contrast, Chiapas, Guerrero, and Oaxaca had literacy levels below 75 percent. National literacy rates improved slightly to 89 percent by 1995.

Besides issues of access and opportunity, observers expressed concern about the quality of instruction. Anecdotal evidence compiled from student test scores by one informed observer, Gilberto Guevara Niebla, pointed to low academic achievement in numerous subjects, including mathematics, languages, and geography. Observers also criticized the highly bureaucratic and centralized nature of Mexico's education system, which traditionally had been centralized. Until 1992 all primary schools, irrespective of regional distinctions, followed a uniform program of study. Fearing a potential loss of political influence, the powerful National Union of Education Workers (Sindicato Nacional de Trabajadores de la Educación—SNTE) strongly opposed efforts to decentralize curriculum and program management and retrain teachers. At the same time, however, the government has earmarked few resources to evaluate school system performance. The result, according to educators, is a system that stifles student creativity.

The deficiencies in the basic education system tend to carry over into public postsecondary education. Observers have identified numerous deficiencies, including faculty salaries, limited research opportunities, and inadequate instructional facilities and curricula. As a result, many employers increasingly look to private educational institutions to provide qualified professional staff.

Responding to these problems, the government established in 1992 the National Accord on the Modernization of Basic Education. Under the accord, the federal government transferred responsibility for primary schools' staff and funding to the states. The federal government, through the Secretariat of Public Education (Secretaría de Educación Pública—SEP), retains authority to establish national policies and to assist schools in poor districts. In addition, a revamped curriculum places renewed emphasis on basic skills, such as reading, writing, and mathematics. The states, for their part, have agreed to commit additional resources to improve teacher salaries and training.

Health Care and Social Security

In the early 1990s, Mexico showed clear signs of having entered a transitional stage in the health of its population. When compared with 1940 or even 1970, Mexico in the 1990s exhibited mortality patterns that more closely approximated those found in developed societies (see table 5, Appendix). Health officials have also reported substantial reductions in morbidity rates for several diseases typically prevalent in poorer countries.

At the same time, however, government officials recognize that this transition is, at best, incomplete. Diseases associated with unsanitary living conditions, minimal access to health care, or inadequate diet continue to affect those in the lowest economic strata. Reductions in government health care expenditures during the economic crisis of the 1980s slowed progress in several areas. In addition, persistent underreporting of diseases in rural areas masks the true dimension of the health care challenge.

Mexico's social security program provides health care to formal-sector workers and their families, some 50 percent of the national population in 1995. This figure represented a drop from the 56 percent coverage rate in 1992. The Mexican Institute of Social Security (Instituto Mexicano de Seguro Social—IMSS) covers approximately 80 percent of these beneficiaries (all employed in the private sector). The Institute of Security and Social Services for State Workers (Instituto de Seguridad y Servicios Sociales para los Trabajadores del Estado—ISSSTE) covers government workers and accounts for 17 percent of the beneficiaries. The Secretariat of National Defense (Secretaría de Defensa Nacional), the Secretariat of the Navy (Secretaría de Marina), and Mexican Petroleum (Petróleos Mexicanos—Pemex) have their own health programs, which cover military and naval personnel, and petroleum workers, respectively (see Personnel, ch. 5). A tripartite funding arrangement finances IMSS operations, with contributions from the employee, employer, and government. ISSSTE programs, as well as those offered by the military and Pemex, are financed through employee and government contributions.

Those outside the social security network—the so-called "open population"—receive health care from a wide array of government agencies. Approximately one-third of the population is served by IMSS-Solidarity (IMSS-Solidaridad), the successor of IMSS-Coplamar (see Structure of Society, this ch.) IMSS-Solidarity is funded by general government revenues, although IMSS provides administrative direction. As part of President de la Madrid's decentralization effort and corresponding federal budget reduction, the population served by IMSS-Coplamar in fourteen states was reassigned to state health agencies under the overall direction of the Secretariat of Health (Secretaría de Salud—SS). The SS also serves as coordinator of the National Health System, which includes the health programs offered by the social security agencies. In keeping with its commitment to a new federal partnership, the Zedillo administration announced that it would transfer facilities and operations of IMSS-Solidaridad and the SS to the states in 1996.

Social security beneficiaries had greater access to health care than did their counterparts among the open population. In 1995 the rates of doctors and hospital beds per 100,000 persons stood at 121 and ninety, respectively, for social security beneficiaries but only 105 and eighty, respectively, for the open population. Social security beneficiaries were also nearly twice as likely as the open population to have consulted a doctor during 1995 and twice as likely to have had surgery that year.

Notable regional disparities in health care are also evident. In 1983 the government surveyed health care access nationwide as measured by thirteen basic indicators, including medical facilities, prenatal consultation, medical attention to various illnesses, and vaccination programs. The Federal District and three northern and northwestern states—Coahuila, Colima, and Nuevo León—recorded levels exceeding eighty out of a possible 100 points. In contrast, Oaxaca, Chiapas, and Puebla in southern and central Mexico averaged between forty and fifty points. Guerrero in the southwest posted a score of only thirty-nine.

Mortality Patterns

In 1940 infectious, parasitic, and respiratory illnesses accounted for nearly 70 percent of all deaths in Mexico. Three decades later, these illnesses still produced more than half of all deaths. By 1990, however, their share of the overall mortality level had dropped to around 20 percent. Cardiovascular illnesses, cancer, accidents, diabetes mellitus, and perinatal complications emerged as the top causes of death in 1990, a sharp change from the previous pattern. Yet despite the progress, health officials recognize the continuing serious threat posed by infectious, parasitic, and respiratory illnesses. Two such illnesses—pneumonia and influenza—and intestinal infections remained within the top ten causes of death in 1990. Among the twenty leading causes of death were such maladies as nutritional deficiencies, chronic bronchitis, measles, tuberculosis, anemia, and severe respiratory infections.

Government census data record a continuous and significant decline in infant mortality from 1930 to 1980 (see table 6, Appendix). The infant mortality rate stood at 145.6 deaths per 1,000 registered live births in 1930. It dropped to 96.2 by 1950, to 68.5 in 1970, and to 40.0 in 1990.

Wide regional variations in infant mortality levels persisted into the 1990s. The 1990 census indicated, for example, that infant mortality rates clustered around the mid-twenties in Baja California Norte, Baja California Sur, the Federal District, and Tamaulipas, and the mid-fifties in Oaxaca, Guerrero, Puebla, and Chiapas (see fig. 8). Even more dramatic variations could be found across municipalities. In general, the lowest levels appeared in highly urban municipalities, especially state capitals and metropolitan areas. In contrast, the highest rates typically were associated with remote, rural, and largely Indian communities.

Nationally, 52 percent of all recorded infant deaths in 1990 occurred during the postneonatal stage, when infants are most susceptible to infections and poor diet. Although perinatal complications accounted for 35 percent of all infant deaths in 1990, intestinal infections and influenza and pneumonia also remained important causes, representing 15 and 13 percent of infant deaths, respectively.

The government reported significant reductions between 1980 and 1990 in early childhood mortality. Early childhood mortality declined from 3.4 per 1,000 preschoolers in 1980 to 2.4 in 1990. Intestinal infections headed the list of causes of death, followed by measles, pneumonia and influenza, and nutritional deficiencies. Preliminary figures for 1991 suggested a sharp decline in early childhood mortality to 1.6 per 1,000 preschoolers. The 1991 figures pointed to notable statewide variations, with rates below one in Coahuila, Durango, Sinaloa,

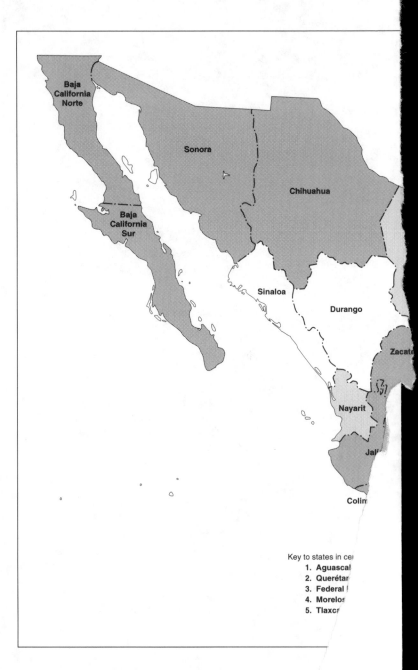

Key to states in cel
1. Aguascal
2. Querétar
3. Federal
4. Morelos
5. Tlaxca

Source: Based on information from Mexico, National Institute of
general de población y vivienda, 1990, Aguascalientes, 1992

Figure 8. Infant Mortality by State, 1990

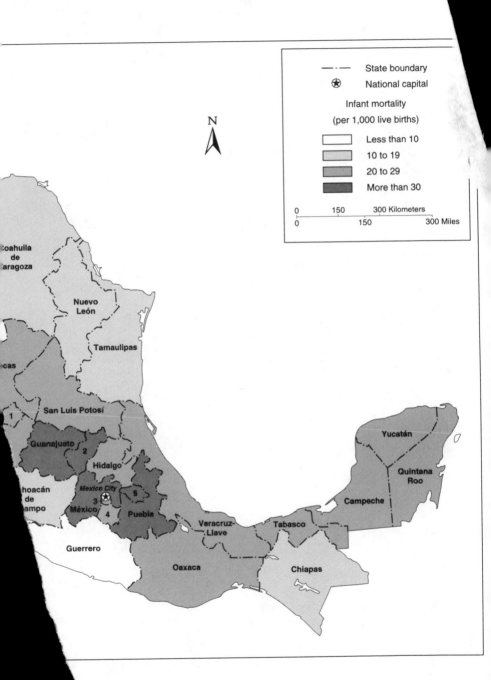

s, Estados Unidos Mexicanos: Resumen general. XI censo

Sonora, Tamaulipas, and the Federal District, and above three in Chiapas, Oaxaca, and Puebla.

Maternal mortality also declined over the same period, with rates falling from 9.4 deaths per 10,000 registered live births in 1980 to 5.4 in 1990, and to 5.1 in preliminary 1991 data. Baja California Sur reported no maternal deaths in 1991, with several, mostly northern states—Chihuahua, Coahuila, Durango, Jalisco, Nayarit, Nuevo León, Sinaloa, Tabasco, and Tamaulipas—indicating rates below three deaths per 10,000 registered live births. In sharp contrast stood Oaxaca, with a rate exceeding fourteen deaths per 10,000 registered live births.

Morbidity Patterns

Although infectious diarrhea and severe respiratory infections have declined significantly as causes of mortality, they remain major illnesses in the early 1990s. Reported cases of infectious diarrhea escalated dramatically from 1,661 per 100,000 residents in 1980 to 2,906 in 1990, and to 4,685 in 1991. During the same period, severe respiratory infections climbed from 3,334 cases per 100,000 residents in 1980 to 10,800 in 1990, and to 13,732 in 1991.

Mexican health officials reported substantial progress in relation to several illnesses controllable by vaccination. Pertussis declined from 122.6 cases per 100,000 residents in 1930 to 4.4 cases in 1980, to 1.3 cases in 1990, and to only 0.2 cases in 1991. Chiapas's rate in 1991 stood at ten times the national average, however. The total number of cases of poliomyelitis declined from 682 in 1980 to seven in 1990 and to zero in 1991. The government recorded only a single case of diphtheria in 1991. Measles epidemics continued to occur, with rates surging from 24.2 cases per 100,000 residents to 80.2 in 1990 before falling sharply to 5.9 in 1991. Even here, however, improvement over past decades could be noted because epidemics occurred only every four or five years as compared with the previous pattern of occurring every other year. Somewhat less progress was apparent in the campaign against tuberculosis, with rates declining from 16.1 cases per 100,000 residents in 1980 to 14.3 in 1990.

Vector-transmitted illnesses remain major public health challenges, especially in southern Mexico. Malaria increased dramatically from 36.9 cases per 100,000 residents in 1980 to 171.5 cases in 1985, before dropping to 31.1 in 1991. Chiapas, Oaxaca, Guerrero, Michoacán, and Sinaloa are priority areas for government antimalarial campaigns. After not a single case of onchocerciasis was reported in 1980 and 1985, the disease reemerged in the late 1980s. Health officials identified 2,905 cases in 1987 and 1,238 cases in 1991, most of them in Oaxaca and Chiapas. In contrast, significant progress occurred in the reduction of dengue, with cases per 100,000 residents declining from 73.8 in 1980 to 6.9 in 1991. The disease is found along the Gulf of Mexico and Pacific coastal regions, the mouth of the Río Balsas, and central Chiapas.

Although most sexually transmitted diseases declined throughout the 1980s, acquired immune deficiency syndrome (AIDS) proved a glaring and deadly exception. Mexico reported its first cases of AIDS in 1983. Both the total number of cases and the ratio increased annually through 1993. In 1993 the government reported 5,095 new cases, or 5.4 cases per 100,000 residents.

Social Security

Mexico's social security agencies are financed through contributions from members, employers, and the government. In the mid-1990s, contributions averaged around 25 percent of members' salaries. Although informal-sector workers may subscribe to the IMSS, they are effectively prevented from doing so because they must pay not only their own share but that of their employers as well. Members are eligible for a wide array of benefits including pension, disability, and maternity coverage. A variety of other services are also available to all Mexicans, including theaters, vacation centers, funeral parlors, and day-care centers. Approximately 1.5 million Mexicans received monthly pensions in the mid-1990s, a higher figure than in previous decades, reflecting gains in average life expectancy.

An actuarial crisis is expected to threaten the fiscal solvency of the social security system by the early twenty-first century. Analyst Carmelo Mesa-Lago has noted numerous problems confronting the system, including rising administrative expenditures, redundant physical plants, the high costs of complex medical technology for IMSS's approximately 1,700 hospitals, and continual transfers of pension funds to cover deficits in disability and maternity programs. In early 1996, IMSS projected its first annual budget deficit. In December 1995, the legislature approved a plan to enhance the viability of social security by expanding its contributory base from the informal sector. In addition, Mexicans can establish privately operated individual retirement accounts. That element of the plan, to take effect in January 1997, was also designed to increase domestic savings to finance future economic growth.

Despite impressive gains in the health care system during the second half of the twentieth century, Mexico's health care and education systems and, indeed, its entire society remain in a profound state of transition. The population of states in northern Mexico and many urban areas exhibits social indicators on a par with those of developed countries, whereas statistics for southern Mexico and most rural areas are comparable to those of the developing world. One of the key challenges for Mexico in the twenty-first century, therefore, will be to meet the needs of a rapidly expanding and urbanizing population while continuing to improve living conditions for the many disadvantaged segments of its society.

*　　*　　*

The various publications of the government's National Institute of Statistics, Geography, and Informatics provide invaluable statistical data on Mexican society. Complete discussions of major environmental issues can be found in the edited work of Enrique Leff, *Medio ambiente y desarrollo en México*, and in *Población, recursos, y medio ambiente en México*, authored by Vicente Sánchez, Margarita Castillejos, and Lenora Rojas Bracho. Alan R. Sandstorm's *Corn Is Our Blood: Culture and Ethnic Identity in a Contemporary Aztec Indian Village* offers an excellent introduction to Indian values and attitudes. Alan Gilbert and Peter M. Ward's *Housing, the State and the Poor: Policy and Practice in Three Latin American Cities*, and Gilbert's edited volume, *Housing and Land in Urban Mexico*, comprehensively examine issues surrounding Mexico's self-help communities. Juan Manuel Ramírez Saiz's edited work, *Normas y prácticas morales y cívicas en la vida cotidiana*, provides a penetrating look at interpersonal relations in Mexico. On the same topic, the edited volume of Alberto Hernández Medina and Luis Narro Rodríguez, *Como somos los mexicanos*, presents rich statistical data of a national survey conducted by the Center for Educational Studies. Continuities and changes in Mexican attitudes in the mid-1990s are ably documented in the UNAM-sponsored *Los mexicanos de los noventa*. Gilberto Guevara Niebla's edited collection, *La catástrofe silenciosa*, is indispensable reading on the problems besetting the Mexican education system. *La salud en México: Tes-*

timonios 1988, edited by Guillermo Soberón, Jesús Kumate, and José Laguna, offers thorough coverage of Mexico's health care system. The Mexican government's internet home page, *www.presidencia.gob.mx,* also contains extensive information on social policy and has links to the various secretariats. (For further information and complete citations, see Bibliography.)

Chapter 3. The Economy

A representation of Mexican campesinos, from a painting by Diego Rivera

FROM THE 1940s UNTIL THE MID-1970s, the Mexican economy enjoyed strong growth averaging more than 6 percent, single-digit inflation, and relatively low external indebtedness. These conditions all began to change during the 1970s. Expansionary government policies generated higher inflation and severe external payments problems while failing to produce sustained growth. Government spending outpaced revenues, generating steep budget deficits and increased external indebtedness. Low real interest rates also discouraged domestic saving.

A brief financial and economic crisis in 1976 signaled the need to address the economy's fundamental problems, but subsequent petroleum discoveries reduced incentives for reform and postponed the inevitable day of reckoning. The government expanded its debt-financed spending in the late 1970s in anticipation of continued low interest rates and high oil revenue. It also maintained a highly overvalued peso (for value of the peso—see Glossary), aggravating balance of payments problems, undermining private-sector confidence, and encouraging capital flight.

External conditions turned sharply against Mexico in the early 1980s, producing a deep recession that forced a fundamental change in the country's decades-old development strategy. Higher interest rates and falling oil prices combined with rising inflation, massive capital flight, and an unserviceable foreign debt to provoke an economic collapse. Lacking access to international capital markets, the government of Miguel de la Madrid Hurtado (1982–88) had to generate huge nonoil trade surpluses to restore macroeconomic balance. Import volume fell sharply at the expense of fixed investment and consumption. As a result of the government's stringent economic stabilization program, the fiscal deficit was eliminated, international reserves rebuilt, and export growth restored, but at the cost of lower real wages and extensive unemployment. Economic output remained flat between 1983 and 1988, and inflation remained high, reaching more than 140 percent in 1987. Real exchange-rate depreciation boosted the country's debt-to-gross domestic product (GDP—see Glossary) ratio by almost 30 percentage points between 1982 and 1987.

To control persistently high inflation and restore growth and international competitiveness, the government pursued a major policy reorientation in the late 1980s. It reduced state involvement in economic production and regulation and integrated Mexico more fully into the world economy. An anti-inflation plan was introduced in late 1987 under which the government, the private sector, and organized labor agreed to limit wage and price increases. In 1989 the government reached agreement with its external creditors on extensive debt restructuring and reduction.

In an effort to restore self-sustaining growth, the administration of Carlos Salinas de Gortari (1988–94) boosted investment as a share of GDP. It also accelerated the privatization of state-owned productive enterprises, both to raise state revenue and to promote economic restructuring and modernization. The government eased foreign investment regulations, stabilized the currency, deregulated the prices of most goods, and enacted extensive trade liberalization measures, including the reduction or elimination of import barriers and the pursuit of free-trade agreements with Mexico's trading partners, especially the United States.

The Salinas government allowed the currency to become increasingly overvalued during 1994, despite mounting trade and current account deficits resulting from trade liberalization and economic growth. It kept real interest rates high to ensure sufficient inflows of foreign (mainly short-term portfolio) investment to cover the current account deficit. During 1994 the government treasury issued a large number of dollar-denominated bonds (*tesebonos*) to reinforce its capital position.

By the end of 1994, the almost total disappearance of Mexico's international reserves made the government's exchange-rate policy no longer tenable. The new administration of President Ernesto Zedillo Ponce de Leon was forced in December 1994 to devalue the new peso (for value of the new peso—see Glossary), despite promises to the contrary. The government's mismanaged new peso devaluation cost the currency nearly half of its value and the government much of its credibility and popular support. Inflation and interest rates rose sharply in subsequent weeks, throwing millions of Mexicans out of work and putting many consumer goods beyond the reach of the middle class, to say nothing of the impoverished majority. Public and private investment plummeted, and Mexico entered its worst economic recession since the 1930s.

By early 1996, however, the economy had begun to recover, as capital inflows increased and most productive sectors registered positive growth rates.

Growth and Structure of the Economy

Early Years

The Mexican wars of independence (1810–21) left a legacy of economic stagnation that persisted until the 1870s. Political instability and foreign invasion deterred foreign investment, risk-taking, and innovation. Most available capital left with its Spanish owners following independence. Instead of investing in productive enterprises and thereby spurring economic growth, many wealthy Mexicans converted their assets into tangible, secure, and often unproductive property.

The seeds of economic modernization were laid under the restored Republic (1867–76) (see The Restoration, 1867–76, ch. 1). President Benito Juárez (1855–72) sought to attract foreign capital to finance Mexico's economic modernization. His government revised the tax and tariff structure to revitalize the mining industry, and it improved the transportation and communications infrastructure to allow fuller exploitation of the country's natural resources. The government let contracts for construction of a new rail line northward to the United States, and it completed the commercially vital Mexico City-Veracruz railroad, begun in 1837. Protected by high tariffs, Mexico's textile industry doubled its production of processed items between 1854 and 1877. But overall, manufacturing grew only modestly, and economic stagnation continued.

During the Porfiriato (1876–1910), however, Mexico underwent rapid and sustained growth, and laid the foundations for a modern economy. Taking "order and progress" as his watchwords, President José de la Cruz Porfirio Díaz established the rule of law, political stability, and social peace, which brought the increased capital investment that would finance national development and modernization. Rural banditry was suppressed, communications and transportation facilities were modernized, and local customs duties that had hindered domestic trade were abolished.

Revolution and Aftermath

The Mexican Revolution (1910–20) severely disrupted the Mexican economy, erasing many of the gains achieved during the Porfiriato. The labor force declined sharply, with the economically active share of the population falling from 35 percent in 1910 to 31 percent in 1930. Between 1910 and 1921, the population suffered an overall net decline of 360,000 people. The livestock supply was severely depleted, as thousands of cattle were lost to the depredations of rival militias. Cotton, coffee, and sugarcane went unharvested as workers abandoned the fields either to join or flee the fighting. The result was a precipitous drop in agricultural output. The disruption of communications and rail transportation made distribution unreliable, prompting further reductions in the production of perishable goods. As agricultural and manufacturing output declined, black markets flourished in the major cities. The banking system was shattered, public credit disappeared, and the currency was destroyed. The mining sector suffered huge losses, with gold production falling some 80 percent between 1910 and 1916, and silver and copper output each declining 65 percent.

The Great Depression

The Great Depression brought Mexico a sharp drop in national income and internal demand after 1929, challenging the country's ability to fulfill its constitutional mandate to promote social equity. Still, Mexico did not feel the effects of the Great Depression as directly as some other countries did.

In the early 1930s, manufacturing and other sectors serving the domestic economy began a slow recovery. The upturn was facilitated by several key structural reforms, notably the railroad nationalization of 1929 and 1930, the nationalization of the petroleum industry in 1938, and the acceleration of land reform, first under President Emilio Portes Gil (1928–30) and then under President Lázaro Cárdenas (1934–40) in the late 1930s. To foster industrial expansion, the administration of Manuel Ávila Camacho (1940–46) in 1941 reorganized the National Finance Bank (Nacional Financiera—Nafinsa), which had originally been created in 1934 as an investment bank.

During the 1930s, agricultural production also rose steadily, and urban employment expanded in response to rising domestic demand. The government offered tax incentives for production directed toward the home market. Import-substitution industrialization (see Glossary) began to make a slow advance during the 1930s, although it was not yet official government policy.

Postwar Economic Growth

Mexico's inward-looking development strategy produced sustained economic growth of 3 to 4 percent and modest 3 percent inflation annually from the 1940s until the late 1960s. The government fostered the development of consumer goods industries directed toward domestic markets by imposing high protective tariffs and other barriers to imports. The share of imports subject to licensing requirements rose from 28 percent in 1956 to an average of more than 60 percent during the 1960s and about 70 percent in the 1970s. Industry accounted for 22 percent of total output in 1950, 24 percent in 1960, and 29 percent in 1970. The share of total output arising from agriculture and other primary activities declined during the same period, while services stayed constant. The government promoted industrial expansion through public investment in agricultural, energy, and transportation infrastructure. Cities grew rapidly during these years, reflecting the shift of employment from agriculture to industry and services. The urban population increased at a high rate after 1940 (see Urban Society, ch. 2). Growth of the urban labor force exceeded even the growth rate of industrial employment, with surplus workers taking low-paying service jobs.

In the years following World War II, President Miguel Alemán Valdés's (1946–52) full-scale import-substitution program stimulated output by boosting internal demand. The government raised import controls on consumer goods but relaxed them on capital goods, which it purchased with international reserves accumulated during the war. The government progressively undervalued the peso to reduce the costs of imported capital goods and expand productive capacity, and it spent heavily on infrastructure. By 1950 Mexico's road network had expanded to 21,000 kilometers, of which some 13,600 were paved.

Mexico's strong economic performance continued into the 1960s, when GDP growth averaged about 7 percent overall and about 3 percent per capita. Consumer price inflation averaged only 3 percent annually. Manufacturing remained the country's dominant growth sector, expanding 7 percent annually and attracting considerable foreign investment. Mining grew at an annual rate of nearly 4 percent, trade at 6 percent, and agriculture at 3 percent. By 1970 Mexico had diversified its export base and become largely self-sufficient in food crops, steel, and most consumer goods. Although its imports remained high, most were capital goods used to expand domestic production.

Deterioration in the 1970s

Although the Mexican economy maintained its rapid growth during most of the 1970s, it was progressively undermined by fiscal mismanagement and a resulting sharp deterioration of the investment climate. The GDP grew more than 6 percent annually during the administration of President Luis Echeverría Álvarez (1970–76), and at about a 6 percent rate during that of his successor, José López Portillo y Pacheco (1976–82). But economic activity fluctuated wildly during the decade, with spurts of rapid growth followed by sharp depressions in 1976 and 1982.

Fiscal profligacy combined with the 1973 oil shock to exacerbate inflation and upset the balance of payments. Moreover, President Echeverría's leftist rhetoric and actions—such as abetting illegal land seizures by peasants—eroded investor confidence and alienated the private sector. The balance of payments disequilibrium became unmanageable as capital flight intensified, forcing the government in 1976 to devalue the peso by 45 percent. The action ended Mexico's twenty-year fixed exchange rate.

Although significant oil discoveries in 1976 allowed a temporary recovery, the windfall from petroleum sales also allowed continuation of Echeverría's destructive fiscal policies. In the mid-1970s, Mexico went from being a net importer of oil and petroleum products to a significant exporter. Oil and petrochemicals became the economy's most dynamic growth sector. Rising oil income allowed the government to continue its expansionary fiscal policy, partially financed by higher foreign borrowing. Between 1978 and 1981, the economy grew more than 8 percent annually, as the government spent heavily on energy, transportation, and basic industries. Manufacturing output expanded modestly during these years, growing by 9 percent in 1978, 9 percent in 1979, and 6 percent in 1980.

This renewed growth rested on shaky foundations. Mexico's external indebtedness mounted, and the peso became increasingly overvalued, hurting nonoil exports in the late 1970s and forcing a second peso devaluation in 1980. Production of basic food crops stagnated, forcing Mexico in the early 1980s to become a net importer of foodstuffs. The portion of import categories subject to controls rose from 20 percent of the total in 1977 to 24 percent in 1979. The government raised tariffs concurrently to shield domestic producers from foreign competition, further hampering the modernization and competitiveness of Mexican industry.

1982 Crisis and Recovery

The macroeconomic policies of the 1970s left Mexico's economy highly vulnerable to external conditions. These turned sharply against Mexico in the early 1980s, and caused the worst recession since the 1930s. By mid-1981, Mexico was beset by falling oil prices, higher world interest rates, rising inflation, a chronically overvalued peso, and a deteriorating balance of payments that spurred massive capital flight. This disequilibrium, along with the virtual disappearance of Mexico's international reserves—by the end of 1982 they were insufficient to cover three weeks' imports—forced the government to devalue the peso three times during 1982. The devaluation further fueled inflation and prevented short-term recovery. The devaluations depressed real wages and increased the private sector's burden in servicing its dollar-denominated debt. Interest payments on long-term debt alone were equal to 28 percent of export revenue. Cut off from additional credit, the government declared an involuntary moratorium on debt payments in August 1982, and the following month it announced the nationalization of Mexico's private banking system.

By late 1982, incoming President Miguel de la Madrid had to reduce public spending drastically, stimulate exports, and foster economic growth to balance the national accounts. Recovery was extremely slow to materialize, however. The economy stagnated throughout the 1980s as a result of continuing negative terms of trade, high domestic interest rates, and scarce credit. Widespread fears that the government might fail to achieve fiscal balance and have to expand the money supply and raise taxes deterred private investment and encouraged massive capital flight that further increased inflationary pressures. The resulting reduction in domestic savings impeded growth, as did the government's rapid and drastic reductions in public investment and its raising of real domestic interest rates to deter capital flight.

Mexico's GDP grew at an average rate of just 0.1 percent per year between 1983 and 1988, while inflation stayed extremely high (see table 7, Appendix). Public consumption grew at an average annual rate of less than 2 percent, and private consumption not at all. Total investment fell at an average annual rate of 4 percent and public investment at an 11 percent pace. Throughout the 1980s, the productive sectors of the economy contributed a decreasing share to GDP, while the services sectors expanded their share, reflecting the rapid growth of the informal economy. De la Madrid's stabilization strategy imposed high social costs: real disposable income per capita fell 5 percent each year between 1983 and 1988. High levels of unemployment and underemployment, especially in rural areas, stimulated migration to Mexico City and to the United States.

By 1988 inflation was at last under control, fiscal and monetary discipline attained, relative price adjustment achieved, structural reform in trade and public-sector management underway, and the preconditions for recovery in place. But these positive developments were inadequate to attract foreign investment and return capital in sufficient quantities for sustained recovery. A shift in development strategy became necessary, predicated on the need to generate a net capital inflow.

In April 1989, President Carlos Salinas de Gortari announced his government's national development plan for 1989–94, which called for annual GDP growth of 6 percent and an inflation rate similar to those of Mexico's main trading partners. Salinas planned to achieve this sustained growth by boosting the investment share of GDP and by encouraging private investment through denationalization of state enterprises and deregulation of the economy. His first priority was to reduce Mexico's external debt; in mid-1989 the government reached agreement with its commercial bank creditors to reduce its medium- and long-term debt. The following year, Salinas took his next step toward higher capital inflows by lowering domestic borrowing costs, reprivatizing the banking system, and broaching the idea of a free-trade agreement with the United States. These announcements were soon followed by increased levels of capital repatriation and foreign investment.

After rising impressively during the early years of Salinas's presidency, the growth rate of real GDP began to slow during the early 1990s. During 1993 the economy grew by a negligible amount, but growth rebounded to almost 4 percent during 1994, as fiscal and monetary policy were relaxed and foreign investment was bolstered by United States ratification of the North American Free Trade Agreement (NAFTA). In 1994 the commerce and services sectors accounted for 22 percent of

Mexico's total GDP. Manufacturing followed at 20 percent; transport and communications at 10 percent; agriculture, forestry, and fishing at 8 percent; construction at 5 percent; mining at 2 percent; and electricity, gas, and water at 2 percent (see fig. 9). Some two-thirds of GDP in 1994 (67 percent) was spent on private consumption, 11 percent on public consumption, and 22 percent on fixed investment. During 1994 private consumption rose by 4 percent, public consumption by 2 percent, public investment by 9 percent, and private investment by 8 percent.

However, the collapse of the new peso in December 1994 and the ensuing economic crisis caused the economy to contract by an estimated 7 percent during 1995. Investment and consumption both fell sharply, the latter by some 10 percent. Agriculture, livestock, and fishing contracted by 4 percent; mining by 1 percent; manufacturing by 6 percent; construction by 22 percent; and transport, storage, and communications by 2 percent. The only sector to register positive growth was utilities, which expanded by 3 percent.

By 1996 Mexican government and independent analysts saw signs that the country had begun to emerge from its economic recession. The economy contracted by a modest 1 percent during the first quarter of 1996. The Mexican government reported strong growth of 7 percent for the second quarter, and the Union Bank of Switzerland forecast economic growth of 4 percent for all of 1996.

Macroeconomic Management

In the 1940s, Mexico adopted a state-led development strategy that relied on public-sector investment to integrate the national economy. Under the policy of "stabilizing development," the state promoted industrialization by encouraging import substitution, mobilizing domestic savings, and directing state credit toward priority investment projects. It followed conservative policies on interest and exchange rates in order to attract external capital to support industrialization. During the 1940s and 1950s, the government channeled public investment toward the agricultural sector, and especially into large-scale irrigation projects. During the 1960s, public spending was redirected toward expanding the nation's industrial capacity.

Although social infrastructure, such as medical and educational facilities, received some 25 percent of public spending, income distribution became steadily more unequal during the

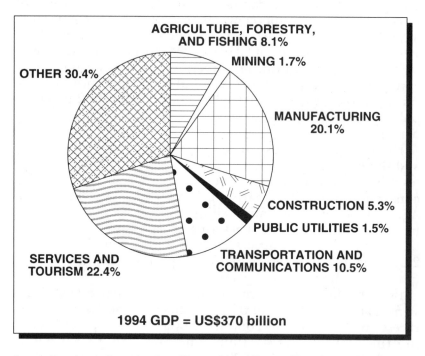

AGRICULTURE, FORESTRY, AND FISHING 8.1%

MINING 1.7%

OTHER 30.4%

MANUFACTURING 20.1%

CONSTRUCTION 5.3%

PUBLIC UTILITIES 1.5%

SERVICES AND TOURISM 22.4%

TRANSPORTATION AND COMMUNICATIONS 10.5%

1994 GDP = US$370 billion

Source: Based on information from Economist Intelligence Unit, *Country Report: Mexico*, London, No. 1, 1996, 3.

Figure 9. Gross Domestic Product (GDP) by Sector, 1994

postwar decades, and the social needs of the rural poor went largely unaddressed. Popular acceptance of Mexico's post-1940 development strategy began to wane by 1970 as its inegalitarian consequences became clear. As public pressure for state redress of social needs rose, presidents Echeverría and López Portillo turned to destructive fiscal policies that nearly bankrupted the state and contributed to Mexico's economic collapse in the early 1980s.

After taking power in 1970, Echeverría turned away from the policy of "stabilizing development" that had closely linked Mexico's economic fortunes to those of the private sector. By expanding the state's role in directing and regulating economic activity, Echeverría hoped to promote both equity and prosperity while easing political pressures on the state. Higher public spending was also intended to alleviate the social and political tensions that had found violent expression in the riots at the Plaza of the Three Cultures in Tlatelolco in 1968 and threatened continued Institutional Revolutionary Party (Partido Revolucionario Institucional—PRI) rule (see Reconciliation and Redistribution, 1970–76, ch. 1).

Echeverría's improvidence produced a growing fiscal imbalance, which he financed through foreign borrowing. Mexico's public-sector deficit rose sharply from 2 percent of GDP in 1970 to 7 percent by 1976. Under Echeverría, Mexico resorted for the first time to massive external borrowing to finance these deficits. Extensive oil discoveries in the mid-1970s gave Mexico access to almost unlimited foreign credits, allowing the government to contract huge loans to finance the fiscal and trade deficits. The share of public-sector spending financed by debt rose from 32 percent in 1971 to 50 percent by 1977. The looming fiscal crisis, together with the president's intemperate rhetorical assaults on the private sector, undermined business confidence and soured the investment climate. The government's determination to maintain a fixed exchange rate despite rising inflation undermined the competitiveness of domestic production, discouraged new investment, and encouraged capital flight.

By the mid-1970s, the balance of payments disequilibrium had become unmanageable. Inflation increased from 3 percent in 1969 to an annual average of 17 percent between 1973 and 1975. The fiscal deficit rose from 3 percent of GDP in 1971 to 10 percent in 1975. During those same years, the current account deficit rose from US$0.9 billion to US$4.4 billion, and the foreign public debt more than doubled from US$6.7 billion to US$15.7 billion. The private sector responded with massive capital flight, both to protect against the expected peso devaluation and to protest Echeverría's attacks on the private sector.

By 1976 the government could no longer ignore the crisis. Complying with International Monetary Fund (IMF—see Glossary) requirements for contingency lending and private-sector demands, the government curbed the expansion of state industry and public-sector spending, restricted credit, and forced the economy into recession. In August 1976, the government allowed the peso to float, ending more than twenty years of exchange-rate stability. The peso quickly depreciated by almost 40 percent against the dollar.

Although the discovery of massive new petroleum deposits in 1977 briefly alleviated the fiscal pressures weighing upon the government, it also led officials to abandon their newly acquired habits of fiscal restraint (see Recovery and Relapse, ch. 1). The fiscally expansionist Secretariat of Programming and Budget (Secretaría de Programación y Presupuesto—SPP), which had been established in 1977 and given responsibility for public investment planning, grew in influence at the expense of technocrats from the Central Bank and Treasury Ministry, who were more concerned with maintaining macroeconomic efficiency and stability.

The dénouement of López Portillo's expansionary policies came in mid-1981. International interest rates rose and oil prices fell. Capital flight accelerated as the government defended the increasingly overvalued peso through short-term external borrowing. Despite the warning signs, López Portillo decided to postpone adjustment measures and maintain existing policy.

In late 1982, the incoming administration of President de la Madrid faced a raft of challenges: huge fiscal imbalances, unsympathetic creditor banks, an alienated private sector, and international institutions inexperienced in managing a global debt crisis (see The de la Madrid *Sexenio*, 1982–88, ch. 1). Mexico's public-sector deficit in 1982 amounted to 18 percent of GDP. Total public spending amounted to nearly 47 percent of GDP, compared with only 30 percent in 1977, while public-sector revenue rose during the same period from 24 percent of GDP in 1977 to only 30 percent in 1982. Both production and economic growth stagnated.

Despite having vowed to defend the peso "like a dog," in February 1982 the president allowed the dollar price of the peso to almost double to discourage foreign-exchange speculation. The exchange rate rose from more than twenty-six pesos per dollar in January 1982 to about forty-five three months later. In August of that year, the government announced three more dramatic devaluations of the peso and a ninety-day suspension of debt principal payments. It also began negotiations for bridge loans and rescheduling agreements with the United States treasury, the IMF, and private commercial banks. In September the government adopted full exchange controls and nationalized the domestic banking system in a mistaken effort to stem capital flight. In November the government concluded a rescheduling accord with the IMF, and in early 1993 it negotiated a US$10 billion rescue package with private banks.

In December 1982, de la Madrid announced what turned out to be his first stabilization package, the Immediate Economic Reorganization Program (Programa Inmediato de Reordenación Económica—PIRE). This two-stage program called for "shock" treatment in 1983 to restore macroeconomic balance, to be followed in 1984 and 1985 by a "gradualist" adjustment program to open the economy to market forces. The first phase was intended to restore price and financial stability by means of a sharp reduction in public spending and a steep peso devaluation. The government instituted a harsh austerity regime that held the growth in domestic spending far below the rise in total output.

De la Madrid's first stabilization package did not work as expected. The government had expected lower inflation and more realistic prices to produce strong economic growth by 1984. This did not take place. From early 1983 until mid-1984, the government adhered closely to the goals of a November 1982 agreement it had reached with the IMF. The agreement maintained highly restrictive fiscal and monetary policies and allowed wages to lag substantially behind inflation. The austerity measures and devaluations of 1983 eliminated both the fiscal and trade deficits, but at the cost of sharply reduced imports and a severe economic recession. Contrary to expectations, the inflation rate did not fall significantly, and voluntary private lending did not resume.

Increasingly concerned about Mexico's growing fiscal deficit and its failure to reach its economic targets, the IMF in September 1985 suspended disbursement of the loan it had approved in late 1982. This announcement led to another run on the peso and a new balance-of-payments crisis. The government reacted to the situation by imposing a series of devaluations and further harsh stabilization measures, including additional reductions in spending and domestic credit. Economic growth slowed and inflation surged, suggesting the failure of de la Madrid's first stabilization package.

In 1985 the Mexican government signaled a fundamental change in development strategy by reorienting economic policy toward trade liberalization and export promotion. It expected renewed export promotion to restore external balance and trade liberalization to restrain domestic prices by encouraging import competition. In July 1985, the government substantially reduced import licensing requirements and raised the share of total imports exempt from licensing. It compensated slightly for these measures by raising tariffs. The government also devalued the peso again, despite the inflationary consequences, to force previously protected domestic firms to become more competitive against imported goods.

In late 1986, the government cautiously relaxed credit to the private sector in an effort to ease the economy out of recession. External financing was again made available in 1987 following approval of a debt rescheduling plan proposed by United States Secretary of the Treasury James A. Baker III. The Baker Plan called for rescheduling some 83 percent of the US$52.2 billion of public-sector debt that Mexico had contracted prior to 1985. The debt would be repaid over a twenty-year period, with a seven-year grace period. Multilateral agencies agreed to lend an additional US$6 billion and commercial banks an additional US$7.7 billion, of which US$1.7 billion was contingency lending. The Baker Plan also provided for rescheduling some US$9.7 billion of private debt owed to commercial banks over a twenty-year period with seven years' grace. In all, the 1986 agreement provided Mexico some US$12.5 billion in new private and official credit.

After 1987 the government finally began to make progress against inflation. Endemic price instability had severely upset economic expectations, deterred much-needed investment, and hindered the country's economic recovery. In an effort to restore price stability, government policy makers decided in late 1987 to stop devaluing the peso at rates equal to or higher than the inflation rate. Even more important, in December 1987 the government forged a joint agreement with official leaders of the labor, peasant, and business sectors to restrain wages and prices. This accord, known as the Economic Solidarity Pact (Pacto de Solidaridad Económica—PSE), promised to reduce Mexico's monthly inflation rate to 2 percent by the end of 1988.

The PSE required further reductions in public spending and credit, higher tax revenue, and a tighter monetary policy. All were intended to reduce the fiscal deficit and curb inflation. The new revenue measures included an increase in the value-added tax (VAT), a new personal income surtax, and elimination of tax exemptions. The government raised prices of public goods and services, and allowed interest rates to rise in order to promote saving and reduce capital flight. The PSE also included a structural adjustment component emphasizing trade liberalization and privatization of state enterprises.

The plan soon produced results. The inflation rate fell considerably, living standards recovered slightly, and economic growth resumed. Annual inflation fell from 159 percent in 1987 to 52 percent in 1988. The gradual recovery of Mexico's international reserves in 1989 and 1990 allowed the government to sustain a credible fixed exchange rate and finance the deterioration in the external account caused by the tariff reductions. Although President de la Madrid was himself not highly popular as he approached the end of his six-year term, his government had sufficient authority and institutional strength to enforce the wage restraints included in the PSE.

President Salinas announced in January 1989 a new version of de la Madrid's PSE, called the Pact for Economic Stability and Growth (Pacto para la Estabilidad y el Crecimiento Económico—PECE), which he hoped would end Mexico's net capital outflow. Salinas's economic program received considerable external support (see President Salinas, ch. 1). In March 1989, Mexico and the United States reached agreement on a long-term plan to restructure Mexico's US$52.7 billion debt owed to commercial creditors. The plan, proposed by United States Secretary of the Treasury Nicholas F. Brady, was intended to attract new foreign investment, encourage return capital, reduce domestic interest rates, and foster higher growth.

In July 1989, Mexico signed an agreement in principle with an advisory committee representing its 500 or so international creditors. The final agreement was signed in February 1990 and went into effect the following month.

Mexico's public finances improved steadily during the early years of Salinas's presidency. Throughout the 1980s, the Mexican government had emphasized fiscal austerity while making little effort to raise tax revenue. This policy mix began to change under Salinas, as Mexican economic policy stopped holding domestic demand below output and began to tighten tax collection. The government broadened the tax base by reducing marginal tax rates, the maximum corporate and personal tax rates, and the number of personal income tax brackets. Between 1989 and 1992, the number of taxpayers increased by 45 percent. As a result in part of improved tax collection, Mexico went from a public-sector deficit of 9 percent of GDP in

1988 to a surplus of 2 percent of GDP in 1992, although the government began to relax fiscal policy thereafter.

In the wake of the currency collapse of late 1994, the government committed itself in March 1995 to reduce public spending by almost 10 percent in real terms; it raised the VAT from 10 percent to 15 percent, and it raised prices for fuel, electricity, and other publicly provided services. Although the anti-inflationary social pact among the government, business, and labor—the PECE—was not renewed in early 1995, the government announced in October 1995 a new pact with labor and business, the Alliance for Economic Recovery (Alianza para la Recuperación Económica—APRE), which established fixed rates of increase for wages and prices. Under the terms of the APRE, the government pledged to maintain a balanced budget during 1996. It also planned a 5 percent real reduction in current spending, as well as regular increases in prices of publicly provided goods and services. Unlike its predecessors, however, this measure was not called a "pact," and it included no provision for a crawling- peg exchange rate. The government's reductions in current spending and public investment during 1995 were especially severe because vastly higher interest rates had boosted the government's interest payments by more than 37 percent in real terms.

These spending reductions helped the government to move from a public-sector deficit of 1.7 billion new pesos in 1994 to a modest surplus of 815 million new pesos in 1995, the latter representing 0.05 percent of GDP. Public expenditure in 1995 totaled 424 billion new pesos, of which 72 billion new pesos (17 percent) went to interest payments, 67 billion (16 percent) to education, 65 billion (15 percent) to energy, and 62 billion (15 percent) to health and social security. For 1996 the government budgeted total public-sector revenue of 558 billion new pesos, of which 237 billion new pesos would come from taxation and 177 billion new pesos from state enterprises. It budgeted total net expenditures of 554 billion new pesos, of which the largest share would go to education, energy, and health and social security, as well as debt service.

External Debt

By the early 1990s, Mexico's debt crisis had largely passed, although the country remained saddled with huge debts. Capital inflows were more than sufficient to service the debt through 1993 as portfolio and foreign direct investment reached unprecedented levels in response to liberalization and the successful negotiation of NAFTA. Despite the use of funds from privatization to retire old public-sector debt, total external debt continued to grow during the early 1990s as current account deficits soared after 1992.

After reaching a low of US$112 billion in 1992, Mexico's total external debt rose steadily thereafter, reaching an estimated US$158 billion in 1995. The large increase during 1995 in Mexico's total public indebtedness resulted in part from loans contracted in the wake of the new peso collapse of late 1994. In early 1995, the United States government made US$20 billion available to Mexico from the United States treasury department's Exchange Stabilization Fund, the Bank for International Settlements contributed US$10 billion, and the IMF offered US$8 billion in standby credit and US$10 billion of other funding.

In 1993 Mexico's total debt service amounted to US$21 billion, including US$14 billion in principal payments and US$7 billion in interest payments. Mexico's total external debt amounted to 356 percent of GDP in 1993.

Inflation

Control of inflation was the main policy objective of the de la Madrid and Salinas administrations between 1987 and 1993, despite the cost of this policy in terms of the currency's continued real appreciation and the resultant need to maintain high interest rates to attract foreign investment and deter capital flight. The government made steady progress against inflation following the PSE's introduction in late 1987 (replaced in 1989 by the PECE, which was revised and updated annually between 1989 and 1993). Largely as a result of the wage and price restraints included in these pacts, inflation fell from 159 percent in 1987 to 20 percent in 1989. In 1990 it rose slightly to 30 percent (double the initial target of 15 percent), as the government eased credit, eliminated price subsidies, and realigned public-sector prices as well as some private-sector prices. Thereafter, the inflation rate fell steadily from 23 percent in 1991 to 7 percent in 1994, Mexico's first single-digit inflation rate in twenty years.

Consumer price inflation rose sharply between January and April 1995 in response to the December 1994 new peso devaluation, then abated between May and August as the new peso appreciated. When the currency came under renewed pressure during the last four months of the year, however, inflation rose more quickly. It soared as high as 52 percent (Mexico's highest inflation rate since 1987) by December 1995, although it averaged 35 percent for the year. A 21 percent increase in the minimum wage and monthly adjustments of public prices contributed to the high inflation. Consumer prices rose by 11 percent during the first four months of 1996, despite Mexico's continued recession and the new peso's real appreciation. The government conservatively projected an inflation rate of 21 percent for all of 1996.

Privatization

Prior to 1970, the Mexican government operated relatively few productive enterprises. The influx of oil revenue during the 1970s, however, allowed the government to vastly expand its patronage resources by assuming ownership of hundreds of unprofitable firms. By 1982 the Mexican government ran 1,155 businesses, among them public enterprises (65 percent with state majority ownership and 6 percent with state minority ownership), trust funds, and decentralized agencies. President de la Madrid announced in February 1985 that 237 parastatal (see Glossary) enterprises would be sold to private buyers as part of the government's campaign to raise state revenues and promote economic efficiency. Privatization of state enterprises accelerated under President Salinas and became a central component of his structural adjustment program. The Salinas team began by selling smaller enterprises, then moved to larger and more complicated firms. In November 1993, Salinas announced that his government had sold a total of 390 state enterprises (63 percent of the firms in state hands in 1988), and that fifty of the remaining 209 enterprises were in the process of being sold, merged, or closed.

Despite its overall success, the privatization program eliminated more than 400,000 jobs between 1983 and 1993. Far more enterprises were closed than sold, and the overwhelming majority of the latter were sold through acceptance of private bids, mainly from wealthy Mexican investors, rather than through stock offerings to employees or the public. Some newly privatized enterprises—such as Astilleros Unidos de Veracruz, Mexico's largest shipyard—subsequently came close to bankruptcy, and several sugar mills closed soon after they were privatized.

The Zedillo government continued its predecessor's search for new privatization opportunities. During 1995 it awarded five concessions to joint ventures between Mexican and foreign companies to operate in the long-distance telecommunications market following the expiration of the Mexican Telephone (Teléfonos de México—Telmex) monopoly in January 1997. New privatization opportunities were expected to boost private capital formation, which had slumped in late 1995. The planned privatization of the secondary petrochemicals operation, Mexican Petroleum (Petróleos Mexicanos—Pemex), however, had not occurred by mid-1996, in part because of opposition from the oil workers' union and elements within the ruling party. The government also delayed its offering of railroad concessions for privatization, partly out of concern about job losses. Moreover, it had to rescue the operators of Mexico's new private toll roads, who had sharply raised tolls to recoup construction costs and then faced insolvency because they had misjudged the volume of traffic.

Labor Force

Mexico's workforce was estimated in the 1990 census at some 24.3 million. Workers constituted a relatively small share of the total population, in part because of the population's relative youth (38 percent were below the minimum working age of fourteen). Slightly more than half of the working-age population (those aged fifteen to sixty-four) had actually entered the formal labor market. In the early 1990s, an estimated 500,000 people entered the labor force each year, expanding the total workforce by some 3 percent annually.

In 1988 employers and the self-employed constituted 29 percent of the labor force, employees 56 percent, and unpaid family workers 15 percent. Agriculture, forestry, and fishing employed some 24 percent of the economically active population; manufacturing, mining, quarrying, and public utilities employed 22 percent; trade, hotels, and restaurants employed 19 percent; construction employed 5 percent; finance and real estate employed 5 percent; transportation and communications employed 4 percent; and 21 percent were engaged in other service work. About half of all manufacturing workers were employed in small and medium-size enterprises.

Partly because of high unemployment in the formal labor sector, the number of informal-sector workers swelled during the 1980s and early 1990s (see Income Distribution, ch. 2).

These informal workers included some 900,000 street vendors in forty-five cities, with annual sales of about US$13 billion. The growth of the informal sector both reduced the state's tax revenue receipts and encouraged corruption among local officials.

Historically, real wages in Mexico have been subject to tacit understandings among government officials, the private sector, and labor union chiefs. During the 1940s and 1950s, these sectors forged an understanding whereby Central Bank and Treasury Ministry technocrats would control macroeconomic policy, business groups would refrain from open political opposition while gaining political access through officially recognized private-sector associations, and labor leaders would restrict real wage demands in exchange for additional patronage for distribution to workers. After falling sharply during the 1940s, real wages began to recover in the mid-1950s and continued to rise until the late 1970s, when the government responded to growing fiscal pressures by shifting resources away from the peasantry and the public sector. The government used its control of employment opportunities and the labor union movement to hold down wages throughout the 1980s in an effort to reduce inflation.

The average real wage in Mexico remained low in 1995, both in historical and international terms (see Income Distribution, ch. 2). The Confederation of Mexican Workers (Confederación de Trabajadores Mexicanos—CTM) noted that the average worker's purchasing power in 1993 was only 65 percent of its 1982 level.

Unemployment rose sharply during the six months following the December 1994 new peso devaluation, then receded somewhat between August and December 1995. Open unemployment (according to the government's narrow definition) dropped from 8 percent to 5 percent during this period, although it subsequently increased to an average of 6 percent during the first quarter of 1996.

Although the government increased the minimum wage by 21 percent during 1995, the cost of living rose by more than 50 percent as a result of the currency collapse. In September 1995, the minimum wage was sufficient to cover only 35 percent of workers' basic necessities, compared to 94 percent in December 1987. The government's anti-inflation APRE program called for the minimum wage to increase in line with projected inflation of 21 percent. The government also pledged to

Street vendor, Mexico City
Courtesy Arturo Salinas

boost employment through fiscal incentives to encourage private investment and tax credits for companies that increased their workforce above the average level for the first three quarters of 1995. It also planned to expand public training programs for workers and to maintain its temporary public works programs (such as rural road conservation, which was expected to employ 140,000 people, as well as other temporary work programs that would employ 700,000).

Partially to increase Mexico's domestic savings, the government proposed legislation in November 1995 to reform the country's pension system by allowing the creation of individual accounts managed by private financial institutions rather than by the government's Mexican Institute of Social Security (Instituto Mexicano de Seguro Social—IMSS). Until 1992 the IMSS had been solely responsible for managing the pension system.

Labor Legislation

Mexico's first comprehensive labor law was promulgated in 1931. The Federal Labor Act of 1970 authorizes the government to regulate all labor contracts and work conditions, including minimum wages, work hours, holidays, paid vacations, employment of women and minors, collective bargaining and strikes, occupational hazards, and profit sharing. The act sets the minimum employment age for children at fourteen years. Children fifteen years old can work but are restricted from certain jobs and have special legal protections and shorter working hours than adults. Medium and large commercial and manufacturing enterprises generally observe child labor laws strictly, although small shops and informal enterprises often do not. Although the law mandates a minimum wage, noncompliance ranges from 30 percent to 50 percent among employers of urban workers and reaches 80 percent in the countryside. Industrial safety laws often are loosely observed in practice, especially in the heavy industry and construction sectors.

The maximum legal workweek is forty-eight hours, and the maximum workday is eight hours. Industrial workers generally work the maximum number of hours per week, whereas office workers typically work forty or forty-four hours. The maximum workweek consists of either six eight-hour day shifts, six seven-hour night shifts, or six seven-and-a-half hour mixed shifts. Employers are required to pay double-time for overtime of up to three hours per day, and they cannot require workers to work overtime more than three times in one week. Each employee has the right to one free day per week, five paid holidays every year, and six to eight days of vacation during each full year of employment. Workers also are entitled to a share of their employers' annual profits.

Labor Unions

More than 90 percent of production workers in industrial enterprises employing more than twenty-five workers belong to labor unions. Relatively few craft or professional workers are organized. Because almost half of all Mexican workers were either unemployed or underemployed and therefore not organizable, Mexico ranked in the early 1990s as a country with a highly organized labor force. The plant or workplace union is the basic unit of Mexican labor organization. Local units (*secciones*) are federated either into national unions (*sindicatos*) or local, regional (intrastate), or state federations. Occasionally these federations join in nationwide confederations. The CTM is the country's largest labor organization. Its secretary general in 1994 was the long-serving Fidel Velásquez. The CTM women's affiliate is the Workers' Federation of Women's Organizations (Federación Obrera de Organizaciones Femininas). Other prominent union federations include the Regional Confederation of Mexican Workers (Confederación Regional de Obreros Mexicanos), the Revolutionary Confederation of Mexican Workers and Peasants (Confederación Revolucionaria de Obreros y Campesinos), the National Federation of Independent Unions (Federacíon Nacional de Sindicatos Independientes), and the Federation of Unions of Workers in the Service of the State (Federación de Sindicatos de Trabajadores al Servicio del Estado). Most of these federations are affiliated with the Congress of Labor (Congreso del Trabajo), which represents 85 percent of all unionized workers.

Most Mexican labor unions have strong ties to the PRI. In the 1930s and 1940s, organized labor became an integral component of the regime. The official unions facilitated Mexico's dramatic postwar economic growth by accepting labor wage increases that did not exceed productivity gains, thus eliminating a major source of inflation. The unions also discouraged industrial conflict, which helped to foster a receptive climate for foreign investment. Unions close to the PRI—especially the CTM—used both coercion and bribery to restrain wage demands. The absence of meaningful union democracy made it hard for the union rank and file to press independently for wage increases. During the 1970s, an increasing number of militant union movements broke away from the control of traditional union bosses, winning considerable autonomy over hiring and firing decisions, internal labor market operations, line speeds, and other working conditions. The government's efforts during the 1980s to promote greater productivity and efficiency in both the public and private sectors led to the reversal of many of these gains. Industrial reorganizations and downsizing resulted in massive layoffs and numerous labor concessions to management regarding work practices.

President Salinas further weakened the traditional unions during his incumbency. In some cases, he forced unions to negotiate at the plant level rather than nationwide. Shortly after taking office, he weakened the official oil workers' union by having its powerful and corrupt chief, Joaquín Hernández Galicia, arrested on corruption and murder charges. Salinas also undercut the 800,000-member official public schoolteachers' union, the National Union of Education Workers (Sindicato Nacional de Trabajadores de la Educación), by transferring authority over education from the central government to the states. By doing so, he restricted the union's power by forcing it to negotiate separate contracts with each state government. The central government's ongoing privatization program eliminated hundreds of thousands of union jobs, and its 1993 decision to link future wage increases to productivity gains denied the CTM the role of bargaining with the government on wage increases for all workers. Instead, the CTM was limited to advising individual union locals as they negotiated new contracts with plant operators.

Financial System

Banking System

Mexico has one of Latin America's most developed banking systems, consisting of a central bank and six types of banking institutions: public development banks, public credit institutions, private commercial banks, private investment banks, savings and loan associations, and mortgage banks. Other components of the financial system include securities market institutions, development trust funds, insurance companies, credit unions, factoring companies, mutual funds, and bonded warehouses.

The central bank, the Bank of Mexico (Banco de México), regulates the money supply and foreign exchange markets, sets reserve requirements for Mexican banks, and enforces credit controls. It serves as the fiscal agent of the federal government, the issuing bank for the new peso, and a discount house for private deposit banks. It supervises the private banking sector through the National Banking Commission, and it provides funds for government development programs. Legislation in 1984 required the Bank of Mexico to limit its lending to the government to an amount fixed at the beginning of each year. To ensure continued control of inflation, the central bank was made autonomous in April 1994.

Mexico has a number of other official banks for agriculture, foreign trade, cooperatives, public works, housing, transportation, and the sugar industry, among other specialized purposes. The most important such development institution is the Nafinsa, which provides financial support for Mexico's industrialization program. Nafinsa provides medium-term financing and equity capital for productive enterprises, promotes Mexican investment companies, oversees the stock market and the issuance of public securities, and serves as the legal depository

Bank of Mexico headquarters, Mexico City
Courtesy Arturo Salinas

of government securities. By 1993 Nafinsa had divested itself of some of its interests, but it remained under state ownership. Mexico's other most important state development bank is the National Bank of Public Works and Services (Banco Nacional de Obras y Servicios Públicos).

The private banking sector consists of more than 200 banks, which together have more than 2,500 branches. The proliferation of banking institutions resulted from regulations that prohibited any single bank from combining more than two banking functions. Mexico's two largest private banks are the Bank of Commerce (Banco de Comercio—Bancomer), comprising thirty-five affiliated banks with more than 500 branches, and the National Bank of Mexico (Banco Nacional de México—Banamex). Development banks, known as *financieras* and organized by commercial banks in association with major industrial enterprises, provide most of the private sector's development financing.

In an effort to stem massive capital flight, President López Portillo decreed the nationalization of the country's private banks in September 1982. In August 1983, the government authorized the return of up to 34 percent of the equity shares in these banks to the private sector, and it eliminated eleven banks and merged fifty others into twenty-nine national credit institutions in an effort to improve the banking system's efficiency. In March 1985, the government announced a further reduction in the number of commercial banks, from twenty-nine to eighteen.

The government took its first actual step toward reprivatizing the commercial banks in 1987, when it returned 34 percent of their capital to private investors in the form of nonvoting stock. In 1990 it allowed the sale to foreign investors of 34 percent of nonvoting shares in state-owned commercial banks. Reprivatization began in earnest in June 1991. By July 1992, all eighteen commercial banks had been sold to private owners, yielding more than US$12 billion. The privatization program dramatically increased the number of investors holding stock in Mexican commercial banks from just 8,000 on the eve of the 1982 nationalization to 80,000 in January 1993.

To improve the availability of credit, the government allowed the establishment of new domestic banks in Mexico in 1993, and the following year it allowed United States and Canadian banks to begin operating in Mexico. At the end of 1994, there were some fifty commercial banks in operation in Mexico, up from nineteen at the end of 1992. Mexico had forty-five brokerage houses, fifty-nine insurance companies, seventy-four leasing companies, sixty-five factoring houses, and forty-nine exchange houses.

Following the currency crisis of late 1994, the government was forced to raise interest rates sharply in order to protect the new peso by retaining existing short-term foreign investment and attracting new capital inflows. High interest rates during 1995 sharply increased the payments owed by Mexican individual and business borrowers, many of whom could not shoulder the increased burden. As a result, the share of nonperforming to performing loans held by Mexican banks rose significantly, creating a major crisis for the financial sector. During the first three quarters of 1995, the ratio of bad debts to the banking system's total loan portfolio increased from 8 percent to 17 percent. Partially as a result, the rate of growth in commercial bank financing of private-sector activities declined to just 1 percent during this period, compared with 19 percent a year earlier.

The interest rate increase also raised the cost to banks and the government of the various efforts to resolve the problem of banks' nonperforming loans. In late 1994, the government took over Banca Cremi, and a year later it was forced to take control of Inverlat. The government also agreed to assume problem loans held by Banamex and Bancomer.

In the wake of the financial sector crisis, the government introduced in mid-1995 a program for rescheduling bank loans using index-linked investment units. In September 1995, the government unveiled another emergency program of aid for bank debtors, which was to provide relief for 8 million bank debtors. By February 1996, 83 percent of eligible loans had been restructured under this program. By mid-1996, the cost of the government's various efforts to prevent a banking system collapse was estimated at 91 billion new pesos. The government held control of 25 percent of bank assets, despite having privatized the banking system only four years earlier. The government's efforts to restore the financial sector's stability were rewarded by a sharp drop in interest rates in late 1995 and early 1996.

Stock Exchange

Shortly after taking office, President de la Madrid allowed the establishment of private brokerage houses with wide latitude to conduct financial transactions in domestic capital markets. That action laid the foundation for the first significant stock market in Mexican history, the Mexican Stock Exchange (Bolsa Mexicana de Valores—BMV). Following several years of dynamic growth, the BMV's leading index fell sharply as a result of the October 1987 United States stock market crash. The BMV recovered slowly in 1988, then surged ahead from 1989 through 1991. By the early 1990s, the BMV had become one of the world's fastest growing stock exchanges. During 1991 the index of traded stocks rose 128 percent in new peso terms and 118 percent in United States dollar terms. Analysts attributed the stock market's buoyancy to increased confidence in the economy and to expectations of lower interest rates and approval of NAFTA.

In 1992, 199 companies were listed as trading on the stock exchange. A total of 11 trillion new pesos were traded, and the exchange had a total capitalization of US$139 billion and a price-to-earnings ratio of more than thirteen. The total value of stocks traded increased by US$191 billion between 1987 and 1993. Treasury bills, bank acceptances, and commercial paper were the most common instruments traded. At the end of

1993, Mexican investors held about 75 percent of the equities traded. Although the value of Mexican-owned stocks rose by about US$143 billion between 1987 and 1993, only 0.2 percent of all Mexicans had brokerage accounts at the end of 1992.

The BMV's market value stood at about US$200 billion at the end of 1993. Analysts attributed the rise partly to expectations of higher profits resulting from a 1 percentage point reduction in the corporate tax rate, lower energy prices for industrial users, and euphoria over the passage of NAFTA. Despite a setback induced by the January 1994 Zapatista rebellion in the state of Chiapas, the BMV continued its strong growth in early 1994. Beginning in March, however, the market was buffeted by a series of political shocks—including two high-profile political assassinations, revelations of high-level corruption in President Salinas's entourage, and continued unrest in Chiapas—that contributed to its high volatility throughout the rest of the year.

The stock market was further buffeted by the collapse of the new peso in early 1995, causing the stock index to fall to less than 1,500 points in February of that year. The main stock index gradually recovered to just under 3,000 points by the end of 1995 and had reached 3,300 by September 1996. Mexican stocks gained 24 percent in dollar terms during the first eight months of 1996. Mexico's stock market had a US$70 billion capitalization in September 1996, according to Morgan Stanley Capital International indices.

Exchange Rate

From December 1982 until November 1991, the Mexican peso had two rates of exchange against the United States dollar—the controlled or "official rate" and the "free rate." The controlled rate applied to income from most merchandise exports, to funds used by *maquiladora* (see Glossary) assembly industries for local expenditure other than fixed assets, to nearly all import payments, and to principal and interest payments and other credit expenses. The free rate applied to most other transactions, such as tourism and profit remittances.

In November 1991, the government eliminated all exchange controls, thereby unifying the various peso exchange rates. The regime freed the peso to float within a band, the bottom of which was fixed at 3,051 pesos per dollar and the top of which was devalued by 0.2 pesos per day. Renewed pressure on the peso forced the authorities in October 1992 to raise the average daily depreciation to 0.4 pesos per dollar, increasing the peso's annual rate of devaluation to less than 5 percent. The peso continued to appreciate in real terms, however, because Mexico's inflation rate exceeded that of the United States by some 8 percentage points. The government was reluctant to devalue the peso to the full extent of the inflation differential with the United States because it feared that a large devaluation would exacerbate domestic inflation and undermine public confidence in the stability of the government's macroeconomic policy. It preferred to compensate for the less competitive position of the peso by increasing productivity within Mexico. In January 1993, the government introduced the new peso, worth 1,000 of the old and divided into 100 centavos, to simplify foreign exchange.

Intense international demand for Mexican stocks and high-yielding two-year treasury certificates, known as *cetes*, kept the new peso at a stable level of 3.1 new pesos per dollar for most of 1993. Uncertainty about NAFTA's passage drove the new peso down to 3.3 per dollar in November 1993, although it soon rallied to 3.1 per dollar as interest rates rose and NAFTA's prospects of ratification appeared to improve. By late 1993, the capital influx had overvalued the new peso against the dollar by some 30 percent, leading some investors to avoid Mexican currency for fear that the new peso's overvaluation would compel the government to impose a large devaluation that would sharply reduce the dollar return of *cetes*. Some leading private-sector figures favored devaluation, expecting it to help reduce the trade deficit, Mexico's need for foreign capital, and thus interest rates.

Political considerations deterred the government from imposing a devaluation that would lower living standards, jeopardize investor confidence, and promote capital flight in the months prior to the August 1994 presidential and congressional elections. The slowdown of capital inflows exerted steady downward pressure on the new peso throughout the year. By late 1994, the government was drawing heavily on international reserves to prop up the new peso.

The almost complete disappearance of Mexico's reserves forced the new Zedillo government to bolster the currency's value. On December 20, 1994, the government raised the ceiling on the exchange rate band from 3.4 to 4.1 new pesos per dollar. However, continued pressure on the new peso, combined with mounting investor concern about the government's intentions, forced the administration two days later to let the currency float. The new peso ended 1994 at 5.3 per dollar. It continued to weaken during early 1995, as investors doubted the government's ability to repay the US$29 billion in short-term *tesebono* debt that would fall due during that year. In 1995 the exchange rate fell to 6.5 new pesos per dollar, and in January 1996 it stood at 7.4 new pesos per dollar.

The average monthly interest rate on twenty-eight-day *cetes* rose from 14 percent in 1995 to 49 percent in 1996. When the new peso came under heavy speculative pressure in late 1995, Mexico's monetary authorities reacted by raising interest rates sharply. Mindful of the need to restore investor confidence in Mexico's early economic recovery, the authorities allowed interest rates to fall at the end of 1995.

Agriculture

Although nearly half of Mexico's total land area is officially classified as agricultural, only 12 percent of the total area is cultivated. In the early 1990s, only some 24 million hectares of a possible 32 million hectares were under cultivation.

Extensive irrigation projects carried out in the 1940s and 1950s greatly expanded Mexico's cropland, especially in the north. The government created areas of intensive irrigated agriculture by constructing storage dams across the valleys of the Río Bravo del Norte (Rio Grande) and the rivers flowing down from the Sierra Madre Occidental, by controlling the lower Río Colorado (Colorado River), and by tapping subterranean aquifers.

These water-control projects allowed Mexico to expand rapidly its total land area under cultivation. Between 1950 and 1965, the total area of irrigated land in Mexico more than doubled, from 1.5 million hectares to 3.5 million hectares. Despite a slowdown in the development of irrigated land after 1965, the total irrigated area had expanded to more than 6 million hectares by 1987. In the early 1990s, 80 percent of Mexico's cultivated land required regular irrigation. Because of the high cost of irrigation, however, the government has emphasized expanding production on existing farmland rather than expanding the area under irrigation.

Agricultural practices in Mexico range from traditional techniques, such as the slash-and-burn cultivation of indigenous plants for family subsistence, to the use of advanced technology and marketing expertise in large-scale, capital-intensive export agriculture. Government extension programs have fostered the wider use of machinery, fertilizers, and soil conservation techniques. Although corn is grown on almost half of Mexico's cropland, the country became a net importer of grain during the 1970s.

Land Tenure

During the first decade of the twentieth century, peasants began to agitate for the return of communal and private lands seized by large-scale commercial producers since the 1870s. The desire to recover lost lands motivated many peasants to join the Revolution that began in 1910. On January 6, 1915, General Venustiano Carranza began the agrarian reform process by decreeing the immediate return to their original owners of all communal lands improperly seized since 1856. Carranza, who became president in 1917, also decreed that previously landless villages receive title to lands expropriated from private hacienda owners or to excess government land. These principles were later incorporated into Article 27 of the constitution of 1917.

The constitution established three different forms of land tenure in Mexico: private, public, and social. Social property was further subdivided into communal (in southern Mexico) and *ejido* (see Glossary) lands. Private lands were worked by owners, sharecroppers, and landless peasants; social lands were worked by *colonos* (settlers) or members of *ejidos*, known as *ejidatarios*. Although the constitution limited private holdings to 100 hectares, by the early 1990s Mexico had more than 40,000 farms of 101 hectares or larger and some 500 farms larger than 50,000 hectares. The constitution prescribed national sovereignty over all land, water, and subsoil mineral resources within national boundaries. It held private ownership of land to be a privilege rather than an absolute right, and it allowed the state to expropriate lands that it judged not to serve a useful social purpose (see Rural Society, ch. 2).

Article 27 and subsequent legislation established the *ejido*, or communal landholding, as the primary form of land tenure in Mexico (see Rural Society, ch. 2). Mexico's most extensive land redistribution took place during the presidency of Lázaro Cárdenas (1934–40). Cárdenas redistributed some 18 million hectares, twice as much as all his predecessors combined. By 1940 most of the country's arable land had been redistributed to peasant farmers, and approximately one-third of all Mexicans had benefited from the agrarian reform program (see Cárdenas and the Revolution Rekindled, 1934–40, ch. 1).

Agrarian reform sharply increased the proportion of Mexico's arable land held by *minifundistas* (smallholders). The share of total crop land held by large estates fell from 70 percent in 1923 to 29 percent by 1960, while that held by small farms of fewer than five hectares rose from 7 percent in 1930 to more than 33 percent by the 1980s. Between 1924 and 1984, the government expropriated and redistributed more than 77 million hectares of large-estate land, amounting to more than one-third of the national territory.

Declining agricultural production and mounting food imports moved President Salinas finally to address the root cause of the problem, the land tenure system. In 1991 Salinas announced a constitutional reform of the *ejido* and land distribution systems intended to overcome the low productivity resulting from the fragmentation of *ejido* farming units, of which 58 percent contained five hectares or fewer. A reform of land tenure rules in February 1992 gave Mexico's 3 million *ejidatarios* formal title to their land, enabling them to lease or sell their plots if a majority of members of their *ejido* agreed. No further land would be distributed, and joint ventures with private capital were legalized and encouraged. The reforms sought to reverse the trend toward smaller and less productive farming units and stimulate rural investment by allowing *ejidatarios* to use their holdings as collateral for raising capital. Implementation was hampered, however, by delays in conducting the necessary land surveys of *ejidos* prior to transfer of title, as well as by other factors.

Government Agricultural Policy

In the years after World War II, Mexico followed a relatively moderate import-substitution policy. By striking a relative balance between industrialization and growth of agricultural output, the government was able to maintain a steady rate of agricultural output and exports and to restrict its external borrowing requirements for many years.

In an effort to resolve Mexico's long-standing conflict between promoting agricultural production for export and for domestic consumption, the government followed a dual strategy between 1940 and 1965; it promoted large-scale commercial agriculture while redistributing land to the rural poor. Government policy favored large producers because export

Ejido, or communal farm, in Chiapas
Courtesy Mexican National Tourist Council

agriculture provided foreign exchange needed to finance industrialization. Extensive public investment in irrigation projects primarily benefited northern areas, where large private farms were concentrated, while rain-fed subsistence farming predominated in the central, southwest, and lower Gulf of Mexico regions. Larger farms produced for the lucrative export and agro-industrial markets, while traditional farmers grew the less profitable staple crops. The government sold basic food crops through its National Company for People's Sustenance (Compañía Nacional de Susistencias Populares—Conasupo) retail outlets, maintaining low purchase prices in order to maintain domestic political stability and justify low urban wages. Until the 1970s, Mexico was largely self-sufficient in basic staple crops.

Partly in response to changing market conditions, the production of staple commodities stagnated and then declined after 1965, while production of feed crops, livestock, and export products expanded. The agriculture sector's problems resulted partly from reduced public investment, as the government shifted resources to urban areas and failed to collect sufficient tax revenue. The government responded to declining staple output in 1971 with new agrarian reform legislation intended both to encourage production and to increase rural employment. The law authorized *ejidos* to move beyond basic crop cultivation into mining, forestry, fishing, agro-industry, commerce, and tourism.

Despite such measures, agricultural output failed to grow by more than 2 percent during the 1970s even though domestic food demand steadily increased as a result of population growth, growth in personal income resulting from the oil boom, and the government's provision of consumer subsidies for basic foods in order to improve the nutrition of the poor. The government raised producer prices and began to increase public spending in support of rain-fed production by small producers. Supply failed to keep pace with demand, however, and by 1980 Mexico had become a net food importer.

In 1980 President López Portillo signaled a new emphasis on production of staple crops for domestic consumption over export-oriented agriculture by establishing the Mexican Food System (Sistema Alimentario Mexicano—SAM) (see Rural Society, ch. 2). This program sought to build a strong productive base for Mexican agriculture in order to reduce the country's dependence on food imports from the United States and restore self-sufficiency in basic staples. Its main beneficiaries included landless peasants and small farmers, mainly in rain-fed areas. Additionally, the program provided subsidized "baskets" of basic foods to some 19 million undernourished Mexicans. Production priorities and goals were set for each region: wheat would be grown in the north, corn in the southeast highlands, rice in the Gulf of Mexico region, and beans throughout. Conasupo's retail outlets would distribute the food. As a result of the debt crisis, the de la Madrid administration abolished SAM in 1982.

In the late 1980s, the Mexican government began to emphasize reform and modernization of the agricultural sector (see table 8, Appendix). President Salinas moved to reduce credit costs, root out corruption and inefficiency in agricultural institutions, and raise guaranteed prices for certain products. The government's increased investment in agriculture and its 1991 reform of the land tenure system helped to attract substantial new private investment to agriculture between 1990 and 1994.

Building upon its 1991 land reform measures, the Salinas administration announced in October 1993 the details of a new agricultural income support plan, the Program of Direct Rural Support or Procampo. Starting with the 1994 growing season, Procampo replaced current price supports for basic grains with direct cash payments of 12 billion new pesos (US$3.5 billion), representing an 83 percent increase over supports paid in 1993. About 70 percent of Mexico's cultivated land was subsidized. The program was initially funded from the fiscal surplus that had accumulated since the late 1980s.

Procampo was intended to improve agricultural planning decisions and promote capitalization of the rural sector. It marked the abandonment of Mexico's traditional policy of agricultural self-sufficiency in favor of a more market-oriented system in which individual producers rather than government bureaucrats would make basic production decisions. The program also sought to offset producer subsidies in other countries, reduce domestic commodity prices to levels consistent with world market prices, encourage crop diversification and conservation, boost the competitiveness of the domestic food processing sector, and encourage the modernization of Mexico's agricultural production and marketing channels.

Initial beneficiaries of Procampo included 3.3 million growers of corn, beans, sorghum, wheat, rice, soybeans, and cotton, which together accounted for 70 percent of Mexico's arable land. Barley and safflower producers were added to the program in autumn 1994. The new subsidies were based on the size and productivity of land holdings and were paid to both commercial and subsistence growers. The government claimed that the new program would cover some 2.5 million farmers who had not benefited from the previous price support system. The 800,000 farmers who did benefit from that system received both the price subsidies and the new Procampo subsidy for an eighteen-month transitional period.

In addition to price supports, growers of program crops received in the spring and summer of 1994 a general support payment of 330 new pesos per hectare, which rose to 350 new pesos per hectare in the fall and winter of 1994. Starting in April 1995, the Procampo support payments were gradually reduced in order to bring food prices into line with market conditions. Meanwhile, direct payments under the program increased, although at a slower rate than the decline in price supports. Total support to agricultural producers fluctuated between a minimum level ensuring adequate income for subsistence farmers and a maximum level that would guarantee profitability for commercial producers.

Funding for Procampo was expected to remain steady for ten years, until 2003, and then decline over an additional five years until the program's termination in 2008. Procampo's fifteen-year duration was intended to give farmers adequate time to adopt new technologies, develop producer associations with other farmers or private agribusiness firms, and rationalize land use. To encourage alternative crop production, Procampo would continue to provide area support payments to growers who decided to change from program crops to alternative crops or livestock, forestry, ecological, and aquaculture activities throughout the fifteen-year phase-out period.

Procampo's reform of agricultural prices was expected to encourage a shift away from production of corn and dry beans and toward wheat, soybeans, and other products such as fruits and vegetables. Its impact was likely to be greatest in northwestern and northeastern Mexico and the Bajío region of west-central Mexico, where in the late 1980s and early 1990s many growers had switched from production of rice, cotton, sorghum, oilseeds, and wheat to the more profitable corn and dry beans. The direct payments were also expected to slow rural migration to cities and provide needed capital to impoverished subsistence farmers. Some government critics alleged that Pro-

Harvesting citrus by hand
Courtesy Inter-American
Development Bank

Packing strawberries for
shipment
Courtesy Inter-American
Development Bank

campo was intended to generate rural support for the ruling PRI.

During 1995 the government introduced a new agricultural support program, the Alliance for the Countryside (Alianza para el Campo), as an adjunct to its APRE program with labor and business. The alliance program presaged the devolution of responsibility for agricultural support to state governments, and it reinforced Procampo by expanding from ten to fifteen years the period during which direct cash subsidies would be paid to producers of various basic food crops. The new program also sought to improve credit flows to farmers from Banrural and other state agencies.

Grain Production

Corn is the staple food of most Mexicans and is grown on about one-third of the country's cultivated land. Central Mexico is the main area of corn cultivation. The size of the corn harvest varies significantly with weather conditions. In the 1992–93 growing season, about 8 million hectares were planted in corn, and 16.5 million tons were harvested, a slight increase over the previous year's output of 16.3 million tons. In 1994 the corn harvest amounted to 19.2 million tons.

Until the late 1980s, Mexico enjoyed corn self-sufficiency during years when the harvest was good. In 1990, however, demand exceeded supply by some 3.3 million tons and was met by imports. Thereafter, Mexico's import needs steadily fell to 1.9 million tons, at a cost of US$178 million in 1991 and 1.1 million tons in 1992. In 1993 Mexico imported just 400,000 tons of corn, almost all from the United States.

Wheat became more widely cultivated than it had been before, as bread replaced corn tortillas among Mexican consumers. There is little correlation between poor harvests of wheat and corn because each has different climatic requirements. The total area sown in wheat declined from 1.1 million hectares in 1986 to 714,000 hectares in 1993. Mexico's wheat output averaged slightly more than 4 million tons annually during the 1980s, fluctuating from 3.2 million tons in 1981, to 3.7 million tons in 1988, and to 4.4 million in 1989. Wheat production fell slightly from 3.7 million tons in 1992 to 3.6 million tons in 1994. For most of the 1980s, domestic wheat output was barely sufficient to satisfy internal demand. Mexico's wheat import requirement steadily grew from 260,000 tons (at a cost of US$46 million) in 1990 to 1.4 million tons in 1993.

Because the climatic requirements of sorghum are similar to those of corn, its output has undergone similar weather-based fluctuations. Mexico's sorghum production declined from 5.4 million tons in 1992 to 3.9 million tons in 1994. The land area sown in sorghum declined by more than half between 1989 and 1993, from 1.3 million hectares to 600,000 hectares. Mexico's import requirements for sorghum (almost all from the United States) consequently rose between the mid-1980s and early 1990s. Mexico imported 3.0 million tons of sorghum (at a cost of US$362 million) in both 1990 and 1991. Its import needs rose further to 5.0 million tons in 1992, then declined to 2.8 million tons in 1993.

The total land area sown in rice decreased from 192,000 hectares in 1986 to 50,000 hectares in 1993. Mexico's domestic output of milled rice fell steadily from 615,000 tons in 1986 to 312,000 tons in 1989. After rising slightly to 431,000 tons in 1990, rice output fell again to 246,000 tons in 1992, then recovered to 371,000 tons in 1993. Mexico imported substantial quantities of rice from the late 1980s through the early 1990s. In 1993 the country imported 350,000 tons of rice.

Beans are a basic staple food for most poor Mexicans. Mexico's domestic production of dry beans fell from 1.4 million tons in 1991 to 719,000 tons in 1992, then recovered to 1.5 million tons in 1994. In 1991 Mexico imported 125,000 tons of beans. The 1991 bean harvest covered 1.9 million hectares, the largest area sown in beans since the early 1980s.

Mexico's barley output fell steadily from 581,000 tons in 1991 to 325,000 tons in 1994. About 450,000 hectares were sown in barley in 1993. Annual production of oats remained steady throughout the early 1990s at 100,000 tons, and some 100,000 hectares were sown in oats each year.

Fresh Fruits and Vegetables

Fruit and vegetable production is concentrated in Mexico's irrigated northeast region and directed mainly to the United States winter market. In 1991 fruit and vegetable exports earned some US$935 million, 40 percent of Mexico's total export revenue. Fresh fruit and vegetables accounted for more of Mexico's agricultural export revenue than did coffee by the early 1990s. Processed food exports grew at an average annual rate of nearly 13 percent in the early 1990s.

Mexico produced 2.7 million tons of oranges in 1993, followed by apples (580,000 tons), table grapes (270,000 tons), tangerines (185,000 tons), grapefruit (118,000 tons), pears (32,000 tons), and raisins (13,000 tons). It also produced considerable quantities of bananas, mangoes, lemons, limes, watermelons, peaches, nectarines, plums, avocados, pineapples, and strawberries.

Mexico's output of fresh tomatoes declined from 1.7 million tons in 1990 to 1.4 million tons in 1993. During the same period,the total area harvested in tomatoes fell from 74,200 hectares to 58,500 hectares.

Other Crops

Between 1990 and 1993, Mexico's soybean output fluctuated with the amount of land sown. For the 1992–93 growing season, 313,000 hectares were sown in soybeans, producing 578,000 tons. Mexico's soybean imports generally exceeded domestic production in the late 1980s and early 1990s, in some years by a wide margin. The country imported 2.1 million tons of soybeans in 1992 and 1993, mainly from the United States. In 1991 Mexico imported US$348 million worth of soybeans.

Between 1989 and 1993, Mexico's cottonseed output fell from 617,000 tons to 75,000 tons, and its total area harvested fell from 255,000 hectares to 42,000 hectares. In 1993 Mexico imported 180,000 tons of cottonseed. Peanut output averaged 104,000 tons between 1988 and 1992; the 1993 harvest of 80,000 hectares produced 108,000 tons of peanuts. Mexico produced 195,000 tons of copra and 10,000 tons of sunflower seed in 1993. Mexico also produced green chilies, green beans, and green peas.

Mexico's raw sugar industry was reorganized and modernized during the early 1980s. As a result, raw sugar production reached 40 million tons in the 1985–86 growing season, exceeding the 1982–83 harvest by 50 percent. Sugar output declined thereafter because of trade liberalization, price controls, and high credit costs. Bad weather in late 1989 and uncertainties resulting from privatization of state sugar mills also depressed production. Sugar output fell from 42 million tons in 1988 to 35 million tons in 1990, then recovered slightly to 40 million tons (from 530,000 hectares of sugarcane) in 1993. Declining domestic production forced Mexico to import large amounts of sugar to satisfy domestic demand. In 1991 it imported 1.3 million tons of sugar. Mexico's sugar harvest in 1994–95 was 4.3 million tons, and the following year's harvest was expected to rise to 4.4 million tons.

Coffee was introduced into Mexico during the nineteenth century. Mexican coffee is mainly the arabica type, which grows particularly well in the Pacific coastal region of Soconusco, near the Guatemalan border. In the early 1990s, the southern state of Chiapas was Mexico's most important coffee-growing area, producing some 45 percent of the annual crop of 275,000 tons. More than 2 million Mexicans grew coffee, most barely subsisting. Seventy-five percent of Mexico's coffee growers worked plots of fewer than two hectares. These small cultivators produced about 30 percent of the country's annual harvest; larger and more efficient farms produced the rest.

During the 1980s, coffee became Mexico's most valuable export crop. In 1985 coffee growers produced 4.9 million sixty-kilogram bags, and coffee exports earned US$882 million at the unusually high world price of US$0.90 per kilogram. Thereafter output fluctuated between 5.6 million bags and 4.4 million bags. As international coffee prices rose further, the government in 1988 encouraged coffee growers, especially in Chiapas, to increase output and expand the area under cultivation. It tried to increase production by offering easy credit to coffee growers and by converting forested land into *ejidos* for cultivation by poor coffee growers.

International coffee prices fell 50 percent between 1989 and 1993. Lower prices combined with the elimination of coffee subsidies to reduce the income of coffee growers by an estimated 65 percent. Lower prices reduced Mexico's export income from coffee to about US$370 million by 1991. They also depressed coffee production, which fell from 5.2 million bags in 1992 to 4.1 million bags in 1993.

Although cotton had lost its traditional overwhelming dominance of the export market by the 1990s, it remained—along with fresh fruits and vegetables—a major cash crop of Mexico's irrigated lands. Cotton output fell from some 1.8 million bales in 1973 to 1.4 million bales in 1989, and to 800,000 bales in 1990. The cotton industry's poor performance in the late 1980s and early 1990s resulted mainly from bad weather, low world prices, and depressed domestic demand resulting from slow growth in Mexico's textile industry. In 1992 the total area sown in cotton was 42,000 hectares, down sharply from 250,000 hectares in 1991. Mexico's cotton output in 1993 was just over 30,000 tons, down from nearly 181,000 tons in 1992. Export revenue from cotton fell from US$113 million in 1988 to US$77 million in 1991. By 1995–96, Mexico's cotton crop had recovered to 193 million tons, and the 1996–97 harvest was forecast at 266 million tons.

Mexico's cocoa production declined from 57,000 tons in 1988 to 43,500 tons in 1993. The total area harvested in tobacco rose from 18,700 hectares in 1992 to 34,000 hectares in 1993, while the total farm sales weight of tobacco fell from 38,250 tons in 1992 to 29,800 tons in 1993. Tobacco exports earned some US$44 million in 1991.

Livestock

In the early 1990s, one-third of Mexican territory was officially designated as grazing land. These lands were located mainly in the north, where Herefords and other breeds were raised on huge cattle ranches for export to the United States, and in the southern, central, and southeastern states, where native beef cattle were raised. During the 1980s, higher domestic food demand encouraged more intensive raising of improved cattle breeds near urban areas for both dairy products and beef. In 1992 the Mexican government announced new measures to assist the meat industry, including deregulation of cattle growers and tighter controls on imported meat. The needs of the livestock industry also have encouraged more extensive cultivation of fodder crops on irrigated lands.

Mexico's livestock industry accounted for some 30 percent of the agriculture sector's annual growth, although animal husbandry contributed less than 1 percent to total GDP. The industry's weak performance in the late 1980s and early 1990s resulted from inadequate investment (which obstructed the adoption of intensive production techniques), high feed costs, low prices fixed by the government, poor weather conditions, epidemics of hoof-and-mouth disease, and fears of expropriation. Weak productivity has forced Mexico to become a net importer of beef.

Mexico's total cattle stock rose slightly from 30 million head in 1992 to 31 million head in 1993, and the total swine stock rose from 10 million head to 11 million head. The number of sheep held steady at 13 million head. Production of beef and veal was 1.7 million tons in 1993. Although lower domestic demand for red meat caused a 0.5 percent decline in total livestock output in 1991, beef exports held steady and earned US$358 million in 1991, compared with US$349 million in 1990. Output of lamb, mutton, and goat meat was 138,000 tons in 1993, and swine meat production was 870,000 tons.

16 of September Market, Mexico City
Courtesy Inter-American Development Bank

Mexico's total flock of chickens rose from 282 million in 1992 to 285 million in 1993, while poultry meat output fell from 936,000 tons in 1992 to 923,000 tons in 1993. Mexico's chicken flock produced 20 billion eggs in 1993.

Forestry

Some 9 percent of Mexico's territory consists of forest or woodland, 59 percent of which is in the tropics, 15 percent in the subtropical zone, and 26 percent in the temperate and cool zones. Forests cover some 49 million hectares, almost one-third of which are open to logging, mainly in the states of Chihuahua, Durango, and Michoacán. About 9 percent of forests are on state or federal lands, 19 percent on *ejido* lands, and 72 percent on municipal or private lands. Although the tropical trees of the southwest rain forests are the most numerous, the coniferous pine forests of the temperate and cool regions are commercially more important, providing pulpwood for processing in Mexico's paper mills. More than 65 percent of Mexico's forests consist of hardwoods, and the rest are softwoods. The major timber stands are mahogany, cedar, primavera (white mahogany), sapote, oak, copa (yaya), and pine.

In 1992 forestry provided 6 percent of total agricultural output but a negligible 1 percent of overall GDP. Lumber production declined by 5 percent in 1990 and by 3 percent in 1991. Lumber companies attributed lower output to more intense foreign competition as a result of trade liberalization. Exports of wood products were valued at US$14 million in 1988.

In the late 1980s, the forestry sector suffered from overexploitation, insufficient investment and planning, and the disappearance of certain species, as well as from forest fires and insect damage (see Environmental Conditions, ch. 2). Deforestation resulted in the loss of some 370,000 hectares annually as land was cleared for cultivation and livestock grazing.

Fishing

Mexico has some 11,500 kilometers of Pacific, Gulf of Mexico, and Caribbean coastline, and its inland waters cover more than 2.9 million hectares. The country's coastal fishing grounds offer a rich variety of fish and other seafood. The Pacific coast has thirty-one ports and produces nearly three-quarters of Mexico's total catch; the states of Sonora and Sinaloa alone account for 40 percent of the total catch. Mexico's Pacific fishing grounds produce mainly lobster, shrimp, croaker, albacore, skipjack, and anchovies, while its Gulf of Mexico and Caribbean waters produce shrimp, jewfish, croaker, snapper, mackerel, snook, and mullet. The Gulf of Mexico is an especially important source of shrimp. Certain species—such as shrimp, lobster, abalone, clam, croaker, grouper, and sea turtle—are reserved for the country's more than 284 fishing cooperatives, which together have more than 39,000 members. The state-owned Mexican Fisheries (Pesqueros Mexicanos) markets about 15 percent of the total catch. In 1989 the fishing subsector employed 288,000 people. The total fishing fleet grew from 48,000 boats in 1984 to 74,000 boats in 1989.

Until about 1970, the relative distance of urban markets from the coasts depressed commercial production of seafood. During the 1970s and 1980s, the government fostered the construction of new plants for freezing and processing fish. The national catch more than doubled after cooperatives were organized. The government's US$5 billion expansion program helped the fishing industry to increase output by more than 30 percent between 1985 and 1990. Despite these efforts, however, Mexico's catch accounted for less than 10 percent of the total catch taken from waters off Mexico's coasts by United States, Canadian, and Japanese boats.

In the late 1980s, Mexico's fishing output averaged a disappointing 1.4 million tons per year, equivalent to just 0.3 percent of GDP. Production increased from 1.1 million tons in 1983 to 1.6 million tons in 1990. Output fell slightly in 1991 as the United States and Europe embargoed Mexican tuna because of concerns about inadequate protection of dolphins. The Salinas administration's National Fishing Plan for 1990–94 promised higher public investment in the fishing industry, despite the government's stated intention to sell Mexican Fisheries to private owners.

In 1992 Mexico produced 251,500 tons of California pilchard (sardine), down from more than 600,000 tons in 1991. The yellowfin tuna catch rose from 116,400 tons in 1991 to 122,200 tons in 1992. Mexico produced 3,400 tons of Californian anchoveta in 1992, down from 12,100 tons in 1991. Output of marine shrimp and prawns declined from 70,600 tons in 1991 to 66,200 tons in 1992. Mexico exported two-thirds of its catch, especially frozen shrimp, prawns, and other shellfish from the Gulf of California and Bahía de Campeche, mainly to the United States. Export earnings amounted to US$389 million in 1989. In 1992 Mexico produced 77,000 tons of cichlids and 88,100 tons of other freshwater fish.

Industry

Manufacturing

In the early 1950s, the manufacturing sector eclipsed agriculture as the largest contributor to Mexico's overall GDP. Largely because of extensive import substitution, manufacturing output expanded rapidly from the 1950s through the 1970s to satisfy rising domestic demand. The value added by manufacturing rose from 20 percent of GDP in 1960 to 24 percent in 1970, and again to 25 percent by 1980. Manufacturing output grew at an annual average of 9 percent during the 1960s, and by a slightly lower annual rate of 7 percent in the 1970s.

This forty-year trend of manufacturing growth abruptly stopped and then reversed itself during the early 1980s. Sharp reductions in both exports and internal demand caused manufacturing output to fall by 10 percent between 1981 and 1983. After recovering briefly in 1985, manufacturing output fell again by 6 percent the following year. Production of consumer durables suffered especially, with the domestic electrical goods and consumer electronics goods sectors losing between 20 percent and 25 percent of their markets during the mid-1980s. Government industrial policies began to favor manufactured goods destined for the export market, in particular machinery and electrical equipment, automobiles and auto parts, basic chemicals, and food products (especially canned vegetables and fruit).

In the late 1980s, the manufacturing sector began to recover. In 1988 manufacturing output grew by a modest 4 percent. After expanding a robust 7 percent in 1989, manufacturing output steadily slowed; it grew by only 2 percent in 1992, as a result of weak export growth and falling domestic demand. After contracting by 2 percent in 1993, manufacturing output expanded by 4 percent in 1994. The most dynamic manufacturing subsectors in 1994 were metal products, machinery, and equipment (9 percent growth), followed by basic metals industries (9 percent growth). In 1994 the manufacturing sector accounted for 20 percent of the country's total GDP and employed about 20 percent of all Mexican workers.

Mexico's export base for manufactured goods is narrow, with three subsectors (vehicles, chemicals, and machinery and equipment) accounting for more than two-thirds of non-*maquiladora* foreign earnings. The value of Mexico's imports of manufactured goods rose sharply following trade liberalization, from US$11 billion in 1987 to US$48 billion in 1992 (US$62 billion including *maquiladora* imports). Increased foreign competition has seriously threatened many Mexican manufacturing enterprises, almost all of which are small and medium-sized companies employing fewer than 250 workers. In 1991 Mexico had 137,200 manufacturing enterprises, some 90 percent of which employed no more than twenty workers.

The principal industrial centers of Mexico include the Mexico City metropolitan area (which includes the Federal District), Monterrey, and Guadalajara. In the early 1990s, the capital area alone accounted for about half of the country's manufacturing activity, nearly half of all manufacturing employment, and almost one-third of all manufacturing enterprises. About one-third of formal-sector workers in the capital area were engaged in manufacturing. Manufacturers have been drawn to greater Mexico City because of its large and highly skilled work force, large consumer market, low distribution costs and proximity to government decision makers and the nation's communications system. In the early 1990s, the chemical, textile, and food processing industries accounted for half of all manufacturing activity in the Federal District, and metal fabrication accounted for another one-quarter. Heavy industry (including paper mills, electrical machinery plants, and basic chemical and cement enterprises) tended to locate in the suburbs of Mexico City, where planning and environmental restrictions were less rigorous.

By the late 1980s, more than two-thirds of all foreign investment in Mexico was concentrated in *maquiladora* zones near the United States border. In 1965 the government began to encourage the establishment of *maquiladora* plants in border areas to take advantage of a United States customs regulation that limited the duty on imported goods assembled abroad from United States components to the value added in the manufacturing process. The *maquiladora* zones offered foreign investors both proximity to the United States market and low labor costs. Most *maquiladora* plants were established in or near the twelve main cities along Mexico's northern border. Some of these enterprises had counterpart plants just across the United States border, while others drew components from the United States interior or from other countries for assembly in Mexico and then reexport.

The *maquiladora* sector grew nearly 30 percent annually between 1988 and 1993. By the latter year, more than 2,000 *maquiladora* businesses were in operation, employing 505,000 workers. These plants generated US$4.8 billion in value added during 1992. Their main activities included the assembly of automobiles, electrical goods, electronics, furniture, chemicals, and textiles. To increase their purchase of domestic materials, the Mexican government decided in December 1989 to exempt local sales to *maquiladoras* from the value-added tax and to let these enterprises sell up to half of their output on the domestic market. Nevertheless, almost all in-bond products have been exported to the United States.

In 1994 food processing, beverages, and tobacco products constituted the leading manufacturing sector in terms of value, accounting for about 26 percent of total manufacturing output and employing 17 percent of manufacturing workers. Food, beverage, and tobacco output expanded by an annual average of 3 percent between 1990 and 1994, largely as a result of export growth. In 1994 it expanded by less than 1 percent. In the early 1980s, well over 50 percent of Mexico's productive units were involved in food processing, and Mexico's beer industry was the world's eighth largest.

Metal products, machinery, and transportation equipment accounted for 24 percent of manufacturing GNP in 1994. The automobile subsector was among the most dynamic manufacturing sectors in the early 1990s and led among manufacturing exporters. Mexico's automobile manufacturers were led by Volkswagen, General Motors (GM), Ford, Nissan, and Chrysler. Ford expanded production by 33 percent during 1991, Chrysler by 17 percent, and GM by 10 percent. Volkswagen controlled 25 to 30 percent of the domestic automobile market, and Nissan another 15 to 20 percent. Mexican automobile exports earned US$6.1 billion in 1992, not counting *maquiladora* production, which earned an additional US$1.3 billion. Export revenue from passenger vehicle sales rose by 21 percent in 1993 and by 22 percent in 1994, while domestic sales fell by some 14 percent in 1993 and rose by less than 1 percent in 1994.

In 1983 the government encouraged the automobile industry to shift from import substitution to export production. It lowered national content requirements for exporters and required assemblers to balance imports of auto parts with an equivalent value of automobile exports. In 1990 the government eliminated restrictions on the number of production lines that automobile producers could maintain and allowed producers to import finished automobiles (although they were required to earn US$2.50 in automobile exports for every US$1 spent on imports).

In the early 1980s, automobile exports increased as domestic demand fell. Export growth leveled off in the early 1990s as the domestic market recovered. Growth of total vehicle output slowed from 21 percent in 1991 to 9 percent in 1992. In 1994 vehicle production totaled more than 1 million units, of which 850,000 were cars. Production fell by 16 percent between January and November 1995. During those months, exports rose by 37 percent to 700,000 units, while domestic sales fell by 70 percent, to 140,000 units.

Textiles, clothing, and footwear together accounted for 9 percent of manufacturing output in 1994 and employed about 7 percent of all manufacturing workers. Textile and clothing production stagnated throughout the 1980s because of low domestic demand, high labor costs, antiquated and inefficient technology, more competitive export markets (especially in

*Mercedes truck assembly
plant, Mexico City
Courtesy Dennis Hanratty*

Asia), and heavy import competition resulting from trade liberalization. In the early 1990s, the textile industry operated at just 60 percent of capacity. Import competition caused footwear and leather output to decline 4 percent annually between 1982 and 1989. In 1990 domestic footwear enterprises produced almost 200,000 pairs of shoes per week. In 1992 footwear and leather goods accounted for 4 percent of manufacturing GDP.

Non-*maquiladora* export earnings for textile, clothing, and footwear sales rose from US$499 million in 1990 to US$890 million in 1992. Imports also rose sharply to almost US$2 billion in 1992. The sector showed signs of strong recovery in late 1993, following its forced modernization.

The chemicals sector (including oil products, rubber, and plastics) accounted for 18 percent of manufacturing GDP in 1994. Its output increased by 5 percent during 1994. In 1990 this sector employed 130,000 workers. Although the chemical industry was the most important foreign-exchange earner in the manufacturing sector, its output fell far short of domestic demand. Exports of non-*maquiladora* chemicals and petrochemicals earned US$2.5 billion in 1992, but the country imported US$5.8 billion worth of chemicals and petrochemicals. The imbalance resulted partly from domestic price controls, inadequate patent protection, and high research and development costs. Chemicals and petrochemicals accounted for 72 percent of total non-*maquiladora* export revenues in 1992. The chemical industry slumped in early 1993, as sales fell by 10 percent, operating profits by 61 percent, and net profits by 59 percent.

Petrochemicals accounted for less than 2 percent of overall GDP in 1992. The state oil monopoly, Mexican Petroleum (Petróleos Mexicanos—Pemex), dominated the country's more than 200 petrochemical companies, which together operated more than 700 plants. The petrochemical subsector enjoyed robust annual growth of 7 percent between 1982 and 1988, but output slowed thereafter. Pemex produced 18.5 million tons of petrochemicals in 1993, down from 19 million tons in 1992. In 1992 the Salinas government reduced the number of basic petrochemicals reserved for Pemex to just eight and lifted restrictions on foreign investment in "secondary" petrochemicals to improve the oil company's cost-effectiveness, raise the industry's productivity, and attract new private investment.

Although Mexico's pharmaceutical industry consisted of some 450 companies, the largest ten enterprises accounted for 30 percent of all sales in 1993. In the early 1990s, some fifty-six firms controlled three-quarters of pharmaceutical production. Nonmetallic minerals (excluding oil) accounted for 7 percent of manufacturing gross national product (GNP—see Glossary) in 1994. The subsector concentrated on production of cement, glass, pottery, china, and earthenware. Total cement output in 1993 was 27 million tons. Cement exports fell from 4.5 million tons in 1988 to 1.4 million tons in 1992 because of higher domestic demand and United States antidumping sanctions. A new cement plant came into operation in Coahuila in early 1993, and the expansion of two other plants in Hidalgo was completed.

Mexico's largest cement producer is the privately owned Mexican Cement (Cementos Mexicanos—Cemex). By 1994 Cemex had become the world's fourth largest cement company, with annual earnings of US$3 billion. In an effort to establish itself as a major multinational corporation, Cemex expanded its operations during the early 1990s into the United States and twenty-five countries in Europe, Asia, and Latin America.

The basic metals subsector (dominated by iron and steel) accounted for 6 percent of manufacturing GNP in 1994. Mexico's iron and steel industry is one of the oldest in Latin America, comprising ten large steel producers and many smaller firms. The industry is centered in Monterrey, where the country's first steel mills opened in 1903. Steel plants in Monterrey (privatized in 1986) and nearby Monclova accounted for about half of Mexico's total steel output in the early 1990s. Most of the rest came from the government's Lázaro Cárdenas-Las Truchas Steel Plant (Sicartsa) and Altos Hornos de México (Ahmsa) steel mills, which were sold to private investors in 1991.

Export revenue from steel and steel products fell from US$1.03 billion in 1991 to US$868 million in 1992. Spurred by rising demand from the automobile industry, crude steel output rose 6 percent to 9 million tons in 1993. During the first half of 1993, output rose 10 percent over the same period in 1992, to 4 million tons. Production of semifinished steel rose 86 percent, reaching 573,000 tons, and rolled steel production expanded 5 percent to more than 2.6 million tons. Pipe production fell 13 percent to 174,400 tons. In 1993 Mexico was Latin America's second largest steel producer after Brazil, accounting for some 20 percent of Latin America's total steel production of 43 million tons.

Paper, printing, and publishing contributed about 5 percent of manufacturing output in 1994. Mexico produced almost 3 million tons of paper and 772,000 tons of cellulose in 1990. The country had some 760 publishing enterprises in 1990, 48 percent of which published books, 44 percent periodicals, and 8 percent both. These companies produced a total of 142 million books and 693 million periodicals. Trade liberalization hurt the domestic publishing industry in 1992, as imports rose to US$1.6 billion from US$1.3 billion in 1991. Exports of Mexican publications declined in value from US$232 million in 1991 to US$217 million in 1992.

Finally, wood products contributed 3 percent of manufacturing GDP in 1994. Although output of wood products fell in the late 1980s because of high investment costs and other adverse conditions in the primary forestry industry, it began to recover in 1993. Output of wood products increased by 2 percent during 1994.

Construction

The construction sector accounted for slightly more than 5 percent of GDP in 1994. In 1991 Mexico had about 18,000 registered construction companies that employed almost 1 million workers. In that year, heavy construction accounted for 44 percent of all construction, residential building 35 percent, and industrial construction 14 percent. Government efforts to promote private-sector investment in physical infrastructure projects (especially road building and new rental housing) helped to increase construction growth. Construction growth slowed from 7 percent in 1990 to 2 percent in 1991. It accelerated to 8 percent in 1992, but slowed again to 3 percent in 1993, partially as a result of continuing high interest rates, which discouraged private investment. In 1993 transport projects accounted for 29 percent of the value of production in the formal construction sector, the installation of water supplies accounted for 11 percent, and electricity and communications projects accounted for 9 percent.

Energy and Mining

Petroleum

Although explorers drilled Mexico's first petroleum well in 1869, oil was not discovered until after the turn of the twentieth century. Commercial production of crude oil began in 1901. By 1910 prospectors had begun to define the Panuco-Ebano and Faja de Oro fields located near the central Gulf of Mexico coast town of Tuxpán, and systematic explorations by foreign companies came to supersede the uncoordinated efforts of speculative prospectors. Mexico began to export oil in 1911.

Article 27 of the constitution of 1917 gives the Mexican government a permanent and inalienable right to all subsoil resources. The government's efforts to assert this right produced a lengthy dispute with foreign oil companies that was not resolved until the companies were nationalized in the late 1930s. The 1923 Bucarelli Agreements committed the United States and Mexico to regard titles held by foreign oil companies as concessions by the Mexican government rather than as outright ownership claims. In 1925 President Plutarco Elías Calles decreed that foreign oil companies must register their titles in Mexico and limited their concessions to a period of fifty years.

Despite disruption caused by the Revolution, Mexico's oil production peaked in 1921 at 193 million barrels (some 25 percent of world production), largely as a result of increased international demand generated by World War I. During much of the 1920s, Mexico was second only to the United States in petroleum output and led the world in oil exports. By the early 1930s, however, output had fallen to just 20 percent of its 1921 level as a consequence of worldwide economic depression, the lack of new oil discoveries, increased taxation, political instability, and Venezuela's emergence as a more attractive source of petroleum. Production began to recover with the 1932 discovery of the Poza Rica field near Veracruz, which became Mexico's main source of petroleum until the late 1950s.

In 1938 President Lázaro Cárdenas nationalized the petroleum industry, giving the Mexican government a monopoly in the exploration, production, refining, and distribution of oil and natural gas, and in the manufacture and sale of basic petrochemicals. Although Cárdenas offered compensation, United States oil companies pressured the United States government to embargo all imports from Mexico in order to discourage similar nationalizations in other countries. The boycott was in effect briefly, but the United States government soon pressured the oil companies to come to terms with Mexico as a result of President Franklin D. Roosevelt's Good Neighbor Policy and United States security needs arising from World War II. In 1943 Mexico and the oil companies reached a final settlement under which the companies received US$24 million (a fraction of the book value of the expropriated facilities) as compensation. Nevertheless, the oil nationalization deprived Mexico of foreign capital and expertise for some twenty years.

Mexico's oil output expanded at an average annual rate of 6 percent between 1938 and 1971. Production increased from 44 million barrels in 1938 to 78 million barrels in 1951. Domestic demand progressively exceeded output, and in 1957 Mexico became a net importer of petroleum products. Production rose to 177 million barrels by 1971 with the exploitation of new oil fields in the isthmus of Tehuantepec and natural gas reserves near the northeastern border city of Reynosa, but the gap between domestic demand and production continued to widen.

Extensive oil discoveries in the 1970s increased Mexico's domestic output and export revenues. In 1972 explorers discovered deep oil wells in the states of Chiapas and Campeche that showed huge reservoirs of petroleum extending for 200 kilometers northeast below the Bahía de Campeche, and possibly in the opposite direction toward Guatemala. Almost every drilling operation conducted after 1972 struck oil. In 1973 oil production surpassed the peak of 190 million barrels achieved in the early 1920s. In 1974 Pemex announced additional petroleum discoveries in Veracruz, Baja California Norte, Chiapas, and Tabasco.

By 1975 Mexico's oil output once again exceeded internal demand, providing a margin for export. President López Portillo announced in 1976 that Mexico's proven hydrocarbon reserves had risen to 11 billion barrels. They rose further to 72.5 billion barrels by 1983. López Portillo decided to increase domestic production and use the value of Mexico's petroleum reserves as collateral for massive international loans, most of which went to Pemex. Between 1977 and 1980, the oil company received US$12.6 billion in international credit, representing 37 percent of Mexico's total foreign debt. It used the money to construct and operate offshore drilling platforms, build onshore processing facilities, enlarge its refineries, engage in further exploration, prove fresh reserves, and purchase capital goods and technical expertise from abroad. These investments helped to increase petroleum output from 400 million barrels in 1977 to 1.1 billion barrels by 1982. Between 1983 and 1991, Mexico's petroleum exports by volume remained roughly constant at 1.4 million barrels per day (bpd), while total production increased from 2.7 million bpd to 3.1 million bpd.

The oil sector's share of total export revenue fell sharply from 61 percent in 1985 to 38 percent in 1990 because of higher domestic demand and lower total output. The volume of exports fell from 1.4 million bpd in 1987 to 1.3 million bpd in 1990. Oil prices rose briefly to more than US$35 per barrel in 1990 as a result of loss of supplies from Iraq and Kuwait, and Mexico's oil export revenues rose significantly to US$10 billion before falling back some 15 percent in 1991. The volume of oil exports rose slightly to 1.4 million bpd in 1991, then held steady along with production in 1992, as the oil price fell to below US$15 per barrel.

By early 1993, both crude oil production and exports had begun to decline. The drop in exports resulted from both increased domestic demand and lower total production. For all of 1993, Mexico's oil exports averaged 1.3 million bpd, 2 percent less than in 1992. Exports fell even more sharply in terms of value—to US$7 billion—because world oil prices fell steadily during much of 1992 and 1993. In 1994 Mexico's revenue from oil exports was more than US$7 billion.

In 1995 the oil sector generated slightly more than 10 percent of Mexico's export income (down from almost 80 percent in 1982). The United States bought 54 percent of Mexico's crude oil exports in 1991, Western Europe bought 25 percent, and Japan bought 11 percent. In mid-1993, heavy Maya crude accounted for 67 percent of total oil exports, the lighter Isthmus crude accounted for 20 percent, and the high-quality Olmeca type accounted for 13 percent.

In 1995 Mexico was the world's sixth-largest producer of crude oil. In the Western Hemisphere, only the United States produced more oil than Mexico. Directly behind Mexico was Venezuela, which in 1992 produced an amount equal to 89 percent of Mexico's crude oil output. The oil sector's share of overall GDP rose slightly from 5 percent in 1985 to more than 6 percent by 1992. In 1993 petroleum provided nearly 30 percent of central government revenues. Oil output rose steadily from 2.5 million bpd in 1989 to 2.7 million bpd in 1991, partly in response to the Persian Gulf crisis. Production held steady in 1992, then began to decline in early 1993. Mexico consumed 61 million tons of oil equivalent in 1992. Its total petroleum consumption amounted to 1.8 million bpd in 1992.

For the first ten months of 1995, total mineral production (including oil) contracted by a modest 1 percent. For all of 1995, oil production fell to an average of 2.6 million bpd from 2.7 million bpd in 1994. However, oil output in the first quarter of 1996 increased by 6 percent over the first quarter of 1995 to an average of 2.8 million bpd.

In 1993 Pemex operated seven oil refineries with a total capacity of more than 1.5 million bpd, the eleventh largest in the world. Mexico's average annual oil refining capacity grew steadily from 63 million tons in 1983 to 84 million tons in 1990. The country's largest oil refineries in terms of refining capacity were those at Salina Cruz (330,000 bpd) and at Tula (320,000 bpd) in the state of Hidalgo. Other refineries were located at Cadereyta (235,0900 bpd refining capacity), Salamanca (235,000 bpd), Minatitlán (200,000 bpd), Ciudad Madero (195,000 bpd), and Reynosa (9,000 bpd).

By the early 1990s, some 40 percent of Mexico's crude petroleum output was refined domestically. The government invested heavily to increase the capacity of existing refineries and construct new ones in order to retain within Mexico the maximum possible amount of value added in processing crude petroleum. In the early 1990s, financial difficulties prevented Pemex from expanding refinery capacity along with demand, forcing Mexico to consume more of its oil output internally and also to import oil. Petroleum imports rose from 2 billion liters in 1991 to almost 5 billion liters in 1992. Fuel oil imports rose from less than 3 million tons in 1991 to almost 4 million tons in 1992.

During the 1980s, Pemex constructed national pipeline distribution systems for crude and refined petroleum products and for natural gas. In 1989 an oil pipeline across the Tehuantepec isthmus opened to carry 550,000 bpd of Maya crude petroleum to Salina Cruz on the Pacific for export to the Far East. Two enormous petrochemical complexes were being built at Pajaritos and La Cangrejera in Veracruz to supply raw materials for manufacturing fertilizers, detergents, acrylic resins, polyester fibers, emulsifying agents, and other petroleum products.

In 1993 Mexico had the world's eighth largest crude petroleum reserves, amounting to some 5 percent of the world's total. Its proven crude oil reserves amounted to some 51 billion barrels in 1993, and it had potential reserves of some 250 billion barrels. The Gulf of Mexico contains approximately 56 percent of Mexico's proven reserves; 24 percent are located in the Chicontepec region, 15 percent are located in Tabasco and Chiapas, and the remainder are elsewhere. Mexico's reserves are sufficient to guarantee current production levels for fifty years.

Since the nationalization of the oil industry in 1938, the state-owned Pemex has monopolized the production and marketing of hydrocarbons. For decades the government tolerated Pemex's waste and inefficiency because the company produced nearly all public revenues. Problems mounted, however, as a result of Pemex's poor administration, low productivity, overstaffing, and corruption. By the late 1980s, Mexico's economic recovery had come to depend heavily on reform of the state oil sector.

After becoming president, Salinas moved swiftly to modernize and reorganize the oil industry. He began by breaking the power of the oil workers' union, which had contributed to Pemex's overall inefficiency by forcing the hiring of tens of thousands of unnecessary workers. In January 1989, Salinas had the union's notoriously corrupt chief, Joaquín Hernandez

*Pemex refinery on Gulf of Mexico
Courtesy Embassy of Mexico,
Washington*

*Pemex headquarters, Mexico City
Courtesy Arturo Salinas*

Galicia (nicknamed La Quina), arrested on weapons and murder charges. He was subsequently convicted and received a thirty-five-year jail sentence. Salinas then ordered Pemex to monitor and account for its internal finances. To reduce expenses, the company began massive employee layoffs, slashing its workforce by 94,000 (some 44 percent of the total payroll) by mid-1993.

In April 1992, natural gas from a Pemex pipeline leaked into the Guadalajara sewer system, triggering an explosion that killed more than 200 people. The tragedy underscored Pemex's bureaucratic unwieldiness and lack of public accountability. Following the explosion, Salinas accelerated the organizational restructuring of Pemex. The restructuring resulted in the company's division in 1992 into four subsidiaries: Pemex-Exploration and Production (E&P), Pemex-Refining, Pemex-Gas and Basic Petrochemicals, and Pemex-Petrochemicals. Each unit became a semiautonomous profit center, directing its own budget, planning, personnel, and other functions. The subsidiaries deal with each other on the basis of formal contracts and market-based transfer prices. The governing board of each subsidiary is composed entirely of public-sector officials.

Pemex's new focus on profitability and cost-cutting allowed the company to save US$50 million in 1990, US$70 million in 1991, and US$100 million in 1992. Moreover, Pemex reduced its total labor force from 210,000 workers in 1989 to 116,000 in 1992, with more dismissals expected later. A new collective contract permitted the company to seek the lowest bidder for maintenance, transport, slop oil disposal, and other work formerly reserved for the official oil workers' union. Pemex's new focus on efficiency and productivity also cleared the way for previously unthinkable foreign involvement in Mexico's oil sector. Several United States oil exploration companies received permission to drill under contract in Mexico, and foreign partnerships were authorized.

In August 1993, it became known that the government was considering proposals to allow private companies to buy, sell, and distribute imported gasoline, natural gas, and petrochemicals, and to invest in new pipelines. Although the government reiterated in 1992 its longstanding pledge not to denationalize the oil industry, some observers viewed the reorganization of Pemex as a move to improve the company's efficiency and profitability as a prelude to privatization. Denationalization would require amending the constitution of 1917, which mandated state ownership and exploitation of hydrocarbons.

During 1995 Pemex proceeded with its plans to divest its secondary petrochemicals plants and allow private investment in the storage, transportation, and distribution of natural gas. In late 1995, Pemex began to divest itself of sixty-one petrochemical plants.

In early 1996, the government unveiled its Program for the Development and Restructuring of the Energy Sector. The program estimates the minimum investment required by the petroleum sector by the year 2000 to be 250 billion new pesos (at 1995 prices). The private sector is expected to provide 49 billion new pesos of this amount. The plan is intended to increase Mexico's petroleum exports, improve its competitiveness in the international energy market, and contribute to more balanced regional development (see table 9, Appendix).

Electricity

Mexico generated a total 127 billion kilowatt-hours (kWh) of electricity in 1991. Of this total, thermal (coal-, oil-, or gas-fired) plants generated 94 billion kWh (74 percent), hydroelectric plants generated 24 billion kWh (19 percent), nuclear plants generated 4 billion kWh (3 percent), and geothermal and other plants generated 5 billion kWh (4 percent). Mexico had more than 27,000 megawatts of electricity generating capacity in 1992, roughly the level of domestic demand. Net domestic electricity consumption in 1992 was 118 billion kWh, including 24 billion kWh of hydroelectric power. In 1992 Mexico's thermal plants generated 95 billion kWh of electricity, hydroelectric plants generated 25 billion kWh, and nuclear plants generated 4 billion kWh.

Interest revived in nuclear power generation during the late 1980s. In 1989 the much-delayed 1,300-megawatt Laguna Verde nuclear reactor began partial operation (654 megawatts), and in 1990 it produced 2.9 million megawatt-hours of electricity. A second reactor with similar capacity became operational at Laguna Verde in 1994.

Mexico's electric power companies were nationalized during the 1960s, and the public sector monopolized electricity generation. In 1992 the state-run Federal Electricity Commission (Comisión Federal de Electricidad—CFE) accounted for about 90 percent of gross electricity generation. In May 1991, the government enacted legal reforms allowing private companies to generate electricity either for their own consumption or for sale to the CFE or small-scale consumers in rural or remote area-megawatt power plants by 2005.

Nonfuel Mining

In 1994 the mining sector accounted for some 2 percent of GDP and 1 percent of export earnings. It employed 230,000 people in 1988. Although Mexico had approximately 2,000 mining companies in 1989, the industry was highly concentrated, with four companies producing two-thirds of the country's total mineral output. These companies were the Mexico Industrial Mining Group, Inc. (Grupo Industrial Minera México, Sociedad Anónima—IMMSA), Sanluís Industrial Corporation (Corporación Industrial Sanluís), Frisco Enterprises (Empresas Frisco), and Peñoles Industries (Industrias Peñoles).

During the 1960s, the government progressively Mexicanized the mining industry, most of which had previously been foreign-owned. A new mining law in 1961 required majority Mexican ownership and management of all mining companies. Within ten years, most companies had been Mexicanized. The government granted new concessions only to Mexican-owned enterprises and encouraged the growth of small and medium-sized operations.

The state vastly expanded its involvement in mining during the 1970s. The 1975 mining law restricted foreign companies to 34 percent participation in mining concessions on national reserves and in exploitation of certain minerals such as coal and iron ore. The government monopolized exploitation of oil and gas, phosphate rock, potassium, sulfur, and uranium. By 1980 it owned more than 40 percent of shareholders' equity in all mining activity. In 1983 mines owned by or affiliated with the state mining development commission were responsible for 87 percent of copper output, 76 percent of sulfur output, 28 percent of gold and silver, 27 percent of iron ore, 25 percent of coal, 18 percent of lead, and 10 percent of zinc.

The mining sector grew at an annual average of only 0.4 percent between 1983 and 1989. This stagnation resulted from outmoded mining technology, heavy government regulation, insufficient investment, and low world prices. The government responded in 1982 with a ten-year program to sell most of the state's forty-two mining properties. By early 1987, 46 percent of total mineral output was privately produced, and 42 percent

Strip mining in northern Mexico
Courtesy Inter-American Development Bank

came from state companies. In 1988 the government sold the Mexican Copper Company (Compañía Mexicana de Cobre) to private buyers, and in 1990 it privatized the country's largest open-pit copper mine, that of the Cananea Mining Company (Compañía Minera de Cananea), now called Mexicana Compañía de Cananea, despite a strike by the company's 3,800 workers to block the sale.

In the early 1990s, silver was the most valuable subsector in Mexico's mining industry (see table 10, Appendix). The country regained its historical position as the world's leading producer of silver following the opening in 1983 of the world's largest silver mine at Real de Ángeles in the state of Zacatecas, which in 1990 produced 290,000 kilograms of silver. Mexico produced 2,300 tons of silver in 1994, representing more than 16 percent of world silver output. Most of Mexico's silver output came from the states of Zacatecas (39 percent), Durango (15 percent), Chihuahua (14 percent), Guanajuato (7 percent), Sonora (6 percent), and Hidalgo (5 percent).

Mexico's gold output stood at 14,400 kilograms in 1994. The Guanajuato area accounted for almost one-third of Mexico's annual gold production. This region's output decreased by about 1,000 kilograms between 1991 and 1992, slightly offsetting the increase of 900 kilograms of gold production from Sonora. Other important gold-producing areas were the San Dimas district of Durango and several small mines in Sinaloa. In 1992 Mexican and foreign mining companies showed increased interest in exploring for gold in the states of Sonora, Baja California Norte, Chihuahua, Durango, and Sinaloa. Some foreign companies established wholly foreign-owned exploration enterprises by means of investment trusts.

In the early 1990s, Mexico was the world's seventh largest producer of copper. Copper ore output fluctuated in the late 1980s and early 1990s, averaging 282,500 tons per year between 1987 and 1991. Output fell slightly to 266,200 tons in 1992. Production of refined copper rose steadily from 140,800 tons in 1988 to 302,600 tons in 1994. Silver prices fell and copper prices rose in the late 1980s and early 1990s, increasing the value of Mexico's copper output over that of silver for the first time in several decades. Mexico's copper output was valued at US$663 million in 1992.

Mexico's western mining zone, which runs from the states of Baja California Norte, Sonora, Sinaloa, and western Chihuahua southward to Chiapas, is the country's main source of copper. The bulk of Mexico's 1992 copper output came from Sonora, where the country's three largest mines—La Caridad, Cananea, and María—are located. The Mexican Copper Company was Mexico's leading copper producer with 52 percent of total output, followed by the Mexican Compañía de Cananea with 23 percent.

In 1994 Mexico produced 163,700 tons of lead and 356,900 tons of zinc. Mexico's production of zinc constituted 4 percent of world output in 1992, and zinc ranked second among domestically mined minerals in terms of value, after copper but ahead of silver. Mine production of lead amounted to 5 percent of world lead output in 1992, and that mineral ranked fifth among domestically mined minerals in terms of value, ahead of gold. The most important producers of zinc and lead were Frisco Enterprises and Peñoles Industries, which together produced more than 80 percent of Mexico's total supply of these minerals. More than 60 percent of Mexico's lead and zinc output came from the state of Chihuahua, while much of the remainder came from the states of Zacatecas, Hidalgo, and San Luis Potosí.

In 1992 Mexico produced some 5.5 million tons of coal, and it had an estimated 1.7 billion tons of coal reserves. Further development, however, was not seen as commercially viable. The country consumed some 5.8 million tons of coal in 1992. In 1990 Mexico produced iron ore with a metal content of 5.3 million tons, most of it from Cerro el Mercado, Las Truchas, and Peña Colorado, at the mouth of the Río Balsas, on the Pacific coast. Most of Mexico's coal came from the Sabinas basin, about 100 kilometers north of Monterrey.

Transportation and Telecommunications

Roads

Mexico has one of the most extensive highway networks in Latin America, linking nearly all areas of the national territory. In 1994 Mexico had 242,000 kilometers of roads, of which 85,000 kilometers were paved (including more than 3,100 kilometers of expressways), 40,000 kilometers were gravel or cobblestone, 62,000 kilometers were improved earth, and 55,000 kilometers were unimproved dirt roads. The highway system includes federal roads, state roads (for which the federal government provides 50 percent of construction costs), and local roads (for which the federal government contributes 30 percent of costs) (see fig. 10).

The most heavily traveled highway routes form a triangle linking Mexico City with the large population and industrial centers of Guadalajara and Monterrey, as well as with the main port city of Veracruz. The Inter-American Highway begins at the northern border city of Nuevo Laredo and runs through Monterrey and Mexico City, where it turns southeastward toward Oaxaca and then directly eastward into Chiapas and northwestern Guatemala. Mexico has three major federal highways: the Baja California Dorsal Highway, which runs the length of the peninsula from Tijuana to Cabo San Lucas; the Trans-Mexico Highway, which roughly parallels the United States border between Tijuana on the Pacific coast and Matamoros on the Gulf of Mexico; and the Pacific Coast Highway, which extends from Tijuana to Tapachula on the Guatemalan border.

Although extensive, much of Mexico's public highway system is in poor condition as a result of insufficient investment in road maintenance and an overreliance on heavy trucks to haul overland cargo. According to the World Bank (see Glossary), in 1994, 61 percent of Mexican public roads were in poor condition, 29 percent were in fair condition, and only 10 percent were in good condition. In the early 1990s, the Salinas government took steps to reduce the strain on the public highway system by granting concessions to the private sector to build 6,600 kilometers of toll roads by 1994. The newly built toll roads are in better condition than the public highways, but tolls, which were driven up as a result of construction cost overruns, have been too expensive to divert a significant share of commercial traffic from the public roads.

In 1992 total vehicle traffic in Mexico included 7.5 million automobiles, 3.9 million trucks, and more than 106,000 buses. In 1995 there were 12.1 million registered vehicles in Mexico. Intercity bus service is extensive, with bus service generally considered fair to good on most intercity routes. Despite the availability of mass transit, the proliferation of buses and automobiles in greater Mexico City has far outpaced the capital's road building and highway expansion capabilities, causing chronic urban traffic congestion and exacerbating Mexico City's legendary smog (see Environmental Conditions, ch. 2).

Railroads

The predominantly state-owned Mexican railroad system is extensive, consisting in 1994 of 20,425 kilometers of 1.435-meter, standard-gauge line and ninety kilometers of 0.914-meter narrow-gauge line. A 102-kilometer section of line between Mexico City and Querétaro is electrified.

The largest rail line is the state-owned Mexican National Railways (Ferrocarriles Nacionales Mexicanos—FNM), which operates on about 70 percent of the total trackage and carries some 80 percent of total rail traffic. The second largest network, also state-owned, is the Pacific Railroad, which links Nogales and Guadalajara. The three smaller government-owned lines are the Chihuahua to Pacific Railroad, the Sonora to Baja California Railroad, and the United Railroads of the Southeast.

Several Mexican cities have rail links with the United States, including Ciudad Juárez, Laredo, Piedras Negras, Reynosa, Matamoros, Nogales, Naco, and Agua Prieta. The Mexican rail system also connects with Central American lines through Guatemala.

In 1992 FNM's rolling stock consisted of 1,575 diesel locomotives and 42,240 freight cars. In addition, some 60,000 pri-

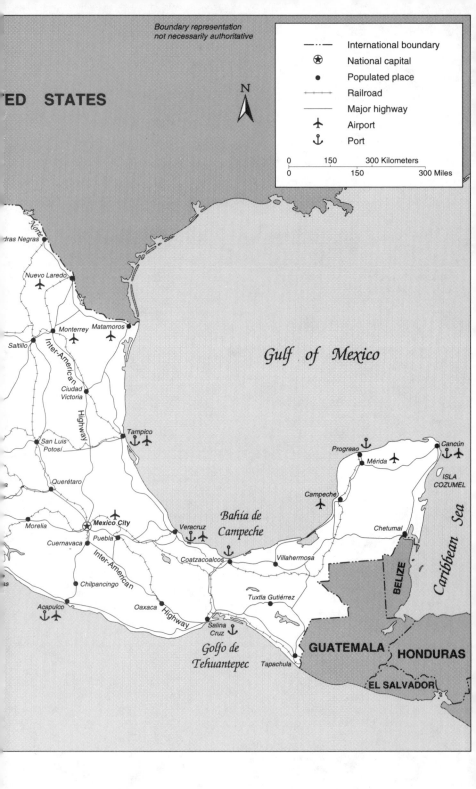

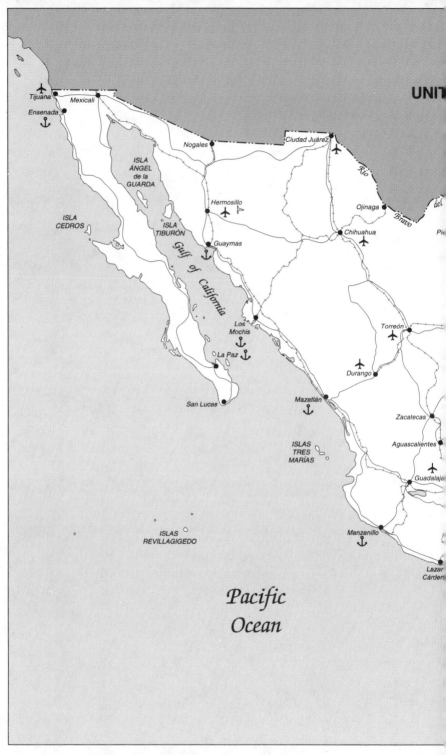

Figure 10. Transportation Network, 1996

vately owned freight cars were in service. In 1992 FNM carried 49 million tons of freight, representing 12 percent of all long-haul freight traffic in Mexico.

Railroads were only lightly used by passengers in the early 1990s, accounting for just 2 percent of total intercity passenger travel. In 1992 FNM carried almost 15 million passengers on its fleet of more than 800 passenger rail vehicles. In 1993 it began gradually privatizing its passenger operations by means of concessions to private carriers. In 1995 the Mexican congress passed legislation allowing private investment in railways under fifty-year concessions. Private enterprises were allowed to operate various portions of the rail network, provide train services, and operate railyards and terminals.

Despite its abundant mileage and rolling stock, the Mexican railroad system was generally considered to be antiquated and inefficient in the early 1990s. Corporate respondents to the World Bank's 1994 survey of commercial users of Mexican transportation services rated the state-owned rail network as the most poorly performing component of Mexico's national transportation system. Inadequate maintenance, mismanagement, and corruption were cited as major impediments to reliable service. In 1991 only 68 percent of locomotives were available for use at any given time, and terminal operations were so poorly managed that only 20 percent of shipment time was spent en route. To avoid delay, spoilage, and loss of merchandise, Mexican companies attempted whenever possible to bypass the rail·system altogether by relying heavily on long-haul trucks, which accounted for 88 percent of all overland cargo travel in 1992. The inefficiency of the railroad system was considered a major impediment to Mexican commercial competitiveness under the new NAFTA trading system.

Rapid Transit

In 1969 Mexico City opened its subway system (Metro). By 1993 it comprised eight lines with 135 stations and a total route length of 158 kilometers (of which ninety-two kilometers were underground). The Metro is a heavy-rail network consisting of more than 250 nine-car trains traveling on 1.435-meter auxiliary-guide rails. A computerized system of traffic control is used in conjunction with human operators on each train. In 1991 the system handled 1.4 billion passenger journeys. The Federal District's System of Electric Transport (Sistema de Transporte Eléctrico—STE), which oversees rapid transit services in greater Mexico City, plans to expand the Metro system to fifteen lines totaling 315 kilometers route-length by 2010. At that point, it predicts daily ridership will exceed 12 million passengers.

In the early 1990s, Guadalajara inaugurated a modest subway system. Two electrified light-rail lines cross in the city's center and extend to nearby suburbs. Tracks are underground in the downtown area and use existing rail right of ways in outlying areas.

Ports and Shipping

Mexico has some 10,000 kilometers of coastline but few navigable rivers and no good natural harbors. The country's 2,900 kilometers of navigable rivers and coastal canals play only a minor role in the transportation system. In the early 1990s, Mexico's seventy-five maritime ports and nine river ports handled 65 percent of imports and 70 percent of nonpetroleum exports. The flow of freight through Mexican ports exceeded 163 million tons of cargo in 1990, representing 31 percent of total freight carried by all modes. The five largest ports—Tampico, Veracruz, Guaymas, Mazatlán, and Manzanillo—handled 80 percent of Mexico's ocean freight.

Veracruz is an important port for general cargo, especially goods headed to and from Mexico City. The port of Tampico primarily handles petroleum and petroleum products. Other important seaports include Coatzacoalcos on the Gulf of Mexico coast and Acapulco on the Pacific. Two new Pacific ports—Pichilingue and Topolobampo—were built in the early 1990s, and another was built on the Gulf of Mexico coast at Progreso, in the state of Yucatán. Between 1989 and 1994, some US$700 million was spent on port development, more than half of that amount provided by the private sector.

Mexico's system of state-owned ports is administered by Mexican Ports (Puertos Mexicanos—PM), a decentralized government agency established in 1989 to oversee the rationalization and streamlining of port operations. To increase the quality of service in the shipping sector and thereby enhance Mexico's export performance, the government announced in 1992 that it would sell management concessions for nine ports—including Acapulco, Lázaro Cárdenas, and Manzanillo—to private buyers. In 1994 ownership of the ports of Altamira, Acapulco, Guaymas, and Tampico passed to the private sector. Mexico expected to complete construction by 1996 of a 437-kilometer

Eastbound train at Orizaba on Mexico City-Veracruz route, Mexico's first rail line
Courtesy Rodolfo García

coastal canal between Matamoros and Tampico, intended to connect with the United States Intracoastal Waterway system through the Río Bravo del Norte (Rio Grande).

In 1994 the Mexican merchant marine consisted of fifty-eight vessels of more than 1,000 gross registered tons, including thirty-two oil tankers owned and operated by Pemex. The state-owned Maritime Transport of Mexico (Transporte Marítimo de México) operated most of the other ships. Maritime freight is about evenly distributed between coastal and ocean shipping, whereas most seaborne passenger travel is coastal.

Air Transportation

Mexico's air transportation system is generally considered adequate to handle projected levels of passenger and freight traffic through the end of the 1990s. In 1994 Mexico had a total of 1,585 operational airfields or airstrips, of which 202 had permanent-surface runways. Forty-four international and thirty-eight domestic airports offer services to all major Mexican cities. Mexico's principal airport and main air transportation hub is Benito Juárez International Airport, on the outskirts of Mexico City. Other major airports at Monterrey, Guadalajara, Mérida, and Cancún also handle large volumes of air traffic.

Air transport services consist overwhelmingly of passenger travel, with air freight representing only 0.03 percent by weight of total cargo transported by all modes in 1994. Mexico's proximity and extensive overland and maritime links to the United States, its main trading partner, account in large measure for the relatively light use of aircraft to transport freight.

In 1992 Mexico had seventy-seven domestic airlines, of which two, Aeronaves de México (Aeroméxico) and Mexican Aviation Company (Compañía Mexicana de Aviación—Mexicana), had international stature. Aeroméxico was sold to private investors in June 1989 after it had declared bankruptcy. Widely known in the past as "Aeromaybe" because of unreliable service, Aeroméxico has maintained consistent on-time performance since its privatization. Also in 1989, the government sold half of its 51 percent stake in Mexicana to private investors.

In 1993 Mexican aircraft flew a total of 325 million kilometers and carried 20 million passengers. Mexico has direct air connections, through Mexicana and Aeroméxico, with the United States, Canada, Europe, Australia, and the rest of Latin America. In 1994 twenty-eight international airlines provided regularly scheduled service from Mexico City to major cities in Europe, Japan, the United States, and the rest of Latin America. In addition, a variety of foreign and domestic air charter services flew directly to the country's major resort areas.

Telecommunications

In December 1990, Mexico sold its state-owned telephone system, Mexican Telephone (Teléfonos de México—Telmex), to private investors in the country's largest and most complicated privatization. The government sold majority voting rights and a 20 percent stake in Telmex to a consortium of investors for US$1.8 billion, and it sold US$3.7 billion in shares to the public in two public offerings. Nevertheless, customers continued to complain about delays in contacting operators, installing new phones, and receiving service upgrades.

In 1995 the Telmex network had some 8.7 million phone lines in service. Almost 13 percent of all international calls from the United States were made to Mexico in 1993, while

Modern port facilities at Veracruz
Courtesy Inter-American Development Bank

more than 90 percent of Mexico's long-distance calls were made to the United States.

To improve service quality, Telmex inaugurated a US$30 billion modernization program in conjunction with its partners, Southwestern Bell Corporation and France Telecom, in 1993. In early 1994, the United States telecommunications company Microwave Communications International (MCI) announced plans to collaborate with Banamex-Accival Financial Group (Grupo Financiero Banamex-Accival—Banacci), Mexico's largest financial group, in building a new long-distance telephone network in Mexico. The two companies valued the joint venture at US$1 billion, of which MCI would invest US$450 million. In early 1994, telephone industry analysts expected Mexico's US$6 billion long-distance telephone market to continue or exceed its 14 percent annual growth rate. The high growth rate stemmed from increased telephone communications between the United States and Mexico resulting from NAFTA and the government's stated intention to open the long-distance market to foreign competition in January 1997.

Mexico uses four Atlantic Ocean satellite ground stations and one Pacific Ocean satellite ground station of the International Telecommunications Satellite Corporation (Intelsat). Mexico is also connected to the Central American Microwave System. In 1985 the Mexican-owned Morelos-B domestic telecommunications satellite was launched from the United States space shuttle Atlantis. Morelos-B was replaced in 1993 by another Mexican-owned domestic telecommunications satellite, Solidarity I.

Radio

In 1993 Mexico had more than 700 commercial amplitude modulation (AM) radio stations, including 679 stations operating on mediumwave, and twenty-two AM shortwave stations. The country has a number of large commercial radio networks, including National Radio Network (Radio Cadena Nacional) and Mexico Radio Programs (Radio Programas de México). Mexico also has some cultural radio stations, operated either by public agencies or by educational institutions. In 1996 Mexico had 21 million radios.

The most important state-run radio systems are the Mexican Radio Institute (Instituto Mexicano de la Radio—IMER), which operates two networks, Mexico Radio (Radio México) and Exact Time Radio (Radio la Hora Exacta); the Education Ministry's Education Radio (Radio Educación), which has a reputation for objectivity; and Radio UNAM (UNAM Radio), run by the National Autonomous University of Mexico (Universidad Nacional Autónoma de México—UNAM). The private commercial sector is dominated by some twenty radio networks. Ninety-two percent of stations belong to a network; 72 percent belong to or are controlled by ten networks; and half are controlled by the top five. The main networks include the Acir Group (Grupo Acir), which controls 140 stations and produces three major news programs daily for national distribution; the Radio Promotional Organization (Organización Impulsora de Radio—OIR); Radio and Television Agency (Agentes de Radio y Televisión—ARTSA), and Mexico Radio Programs.

Television

Introduced in 1950, television reached some 70 percent of the Mexican population by the early 1990s. In 1995 Mexico had 326 television stations (almost 25 percent of all stations in Latin America), most of them owned by or affiliated with the Mexican Telesystem (Telesistema Mexicano—known popularly as Televisa) and the state-run Mexican Institute of Television (Instituto Mexicano de Televisión—Imevisión). In 1996 Mexico had about 800 television transmitters and an average of one television set per 8.9 viewers.

In the early 1990s, Televisa was reportedly the largest communications conglomerate in the developing world. Although a private corporation, Televisa is very close to the ruling PRI. It operates three commercial television networks in Mexico and four stations in the United States. Its main network broadcasts twenty-four hours a day, and the others broadcast between twelve and eighteen hours daily. Televisa's flagship news program is "24 Horas," which has long been the most important source of news for many Mexicans. Televisa exports 20,000 hours of television programming to other Latin American countries. In addition to television and radio, Televisa has interests in newspaper and book publishing; production of records and home videos; motion picture distribution, advertising and marketing; and real estate, tourism, and hotels.

The state-run Imevisión operates two national television networks, as well as several regional and specialized channels. The government also operates Mexican Republic Television (Televisión de la República Mexicana), which broadcasts news and educational and cultural programs to rural areas, and Cultural Television of Mexico (Televisión Cultural de México). A competing network, Televisión Independiente, operates seven stations. There are also some twenty independent stations.

In November 1993, the government granted licenses for sixty-two new local television stations, increasing Televisa's total number of stations from 229 to 291. Most of the new stations are concentrated in northern Mexico. Televisa showed considerable financial strength in 1993, with third-quarter profits of some US$120 million, up 43 percent from the same period of 1992. The company planned additional large investments in an effort to maintain its 90 percent share of Mexico's television market. Televisa's main competitor is Televisión Azteca, which owns 179 stations in two national networks. Although it commanded less than 10 percent of the national television market in 1993, it is attempting to increase its market share to 24 percent by 2000.

Tourism

During the 1970s and 1980s, tourism generated more than 3 percent of Mexico's GNP and between 9 percent and 13 percent of its foreign-exchange earnings. Only petroleum generated more net foreign exchange. The number of arriving tourists rose steadily from more than 5 million in 1987 to 7 million in 1990, despite the peso's overvaluation during those years. The number of arrivals subsequently fell to about 6 million in 1991 and 1992 as the overvalued peso raised costs for United States visitors. Mexico had 7 million foreign arrivals in 1994, and tourism generated total revenue of US$4.2 billion.

Eighty-three percent of foreign visitors to Mexico in 1993 came from the United States, many of them from the border states for short visits. Eight percent of foreign visitors came from Europe, and 6 percent from other Latin American countries. In 1990 United States residents made some 70 million visits to Mexico's border towns, and Mexicans made 88 million visits to United States border towns. In 1984 visitors to Mexican border areas spent some US$1.3 billion, compared with US$2.0 billion spent by all tourists in the interior. By 1990 border visitors spent more than US$2.5 billion, while visitors to the interior spent approximately US$4.0 billion. In 1991 each foreign tourist spent an average amount of US$594. In 1992 Mexico had some 8,000 hotels and some 353,000 hotel rooms.

In the early 1990s, Mexico City was the most popular destination for foreign tourists, followed by Acapulco. In the mid-1970s, the official tourist development agency, Fonatur, began to promote new tourist areas, including Zihuatanejo, Ixtapa, and Puerto Escondido on the Pacific coast, and Cancún on the Caribbean coast. In 1986 and 1987, work began on the new Pacific coast tourist resort of Huatulco. Mexico's tourist industry is particularly vulnerable to external shocks such as natural disasters and bad weather, international incidents, and variations in the exchange rate, as well as changes in national regulations. For instance, a 1985 earthquake that had an epicenter near Acapulco damaged many of Mexico City's central hotels. In September 1987, Hurricane Gilbert struck Cancún, causing US$80 million worth of damage that took three months to repair.

Foreign Trade

Stabilization and adjustment policies implemented by the Mexican government during the 1980s caused a sharp fall in imports and a corresponding increase in exports. Average real exchange rates rose, domestic demand contracted, and the government provided lucrative export incentives, making exportation the principal path to profitable growth. The 1982 peso devaluation caused Mexico's imports to decline 60 percent in value to US$8.6 billion by the end of 1983. After years of running chronic trade deficits, Mexico achieved a net trade surplus of US$13.8 billion in 1993.

Imports

After 1983 the government eliminated import license requirements, official import prices, and quantitative restrictions. This trade liberalization program sought to make Mexican producers more competitive by giving them access to affordable inputs. By 1985 the share of total imports subject to licensing requirements had fallen from 75 percent to 38 percent. In 1986 Mexico acceded to the General Agreement on Tariffs and Trade (GATT), now the World Trade Organization (WTO), and in 1987 it agreed to a major liberalization of bilateral trade relations with the United States.

As a consequence of trade liberalization, the share of domestic output protected by import licenses fell from 92 percent in June 1985 to 18 percent by the end of 1990. The maximum tariff was lowered from 100 percent in 1985 to 20 percent in 1987, and the weighted average tariff fell from 29 percent in 1985 to 12 percent by the end of 1990. The volume of imports subject to entry permits was reduced from 96 percent of the total in 1982 to 4 percent by 1992. The remaining export controls applied mainly to food products, pharmaceuticals, and petroleum and oil derivatives.

The value of Mexico's imports rose steadily from US$50 billion in 1991 to US$79 billion in 1994 (19 percent of GDP). It rose in response to the recovery of domestic demand (especially for food products); the new peso's new stability; trade liberalization; and growth of the nontraditional export sector, which required significant capital and intermediate inputs (see table 11, Appendix). As a result of the new peso devaluation of December 1994, Mexico's imports in 1995 were US$73 billion, 9 percent lower than the 1994 figure. In 1995 Mexico imported US$5 billion worth of consumer goods (7 percent of total imports), US$9 billion worth of capital goods (12 percent), and US$59 billion worth of intermediate goods (81 percent). Renewed growth and the new peso's real appreciation were expected to increase demand for foreign products during 1996. Imports rose by 12 percent in the first quarter of 1996 to US$20 billion.

The government tried to curb the early 1990s' rise in imports by acting against perceived unfair trade practices by other countries. In early 1993, Mexico retaliated against alleged dumping of United States, Republic of Korea (South Korean), and Chinese goods by imposing compensatory quotas on brass locks, pencils, candles, fiber products, sodium carbonate, and hydrogen peroxide. Antidumping duties were applied to steel products, and all importers were required to produce certification of origin.

But Mexico also was subject to complaints by other countries, which charged that Mexico itself engaged in unfair practices. The European Community (now the European Union— EU) and Japan lodged complaints with the GATT about Mexico's invocation of sanitary standards in late 1992 to limit meat imports.

Exports

The mid-1980s decline in world petroleum prices caused the value of Mexico's exports to fall from US$24 billion in 1984 to US$16 billion in 1986, reflecting the country's continued heavy dependence on petroleum export revenue. Lower oil earnings helped to reduce Mexico's trade surplus to almost US$5 billion in 1986. Export revenue rose slightly to US$21 billion in 1987, as oil prices began to recover. Exports continued to rise modestly but steadily thereafter, reaching US$28 billion in 1992. The government promoted exports vigorously in an effort to close a trade gap that began in 1989 and widened in subsequent years. The state-run Foreign Commerce Bank channeled finance to a wide range of potential exporters, especially small and medium-sized firms and agricultural and fishing enterprises. In 1993 it provided US$350 million for the tourist sector, representing a 35 percent increase over 1992.

The value of Mexico's exports rose steadily from US$43 billion in 1991 to US$61 billion in 1994, despite the new peso's overvaluation. The currency devaluation of late 1994 contributed to a significant jump in the value of Mexico's exports to US$80 billion in 1995, a 31 percent increase over the previous year.

Total export earnings for the first quarter of 1996 were US$22 billion. Manufactures accounted for US$67 billion (84 percent) of Mexico's exports in 1995, followed by oil exports (US$9 billion or 11 percent), agricultural products (US$4 billion, or 5 percent), and mining products (US$545 million, or less than 1 percent). This improved export performance resulted from the new peso devaluation, weak domestic demand because of the recession, new export opportunities opened by NAFTA, and improved commodity prices. Export growth was expected to slow during 1996, as a result of recovery of domestic demand, expected drops in the prices of oil and other nonfood items, capacity constraints, and strengthening of the new peso.

Composition of Exports

The 1985 peso devaluations and the 1986 oil price collapse produced a dramatic shift in the composition of Mexico's exports. The value of Mexico's oil exports plummeted from US$13 billion in 1985 to less than US$6 billion in 1986. The oil sector's share of total export revenue consequently fell from 78 percent in 1982 to 42 percent in 1987. Oil export revenue recovered in 1987 to US$7.9 billion as petroleum prices rose. Prompted by the peso devaluation and low domestic demand, nonoil exports rose 41 percent in 1986 and an additional 24 percent in 1987. In 1987 manufactured exports (especially engineering and chemical products) constituted 48 percent of total exports by value, eclipsing petroleum and reducing Mexico's vulnerability to fluctuations in the world oil price. Between 1988 and 1991, petroleum exports fell 22 percent in value because of lower world oil prices and declining sales, while nonoil exports rose 15 percent in value. By 1992 petroleum contributed only 30 percent of total exports by value.

In 1994 petroleum and its derivatives accounted for US$7 billion, or 12 percent, of Mexico's total export revenue of US$62 billion. Transport equipment and machinery exports earned US$33 billion, or 54 percent of total exports. Chemicals earned US$3 billion, or 5 percent, and metals and manufactured metal products earned US$3 billion, or 5 percent. Agricultural, processed food, beverage, and tobacco products accounted for US$3 billion, or 5 percent of total exports.

Trade Balance

Import growth outstripped export performance in the early 1990s, producing a steadily widening trade deficit. In 1988 Mexico's trade surplus had fallen to US$1.7 billion, and the following year it turned into a US$645 million deficit as imports rose 24 percent against export growth of 11 percent. In 1990 the trade deficit widened to US$4.4 billion, despite a rise in international oil prices resulting from the Persian Gulf War. Petroleum exports rose slightly, and nonoil exports grew 12 percent in 1990, producing total export earnings growth of 18 percent. But total imports increased a much more rapid 34 percent. In 1991 the trade gap widened further to US$7.3 billion, as the level of exports remained steady while imports grew 22 percent. Mexico's trade deficit widened again to US$15.9 billion in 1992. Following a slowdown in import growth in 1993, the trade deficit increased substantially in 1994, the first year under NAFTA. Low interest rates and an overvalued new peso bolstered demand for foreign goods, causing imports to grow an estimated 19 percent. Spurred by the newly devalued currency, Mexico's foreign trade balance swung dramatically back to a US$7.1 billion surplus in 1995, effectively eliminating the country's current account deficit. The trade surplus was US$1.7 billion for the first quarter of 1996, compared with the first quarter of 1995 figure of US$647 million.

Direction of Trade

Largely as a result of trade liberalization, two-way trade between Mexico and the United States doubled between 1986 and 1990. In the late 1980s, Mexico expanded its exports to the United States at an average annual rate of 15 percent. Even prior to NAFTA, more than 85 percent of Mexican exports entered the United States duty-free (see table 12, Appendix).

In 1994 the value of two-way United States-Mexico trade amounted to more than US$100 billion. Mexico exported US$53 billion worth of products to the United States and imported US$56 billion worth of United States goods. Mexico's commercial reliance on the United States has increased in recent years, despite efforts to diversify its export markets and import sources. In 1994 the United States took 85 percent of all Mexican exports (up from 83 percent in 1993). Sales to Mexico accounted for only 8 percent of all United States exports in 1991. Sales to Canada amounted to more than US$1.5 billion, or 2 percent of Mexican exports in 1994; sales to Japan amounted to US$997 million, or less than 2 percent. Spain, Germany, and France together accounted for nearly US$2 billion, or 3 percent, of Mexico's export revenue in 1994. In 1994 the United States provided 69 percent of Mexico's imports, Japan 6 percent, Germany 4 percent, Canada 2 percent, and France 2 percent.

Mexico's sales to other Latin American countries totaled US$2.9 billion in 1993, a 65 percent increase over 1988. Nevertheless, these sales constituted only some 10 percent of Mexico's total exports by value. Two-way trade between Mexico and the rest of Latin America increased to about 250 percent between 1988 and 1993. Mexico's most important trading partners in Latin America were Argentina and Brazil.

Trade Agreements

In 1991 Mexico and Chile signed a bilateral free-trade agreement under which each country would gradually reduce tariffs on three categories of products. As a result, Chilean exports to Mexico increased 112 percent between 1991 and 1993, and an additional 33 percent (US$89 million in value) between January and August 1993.

Mexico also formed a trilateral free-trade association with Colombia and Venezuela known as the Group of Three (G–3). Negotiations were concluded in 1993, and the agreement took effect during 1994. Tariffs on most products were to be gradually eliminated over ten years (twelve years for automobiles). The agreement was expected to create a US$373 billion economic market encompassing some 145 million people. In October 1993, the G–3 countries announced their intention to establish a wider Association of Caribbean States (ACS). In March 1994, Mexico and Costa Rica negotiated a bilateral free-trade agreement that was expected to provide a model for similar agreements between Mexico and other Central American countries. Mexico also discussed a free-trade agreement with the EU and membership in the new Asia-Pacific Economic Cooperation forum.

President Salinas's most significant commercial achievement, however, was the successful conclusion of NAFTA negotiations with the United States and Canada in 1993. Salinas sought free trade with the United States largely in order to increase private investment, attract new technology, and ensure continued access for Mexican goods to the United States market. Mexico's neoliberal development strategy depended on promotion of manufactured exports, which in turn required expanded United States-Mexican trade. Salinas also sought a free-trade agreement with the United States and Canada to reassure potential investors of the continuity and stability of Mexican economic policy, and to provide formal legal procedures for resolving commercial disputes. The agreement provided for ongoing consultation on issues of mutual concern to member countries, including health regulations, product subsidies, rules of origin, and quality standards (see President Salinas, ch. 1).

NAFTA provides for the elimination of Mexican tariffs on 5,900 categories of imports from the United States and Canada (mostly machinery and intermediate goods), representing more than 40 percent of Mexico's overall trade. Other products are reclassified in a simplified tariff list having four rate bands—5 percent, 10 percent, 15 percent, and 20 percent. The United States eliminated tariffs on 3,100 additional categories of Mexican goods, bringing to 80 percent the portion of all Mexican exports to the United States that will be free from tariffs. Some 4,200 categories already had been included in the General System of Preferences (GSP) and were thus already exempt from tariffs. The treaty eliminates some tariffs immediately and phases out the rest over five, ten, or fifteen years, with vulnerable industries in the United States and Mexico receiving the longest protection.

Mexico's deadlines for lowering trade barriers are generally longer than those for Canada and the United States. The latter countries are required to lift immediately their tariffs on some 80 percent of Mexico's nonoil exports, while Mexico must grant immediate free entry to 42 percent of United States and Canadian exports. Special rules apply for trade in textiles, vehicles and auto parts, and agricultural products. The treaty also governs trade in services, including overland transport, telecommunications, and financial services, and it includes provisions for the liberalization of government procurement.

NAFTA requires Mexico to abolish protectionist limitations on foreign investment (except in the energy sector), allow free profit repatriation by United States and Canadian firms, and guarantee investors against property seizure without full compensation. The treaty allows foreign banks to take up to 25 percent of Mexico's banking market and allows foreign brokerages to take 30 percent of the securities business by 2004, after which all restrictions are to be eliminated.

NAFTA is expected to create a free-trade area with a combined population of 356 million and a GDP of more than US$6 trillion. It commits future Mexican governments to preserve liberal trade and investment policies, and it maintains pressure on Mexico to increase its trade competitiveness. The agreement is likely to spur both foreign investment and increased

Interior of shopping mall, Monterrey
Courtesy Inter-American Development Bank

exports, which will allow expansion of private consumption and domestic investment as monetary controls are relaxed and interest rates fall. NAFTA's accession clause (Article 2005) allows any country or group of countries to join the treaty provided it negotiates mutually acceptable terms. New accessions are to be ratified according to each member's "standard approval procedures." Each current member enjoys an effective veto over admission of new members. Although Mexico has not opposed Chilean accession, it is unlikely to support a Central American application for fear of competition from these countries for new textile factories and other light industrial installations.

Balance of Payments

Current Account

From the mid-1970s through the early 1980s, Mexico faced persistent balance-of-payments problems resulting from the government's efforts to defend the overvalued peso while incurring massive external debts. By the late 1970s, oil prices had begun to fall, and international interest rates rose sharply, throwing Mexico's external payments so far out of balance that by mid-1982 the country could no longer service its external debt. The government was forced to declare a unilateral moratorium on debt service, devalue the peso, and drastically reduce public spending. By 1985 these measures had brought the current account back into surplus and eliminated the government's fiscal deficit, but at the cost of foregone economic growth and a sharp deterioration in the capital account. Throughout the early and mid-1980s, Mexico suffered a net capital outflow as a result of external debt service, high domestic capital flight, and weak foreign investment.

International oil prices collapsed in 1986, pushing Mexico's current account back into deficit. Meanwhile, debt-equity exchanges and capital repatriation produced a significant capital inflow and brought the capital account back into surplus. The external account balance was again reversed in 1987, as higher oil prices, increased nonoil revenue, a new commercial bank loan, and continued capital repatriation generated a US$4 billion current-account surplus, while heavy debt service obligations forced the capital account into a US$2.5 billion deficit.

Mexico's trade deficit rose sharply between 1989 and 1994, pushing the current account deeply into deficit. The current-account deficit ballooned from US$4 billion in 1989 to US$29 billion in 1994. Capital inflows were adequate to cover the current-account deficit through 1993, but began to falter in response to a series of political crises in 1994. The dramatic improvement in Mexico's trade balance between 1994 and 1995 enabled the current-account deficit to fall to US$654 million in 1995 and to be nearly eliminated by early 1996. This development increased the likelihood that the new peso would be strengthened by capital inflows, especially portfolio investment.

Capital Account

Mexico hemorrhaged capital through most of the 1980s. According to Morgan Guaranty, some US$53 billion fled the country between 1975 and 1985. Total capital flight from Mexico between 1983 and 1988 was approximately US$18 billion. Debt amortization was another major negative item in the capital account. According to the World Bank, debt repayments averaged US$5 billion annually between 1985 and 1990. Capital began to return to Mexico in 1986 and 1987, as investors and lenders were attracted by high domestic interest rates.

The trend was reversed in 1988 as a result of an exchange-rate freeze, domestic interest-rate reductions, competition from higher United States interest rates, and political uncertainty. But capital flows were positive again between 1989 and 1993.

In November 1993, the Mexican government announced that cumulative foreign investment between December 1988 and November 1993 was US$34 billion, exceeding by 40 percent the government's original target. United States direct investment in Mexico more than doubled between 1986 and 1993, to US$23 billion. United States-based multinationals provided more than 60 percent of foreign direct investment in Mexico at the end of 1992. During 1993 foreign investors vastly increased their holdings of Mexican stocks and bonds, producing a huge inflow of portfolio investment. In October 1993, foreign investors held 29 percent of Mexican stocks and 74 percent of bonds.

Foreign investment for all of 1993 reached a record US$16 billion, an increase of 87 percent over 1992. Some two-thirds of this amount (US$11 billion) was portfolio investment, while US$12 billion went to projects approved by the National Foreign Investment Commission (Comisión Nacional de Inversión Extranjera—CNIE) and the remaining US$3 billion went to investments approved in the government's official register. The manufacturing sector received 47 percent of the new investment, and the services sector received 30 percent. The capital inflow boosted Mexico's capital-account surplus to US$16 billion between January and June 1993, representing a 35 percent increase over the same period of 1992. The government was counting on the capital inflow to ensure a continued large capital account surplus with which to balance the current-account deficit.

Mexico's capital account registered a US$15 billion surplus in 1995, mainly because of the country's huge increase in borrowing. Loan disbursements to Mexico rose from US$7 billion in 1994 to US$27 billion in 1995. Foreign direct investment dropped by US$4 billion to a total of US$7 billion for the year, while stock-market investment plunged from US$4 billion in 1994 to US$519 million in 1995. The capital-account surplus allowed Mexico's international reserves to recover from a low of US$3.5 billion in January 1995 to US$15.7 billion by year's end.

Foreign Investment Regulation

Restrictions on direct foreign investment were eased during the administrations of presidents de la Madrid and Salinas. In 1990 the government revised Mexico's 1973 foreign investment law, opening up to foreign investment certain sectors of the economy that previously had been restricted to Mexican nationals or to the state. The new regulations permitted up to 100 percent foreign ownership in many industries.

However, in 1992 the government continued to retain sole rights to large parts of the economy, including oil and natural gas production, uranium production and treatment, basic petrochemical production, rail transport, and electricity distribution. Economic sectors reserved for Mexican nationals included radio and television, gas distribution, forestry, road transport, and domestic sea and air transport. The government limited foreign investors to 30 percent ownership of commercial banks, 40 percent ownership of secondary petrochemical and automotive plants, and 49 percent ownership of financial services, insurance, and telecommunications enterprises. However, foreign investors could obtain majority ownership of certain activities by means of a *fideicomiso,* or trust.

In November 1993, the government announced a new foreign-investment law that vastly expanded foreign-investment opportunities in Mexico. The new law replaced Mexico's protectionist 1973 investment code and united numerous regulatory changes that Salinas previously had imposed by decree without congressional approval. The new law allowed foreigners to invest directly in industrial, commercial, hotel, and time-share developments along Mexico's coast and borders, although such investment had to be carried out through Mexican companies. Foreigners previously had been prohibited from owning property within fifty kilometers of Mexico's borders, and their investments in areas beyond fifty kilometers had to be carried out through bank trusts. In practice, however, foreigners already had invested in many of the listed border industries and areas through complex trust and stock ownership arrangements, although risk and bureaucratic requirements had deterred some potential investors and financiers.

The new investment code also opened the air transportation sector to 25 percent direct foreign investment and the secondary petrochemical sector to full 100 percent direct foreign investment. Mining also was opened to 100 percent direct foreign ownership; previously foreigners could provide 100 percent investment but had to invest through bank trusts for limited periods of time. Other sectors opened to foreign investors included railroad-related services, ports, farmland, courier services, and cross-border cargo transport. The new code eliminated performance requirements previously imposed upon foreign investors, along with minimum domestic content requirements.

The Future of the Economy

The market-oriented structural reforms of the 1980s and early 1990s transformed Mexico's economy from a highly protectionist, public-sector-dominated system to a generally open, deregulated "emerging market." President Salinas's moves to privatize and deregulate large sectors of the Mexican economy elicited widespread support from international investors and the advanced industrial nations. With its positive effect on trade and capital flows, NAFTA was widely interpreted by Mexican decision makers as a validation of their market-oriented economic policies. The currency collapse of December 1994 and the ensuing deep recession, however, erased the economic gains that Mexico had achieved in previous years, shook the nation's political stability, and depressed hopes for an early return to growth.

Although Mexico remained in a difficult economic condition in mid-1996, the worst of the recession had passed and the country appeared headed toward recovery. The economy registered positive growth in the second quarter of 1996, inflation and interest rates abated, and portfolio investment returned, as reflected in Mexico's rising stock exchange index. Despite continuing problems exacerbated by low investor confidence, analysts agreed that Mexico's economy in the mid-1990s was fundamentally sound and capable of long-term expansion.

*   *   *

Mexico's postwar economic growth and development policies are reviewed in James M. Cypher's *State and Capital in Mexico,* Roger Hansen's *The Politics of Mexican Development,* and Clark W. Reynolds's *The Mexican Economy.* The best examinations of Mexican economic policy during the 1970s and 1980s are John Sheahan's *Conflict and Change in Mexican Economic Strategy* and Nora Lustig's *Mexico: The Remaking of an Economy.*

Denise Dresser's *Neopopulist Solutions to Neoliberal Problems: Mexico's National Solidarity Program* offers an in-depth analysis of the structure and political implications of Pronasol, the Salinas administration's major anti-poverty program.

The United States Department of Agriculture maintains extensive statistical data on a variety of Mexican agricultural products, and its annual reports on various crops provide detailed information on specific sectors. Among the best treatments of Mexico's agricultural policy are the volume edited by James Austin and Gustavo Esteva, *Food Policy in Mexico,* and Steven Sanderson's *The Transformation of Mexican Agriculture.* Government-business relations are examined in Roderic A. Camp's *Entrepreneurs and Politics in Twentieth-Century Mexico* and *The Government and Private Sector in Contemporary Mexico,* edited by Sylvia Maxfield and Ricardo Anzaldua.

The United States Department of Energy's *International Energy Annual* provides statistical data on Mexican oil production and reserves. Petroleum policy is examined in Judith Gentleman's *Mexican Oil and Dependent Development* and Laura Randall's *The Political Economy of Mexican Oil.* Among the best examinations of Mexico's international economic relations are David Barkin's *Distorted Development* and Van R. Whiting, Jr.'s *The Political Economy of Foreign Investment in Mexico.* (For further information and complete citations, see Bibliography.)

Chapter 4. Government and Politics

A representation of the Mexican coat of arms—an eagle standing on a cactus, with a snake in its mouth—from a painting by Diego Rivera

FOR MORE THAN THREE GENERATIONS, Mexicans have attributed the origins of their political system to the Revolution of 1910–20. They cite the constitution of 1917, a sweeping document that capped nearly a decade of civil war among rival regional militias, as the foundation of their modern political institutions and practices. Mexico's governing institutions and political culture also bear the imprint of three centuries of Spanish colonial rule. Mexicans' adherence to a highly codified civil law tradition, their acceptance of heavy state involvement in business and civic affairs, and the deference accorded the executive over other branches of government can be traced to the administrative and legal practices of the colonial period. Finally, the traumatic experiences of the nineteenth century, including foreign military occupations and the loss of half of the national territory to the United States, as well as the disillusion sown by a series of unconstitutional regimes, continue to have a profound impact on contemporary political culture.

During the 1920s, President Plutarco Elías Calles (1924–28) reorganized Mexican politics along corporatist (see Glossary) lines as a way to contain latent social conflicts. Calles expanded the government bureaucracy to enable it to mediate among rival constituencies and to dispense state funds to organizations supportive of the "official" party. Calles also created new umbrella organizations that lumped together disparate groups according to broad functional categories. The newly created interest groups depended heavily on the state for their financing and were required to maintain strong ties to the ruling party. By grafting corporatist institutions onto Mexico's historically fractious political system at a time when ideologies of the extreme left and right were gaining support throughout the world, Mexico's leaders avoided a return to the widespread violence that had engulfed their country during the 1910s and early 1920s. Subsequently, the relatively inclusive nature of Mexican corporatism and the firm foundations of civilian supremacy over the military prevented Mexico from following the pattern of alternating civilian and military regimes that characterized most other Latin American countries in the twentieth century.

One of Calles's successors, Lázaro Cárdenas (1934–40), revived populism as a force in national politics by redistributing land to landless peasants under a state-sponsored reincarnation of communal farming known as the *ejido* (see Glossary) system. Cárdenas also emphasized nationalism as a force in Mexican politics by expropriating the holdings of foreign oil corporations and creating a new national oil company. Cardenas's reforms of the late 1930s bolstered the legitimacy of the government while further concentrating power in the president and the Institutional Revolutionary Party (Partido Revolucionario Institucional—PRI), the "official" party of the Revolution. By the early 1940s, the political processes and institutions that would broadly define Mexican politics for the next forty years were well established: a strong federal government dominated by a civilian president and his loyalists within the ruling party, a symbiotic relationship between the state and the official party, a regular and orderly rotation of power among rival factions within a de facto single-party system, and a highly structured corporatist relationship between the state and government-sponsored constituent groups.

During the financial crisis of the 1980s, the stable, ritualistic pattern of Mexican politics instituted by Calles and Cárdenas began to break down. As public funding for a variety of programs dried up, the state's role in the economy was scaled back, and the clientelist relationships developed over four decades between government agencies and legally recognized constituent groups were weakened. Seeking to establish a basis for future economic growth, the governments of Miguel de la Madrid Hurtado (1982–88) and Carlos Salinas de Gortari (1988–94) carried out a structural adjustment program that systematically rolled back state ownership and regulation of key industries. They also eliminated long-standing protectionist legislation that had made Mexico one of the most closed economies in the world and lifted the constitutional prohibition on the sale of *ejido* land to allow it to be converted to larger, more efficient farms. In the mid-1980s, an internal rift emerged between the populist and the more technocratic wings of the ruling party over the market reforms and the authoritarian nature of the PRI-dominated political system. The economic reforms initiated by President de la Madrid had been opposed by many members of the PRI's core agrarian and labor constituencies. These groups rejected privatization and the elimination of economic subsidies for consumer goods and services. The naming of Salinas, a United States-educated technocrat, as de la Madrid's successor was also repudiated by the leftist faction of the PRI leadership. This internal rift developed into the first major mass defection from the PRI ranks when Cuauhtémoc Cárdenas Solórzano, son of the former president, left the party to contest the 1988 presidential election as head of a coalition of leftist parties.

Since the late 1980s, the PRI has defeated serious electoral challenges to its central role in Mexican politics from parties of the left and right. During his presidency, Salinas liberalized the electoral system but further concentrated power in the executive. The main objectives of the Salinas administration were to restructure the Mexican economy and to integrate Mexico into the global market, rather than to democratize the political system. Nevertheless, the electoral reforms enacted by Salinas under domestic and international pressure for democratization set the stage for competitive, internationally monitored presidential and congressional elections in 1994.

After a strongly contested presidential campaign marred by the assassination of its original candidate, the PRI maintained its hold on the presidency with the election of yet another United States-educated technocrat, Ernesto Zedillo Ponce de León, in August 1994. Zedillo's victory preserved the PRI's dubious distinction as the world's longest-ruling political party. The PRI victory also presented Zedillo and his party with the unenviable challenge of guiding Mexico through a difficult and uncertain period of economic dislocation and broad political realignments. By the mid-1990s, most observers believed that the PRI-dominated political system begun in the 1920s was in an advanced state of decay and that a transitional period marked by a greater pluralism of organized political activity was at hand. How this transition would unfold, and whether it would ultimately lead to a more participatory and competitive political process across the spectrum of Mexican society, was yet to be determined.

Constitutional History

Nineteenth-Century Constitutions

The roots of the Mexican republic can be traced to two documents drafted during the early independence struggle against Spain: *Los sentimientos de la nación* (1813), by José María Morelos y Pavón, and the Constitution of Apatzingán (1814). These tracts introduced the ideal of a republic based on liberal political institutions and respect for individual rights. Mexico's independence was attained, however, by an alliance of liberal and ultraconservative forces under the leadership of Agustín de Iturbide (see Wars of Independence, 1810-21, ch. 1). Iturbide's Plan of Iguala proposed an indigenous constitutional monarchy, rather than a republic, as the alternative to Spanish rule. By assuming imperial powers following the victory over Spanish colonial forces in 1821, Iturbide continued the Iberian practice of plenipotentiary rule by the chief executive.

Mexico's first republican constitution was the Acta Constitutiva de la Federación Mexicana (Constituent Act of the Mexican Federation), which was promulgated in 1824, following the forced resignation of Iturbide and the breakup of the short-lived Mexican Empire (see The Abortive Empire, 1821–23, ch. 1). A liberal document modeled largely on the United States constitution, the constitution of 1824 established a federal republic with a divided central government. To avoid the abuses of executive authority experienced under Iturbide, the constitution required the president to share power and responsibility with a bicameral congress and the federal judiciary. Breaking with the Spanish colonial legacy of centralism, the constitution instituted a strong federal system, wherein presidents were to be indirectly elected every four years by a simple majority vote of the republic's nineteen state legislatures.

A document of dubious relevance, the constitution of 1824 was never fully observed by the politico-military leadership of the early Mexican republic. The survival of two of its most important principles, federalism and congressional authority, was more a reflection of the de facto decentralization of power in early nineteenth-century Mexico than of a generalized observance of the rule of law. Many provisions of the constitution of 1824 and subsequent nineteenth-century constitutions were simply ignored by the combative regional caudillos (strongmen) who dominated national politics. The most commonly breached constitutional principle was that of an orderly, electoral process of presidential succession. The violent overthrow of governments and the perpetuation in office of powerful presidents were problems that would plague Mexico throughout the rest of the nineteenth century and into the revolutionary period. Between 1824 and 1857, only one president, Guadalupe Victoria, completed his term and handed over power to an elected successor (see Centralism and the Caudillo State, 1836–55, ch. 1).

In 1833 the conservative president and military caudillo, Antonio López de Santa Anna Pérez de Lebrón, suspended the 1824 constitution and imposed a new national charter known as the Siete Leyes (Seven Laws). The Siete Leyes was a reactionary document that strengthened the powers of the presidency, militarized the federal government, and raised property qualifications for voting.

After three decades of political instability stemming from unrestrained power struggles between liberal and conservative elites, a new reformist constitution was promulgated in 1857 by the liberals, who had gained the upper hand. The 1857 constitution was reminiscent of the 1824 charter but was noteworthy for its introduction of major reform laws restricting military and clerical *fueros* (privileges) and clerical property rights. The new constitution also introduced a bill of rights, abolished slavery, and reestablished a strong national congress as a unicameral body. The clerical reform laws, moderate in comparison to the strongly anticlerical constitution of 1917, nevertheless galvanized the conservative opposition and led to a three-year civil war. Although the liberal forces under President Benito Juárez eventually prevailed, the conflict left Mexico divided and deeply in debt.

Using the excuse of collecting compensation for damage incurred during the civil war, the French landed troops in Veracruz. The French government, hoping to reestablish a French empire in the Americas, allied itself with conservative and church forces in Mexico and sent French troops to take Mexico City (see Civil War and the French Intervention, ch. 1). French troops entered the capital in 1863, and an empire under the Austrian archduke Ferdinand Maximilian Joseph von Habsburg was declared. Republican forces retreated to the far north, and for four years Mexico had two governments.

Bowing to pressure from the United States and responding to the increased belligerency of Prussia, Napoleon III of France decided to withdraw French troops at the end of 1866. The conservative forces in Mexico, disillusioned by Maximilian, threw their support to Juárez. Before the last French troops had boarded their ships in Veracruz, Maximilian had surrendered, and the republican forces again controlled the entire country.

Although the constitution of 1857 was restored, its democratic principles were increasingly violated in the decades to follow. Juárez was reelected twice amidst charges that his administrations were becoming increasingly dictatorial. After Juárez's death in 1872, Sebastián Lerdo de Tejada assumed the presidency. Under Lerdo, a bicameral congress was reinstated. When Lerdo announced he would run for reelection in 1876, José de la Cruz Porfirio Díaz took control as dictator. For more than a third of a century, either directly of indirectly, Díaz ruled Mexico (see The Porfiriato, ch. 1).

The revolutionary years from 1910 to 1917 were a period of governmental chaos (see The Revolution, 1910–20, ch. 1). Various groups espousing populist and revolutionary ideals roamed the country. By 1917 forces under Venustiano Carranza gradually had consolidated their control of the nation. Carranza then called a constitutional convention and presented a draft constitution, similar to the constitution of 1857, to the delegates. Carranza's moderate faction was outnumbered by the radicals, however, and numerous anticlerical and social reform articles were added.

Constitution of 1917

The constitution of 1917, proclaimed on February 5, 1917, is considered by many to be one of the most radical and comprehensive constitutions in modern political history. Although its social content gave it the title of the first modern socialist constitution—it preceded the constitution of the former Soviet Union—the Mexican document replicates many liberal principles and concepts of the constitution of the United States. The liberal concepts include federalism, separation of powers, and a bill of rights. In addition to reaffirming the liberal principles of the nineteenth-century documents, the 1917 constitution adds a strong nationalist proclamation, asserting Mexico's control over its natural resources. It also recognizes social and labor rights, separation of church and state, and universal male suffrage. Reflecting the varied social backgrounds and political philosophies of its framers, the constitution of 1917 includes various contradictory provisions, endorsing within the same text socialism, capitalism, liberal democracy, authoritarian corporatism, and a host of unimplemented provisions for specific social reforms.

Formally, the constitution prescribes a federal republic consisting of thirty-one states and a federal district. The federal government is divided into executive, legislative, and judicial branches, but these branches do not have comparable powers. Only the president may promulgate a law, by signing it and ordering its publication. The executive can veto bills passed by the legislature, either in whole or by item, and although a veto may be overridden, there is no constitutional way in which the president may be forced to sign a bill into law. In addition, executive-sponsored bills submitted to the Congress take precedence over other business, and the constitution gives the president broad authority to issue basic rules (*reglamentos*). *Reglamentos* have the same legal force as laws and are the source of most statutory regulations.

The constitution treats many matters of public policy explicitly. For example, before being amended in 1992, Article 27 placed stringent restrictions on the ownership of property by foreigners and the Roman Catholic Church and declared national ownership of the country's natural resources (see Church-State Relations, ch. 2). Religious groups were excluded from any kind of political activity and were not allowed to participate in public education, conduct services outside churches, or wear clerical dress in public. In its original form, Article 27 also granted the government broad powers to expropriate private property in the public interest and to redistribute land.

The constitution prescribes an activist state that will ensure national autonomy and social justice. Thus, in addition to a charter of individual rights, the constitution provides for a number of social rights for workers and peasants and their organizations. In Article 123, the constitution provides what has been described as "the most advanced labor code in the world at its time." It guarantees the right to organize, as well as an eight-hour workday, and provides for the protection of women and minors in the workplace. It mandates that the minimum wage "should be sufficient to satisfy the normal necessities of life of the worker," and establishes the principle of equal pay for equal work regardless of gender, race, or ethnicity. In addition, Article 123 clarifies the right to strike. Strikes are legal when their purpose is to "establish equilibrium between the diverse factors of production, harmonizing the rights of labor with those of capital." The article further establishes arbitration and conciliation boards made up of equal numbers of management, labor representatives, and one government representative. Although many of these provisions were not implemented until 1931, Article 123 mandates the incorporation of organized labor into the formal political process and serves as a basis for labor's claim to a preeminent status in national politics.

Government Structure

Executive

The presidency is the paramount institution, not only of the Mexican state, but of the entire Mexican political system. Critics have pejoratively labeled the presidency the "six-year monarchy" because of the seemingly unchecked power that historically has resided in the office. Much of the aura of presidential power derives from the president's direct and unchallenged control over both the state apparatus and the ruling political party, the PRI.

Presidents are directly elected by a simple majority of registered voters in the thirty-one states and the Federal District. The president holds the formal titles of chief of state, head of government, and commander in chief of the armed forces (see fig. 11). Presidential candidates must be at least thirty-five years old on election day and must be not only Mexican citizens by birth but also the offspring of Mexican citizens by birth (this clause was amended in 1994 to make the children of naturalized citizens eligible for the presidency, effective in 1999). To be eligible for the presidency, a candidate must reside legally in Mexico during the year preceding the election. The candidate cannot have held a cabinet post or a governorship, nor have been on active military duty during the six months prior to the election. Priests and ministers of religious denominations are barred from holding public office.

The presidential term of six years, commonly known as the *sexenio,* has determined the cyclical character of Mexican politics since the late 1930s. A president can never be reelected, and there is no vice president. If the presidential office falls vacant during the first two years of a *sexenio,* the congress designates an interim president, who, in turn, must call a special presidential election to complete the term. If the vacancy occurs during the latter four years of a *sexenio,* the congress designates a provisional president for the remainder of the term.

In addition to the president's prerogatives in legislative matters, he or she may freely appoint and dismiss cabinet officials and almost all employees of the executive branch. Subject to traditionally routine ratification by the Senate, the president appoints ambassadors, consuls general, magistrates of the

Supreme Court, and the mayor of the Federal District. The president also appoints the magistrates of the Supreme Court of the Federal District, subject to ratification by the Chamber of Deputies. Presidential appointment authority also extends downward through the federal bureaucracy to a wide assortment of midlevel offices in the secretariats, other cabinet-level agencies, semiautonomous agencies, and parastatal (see Glossary) enterprises. This extensive appointment authority provides a formidable source of patronage for incoming administrations and has been an important factor in ensuring the regular, orderly turnover in office of competing elite factions within the official party.

Despite the nominally federal character of the Mexican state, presidents have historically played a decisive role in the selection and removal of state governors, all of whom, until 1991, were members of the PRI. President Salinas was particularly assertive in bringing about the resignations of PRI governors widely believed to have been elected through blatant fraud. In some cases, Salinas annuled the election and appointed the opposition candidate governor.

The president confers broad powers on cabinet secretaries, although the cabinet rarely meets as a single body. There is a hierarchy of influence among the different cabinet posts, and the power of a minister or secretary varies, depending on the priorities set by a particular president as well as the resources available at the time. Traditionally, the secretary of interior has been an influential figure and often has been chosen to succeed the president. During the José López Portillo y Pachecho *sexenio* (1976–82), the Secretariat of Programming and Budget (Secretaría de Programación y Presupuesto—SPP) was reorganized to coordinate all government agencies, supervise the budget, and design the national development program. Until its merger with the Secretariat of Finance and Public Credit (Secretaría de Hacienda y Crédito Público) in 1992, the SPP was extremely influential, becoming the launching point for the presidencies of de la Madrid and Salinas.

In 1994, President Salinas broke with the pattern of selecting SPP economists by designating the Secretary of Social Development, Luis Donaldo Colosio Murrieta, as the PRI presidential nominee. This departure from the established practice of nominating ministers with economic portfolios appeared to reflect a reemergence of a social welfare agenda within the PRI after years of orthodox economic policies. When Colosio was assassi-

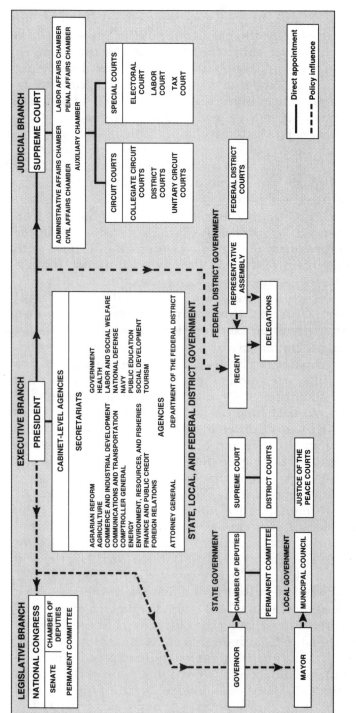

Figure 11. Government Structure, 1996

nated during the presidential campaign, Salinas returned to the fold by selecting Zedillo, a former education and SPP secretary who was then serving as Colosio's campaign manager, to replace the fallen candidate.

One of the unique features of the Mexican presidency has been the highly secretive and mysterious process of presidential succession. Since the 1930s, Mexico's PRI presidents have enjoyed the right to personally name their successor, a privilege known as the *dedazo* (tap). The prerogative of choosing one's successor has allowed outgoing presidents to select individuals who embody either change or continuity with past policies, as demanded by circumstances and public opinion. Over the years, the skillful selection of a successor to the president has become an important element of the adaptability that has characterized the PRI-dominated system.

During the last two years of a *sexenio*, a president selects a short list of candidates for the PRI nomination from among an inner circle within the cabinet. Before announcing the nominee, an event known as the *destape* (unveiling), a president gauges public opinion of the candidates. The *destape* has been criticized for being undemocratic and anachronistic in the age of mass communications. Beginning with the elections of 2000, the PRI's presidential candidate will be selected by a nominating convention, similar to that followed by the other major parties.

Legislative

The legislative branch of the Mexican government consists of a bicameral congress (Congreso de la Unión) divided into an upper chamber, or Senate (Cámara de Senadores), and a lower chamber, or Chamber of Deputies (Cámara de Diputados). As in the United States, both chambers are responsible for the discussion and approval of legislation and the ratification of high-level presidential appointments. In theory, the power of introducing bills is shared with the executive, although in practice the executive initiates about 90 percent of all legislation.

The congress holds two ordinary sessions per year. The first session begins on November 1 and continues until no later than December 31; the second session begins on April 15 and may continue until July 15. A Permanent Committee (Comisión Permanente), consisting of thirty-seven members (eighteen senators and nineteen deputies), assumes legislative responsibilities during congressional recesses. The president may call for extraordinary sessions of congress to deal with important legislation.

Historically, the Senate consisted of sixty-four members, two members for each state and two representing the Federal District elected by direct vote for six-year terms. However, as part of the electoral reforms enacted by the Salinas government in 1993, the Senate was doubled in size to 128 members, with one of each state's four seats going to whichever party comes in second in that state. Since 1986 the Chamber of Deputies has consisted of 500 members, 200 of whom are elected by proportional representation from among large plurinominal districts, and the remainder from single-member districts. Members of the Chamber of Deputies serve three-year terms. All members of the congress are barred from immediate reelection but may serve nonconsecutive terms.

The powers of the congress include the right to pass laws, impose taxes, declare war, approve the national budget, approve or reject treaties and conventions made with foreign countries, and ratify diplomatic appointments. The Senate addresses all matters concerning foreign policy, approves international agreements, and confirms presidential appointments. The Chamber of Deputies, much like the United States House of Representatives, addresses all matters pertaining to the government's budget and public expenditures. As in the United States, in cases of impeachment, the Chamber of Deputies has the power to prosecute, and the Senate acts as the jury. In some instances, both chambers share certain powers, such as establishing committees to discuss particular government issues and question government officials. The deputies have the power to appoint a provisional president. In the event of impeachment, the two chambers are convened jointly as a General Congress. Each legislative chamber has a number of committees that study and recommend bills. If there is disagreement between the chambers, a joint committee is appointed to draft a compromise version.

Judicial

The judicial branch of the Mexican government is divided into federal and state systems. Mexico's highest court is the Supreme Court of Justice, located in Mexico City. It consists of twenty-one magistrates and five auxiliary judges, all appointed

The National Palace, the president's official work place
Courtesy Arturo Salinas

by the president and confirmed by the Senate or the Permanent Committee.

Mexican supreme court justices must be Mexican citizens by birth, thirty-five to sixty-five years old, and must have resided in Mexico and held a law degree during the five years preceding their nomination. According to the constitution, supreme court justices are appointed for life but are subject to impeachment by the Chamber of Deputies. In practice, the justices, along with the entire federal judiciary, traditionally submit their resignations at the beginning of each *sexenio.*

The Supreme Court of Justice may meet in joint session or in separate chambers, depending on the type of case before it. The high court is divided into four chambers, each with five justices. These are the Penal Affairs Chamber, Administrative Affairs Chamber, Civil Affairs Chamber, and Labor Affairs Chamber. A fifth chamber, the Auxiliary Chamber, is responsible for the overload of the four regular chambers. Court rulings of both the whole, or plenary, court and the separate chambers are decided on the basis of majority opinion. Rulings by the separate chambers may be overturned by the full court.

There are three levels of federal courts under the Supreme Court of Justice: twelve Collegiate Circuit Courts, each with three magistrates; nine Unitary Circuit Courts, each with six magistrates; and sixty-eight District Courts, each with one judge. Federal judges for the lower courts are appointed by the Supreme Court of Justice. The Collegiate Circuit Courts are comparable to the United States Courts of Appeals. The Collegiate Circuit Courts deal with the protection of individual rights, most commonly hearing cases where an individual seeks a writ of *amparo,* a category of legal protection comparable to a broad form of habeas corpus that safeguards individual civil liberties and property rights. The Unitary Circuit Courts also handle appeals cases. The Collegiate Circuit Courts are located in Mexico City, Toluca, Guadalajara, Monterrey, Hermosillo, Puebla, Veracruz, Torreón, San Luis Potosí, Villahermosa, Morelia, and Mazatlán. The Unitary Circuit Courts are located in Mexico City, Toluca, Guadalajara, Monterrey, Hermosillo, Puebla, Mérida, Torreón, and Mazatlán.

The Mexican legal system is based on Spanish civil law with some influence of the common law tradition. Unlike the United States version of the common law system, under which the judiciary enjoys broad powers of jurisprudence, Spanish civil law is based upon strict adherence to legal codes and minimal jurisprudence. The most powerful juridical instrument is the writ of *amparo,* which can be invoked against acts by any government official, including the president. Unlike the United States system, where courts may rule on basic constitutional matters, the Mexican Supreme Court of Justice is prohibited by the constitution from applying its rulings beyond any individual case. Within this restricted sphere, the Supreme Court of Justice generally displays greater independence in relation to the president than does the legislature, often deciding against the executive in *amparo* cases. Nevertheless, the judiciary seldom attempts to thwart the will of the president on major issues.

State Government

Mexico is divided into thirty-one states and a Federal District that encompasses Mexico City and its immediate environs. Each state has its own constitution, modeled on the national charter, with the right to legislate and levy taxes other than interstate customs duties. Following the federal organization at the national level, state (and local) governments also have

Congress building
Courtesy Arturo Salinas
Supreme Court of Justice building
Courtesy Arturo Salinas

executive, legislative, and judicial branches. Despite its federal structure, Mexico's political system is highly centralized. State governments depend on Mexico City for much of their revenue, which they, in turn, funnel to municipal governments in a clientelist fashion. Mexican presidents have historically played a prominent role in selecting PRI gubernatorial candidates and in settling state-level electoral disputes. President Salinas was especially assertive in this regard, having removed or prevented the seating of eight PRI governors widely believed to have been fraudulently elected.

The state executive branch is headed by a governor, who is directly elected by simple majority vote for a six-year term, and, like the president, may not be reelected. State legislatures are unicameral, consisting of a single Chamber of Deputies that meets in two ordinary sessions per year, with extended periods and extraordinary sessions when needed. Deputies serve three-year terms and may not be immediately reelected. Legislative bills may be introduced by the deputies, the state governor, the state Superior Court of Justice, or by a municipality within a given state. Replicating the pattern of executive dominance at the national level, most policy-making authority at the state level has historically resided in the governor. The state judiciary is headed by a Superior Court of Justice. Justices of the Superior Courts of Justice are appointed by governors with approval of the state legislatures. The superior court magistrates, in turn, appoint all lower state court judges.

The Federal District, which encompasses Mexico City and its southern suburbs, has traditionally fallen under the supervision of the president, who appoints a mayor (*regente*). In addition to performing his municipal duties, the mayor also holds cabinet rank as head of the Department of the Federal District. In September 1993, the congress approved an electoral reform package that introduced the indirect election of the mayor of the Federal District.

The Federal District has local courts and a Representative Assembly, whose members are elected by proportional representation. The assembly, historically a local advisory body with no real legislative power, is scheduled to elect Federal District mayors beginning in late 1996.

Local Government

The basic unit of Mexican government is the municipality (*municipio*), more than 2,000 of which were legally in existence in 1996. Municipal governments are responsible for a variety of public services, including water and sewerage; street lighting; cleaning and maintenance; public safety and traffic; supervision of slaughterhouses; and the maintenance of parks, gardens, and cemeteries. Municipalities are also free to assist state and federal governments in the provision of elementary education, emergency fire and medical services, environmental protection, and the maintenance of historical landmarks.

Municipal governments, headed by a mayor or municipal president (*regente*) and a municipal council (*ayuntamiento*), are popularly elected for three-year terms. Article 115 of the 1917 constitution proclaims the autonomy of local governments according to the principle of the free municipality (*municipio libre*). Although they are authorized to collect property taxes and user fees, municipalities have historically lacked the means to do so, relying mainly on transfers from higher levels of government for approximately 80 percent of their revenues. Responding to concerns that excessive centralization of political power and financial resources would jeopardize long-term popular support for the PRI, President de la Madrid advocated reforming intergovernmental relations to allow greater municipal autonomy. De la Madrid's municipal reform culminated in the 1984 amendments to Article 115, which expanded municipalities' authority to raise revenue and formulate budgets. The Salinas administration's National Solidarity Program (Programa Nacional de Solidaridad—Pronasol) provided another source of revenue for municipal governments (see Social Spending, ch. 2). By bypassing state bureaucracies and channeling federal funds directly to municipalities and community organizations, Pronasol undermined state governments' control over municipal finances, albeit by promoting municipalities' dependence on the federal government.

The Party System

Institutional Revolutionary Party

The PRI, Mexico's "official" party, was the country's preeminent political organization from 1929 until the early 1990s. In terms of power, it was second only to the president, who also serves as the party's effective chief. Until the early 1980s, the PRI's position in the Mexican political system was hegemonic, with opposition parties posing little or no threat to its power base or its near monopoly of public office. This situation changed during the mid-1980s, as opposition parties of the left and right began to seriously challenge PRI candidates for local, state, and national-level offices.

The PRI was founded by Calles in 1929 as the National Revolutionary Party (Partido Nacional Revolucionario—PNR), a loose confederation of local political bosses and military strongmen grouped together with labor unions, peasant organizations, and regional political parties. In its early years, it served primarily as a means of organizing and containing the political competition among the leaders of the various revolutionary factions. Calles, operating through the party organization, was able to undermine much of the strength of peasant and labor organizations that affiliated with the party and to weaken the regional military commanders who had operated with great autonomy throughout the 1920s. By 1934 Calles was in control of Mexican politics and government, even after he left the presidency, largely through his manipulation of the PNR.

Between 1934 and 1940, an intense struggle for political control developed between Calles and the new president, Cárdenas. At the time, Calles represented the conservative elements of the revolutionary coalition, while Cárdenas drew his support from the more radical political elements. To strengthen his hand against Calles, Cárdenas reunited the labor and peasant organizations that Calles had earlier fragmented and formed two national federations, the National Peasant Confederation (Confederación Nacional Campesina—CNC) and the Confederation of Mexican Workers (Confederación de Trabajadores Mexicanos—CTM). Using these organizations as the bases of his support, Cárdenas then reorganized the PNR in 1938, renaming it the Party of the Mexican Revolution (Partido de la Revolución Mexicana—PRM), incorporating the CTM and the CNC and giving the PRM an organization by sectors: labor, agrarian, popular, and military. The creation of these groups and their integration into the party marked the legitimation of the existing interest group organizations and the transformation of the political system from an elite to a mass-based system. Within a year, the PRM claimed some 4.3 million members: 2.5 million peasants, 1.3 million workers, and 500,000 in the popular sector. In 1946 President Manuel Ávila Camacho abolished the military sector, shifted its members into the popular sector, and renamed the party the PRI.

Beginning with the Cárdenas administration in the late 1930s, the PRI and its predecessors engineered an unprecedented political peace. The overt political intervention by the military that had characterized the country's politics throughout the nineteenth and early twentieth centuries largely disappeared when Ávila Camacho, the last president who came from a military background, left office in 1946. For nearly five decades, there were few episodes of large-scale organized violence and no revolutionary movements that enjoyed widespread support, despite considerable economic strains between 1968 and 1975 and a difficult period of economic austerity beginning in 1982.

For the middle class, whose members typically had led rebellions in the past, the PRI provided upward mobility either through politics (the rule of no reelection opened frequent opportunities for public office) or through business during the high-growth period of "stabilizing development" that lasted from the early 1950s until the late 1960s. The PRI also integrated workers and peasants into the political system by claiming to be the only vehicle able to realize their demands for labor union rights and land reform. The party operated much like an urban political machine in the United States. It weakened attempts to form horizontal class- or interest-based political alliances within the lower class by dispensing services to individuals in exchange for their votes. The PRI emphasized personal relationships between individuals of the lower class and party and government officials. It distributed political patronage from the top down to members of organized labor, the agrarian movement, and the popular sector in accordance with each group's relative strength in a given area. Finally, it used electoral fraud, corruption, bribery, and repression when necessary to maintain control over individuals and groups.

The PRI has been widely described as a coalition of networks of aspiring politicians seeking not only positions of power and prestige but also the concomitant opportunity for personal enrichment. At the highest levels of the political system, the major vehicles for corruption have been illegal landholdings and the manipulation of public-sector enterprises. In the lower reaches of the party and governmental hierarchies, the preferred methods of corruption have been bribery, charging the public for legally free public services, charging members of unions for positions, nepotism, and outright theft of public money. This corruption, although condemned by Mexican and foreign observers alike, historically served an important function in the political system by providing a means of upward mobility within the system and ensuring that those who were forced to retire from politics by the principle of no reelection would have little incentive to seek alternatives outside the PRI structure.

Official corruption reached unprecedented levels during the 1970s when petroleum revenues surged as a result of higher oil prices and when newly discovered oil fields in Chiapas and the Bahía de Campeche began producing. Much of the wealth that flowed into the country through the state oil monopoly, Mexican Petroleum (Petróleos Mexicanos— Pemex), was squandered in wasteful and unnecessary projects and the inflation of payrolls. The main beneficiaries of high-level graft during this period were the senior executives of the national oil workers union and high-level PRI functionaries. This brand of official corruption reached new heights during the presidency of López Portillo (1976–82), who allegedly acquired a US$2 million house as a "gift" from the oil workers' union and was subsequently vilified by the media and the public as a symbol of PRI graft.

Public disclosure of the excesses of the López Portillo years, which came to light during the severe financial crisis of the early 1980s, had a significant impact on the PRI's internal politics as well as on its overall level of public support. Internally, the severe public backlash against the PRI discredited many career politicians within the party who had personally benefited from the fiscal profligacy of the López Portillo *sexenio,* and created opportunities for an emerging generation of *técnicos* (technocrats) to assume high-level government posts. Many of these *técnicos* were brought into the cabinet by President de la Madrid to help restore the integrity of the public accounts during the early 1980s financial crisis.

During the de la Madrid *sexenio* (1982–88), the PRI began to downplay its traditional populist and nationalist agenda and adopted a probusiness, free-market platform. These changes produced an intraparty split between the populist wing dominated by *políticos* (career politicians) and the politically inexperienced *técnicos*. The nomination of Salinas, a Harvard-educated political economist, as the PRI candidate for the 1988 presidential election triggered the final rupture between these two groups. Salinas's nomination prompted two important party leaders, Cuauhtémoc Cárdenas (the son of President

Cárdenas and himself a former governor of Michoacán) and Porfirio Muñoz Ledo (a former PRI secretary general), to resign from the PRI and create a broad coalition of leftist parties, labor unions, and grassroots organizations united in support of a presidential bid by Cárdenas (see Party of the Democratic Revolution, this ch.). This leftist faction criticized the "neoliberal" policies of the de la Madrid government and called for a return to the party's traditional populist platform.

Although the PRI party bosses remained loyal to Salinas, allowing the party to win the July 1988 presidential election, the 1988 vote was a major psychological blow to the ruling party. With the 1988 vote, the PRI saw its fifty-year dominance over the political system come to an almost disastrous end. The PRI received its lowest margin of victory ever, a dubious 50.7 percent of all votes cast, down from 71.6 percent in 1982 and 98.7 percent in 1976. For the first time since the consolidation of single-party rule in the 1940s, opposition leaders were elected to the Senate, and the PRI lost more than one-third of the seats in the Chamber of Deputies to the two main opposition forces, the National Action Party (Partido de Acción Nacional—PAN) and the Cárdenas-led coalition. The results of the 1988 elections were widely viewed as marking the end of single-party hegemony by the PRI and were even interpreted by some observers as a prelude to the fragmentation and collapse of the ruling coalition.

Responding to public pressure for political renewal and seeking to avoid further rupture in the party ranks, President Salinas attempted to improve the PRI's public image without fundamentally challenging its authoritarian and clientelist practices. Salinas took steps to clean up the electoral process and moved forcefully against those elements of the party and organized labor most closely associated with corruption. However, Salinas's anticorruption efforts were by no means systematic. In many instances, corrupt officials were dismissed because of their defiance of the new president rather than for their venality. Although he continued de la Madrid's practice of tapping highly trained technocrats to fill cabinet posts, Salinas took care not to completely disavow the party's *político* wing in filling high-level posts. In addition, the new president shrewdly manipulated state resources through popular programs, such as Pronasol, in order to recover the support of low-income Mexicans who had backed Cárdenas in 1988.

President Salinas's political maneuvers and a modest economic recovery resulted in a better showing for the PRI in the midterm elections of August 1991. In the races for 300 electoral districts in the Chamber of Deputies, thirty-two Senate seats, and six governorships, the PRI won 61.4 percent of the votes cast. This was a sizable increase from the 50 percent received in the 1988 national election. Overall, the PRI won 290 seats in the Chamber of Deputies, all but one seat in the Senate, and five of the six contested governorships.

During his administration, Salinas downplayed the corporatist relationships between the state and society instituted by Cárdenas while reaching out to more traditional interest groups. In his efforts to broaden and democratize the PRI, Salinas distanced the party from the PRI-affiliated labor unions and *ejido* associations, while seeking a reconciliation between the PRI and its historical adversaries, such as foreign investors, agribusiness, private banks, the Roman Catholic Church, and export industries. In foreign affairs, the PRI shed much of its economic nationalism under Salinas, while retaining its independence from the United States on regional security matters. However, even President Salinas was unwilling to seek a constitutional amendment to end public ownership of petroleum and natural gas deposits, a mainstay of PRI nationalism for more than sixty years.

The executive organization of the PRI is pyramidal, with the president of the Republic at the top. The party is headed by a president and a secretary general, who together direct a National Executive Committee of the party's top leaders. At the party base, there is a National Assembly, which meets every six years to discuss and review the party's platform as well as to formally nominate the party's candidate for the presidency. The National Assembly also elects the members of the National Executive Council. Although the party's presidential candidate is formally nominated at the National Assembly Congress, in practice the assembly has served only to ratify the candidate handpicked by the president through the *dedazo*. In accordance with political reforms approved in the early 1990s, the PRI's National Assembly is expected to assume a much more significant role in nominating the party's presidential candidate for the election to be held in the year 2000.

National Action Party

Founded in 1939 by Manuel Gómez Morán, the National

Action Party (Partido de Acción Nacional—PAN) was the first genuine opposition party to develop in Mexico. The PAN emerged as a conservative reaction against the nationalizations and land confiscations undertaken by the Cárdenas government during the 1930s. The PAN resembled a standard Christian Democratic party, and its early support derived primarily from the Roman Catholic Church, the business sector, and other groups alienated by the left-wing populist reforms of the Cárdenas government. Although the PAN is much more conservative than the PRI on social issues, since the mid-1980s the PAN's economic program has been almost indistinguishable from that of the PRI governments it has attempted to supplant.

The PAN has traditionally favored a limited role of the government in the economy, an orientation that has been adopted by the PRI during the past fifteen years under presidents de la Madrid, Salinas, and Zedillo. Historically, the PAN also has campaigned in favor of a breakup of the communal *ejidos* into individually owned plots of land. In 1992 the Salinas administration introduced radical reforms to the land tenure law that allowed *ejidatarios* to sell their plots and to consolidate their holdings (see Rural Society, ch. 2). This convergence of PRI and PAN economic programs encouraged the PAN congressional delegation to work closely with the Salinas administration to pass the government's sweeping economic reforms. In an effort to distance itself from the PRI, in the mid-1990s, the PAN has stressed issues such as the need for democratization, eradication of government corruption, and additional electoral reforms.

Traditionally, the PAN has had strong support in the country's wealthiest and most urbanized regions of the north and center, particularly in the Federal District, Jalisco, Nuevo León, Puebla, and Sonora. The effects of PAN victories in the northern part of the country since the 1980s are highly significant, particularly in the states of Baja California Norte, Chihuahua, Durango, Nuevo León, Sinaloa, and Sonora. The PAN has also displayed political strength in the states of Guanajuato, Jalisco, and Yucatán. The PAN won the governorships and congressional majorities in Baja California Norte and Chihuahua during the Salinas administration, and the local congress in the state of Guanajuato gave a third governorship to the PAN after a state election had been plagued with irregularities. The PAN's major handicap has been its lack of appeal to urban labor and peasant groups.

The PAN has presented a candidate in every presidential race since 1946 with the exception of 1976, when its leadership could not reach consensus on a candidate. It has always been the main opposition to the PRI, although in the 1988 presidential election its presidential candidate, Manuel Clouthier, ran third to Salinas and Cárdenas. By 1992 the PAN controlled more than 100 municipal governments in addition to the three governorships. With Diego Fernández de Cevallos as its candidate and "por un México sin mentiras" ("for a Mexico without lies") as its campaign slogan, the PAN won a comfortable second place in the 1994 presidential race. The second-place win consolidated the PAN's role as the main opposition political force in the country.

Democratic Revolutionary Party

The Democratic Revolutionary Party (Partido Revolucionario Democrático—PRD), established in 1989, evolved from the National Democratic Front (Frente Democrático Nacional—FDN), under the leadership of Cuauhtémoc Cárdenas. Cárdenas left the PRI in 1988 in protest over its choice of Salinas, a free-market reformer, as the PRI's presidential nominee. The PRD's party program emphasizes social welfare concerns and opposes most of the economic reforms implemented since the mid-1980s.

The PRD's agenda dates back to the populist and nationalist measures implemented by President Lázaro Cárdenas during the 1930s. The party promotes economic nationalism, as opposed to the structural neoliberal changes that focus on increasing trade and foreign investment to boost the Mexican economy introduced by the PRI during President de la Madrid's administration. Although the PRD holds a good part of the former communist and socialist parties' rank and file, the PRD is controlled by former PRI leaders. An estimated 70 percent of its leadership consists of former PRI members, while 30 percent consists of former members of the Mexican communist and socialist parties. The PRD president, Porfirio Muñoz Ledo, served as president of the PRI during the *sexenio* of Luis Echeverría Álvarez. The PRD opposed most of the constitutional amendments passed during the Salinas government, the most important being the ecclesiastical, agrarian, and electoral system reforms. Although the PRD is currently recognized as an opposition voice in the national debate, it remains in a distant third place in the electoral scenario. Toward the end of

the 1994 presidential race, the left strongly criticized Cuauhtémoc Cárdenas for having lent qualified support to the broad
principles of the North American Free Trade Agreement
(NAFTA) and the privatization of some state-owned companies. Despite these changes, Cárdenas and the PRD are committed to greater state control of the economy and propose the
renegotiation of parts of NAFTA with the United States and
Canada.

Minor Opposition Parties

In 1954 dissident members of the PRI established the
Authentic Party of the Mexican Revolution (Partido Auténtico
de la Revolución Mexicana—PARM). Its political platform,
which is based on the principles of the Mexican Revolution
and the constitution of 1917, is strongly nationalistic. The
PARM has a limited role in national politics, although it was
able to maintain its electoral registration status as well as its
minority representation in the lower chamber until the 1994
elections, when it received less than 0.5 percent of the vote.
The PARM temporarily joined the FDN during the 1988 elections but broke with the party coalition in 1989.

The Popular Socialist Party (Partido Popular Socialista—
PPS) was first organized in 1948 by a radical sector of the PRI
led by Vicente Lombardo Toledano, the founder of the PRI's
labor organization. Despite the PPS's Marxist orientation, its
membership has traditionally supported the official party's candidate in presidential elections, while working closely with the
PRI in most initiatives dealing with the expansion of the government's role in the economy. In 1988, however, the PPS
broke with tradition and joined the FDN in support of Cárdenas's presidential bid. The PPS fielded its own candidate, Mar-
cela Lombardo Otero, in the 1994 presidential election. Otero
received 0.46 percent of the total vote.

The Cárdenas Front of the National Reconstruction Party
(Partido del Frente Cardenista de Reconstrucción Nacional—
PFCRN), formerly the Socialist Workers' Party, was established
in 1973 with labor support. It traditionally had worked closely
with the PRI, but joined the FDN in supporting the candidacy
of Cárdenas in 1988. The PFCRN ran its own candidate, Rafael
Aguilar Talamantes, in the 1994 presidential race, receiving
0.77 percent of the vote.

Other small political parties that registered for the 1994
presidential election included the Mexican Green Ecologist

Party (Partido Verde Ecologista Mexicano—PVEM), the Labor Party (Partido del Trabajo—PT), and the National Opposition Union (Unión Nacional Opositora—UNO). Support for the PT and the PVEM is found predominantly in urban areas. The PT operates mainly in the Federal District, where it made a surprisingly strong showing in 1994.

Of the six small political parties that participated in the 1994 elections (PARM, PFCRN, PPS, PT, PVEM, and UNO), only the PT and its candidate, Cecilia Soto González, received more than 3 percent of the vote. Under current electoral law, the PT is the only minor party that may legally contest the next presidential election in 2000.

Institutions of Civil Society

Organized Labor

Labor unions are mostly representative of workers in urban areas. Most labor unions are affiliated with the PRI through the Confederation of Mexican Workers (Confederación de Trabajadores Mexicanos—CTM), which is associated with some independent unions and federations in an umbrella organization known as the Congress of Labor (Congreso del Trabajo—CT). During August 1991, the CT confirmed its direct relationship with the government party in a document called the Political Agreement Between the PRI and the Organization of the CT.

The CT, considered the labor sector of the PRI, consists of more than thirty organizations encompassing 85 percent of the unionized workforce. In the early 1990s, Mexico had an estimated 9.5 million unionized workers. The CT mediates between the labor unions and the government. At the same time, it provides the state with a formal mechanism for political manipulation of the labor force.

The CTM is the largest and most influential organization in the CT, comprising over 11,000 labor unions with more than 5 million union members. It is considered the spearhead of the Mexican labor movement. Since 1941 the CTM has been tightly controlled by its secretary general, Fidel Velázquez, considered one of the most influential political figures in Mexico.

The second organization within the CT is the Federation of Unions of Workers in the Service of the State (Federación de Sindicatos de Trabajadores al Servicio del Estado—FSTSE). The FSTSE was established in 1938 as an umbrella organization for labor unions within the federal civil system and other government-related organizations. In 1990 the FSTSE consisted of eighty-nine unions with a total membership of 1.8 million employees.

The Revolutionary Confederation of Workers and Peasants (Confederación Revolucionaria de Obreros y Campesinos—CROC) is the third largest labor organization within the CT. The CROC was established in 1952; since 1980, it has been under the leadership of Alberto Juárez Blancas. During the 1990s, the CROC had an estimated membership of some 600,000. Other important labor organizations are the Regional Confederation of Mexican Workers (Confederación Regional de Obreros Mexicanos—CROM), the National Federation of Independent Unions (Federación Nacional de Sindicatos Independientes—FNSI), the Confederation of Workers and Peasants (Confederación de Trabajadores y Campesinos—CTC), the International Proletarian Movement (Movimiento Proletario Internacional—MPI), the Confederation of Revolutionary Workers (Confederación de Obreros Revolucionarios—COR), the General Confederation of Workers (Confederación General de Trabajadores—CGT), the Authentic Labor Front (Frente Auténtico del Trabajo—FAT), and the Revolutionary Confederation of Workers (Confederación Revolucionaria de Trabajadores—CRT). There are, in addition, some 1.5 million members of independent unions and company labor organizations.

In theory, labor-management relations are well defined by the Labor Code, which leaves little margin for bargaining in labor disputes. All labor unions receive official recognition by applying to the Secretariat of Labor and Social Welfare. Once it is officially recognized, a union is protected by the Labor Code, which details the rights of each official organization to receive social security payments, to participate in profit sharing, and to use meeting halls, among many other benefits. The code stipulates that strikes are illegal if unauthorized by the secretariat and that workers participating in an illegal strike will be subject to government sanctions and dismissal by their employers.

Corruption, paternalism, and abuse of union funds have traditionally been rampant in the labor movement. In recent years, however, the traditional oligarchic leadership of most Mexican labor unions has been challenged by the rank and file, as well as by independent unions wishing to end the use of leadership positions to amass wealth and power. The lack of support for Salinas's presidential bid by the leadership of some powerful unions, in particular that of the union of oil workers, contributed to a change in government relations with union groups. President Salinas launched an anticorruption campaign during his first year in government, toppling from power strong labor leaders in corruption-related scandals. Although the level of corruption and abuse of power has not been substantially reduced, the political relationship and corporatist structure between the labor sector and the party are currently undergoing profound changes. There is a sharp distinction between two clashing forces in the labor movement: the traditional leadership that forcefully resists political change and a new generation that strongly supports the government's neoliberal policies currently in place. In the mid-1990s, labor groups have less impact on Mexican politics than they did in the past.

Business Organizations

Traditionally, business interests in Mexico are driven by government policies and interests. In addition to participation of individual businessmen in politics, many business groups are represented in government agencies and commissions. There has always been a close connection between the business community and the different economic cabinets. The most influential of all business associations is the Confederation of National Chambers of Commerce (Confederación de Cámaras Nacionales de Comercio—Concanaco). The Confederation of Chambers of Industry (Confederación de Cámaras de Industria—Concamin) serves as the umbrella organization for industrial associations. There is also the National Chamber of Manufacturing Industries (Cámara Nacional de la Industria de la Transformación—Canacintra), which historically has represented small and medium-sized businesses. A sharp distinction exists between small and big business in Mexican politics. Although technically these organizations are not integrated into a particular political party, contributions of big business go first to the PRI to reward government policies that benefit big business and to make sure that such policies continue. According to PRI Finance Secretary Oscar Espinoza Villareal, the Mexican private sector contributed between 54 and 67 billion new pesos (for value of the new peso—see Glossary) to the campaigns of government party candidates for the August 1994 elections.

Business associations such as Concanaco play an active role in government policy debates. Most of the business sector currently supports the reduction of trade barriers, liberal economic policies, and conservative labor legislation. The success of the liberal policies launched during the Salinas *sexenio* greatly benefited the Mexican private sector. Thus, relations between the business community and the PRI improved significantly. A clear example of the improved relationship was a well-publicized gathering held in February 1993, when thirty of Mexico's multimillionaires pledged an average US$25 million each in support of the 1994 PRI election campaign. At the fund-raising dinner, television baron Emilio Azcarrago, considered the richest man in Latin America, pledged US$70 million to the government's party "in gratitude" for his prosperity during the Salinas administration. The great disparity in funding between the PRI and the opposition during the 1994 electoral race was clearly attributable to generous contributions from domestic private enterprises to the PRI.

The Church

Although there has been conflict between church and state in Mexico since the country's independence, more than 90 percent of the population remains Roman Catholic, according to 1990 census estimates. The state feud with the Roman Catholic Church is reflected in the 1917 constitution, which imposes many restrictions on the influence and privileges of the clergy in Mexico. The early drafts of the 1917 constitution banned public religious ceremonies, the establishment of monastic orders, and property ownership by the Roman Catholic Church, and forbade the clergy from participating in elections. All church buildings, according to law, were considered national property, and church ministers had to be Mexican nationals. The law also prohibited criticism of public law and institutions, both public and private, by members of the clergy.

Far from bring a traditional conservative force, however, the Roman Catholic Church has been a strong advocate for social and political change. In the late 1980s, for example, the clergy were active in the northern states, condemning electoral fraud to the extent of threatening to cease celebrating masses unless there were a recount of the vote. The Roman Catholic Church was also instrumental throughout the 1980s in demanding recognition of its legal status and electoral participation for the clergy. Despite the traditional view of the Roman Catholic Church as representative or supporter of the elites, the Mexican Roman Catholic Church has emerged during the last decades as the defender of social justice, and the more progressive clergy have worked closely with underprivileged sectors to increase economic and social reform.

The Salinas administration changed dramatically the relations between church and state in Mexico (see Church-State Relations, ch. 2). During the fall of 1991, Salinas's government took the first steps toward lifting some restrictions on church activities and introduced a reform proposal to end constitutional limits on the church. The new law, approved by the Congress in December 1991 and promulgated in January 1992, amended the constitution of 1917. Under the new law, the Roman Catholic Church is formally recognized by the state, the clergy are allowed to vote, the possession of property by churches is legal, and religion may be taught in private schools. Mexico also established diplomatic relations with the Vatican, relations that had been broken in 1867. State and church, nevertheless, remain separate, and church buildings remain state property.

Protestant groups in Mexico have tended to support the PRI, in light of the party's broad appeal. The political alternatives are not viable options for Mexican Protestants because the opposition on the right, the PAN, openly represents Roman Catholicism and groups on the left exclude religion from their political goals. Toward the latter part of the twentieth century, the participation of Protestant groups in Mexican politics increased as Protestants supported efforts aimed at political change.

Given the country's anticlerical history, it is highly unlikely that the Roman Catholic Church will assume a direct role in Mexican politics in the near future. However, the church's traditional commitment to social justice and economic development, along with the government redefinition of its institutional responsibilities, provides the Roman Catholic Church with a strong voice on future political issues.

The Media

Based on the number of newspapers, publishers, radio stations, and television networks in the country, Mexico is considered the media power center of Spanish-speaking Latin America. Mexico's mainstream newspapers and periodicals range in political ideology and independence from the official government newspaper *El Nacional* to the left-wing independent *El Proceso*. Although the press was for many years generally pro-establishment and supportive of the PRI, it diversified during the 1980s to reflect a wider spectrum of opinion. In early 1994, the government postponed its stated plans to sell *El Nacional* to private owners but declared that the newspaper would no longer receive public funding.

The constitution of 1917 explicitly guarantees freedom of the press. Article 7 forbids prior censorship, and an amendment to Article 6 adopted in 1977 declares that "the right of information will be guaranteed by the state." However, these guarantees are highly qualified in practice. The Press Law of 1917, for instance, restricts the press on matters of personal privacy, morality, and public health. Many other regulations govern the news media. The 1960 Law on Radio and Television, for instance, forbids the broadcast of material deemed offensive to national heroes.

Although nominally independent, the news media are subject to a variety of mainly indirect economic and political pressures from the government. The Secretariat of Communications and Transport supervises the news media, granting publishing and broadcast licenses and ensuring adherence to the media laws. Successive PRI governments have influenced the news media by paying individual journalists for favorable coverage, by restricting access to newsprint and ink (the state monopolizes the production of both, although this control was somewhat reduced under President Salinas), by withholding information from critical journalists, and especially by granting or withholding government advertising, an important source of revenue for the press. Many newspapers accept government payments for the insertion of official announcements disguised as editorials. Occasionally, the government provides indirect financial inducements to particular journalists (for example, by offering them part of the payment for official advertising run by their newspapers). Some journalists and opposition political parties have accused the government of trying to conceal the extent of official subsidies to journalists by redirecting payoffs through the PRI's Office of Information.

Government tolerance of press freedoms varies according to the sensitivities of the president in office. Traditionally, the media avoid direct criticism of an incumbent president. On sensitive issues affecting the government, the press provides only minimal coverage. Among the many unwritten rules is one that says that journalists are expected to respect the image of the president and other high-level government officials.

In essence, government policies may be criticized, but elected individuals must not be ridiculed. Since the early 1980s, the trend toward a more open political debate has brought greater tolerance of criticism in the media. Some argue that this tolerance, which has occurred faster than the increasing democratization of the political system, has definitively contributed to increasing public awareness of the need for changes within the Mexican political system.

Television is highly biased toward the official party, as illustrated by the open support the Televisa network gives to the government. Televisa is part of Mexican Telesystem (Telesistema Mexicano), considered the biggest communications conglomerate in the developing world, as well as one of the world's major transnational media empires. Televisa's political and economic influence in Mexico is extensive. Aside from the ownership of television and radio stations, it has significant interests in newsprint and publishing, record production, home videos, cinemas, advertising and marketing, real estate, tourism, sports, and the food processing and transport industries.

Mexico City has fifteen newspapers; its dailies account for more than 50 percent of the national circulation. In 1994 there were eight newspapers in Mexico City with a daily circulation of more than 100,000 issues: *Esto* (450,000), *La Prensa* (300,000), *Novedades* (240,000), *Ovaciones* (220,000), *El Heraldo de México* (209,600), *Excélsior* (200,000), *El Financiero* (135,000), and *El Universal* (122,000). *Excélsior* is the most prestigious national daily and one of the most prominent newspapers in Latin America, known for its breadth of coverage, analytical style, and relative independence. The oldest of the traditional newspapers is *El Universal*, closely associated with the government throughout the 1970s, but currently known for its independence in reporting. *El Nacional* is the official newspaper of the federal government. The largest newspaper group is the Organización Editorial Mexicana (OEM), which owns some ninety newspapers throughout the country. The second largest publishing group is Novedades Editores, which is part of the Telesistema Mexicano conglomerate. Some of the leading daily newspapers, such as *Excélsior* and *La Prensa*, are run as cooperatives.

There are five national news agencies: Notimex, Infomex, Noti-Acción, Notipress, and Agencia Mexicana de Información. Infomex is the largest, with almost 100 offices throughout the country and some twenty foreign correspondents. All leading international agencies have bureaus in Mexico City.

National broadcasting stations are divided into commercial and cultural networks. All commercial stations are financed by advertising (both public and private) but must provide 12 percent of broadcasting time for government use. All cultural stations are operated by government agencies or by educational institutions. Media analysts expect that the economic policies pursued by the Salinas and Zedillo administrations will have a major impact on the media by further reducing state intervention and promoting the concentration of private ownership.

The Electoral Process and Political Dynamics

The Electoral Process

Article 41 of the constitution of 1917 and subsequent amendments regulate electoral politics in Mexico. Suffrage is universal for all citizens eighteen or older, and voting is compulsory, although this provision is rarely enforced. The Mexican constitution enshrines the principle of direct election by popular vote of the president and most other elected officials. Executive officeholders may not be reelected, and legislators may not serve consecutive terms. Ordinary elections are held every six years for president and members of the Senate, and every three years for deputies. Since 1986 midterm elections have renewed one-half of the Senate, in addition to the entire Chamber of Deputies. Gubernatorial elections are evenly distributed throughout a *sexenio*, so that ordinarily no more than six governorships are contested in any given year.

Although holding multicandidate elections in which the electorate makes the final choice is one of the basic principles of the Mexican Revolution, the electoral process in Mexico has historically fallen short of this liberal ideal. During the sixty-year period of single-party hegemony that followed the consolidation of the revolutionary regime, regular elections became an important symbol of stability and of the regime's self-ascribed democratic character. Beyond fulfilling an ambiguous plebiscitary function, however, elections were not intended as a means of selecting new leaders, nor were they usually relevant to the public policy process. Instead, leadership turnover was centrally controlled by the president, while most significant interaction between public officials and the citizenry took place within the context of day-to-day corporatist bargaining and informal clientelist relationships.

As the beneficiary of a noncompetitive electoral process, the official party has historically enjoyed a near monopoly of all levels of public office. For almost six decades, the principal political battles in Mexico were fought among elite factions and interest groups within the PRI party structure, with little or no meaningful participation by independent organizations or opposition parties. During this prolonged period of one-party hegemony, several modest electoral reforms were implemented by the government in order to maintain the appearance of electoral democracy and undercut the appeal of latent opposition movements. Electoral reforms enacted during the 1970s included the allotment of a minimum number of congressional seats to both legitimate and "satellite" opposition parties. Additional steps toward greater political pluralism were taken during the early 1980s, when President de la Madrid embarked on a campaign to make local-level politics more competitive.

By the mid-1980s, the electoral arena had been liberalized and the political space for opposition had expanded to such an extent that the PRI found itself increasingly challenged at the ballot box. In 1985 the landslide victories of PRI candidates in gubernatorial and municipal elections in the northern state of Chihuahua led to widespread allegations of electoral fraud by the opposition PAN, which had expected major wins in one of its traditional strongholds. In an unprecedented series of public protests, a variety of civic groups, with support from the Roman Catholic Church, staged massive demonstrations denouncing the official tallies.

Responding to increasing popular pressure for democratization, the de la Madrid administration in 1986 introduced an electoral reform package that expanded opportunities for an opposition presence in the congress. The 1986 Electoral Reform Law enlarged the Chamber of Deputies from 400 to 500 seats and doubled the number of congressional seats filled by proportional representation to 200. Of the 500 deputyships, one each is allocated to 300 electoral districts, elected by simple plurality in single-member districts comparable to those in the United States. The remaining 200 seats are assigned by proportional representation based on a party's share of the national vote tally. The proportional seats give opposition parties an opportunity to be represented in the congress even if they lose all of the district races. The PRI assured, however, that the distribution of proportional seats would not become a means for a coalition of parties without a plurality of the overall vote to take control of the lower house. A clause in the electoral law provides that enough proportional seats in the Chamber of Deputies be assigned to the party winning an overall plurality in the election to give that party a majority in the Chamber of Deputies.

Theoretically, no party is barred from holding a single-member district seat, although in practice an overwhelming number of such seats have been held by the PRI. The increase in the number of proportional seats was a concession to the opposition, which relies heavily on proportional seating for its representation in the congress. The 1986 reform also introduced proportional representation in state legislatures as well as government funding for all registered political parties.

The 1988 Elections

The 1988 elections were a watershed in the history of Mexican politics, marking a radical shift in the country's political dynamics and providing the first test of the 1986 electoral reforms. The emergence of two nationally prominent opposition candidates afforded an unprecedented challenge to the PRI's electoral machine, which until that time had faced mostly obscure and poorly financed adversaries.

Assailed by a partisan rupture over the nomination of Salinas, which ultimately led to the defection of much of the PRI's populist wing to the leftist opposition, the PRI party apparatus was under intense pressure to produce a victory or face disintegration. Within the context of a national economic crisis, an intraparty split, and a hotly contested presidential race, many observers expected the PRI to resort to fraud to secure a decisive win.

Although the PRI maintained control of the presidency and preserved its congressional majority in the July 1988 balloting, the elections were a blow to the PRI's preeminent position in Mexican politics. The PRI suffered a dramatic erosion of 18 percent in its share of the presidential vote from the previous election and surrendered an unprecedented 48 percent of seats in the Chamber of Deputies to the opposition. The official tally, which showed Salinas winning a bare majority of 50.7 percent of the vote, was questioned by an unexpected weeklong delay in the computerized tally and widespread reports of vote fraud and irregularities. As a result, the new administration began its term in office as one of the most unpopular in recent Mexican history.

The Salinas Presidency: Reform and Retrenchment

Upon assuming office in December 1988, Salinas faced grave challenges to his authority as president. Among his most pressing concerns was the need to defuse political tensions that had arisen in the highly polarized climate of the election. The defection of many former PRI stalwarts and the threat of further erosion of the party ranks also placed enormous pressure on Salinas to relax the economic austerity measures put in place by his predecessor. Compounding the new government's problems was the fact that, for the first time in its history, the PRI did not command the two-thirds majority in the Chamber of Deputies required to amend the constitution. To continue liberalizing the economy, the government would need to negotiate with the 101 delegates of the "moderate" opposition (the center-right PAN) to remove the remaining constitutional barriers to reform.

Perhaps the most formidable political challenge faced by the new Salinas administration was mistrust of the official party's leadership and its lack of credibility among a likely majority of the electorate in light of the questionable results of the 1988 presidential vote. In the aftermath of the narrow PRI presidential victory and facing widespread charges of electoral fraud, President Salinas sought limited reforms of the electoral process without disavowing the PRI's many legal and financial advantages in the political system.

Seeking to restore the government's credibility and to pacify the opposition, Salinas increased the opportunities for opposition politicians to take office at the state and local levels. This strategy benefited mainly the PAN, whose free-market economic policies closely resembled those of the modernizing *técnico* wing of the PRI. Whereas previous PRI administrations had been willing to concede some municipalities to the PAN, the growth of opposition strength after the 1988 elections compelled the PRI to begin surrendering state governments as well.

The first test of Salinas's commitment to cleaner gubernatorial elections came in 1989, when the PRI conceded its first governorship to an opposition party by accepting a PAN victory in Baja California Norte. In 1991 PRI victories in the gubernatorial elections in Guanajuato and San Luis Potosí sparked widespread allegations of fraud. In both cases, the president

Carlos Salinas de Gortari,
president, 1988–94
Courtesy Embassy of Mexico,
Washington

intervened by forcing the local PRI candidate to step down. Whereas in San Luis Potosí another PRI leader was installed as interim governor, in Guanajuato the interim governorship was handed to the PAN candidate.

The 1992 gubernatorial elections in Chihuahua and Michoacán illustrated the Salinas administration's ambivalent approach toward the opposition in general. Although the PAN candidate won and was allowed to take office in Chihuahua, the PRI spent vast amounts of party and government funds to defeat the PRD in its regional stronghold of Michoacán. Following months of strident PRD protests over the official results, Salinas faced the prospect of a massive protest march on Mexico City. The president was finally compelled to intervene and replace the sitting governor with a more suitable PRI substitute.

Although President Salinas's rejection of overt electoral fraud was by no means novel or systematic, his admonitions concerning fraud in state and local elections did help curb some of the more conspicuous abuses. In addition, the president's moves against individuals associated with corruption served as a powerful weapon in his reformist struggles against the most recalcitrant factions of the PRI old guard. Many members of the PRI's *político* wing opposed the president's economic policies and resented central government interference in state and local politics.

Contradicting his moves on behalf of more transparent and competitive elections, Salinas took some measures that made it more difficult for the opposition to contest the PRI's public policy initiatives. In the name of preserving "governability," Salinas resorted frequently to his executive prerogatives in pushing legislation through the Congress with a minimum of public debate. Although the 1990 electoral reform created institutions and a legal framework to fight electoral fraud and abuses, it also contained a new formula for legislative seating that made it more difficult for the opposition to gain seats in the Chamber of Deputies. Under the 1990 electoral code, the threshold for obtaining an automatic majority of seats in the chamber was reduced to 35 percent of the national vote. This threshold practically ensured that any future PRI administration could count on a PRI-controlled Chamber of Deputies to pass its legislative initiatives. This highly unpopular electoral law was rescinded in 1994 during the reforms leading to the August elections.

One of the key features of the 1990 electoral code was the abolition of the discredited Federal Electoral Commission and its replacement with a new Federal Electoral Institute (Instituto Federal Electoral—IFE). The IFE is a semiautononomous organization, consisting of representatives from government and the major political parties. It supervises elections and investigates complaints of irregularities. The IFE also administers the entire electoral process at the federal, state, and local levels. During the early 1990s, reforms of the IFE strengthened its capacity to serve as a nonpartisan electoral commission. These reforms included the introduction of majority nonpartisan representation (six out of eleven seats) in the IFE governing board, a legal framework for Mexican and foreign observers to monitor the elections, and an independent audit of the national voter list. Other electoral rules implemented during the Salinas *sexenio* included the compilation of a new and more accurate national electoral roll, and the issue of new voter registration cards bearing voter photographs and fingerprints.

The Salinas government reform program was twofold. It focused on economic growth and the replacement of wide-ranging subsidies to the middle class by a welfare program targeted at the poorest sectors of Mexican society. In a coordinated effort to stimulate economic growth and restructure the economy, Salinas promoted the privatization of state firms that brought more than US$10 billion to the Mexican government. The administration also launched an active campaign to increase foreign investment in Mexico. A second approach involved the massive National Solidarity Program (Programa Nacional de Solidaridad—Pronasol), which was to help the poor and attract political support (see Social Spending, ch. 2). Pronasol distributed several billion dollars, derived from privatization funds, aimed at delivering public works projects to poor areas within the country. Heavy government spending on social projects (schools, health clinics, and roads, among others) contributed to PRI victories in the 1991 midterm elections.

Two important events in 1994 led to dramatic political reforms. First came the Chiapas rebellion on New Year's Day, in which an army of some 2,000 peasants led by the masked Subcommander Marcos demanded social justice and democratization of the Mexican political system (see President Salinas, ch. 1). Two months later, PRI presidential candidate Colosio was assassinated while campaigning in Tijuana.

Despite the rhetoric calling for political reform and democratization, President Salinas actually strengthened the traditional pattern of centralized authority in the decision-making process. A clear example of the continuation of the *dedazo* was the tight control and secrecy around the unveiling of the second PRI presidential candidate, Zedillo, soon after Colosio's assassination. Critics charged that much of the effort to curb voting fraud stemmed not from a change in institutions but from the personal intervention of President Salinas. Electoral reform was also inhibited by a lack of meaningful political participation by women (who did not attain voting rights until 1954) and by ethnic minorities. Despite the glorification of Mexico's indigenous history in popular art and literature, Mexico's indigenous peoples have been largely marginalized in national politics.

Foreign Relations

The principles of Mexican foreign policy are respect for international law and the judicial equality of states, respect for the sovereignty and independence of nations, nonintervention in the domestic affairs of other countries, the peaceful resolution of conflicts, and the promotion of collective security through participation in international organizations. Traditionally, Mexico's foreign policy has been considered leftist, prorevolutionary, and nationalistic. Demonstrating independence from United States foreign policy, Mexico supported the Cuban government during the 1960s, the Sandinista (see Glossary) revolution in Nicaragua during the late 1970s, and leftist revolutionary groups in El Salvador during the 1980s.

Mexico has played a minor role in international affairs through most of its history. Since the mid-nineteenth century, Mexican foreign policy has focused primarily on the United States, its northern neighbor, largest trading partner, and the most powerful actor in hemispheric and world affairs. Mexico's role in international affairs was limited until the 1970s, mainly because of the country's need to concentrate on domestic issues, particularly on internal stability and economic growth.

The discovery of vast petroleum reserves during the 1970s, however, placed Mexico in the forefront of oil producers and exporters. Mexico soon became the principal supplier of oil to the United States after the 1973 energy crisis. The heavy inflow of dollars contributed to changing Mexico's perceptions of its role in world affairs while increasing its potential of becoming an important regional power. Mexico has maintained an independent oil policy, however, refusing to join the Organization of the Petroleum Exporting Countries (OPEC) during the 1970s, but participating in the Organization of Latin American Petroleum Exporting Countries (OLAPEC) during the 1980s.

Beginning with the presidency of Luis Echeverría (1970–76), Mexico developed and implemented a more independent and assertive foreign policy. Following an activist policy independent of the United States, the Echeverría government asserted Mexico's position as a leader in the developing world's affairs, particularly on discussions for establishing a new international economic order as part of the so-called "North-South Dialogue." The Echeverría administration boycotted the General Assembly meeting of the Organization of American States (OAS) in 1973 to protest the military coup in Chile that deposed the popularly elected government of Salvador Allende Gossens and suspended diplomatic relations with Chile and South Africa because of these governments' human rights violations. The Mexican government frequently criticized United States foreign policy for favoring military regimes throughout the Third World. Most distinctively, Mexico adopted an aggressive role as a leader within Latin America in concerted efforts

Ernesto Zedillo Ponce de León,
president, 1994–
Courtesy Embassy of Mexico,
Washington

to adopt a unified position in regional relations against the United States.

During the late 1970s, Mexico broke diplomatic relations with the Somoza regime in Nicaragua on the advent of the Sandinista revolution and in 1980 joined Venezuela in the San José Accords, providing favorable trade conditions for oil supply to the depressed economies of Caribbean and Central American countries. In 1983 Mexico was instrumental in the establishment of the Contadora (see Glossary) Group, a diplomatic effort by four regional governments (Colombia, Mexico, Panama, and Venezuela) to present a Latin American solution to the crisis in Central America. The document developed by the Contadora Group was instrumental in the final Central American Peace Plan (see The United States and the Crisis in Mexico, ch. 1).

During the Salinas administration, the central theme of Mexican foreign policy became free trade, especially NAFTA. Mexico focused on bilateral discussions with countries within the hemisphere in an effort to improve trade and investment potential. By 1994 it had signed free-trade agreements with Venezuela and Colombia (effective January 1, 1995) as well as with Bolivia. Under President Salinas, Mexican nationalism was redefined as "progressive nationalism," or the pursuit of economic development while strengthening Mexico's international role. Salinas felt that national independence demanded that Mexico effectively insert itself into the international market. In the mid-1990s, President Ernesto Zedillo continued to stress Mexico's strategic position and market potential worldwide.

Relations with the United States

Throughout its history, Mexico has had an ambivalent love-hate relationship with its northern neighbor. Nationalist rhetoric continuously highlights the loss of one-half of Mexico's territory and natural resources to the United States in the 1800s. Even at times when United States-Mexican relations have been at their best, this loss is still present in Mexican rhetoric. During the Rio Group summit in September 1994, for example, President Salinas commented on the United Nations-sponsored United States intervention in Haiti, "Having suffered an external intervention by the United States, in which we lost more than half of our territory, Mexico cannot accept any proposal for intervention by any nation of the region." In economic terms, good relations with the United States have long been critical for Mexico, given that its northern neighbor is its principal trading partner, both for exports and imports. For its part, the United States gives serious consideration to its relations with Mexico because of Mexico's strategic location on the United States southern border as well as the fact that Mexico has the largest oil deposits in Latin America.

Relations between the countries often have been characterized by conflict. Analysts attribute much of the antagonism to the great disparities in wealth between the two countries; a history of intervention by the United States that makes Mexico highly critical and suspicious of United States positions; cultural differences and stereotypes of both nations; and the high levels of interdependence on many socioeconomic and political issues, both at the national level and in border areas.

In the past, Mexico defied the United States on a number of crucial hemispheric issues. Mexico never broke relations with the Cuban communist regime as did the rest of Latin America in the early 1960s. During President Echeverría's *sexenio*, Mexico took a leading role in demands for a new international economic order. During the 1970s, Mexico challenged the United States position in Central America and led a concerted regional effort that excluded the United States to bring a peaceful end to regional conflicts. During the 1980s, Mexico was highly critical of United States policy in El Salvador and, along with the French government, called for formal recognition of the Salvadoran guerrillas in the peace process.

The most important bilateral issues in the 1990s are drugs, trade, and illegal immigration into the United States. Drug trafficking is a pressing issue for both Mexico, as a producer and point of entry of the drug trade from South America into the United States drug market, and the United States, as a major consumer. Mexico insists that the trafficking of drugs would not exist without the enormous and growing market in the United States, thus placing responsibility on its northern neighbor. Nevertheless, the corruption and crime provoked by the growing drug business in Mexico have led the Mexican government to take domestic antidrug measures. The Salinas government launched a massive military campaign to counter the threat posed by the narcotics trade within the country. In 1989 Mexico signed a cooperation agreement with the United States on fighting the illegal drug trade (see President Salinas, ch. 1). Mexico's position on drug trafficking consists of two major contentions: Mexico will make a good-faith effort to eradicate the production and trade of drugs, and it will not, under any circumstances, allow the consolidation of narcotics groups within its territory. Currently, Mexico has a large portion of its army involved in the government's drug eradication program (see Narcotics Trafficking, ch. 5).

Trade between the two nations remains an important issue. A trade and environmental agreement signed in late 1989 paved the way for an expansion of bilateral trade and investment with the United States. In 1990 Mexico began negotiations over NAFTA with the United States and Canada. The main objective of NAFTA was to remove all trade barriers and investment obstacles among the three countries over a fifteen-year period. Negotiations concluded in 1992, and NAFTA was approved in 1993. The agreement was activated on January 1, 1994, creating the world's richest and largest trading bloc, consisting of 360 million consumers in a US$6.6 trillion market (see Foreign Trade, ch. 3).

A third pressing issue between the two countries continues to be illegal immigration of Mexicans into the United States. By the mid-1990s, this issue occupied center stage in United States-Mexican relations. Since the 1960s, the number of Mexican illegal immigrants into the United States has soared to an average of 300,000 to 500,000 per year. These groups are concentrated in the southwestern states of the United States, especially California. Although NAFTA may help to decrease this trend in the long run, the presence of a large number of illegal residents in the United States—many of whom benefit from local and federal programs—triggered a legislative proposal in 1995 in the state of California to deprive these groups of any United States government support. In particular, legislation in the state of California has revived anti-United States feelings among Mexicans.

Relations with Cuba

Mexican policy toward Cuba has been the cornerstone of its assertive independence from United States policies. Mexico's closeness with Cuba also set it apart from its Latin American neighbors, especially in the 1960s when Mexico was the only Latin American country that did not break diplomatic relations with the Cuban government. Mexico also opposed any foreign interference in Cuban affairs, including the United States-backed Bay of Pigs invasion in 1961 and the expulsion of Cuba from international organizations—for example, the suspension of Cuba from the OAS in 1962. As part of asserting Mexican independence from United States policy toward Cuba, the Mexican president pays an official visit to Cuba during the last year of his term. This practice was established by President Echeverría in 1975 and continued by presidents López Portillo in 1980, de la Madrid in 1988, and Salinas in 1994. Mexico and Cuba currently hold many formal agreements on economic, educational, and cultural issues.

Relations with Guatemala

Mexico's shared border with Guatemala has led to tensions between the countries. Because of the disparity between the two countries in economic levels and power, some critics draw parallels to United States-Mexican relations. Traditionally, Guatemalans have crossed the border seasonally to work in the coffee fields of southern Mexico. During the early 1980s, however, a military campaign against indigenous Mayan peasants in northern Guatemala forced an exodus of refugees, who crossed the Mexican border to get away from the violent displacement of their communities. From 1982 to 1993, more than 40,000 Maya lived in refugee camps along the southern border of Mexico, creating a problem for local authorities. The

Mexican government, at both the national and local levels, was unprepared and unwilling to support such mass immigration into its territory. The emergence of the Zapatista guerrilla movement and alleged drug trafficking in the region exacerbated the situation. The Mexican government was criticized for its neglect and selectiveness regarding political asylum issues. Repatriation agreements between the Guatemalan government and organized refugee groups were reached during 1992, providing for the return of these groups to their country. Repatriation has proceeded slowly since then.

Relations with Other Latin American Countries

Mexico is a founding and active member of various hemispheric fora that support regional political and economic cooperation within Latin America. Mexico is, for example, a founding member of the OAS and the Inter-American Treaty of Reciprocal Assistance (Rio Treaty). But although Mexico is an active participant in many regional organizations, it maintains an independent view and often dissents from decisions taken by the international forum. Its record within the OAS consistently shows an independent Mexican policy: Mexico dissented from the United States-sponsored 1954 Caracas Resolution, which was directed at the leftist government of Jacobo Arbenz Guzmán in Guatemala; it systematically opposed the United States-led imposition by the OAS of economic sanctions against Cuba during the 1960s; and it opposed United States interventions in the Dominican Republic (1965), Grenada (1983), Panama (1990), and Haiti (1994).

Through most of the 1980s, Mexico was among the leaders of an intra-Latin American cooperation effort that excluded the United States. As a member of the Contadora Group established in 1983 with Colombia, Panama, and Venezuela, Mexico advocated a negotiated settlement of the Central American conflict and called for the withdrawal of foreign influence— including that of the United States and the Soviet Union— from the region. Mexico was also a founding member of the Cartagena Group (1984), an informal Latin American forum established to deal collectively with issues concerning foreign debt. Along with Venezuela, Mexico established the San José Accords, a cooperative effort to supply Central American nations, Barbados, the Dominican Republic, and Jamaica with oil on concessionary terms. Currently, Mexico is an active participant in the Group of Eight (derived from the Contadora

Group), which includes Argentina, Brazil, Colombia, Mexico, Panama, Peru, Uruguay, and Venezuela; and in the Group of Three, along with Colombia and Venezuela.

Membership in International Organizations

Mexico has always been a staunch supporter of international cooperation through multilateral institutions. Mexico maintains diplomatic relations with 176 countries. Mexico also is a founding member of the United Nations and participates as an active member in more than seventy other international fora, including the General Agreement on Tariffs and Trade (GATT; now the World Trade Organization—WTO), the Organisation for Economic Co-operation and Development (OECD), the Asia Pacific Economic Cooperation (APEC) forum, NAFTA, and the Rio Group. In addition, the Mexican government was among the leading members of the Inter-American System that drafted the Treaty of Tlatelolco, which prohibits Latin American countries from acquiring nuclear weapons.

Prospects for the Future

The presidential election of 1994 was unlike any election of the twentieth century. With more than 80,000 Mexican observers and 1,000 foreign poll watchers stationed around the country, the 1994 presidential election was, by far, the most open and honest in modern Mexican history. A high voter turnout (70 percent of the electorate) provided credibility to the election process and confirmed the government's commitment to, and the legitimacy of, democratic practices in Mexico. In his campaign, the new Mexican president, albeit representing the traditional forces within the official party, promised to divert powers from the executive branch to the other two branches of government. He also promised to democratize the PRI's presidential selection process.

Although significant changes during the 1990s have contributed to the development of a more competitive and democratic Mexican political system, a strong executive branch, as well as a close connection between the PRI and the government, continues to prevail as the official party enters its seventh decade in power. Most analysts agree that the period of PRI hegemony is over. The outcome of this new pluralism, however, is a matter for conjecture. Mexico today faces the challenge of maintaining political and economic stability while pursuing a dramatic transition toward an open economy and a competitive, pluralist political system.

*   *   *

The body of work on Mexican politics is extensive. Recent books include Roderic A. Camp's *Politics in Mexico*, Wayne A. Cornelius and Ann L. Craig's *The Mexican Political System in Transition*, Dan A. Cothran's *Political Stability and Democracy in Mexico*, and Jaime E. Rodríguez's *The Evolution of the Mexican Political System*. Roger Hansen's *The Politics of Mexican Development*, although becoming dated, continues to provide the best analysis of the PRI. The articles on Mexico in *Latin America and Caribbean Contemporary Record* provide useful information on political and economic events, as do the articles on Mexico in the yearly special issue of *Current History*. Information on contemporary events is available in the *Latin America Regional Reports: Mexico and Central America Report* and *Latin America Weekly Report*, both published by Latin American Newsletters of London, and in various issues of the *Financial Times*, the *Los Angeles Times*, the *New York Times*, the *Wall Street Journal*, the *Washington Post*, and the Mexican newspapers *Excélsior*, the *News*, and *Uno Más Uno*. (For further information and complete citations, see Bibliography.)

Chapter 5. National Security

MEXICO'S EXTERNAL SECURITY ENVIRONMENT is peaceful. Mexico has no foreign adversaries and little ambition to impose itself upon other nations. It repudiates the use of force to settle disputes and rejects interference by one nation in the affairs of another. It sees no regional security problems justifying military alliances.

The traditional Mexican definition of national security has constrained the role played by the armed forces. The military is essentially passive in matters of external defense. It has been relegated to internal missions of guaranteeing domestic political stability, contributing to the antinarcotics campaign, and carrying out development-oriented civic-action programs in fulfillment of its duties as the "servant of the people." Since the end of World War II, a succession of civilian presidents has divested the military establishment of political power. The ruling civilian elite that guides national security policy focuses on maintaining social order and overcoming local uprisings.

Because of these limited national security goals, Mexico long maintained a military establishment that was relatively small for a regional power. The picture began to change in the late 1970s, however. The discovery and exploitation of new petroleum reserves gave Mexico added stature as a world energy supplier. Violence in Central America brought tens of thousands of refugees, mainly Guatemalans, to Mexico. This influx of refugees was part of a regional upheaval that Mexico feared might spread northward to Mexican soil. Given the situation, the nation's armed forces, which until the 1970s were one of the most poorly paid and ill-equipped in the Western Hemisphere, took on new significance.

As a result, Mexico launched an ambitious military modernization program with the goals of increasing the size of the armed forces, improving education and training, and upgrading military equipment. The plan had to be scaled back because of a serious international financial crisis and domestic economic distress in the 1980s, but important changes were realized. The number of armed services personnel doubled in less than two decades, reaching 175,000 in 1996. In addition to keeping independent regiments and battalions in garrisons throughout the country, the army formed an armored brigade, bringing its combat forces to six brigades. There was also an elite Presidential Guard brigade. The army also enlarged its inventory of armored vehicles, although it still had no tanks. The air force expanded by adding a jet fighter squadron, in addition to less sophisticated planes, and armed helicopters that have been used in counterinsurgency operations. The navy acquired modern patrol vessels to provide increased protection of offshore oil installations and the country's fishery resources.

Violence in nearby Central American countries slackened in the early 1990s. A 1994 peasant rebellion in the southernmost state of Chiapas, however, demonstrated the potential for revolutionary activity by people not sharing in the country's economic and social progress. Although the lightly armed insurgents inflicted relatively few casualties, troop units were heavily deployed in the area. The possibility that localized uprisings could become more widespread underscores the need for modern, well-trained armed forces to ensure the country's stability.

History and Traditions of the Armed Forces

Mexico's military claims a rich heritage dating back to the pre-Columbian era. As early as the beginning of the fifteenth century, the Aztec army achieved a high degree of military organization that included formal education and training, weapons production, war planning, and the execution of coordinated operations (see The Aztec, ch. 1). The importance of military service was impressed upon each young male in the ritual of declaring to him, shortly after birth, that his destiny was to be a warrior and to die in combat, the most honorable death in Aztec culture. The powers of the Triple Alliance, formed by the urban centers of Tenochtitlán, Texcoco, and Tlacopán (now known as Tacuba)—all three of which are in the area of present-day Mexico City—reportedly could assemble a force of between 16,000 and 18,000 combatants, roughly 10 percent of the male population, on an hour's notice. Evidence of this indigenous influence on the modern military is found in the profile of an eagle warrior, the name given Aztec society's fighting elite, on the insignia of the Superior War College (Escuela Superior de Guerra).

At the beginning of the sixteenth century, the forces of the Triple Alliance were at the peak of their military development. Nevertheless, when the Spanish conquistadors under Hernán Cortés arrived in 1519, the native warriors put up little resistance. The two decisive factors in the Spanish victories were the conquistadors' possession of firearms and the mobility they gained from horses, elements of battle hitherto unknown to the Aztec. The cruelty of the Spanish induced the Aztec to rebel in 1520, and Cortés was forced to abandon the Aztec capital of Tenochtitlán. After launching a new offensive, the Spanish regained control, destroying the magnificent city (see The Spanish Conquest, ch. 1). An alliance with indigenous peoples opposed to the Aztec; the belief of Aztec ruler Moctezuma II (Montezuma) that Cortés was a Toltec god, Quetzalcóatl, whose return was predicted by legend; and the rapid spread of smallpox, which had been carried by the Spanish, also contributed to the Spanish victory. Despite the Aztec's continued battles and subterfuge, the Spanish succeeded in superimposing their own theocratic-militaristic traditions on the conquered society.

The Spanish organized the new colony as the Viceroyalty of New Spain and established an army there in the latter part of the eighteenth century. By 1800 the army's main components were four infantry regiments and two dragoon regiments rotated periodically from Spain. These were supported by ten militia regiments of infantry and nine regiments of dragoons recruited locally. In all, the army numbered about 30,000 members.

After independence, the Mexican armed forces gradually eliminated many practices of the Spanish colonial army. The practice of granting military officers special rights or privileges (*fueros*) that enabled them to "make sport of justice, avoid payment of their debts, establish gambling houses, and lead a dissolute life under the protection of their epaulets" was abolished in 1855. The military also phased out the nineteenth-century practice of forced conscription, which often filled the ranks with criminals or other social undesirables whom local caudillos (strongmen) wished to be rid of. These practices led to a sharp division between the officer corps and the enlisted ranks, a division that has slowly abated in the twentieth century in response to the egalitarian influence and myths of the Mexican Revolution (1910–20). Two legacies still remain from the years of colonial rule, however: the use of Spanish military ranks, some of which have no direct equivalent in the United States armed forces, and the high prestige traditionally accorded to cavalry units.

The Wars of Independence, 1810–21

According to one historical account, the struggle for independence involved four phases of military operations. In the first phase, Father Miguel Hidalgo y Costilla, a parish priest, formed the precursor of the first independent Mexican military force when he issued the now-famous Grito de Dolores on September 16, 1810, calling for an end to Spanish rule (see Wars of Independence, 1810–21, ch. 1). Hidalgo led a poorly armed force of native and mestizo peasants in disorganized attacks on Spanish-controlled towns and villages throughout central Mexico. The second phase began after Hidalgo's capture and execution in 1811, when Father José María Morelos y Pavón assumed leadership of the independence movement. Morelos led guerrilla-style operations at the head of a small army equipped with weapons captured from the Spanish. He was able to establish an independent republic from central Mexico to the Pacific coast and to encircle Mexico City by early 1813. The third phase, following Morelos's capture and execution in 1815, consisted of attacks by uncoordinated rebel bands led by guerrilla chieftains—among them Guadalupe (Manuel Félix Fernández) Victoria and Vicente Guerrero, both of whom later became presidents. Their operations further undermined Spanish control.

The final phase of the independence struggle began in 1821, when a loyalist officer, Augustín de Iturbide, revolted against his superiors and formed a tenuous military alliance with Guerrero. The temporary establishment of a liberal monarchy in Spain had provoked many Mexican conservatives like Iturbide to switch their sympathies to the revolutionaries. Iturbide's Army of the Three Guarantees, composed of approximately 16,000 men, quickly succeeded in routing those of the regular Spanish forces who resisted (see Iturbide and the Plan of Iguala, ch. 1). Full independence in 1821 was followed by the 1822 coronation of Iturbide as the "constitutional emperor" of Mexico. The revolutionary force became the first standing Mexican military body. Known as the Mexican Imperial Army, it was almost an exact copy of the Spanish colonial militia. Its officers were of direct Spanish descent, but the rank and file were mainly peasants recruited by raids on villages in the mountains and brought down in chains to the cities. The desertion rate was high among these "recruits," who remained ill-trained and poorly equipped for military action.

For the first thirty years following independence, military officers dominated the country's chaotic political life (see Empire and the Early Republic, 1821–55, ch. 1). Repeatedly, groups of generals led by a caudillo issued "pronouncements" (*pronunciamientos*) denouncing the government and promising reform and rewards for those who would join their revolt. One of the most vilified and cunning of the military caudillos was General Antonio López de Santa Anna Pérez de Lebrón, who led the first revolt against Iturbide and, between 1833 and 1855, served as president on eleven different occasions.

War with the United States, 1846

In spite of his military talents, Santa Anna is most remembered for his defeats that led to the cession of roughly one-half of Mexican territory to the United States under the 1848 peace settlement (see Centralism and the Caudillo State, 1836–55, ch. 1). After Texas declared its independence in 1836, Texan forces initially suffered a series of military reverses that culminated in the disaster at the Alamo in San Antonio. But later, bolstered by volunteer fighters from throughout the United States, they soundly defeated the Mexicans and captured Santa Anna at the Battle of San Jacinto. After nine years of independence (unrecognized by Mexico), Texas was admitted to the United States in 1845. The next year, the administration of President James K. Polk, eager to fulfill the United States claim to "manifest destiny," found a pretext to declare war on Mexico. After occupying Santa Fe without a struggle, United States forces under General Stephen Kearney advanced west to present-day California, while forces under Alexander Doniplan occupied Chihuahua. Another United States force under General Zachary Taylor defeated Santa Anna's army at the Battle of Buena Vista near Monterrey. The decisive battles, however, were waged by General Winfield Scott's 15,000-man Army of Occupation after it opened another front by landing at Veracruz. Scott's army continued toward the Mexican capital, winning a series of engagements with Santa Anna, who had assumed the Mexican presidency. United States forces took Mexico City after a three-week siege that culminated in the decisive Battle of Chapultepec. By Mexican accounts, some 1,100 Mexican troops and cadets fought in hand-to-hand combat against 7,000 United States soldiers at Chapultepec Castle, the site of the Heroic Military College on the western outskirts of the city. The legend of the Boy Heroes (Niños Héroes) was born when young cadets, among the last defenders of Chapultepec, reputedly threw themselves over the ramparts to their deaths rather than surrender to Scott's troops.

The internal disorder that followed Mexico's defeat depleted the country's treasury and destroyed much of its commerce and agriculture. Mounting unpaid foreign debts created a pretext for Britain, France, and Spain to land troops at Veracruz in 1861. Dreaming of expanding his influence to the New World, the French ruler, Napoleon III, sent an expeditionary force inland to capture Mexico City in early 1862. Although initially defeated at the bloody Battle of Puebla on May 5, 1862, the French, aided by Mexican conservative troops, eventually succeeded in installing the Habsburg archduke Ferdinand Maximilian Joseph as the second emperor of Mexico (see Civil War and the French Intervention, 1855–67, ch. 1). By late 1862, the legitimate government of Benito Juárez was left with control of only a small enclave along the border with Texas.

General José de la Cruz Porfirio Díaz had played a decisive role in the early victory of Juárez's forces at Puebla and commanded troops in the republican stronghold of Oaxaca until it was captured by the French in 1865. After escaping from a French military prison, Díaz commanded republican troops in the final campaigns leading to the surrender of Maximilian's remaining forces at Querétaro in 1867. After Juárez was returned to the presidency, Díaz managed to slowly parlay his military prowess into political strength.

Díaz's allegiance to Juárez ended soon after the restoration of the republic when the newly reinstalled president discharged two-thirds of the 60,000- to 90,000-member army. During the next several years, Díaz championed the cause of the dismissed troops and unsuccessfully challenged Juárez in the 1867 and 1871 presidential elections. The presidential succession after Juárez's death finally provoked Díaz to move against the government by issuing the 1876 Plan of Tuxtepec. Using recruits and funds gathered in the United States, Díaz defeated the government troops and, in November of that year, assumed the presidency, a position he would hold for all but four of the next thirty-four years (see The Restoration, 1867–76, ch. 1).

Established as the national caudillo, Díaz based his power on military might as he ruthlessly eliminated those who challenged his authority. When the United States and Mexico came close to war in 1877 over raids into United States territory by Mexican bandits and cattle rustlers, Díaz halted the brigandage and averted war by sending in federal army troops and the *rurales*, the feared paramilitary corps composed largely of criminals that also served as a counterweight to the regular military's power. Díaz resumed the practice of forced conscription and used his troops to brutally suppress antigovernment riots in Mexico City. Although state governorships were regularly offered to loyal officers, Díaz rotated the command of the army's military zones as a means of preventing generals from acquiring a local power base.

The Military Phase of the Revolution, 1910–17

Opposition to Díaz grew during the later years of Díaz's rule, and liberal reformers rose against Díaz in 1910, following yet another fraudulent reelection. Using the United States as a base of operations, the liberal democratic opposition forces laid siege to the federal garrison at Ciudad Juárez. Díaz's liberal presidential opponent, Francisco I. Madero, issued a manifesto in San Antonio, Texas, declaring himself provisional president and creating the Army of Liberation, which later became the Constitutionalist Army (see The Revolution, 1910–20, ch. 1).

Regional caudillos, some of whom were little more than bandits, soon joined the movement. Rebels led by Pascual Orozco and Francisco (Pancho) Villa, armed with Winchester rifles smuggled from the United States, quickly gained the advantage over federal troops, who depended on long supply lines from the capital. As rebel successes mounted, government troops began deserting. Under pressure, Díaz resigned in 1911 and fled to exile in France.

The Madero government, which succeeded Díaz, was forced to deal with uprisings throughout the country. Rebel military leaders (most notably Orozco) were dissatisfied with the rewards that the new Madero government offered them for defeating the dictatorship. A coup ousted Madero in 1913 and set the Mexican Revolution on a bloody course that would last for the next four years.

Various rival factions struggled for supremacy in confused fighting. The principal leaders were Villa, Orozco, Emiliano Zapata, Venustiano Carranza, and Álvaro Obregón. Villa deliberately provoked United States intervention by launching cross-border raids. A 7,000-man expeditionary force under United States General John J. "Blackjack" Pershing was dispatched in 1916 but failed to capture Villa. In spite of the chaotic conditions, the military phase of the Mexican Revolution provided the Mexican armed forces with a unifying ideology. This new ideology stressed the military's peasant origins and established the military as the defender of the popular will. Drawing on this heritage, the modern Mexican military identifies itself as the "silent and anonymous guardian" that has provided the security essential to the subsequent development of the nation.

Professionalization of the Armed Forces, 1920–46

The first serious efforts at depoliticizing and professionalizing the military began in 1920 under the government of Obregón, himself a general who had been elected president with the support of the old revolutionary chiefs. Obregón saw the need to consolidate his political position by diminishing the power and influence of the regional caudillos. Military uprisings in 1923, 1927, and 1929 resulted in purges of large numbers of rebellious generals. The army was reduced by two-thirds, to 14,000 officers and 70,000 troops in 1921. The demobilization principally dismantled the excessive number of cavalry regiments. Pay and living conditions of the enlisted ranks were improved, and the military's share of the national budget was slashed from 61 percent in 1921 to 25 percent by 1926. Many officers and men were weeded out by new laws on competitive promotion and mandatory retirement ages. Nevertheless, unqualified revolutionary-era generals continued to be carried on the rolls. The Organic Law of 1926 provided the legal base for the army, defined its missions, and established regulations and formal procedures.

General Plutarco Elías Calles (president, 1924–28) continued Obregón's efforts to reduce the political influence of the military and ensure the army's loyalty to the central government. Calles's policies were carried out by General Joaquín Amaro, the secretary of war and navy. Amaro promoted education of officers and enlisted men in the belief that it would increase loyalty and obedience to civilian authorities. Officers were sent for professional training in the United States and Western Europe. The curriculum of the Heroic Military College, founded in 1823, was reformed, and the Superior War College, a command and general staff college for promising officers, was created. Schools providing specialized training in the various service branches also were established (see Education and Training, this ch.).

General Lázaro Cárdenas, who assumed the presidency in 1934, divided the Secretariat of War and the Navy into two autonomous defense ministries, the Secretariat of National Defense (Secretaría de Defensa Nacional), which controlled the army and air force, and the Secretariat of the Navy (Secretaría de Marina Armada). As the possibility of Mexican involvement in World War II increased, Cárdenas drafted the Law of National Military Service, which established, through a lottery system, compulsory basic military training for eighteen-year-old males.

The Mexican Military in World War II

General Manuel Ávila Camacho, who came to office in 1940 and was the last general elected president of Mexico, continued Cárdenas's and Obregón's efforts to institutionalize the army and remove the military from politics. In February 1942, soon after the Japanese attack on United States forces at Pearl Harbor, the Joint Mexican-United States Commission on Continental Defense was established. The commission coordinated planning for the defense of Mexico and the adjacent southwestern United States. The sinking of two Mexican tankers in the Gulf of Mexico by German submarines provoked Ávila Camacho to declare war on the Axis powers in May 1942. In response to the Mexican government's expressed desire to fight the Japanese, a Mexican air squadron was readied for duty in the Pacific theater. After a year's training in the United States, Squadron 201 of the Mexican Expeditionary Air Force arrived in the Philippines in April 1945. Flying P–47 Thunderbolt fighters, the Mexican pilots participated in bombing and strafing runs to support ground forces and in long-range reconnaissance missions over Taiwan. Of thirty-two pilots in the expeditionary squadron, seven were killed.

The immediate postwar years were a peak period of United States influence on the Mexican armed forces. The Mexican military reorganized, using the United States armed forces as a model. The military training program incorporated United States army field manuals. United States arms transferred to Mexico just after World War II were the country's last major acquisitions of military hardware for a period of three decades, however. In the mid-1970s, the government accepted the need for a larger, modernized army because of growing concerns over potential threats to its oil resources.

The Military in Civilian Politics

Despite the military's prominent role in the history of the country, the Mexican armed forces have steadily retreated from direct involvement in political matters since the 1940s. The typical Mexican officer is deliberately removed from political issues, and there has been a decline in military representation in government offices outside the armed services. Since World War II, the number of persons with military backgrounds serving in the cabinet, subcabinet, state governorships, and in the bureaucracy has steadily declined.

Mexican political observer Adolfo Aguilar Zinser believes there is little reason to expect the officer corps to change its deeply rooted loyalty to civil authority. Serious domestic turmoil might cause a conservative middle class and business interests to pressure the army to intervene in the government. As long as the military remains assured of the civilian leadership's ability to deal with any crisis threatening the established system, however, the military is unlikely to be drawn into political affairs.

National Security Concerns

Under the constitution of 1917, the armed forces have responsibility for defending the sovereignty and independence of the nation, maintaining the constitution and its laws, and preserving internal order. At various times during the first century of independence, Mexico was subjected to foreign attacks by the United States, France, and, for a brief period, Spain and Britain. Mexico's principal national security concerns since 1910 have been to preserve domestic political stability and to prevent foreign economic domination. The last time Mexico faced a foreign threat was when it joined the war against the Axis in World War II. During World War II and in the subsequent years of the Cold War, however, Mexico's proximity to the United States allowed it to fall under the protective shield of its northern neighbor.

Bilateral relations with the United States have been strongly affected by the bitter legacy left by Mexico's loss of more than one-half of its territory in 1848 and subsequent incidents of United States infringement of its sovereignty. General Winfield Scott's 1847 siege of the capital, the United States marines' 1914 occupation of Veracruz, and General Pershing's 1916 punitive expedition in northern Mexico against Pancho Villa were traumatic episodes in Mexican history. Even in the post-World War II era, most Mexicans viewed United States domination, not Soviet-Cuban designs in the Western Hemisphere or revolutionary regimes in Central America, as the major foreign threat to national sovereignty. Although fears of armed intervention by the United States have receded, concerns over United States economic and political penetration persist.

The Mexican military is primarily organized to meet challenges to internal order and the existing political system. Since the 1940s, Mexico has remained remarkably free from domestic upheaval, perhaps more so than any other Latin American nation. For the most part, the military has been reluctant to become involved in law enforcement. The armed forces have given the responsibility of preventing violence to federal and state police authorities except when faced with a large-scale breakdown of civil order. Troops are not fully equipped or trained to deal directly with protesters, and, with its reputation at risk, the military leadership seems inclined to register its influence more as a presence than an active force.

In 1968 the military was called upon to put down massive student-led protests associated with strongly felt economic grievances. Fearful of losing control of the situation, the army violently suppressed the movement by opening fire on thousands of demonstrators at Tlatelolco, in northern Mexico City. The brutality of the action, in which hundreds of demonstrators were killed or wounded, was severely criticized and had a lasting effect on the public's perception of the military.

The January 1994 uprising in the state of Chiapas by a previously unknown guerrilla group, the Zapatista National Liberation Army (Ejército Zapatista de Liberación Nacional—EZLN), has been the only outbreak in recent years that has necessitated major troop deployments (see Public Order and Internal Security, this ch.). Both army and air force units were shifted to the scene to drive the insurgents out of towns they occupied. After widespread skirmishes in which several hundred persons were reportedly killed, the army was able to regain control of most towns in the area within a matter of hours, forcing the guerrillas to retreat into remote mountain strongholds. Except for a brief army offensive in February 1995, several consecutive cease-fires prevented any further fighting after the initial actions of 1994. By early 1996, the military situation in Chiapas was stalemated: the army occupied the towns, and the rebels were largely confined to the thinly populated highlands.

In dealing with potential regional hostilities, the Mexican military has adopted a reserved posture that reflects the country's foreign policy traditions. Neither Cuban-style communism nor the possibility of conflict spreading northward from Central America has been regarded as directly threatening to Mexico. No effort has been made to erect defenses along the 3,200-kilometer land border Mexico shares with the United States. Mexico's 970-kilometer border with Guatemala also remains unguarded despite occasional clashes between Mexican and Guatemalan forces. When Guatemalan army units carried out raids in the early 1980s against Guatemalan refugees and Mexican communities that were aiding them, the Mexican military reacted mildly to avoid confrontation. Mexican coastal areas and its 320-kilometer Exclusive Economic Zone (EEZ) are lightly patrolled by Mexican fleet units. The security of Mexico's coasts is effectively guaranteed since they are within the orbit of United States hemispheric defense.

Tasks and Missions

In the half-century following World War II, the Mexican armed forces have never been called upon to exercise an external defense role. Their primary mission has been to deter and prevent violence threatening public order, including outbreaks arising from strikes and protests, rural political grievances, guerrilla insurgency, and urban terrorism. Since the 1920s, the military has devoted a considerable share of its resources to civic-action programs to improve socioeconomic conditions and relieve human distress, particularly in rural areas that otherwise have little contact with government representatives (see Civic Action, this ch.). The army has often been called upon to respond to natural disasters, its responsibilities set forth in a plan known as National Defense III (Defensa Nacional III—DN III), and to coordinate the work of other agencies during the course of the emergency. The army took charge of relief operations after the volcanic eruption in Chiapas in 1982. When parts of the capital were devastated by the powerful earthquake of 1985, however, the army played a lesser role because the civil authorities did not wish to appear incapable of dealing with the crisis without military help.

The army assigns large numbers of personnel to the antinarcotics campaign, carrying out crop eradication as well as supporting law enforcement agencies in interdiction missions. The navy is responsible for maritime drug interdiction, and the ground-based radar system of the air force supports air inter-diction efforts (see Narcotics Trafficking, this ch.).

Under the Mexican code for federal elections, the army has a limited but important part in the administration of elections, monitoring polling stations and protecting ballot boxes on election day. Although the military has generally remained impartial in carrying out its election duties, it faced accusations in 1985 and 1986 that it assisted in manipulating ballot counts in the northern states to ensure victories by the government party, the Institutional Revolutionary Party (Partido Revolucio-nario Institucional—PRI).

As part of its domestic security functions, the army is also responsible for protecting strategic economic installations such as electric power plants, oil fields, petroleum complexes, ports, and airports. All regions where the country's petroleum reserves are located are regarded as of high strategic signifi-cance. Petroleum fields are found primarily in the southeast-ern states of Veracruz and Tabasco and offshore in the Gulf of Mexico. The threat of spreading conflict in Central America and the strategic importance attached to Mexico's oil fields were the decisive factors in the government's decision to assign additional military personnel to the southernmost areas in the mid-1980s and to relocate Guatemalans living in refugee camps there so as to remove any pretext for Guatemalan border incur-sions.

Along with protection of Mexico's fisheries and detection of vessels transporting contraband, the Mexican navy is charged with the defense of offshore oil installations and other mari-time resources. The campaign against drug smuggling has placed an increasing burden on the navy's resources. These heightened priorities led the government to dedicate a signifi-cantly greater portion of its budget to the Secretariat of the Navy during the 1980s. Between 1980 and 1984, the United States and Mexico were at odds over the Mexican navy's appre-hending of United States fishing vessels—mainly tuna boats—within Mexico's EEZ. In 1993 three smuggling ships carrying several hundred illegal Chinese immigrants were forced to land in Mexico after the ships had been detected off the Cali-fornia coast, adding another dimension to the navy's mission.

United States Concerns

Mexico has enjoyed peaceful relations with its northern neighbor for many decades. In the United States, national security issues involving Mexico gained increased attention during the 1980s because of the growing importance of Mexico's oil reserves and installations and because of the fear that leftist-inspired turbulence in Central America might spread northward. Mexico's economic difficulties and societal frictions intensified fears that the long period of stable border conditions might be ending. By the early 1990s, however, unrest had abated in Central America. Radical movements were no longer threatening the government of El Salvador, and the leftist Sandinista (see Glossary) government was out of power in Nicaragua. In Guatemala, the civilian government had largely overcome the left-wing insurgency and had begun to engage in serious peace negotiations under United Nations auspices. The Mexican military leadership, although conservative and anticommunist in outlook, had never been persuaded that it faced a security threat arising from the spread of violence in Central America or that popular discontent in Mexico had gathered sufficient force to provoke widespread domestic disorder and revolutionary violence.

Historically, relations between the military establishments of Mexico and the United States have not been close. Cooperation reached its peak for a brief period during and after World War II. In the Cold War atmosphere that followed, Mexico opposed the United States concepts of regional security; in particular, it did not support the United States intervention in Guatemala in 1954 and the trade embargo imposed against Castro-led Cuba in the early 1960s. The country's leaders felt that the roots of violence in Central America could be found in social and economic problems and in right-wing dictatorships, rather than any Cuban and Soviet subversion. The defense commission with the United States formed in World War II became inactive, and military assistance—under which the United States transferred US$40 million worth of modern equipment to Mexico in the late 1940s—ended in 1950.

By the late 1980s, relations between the military establishments of Mexico and the United States became somewhat warmer as cooperation expanded in the fight against illicit drugs. Purchases of United States military items, which had amounted to US$140 million in the five-year period 1982 to 1986, rose steeply to US$410 million over the period from 1987 to 1991, accounting for three-quarters of all of Mexico's arms imports. Numerous Mexican officers received training in the United States and became well acquainted with United States military doctrine. On the whole, however, the Mexican armed forces were less influenced by the United States military than were the armed forces of other countries of Latin America. In the mid-1990s, military assistance and concessional military credits from the United States to Mexico still had not been resumed. About US$500,000 was allocated by the United States government for military education and training each year, enabling more than 900 Mexican officers to attend United States military institutions between 1977 and 1991. This figure was exclusive of training funded by Mexico in connection with weapons procurements.

Treaty Obligations

Mexico is a signatory to the principal defense-related multilateral treaties and agreements in the Western Hemisphere but has refrained from entering into alliances or collective security arrangements that could be viewed as inconsistent with its principles of nonintervention and self-determination. In early 1945, Mexico, along with nineteen other nations of the hemisphere, signed the Act of Chapultepec. Under the act, the first hemispheric defense agreement, signatory nations agreed that if any aggression across treaty-established boundaries occurred or was threatened, a meeting would be convened to determine what steps, up to and including the use of armed force, should be taken to prevent or repel such aggression.

Mexico signed the Inter-American Treaty of Reciprocal Assistance, also known as the Rio Treaty, in September 1947. The Rio Treaty, which expanded the responsibilities of nations under the Act of Chapultepec, emphasized the peaceful settlement of disputes among Western Hemisphere nations and provided for collective defense should any signatory be subject to external aggression. Although the treaty was conceived as a means to protect the nations of the hemisphere from possible communist aggression, Mexico chose to interpret it as a juridical association of states, not as a military alliance. Each time that the treaty has been invoked, Mexico has voted against the adoption of collective security measures (see Foreign Relations, ch. 4).

Upon formation of the Organization of American States (OAS) in April 1948, Mexico actively opposed proposals to create a standing military force under OAS supervision. Mexico insisted on limiting the newly created OAS defense body—now known as the Inter-American Defense Board—to serving in a consultative capacity to OAS member nations. Subsequent amendments to the charter have underscored the goal of peaceful resolution of disputes among member states.

Mexico initially proposed and then became a signatory to the 1967 Treaty of Tlatelolco, which prohibits the introduction of nuclear weapons into Latin America. Similarly, it is a signatory to the 1968 Nuclear Non-Proliferation Treaty, which limits the application of nuclear technology to peaceful purposes. Mexico has accepted the safeguard agreements of the International Atomic Energy Agency, which include the accounting and control of nuclear reactor by-products that could be used to make weapons, but has refused to permit on-site inspections of its nuclear facilities.

Armed Forces

Constitutional and Legal Basis

The constitution of 1917 established the guiding principles for the armed forces and placed restrictions on their activities. Article 89 places the military under the control of the president of the republic, who, as commander in chief, is responsible for seeing that the armed forces fulfill their obligation to guarantee "internal order and external defense." The restriction on peacetime interference by military authorities in civilian affairs or other activities not "directly connected with the military discipline," set forth by Article 129, has often been abused, however, usually on the order of the president. The final constitutional provision for establishing government control of the armed forces, Article 132, places all military facilities and properties under federal jurisdiction.

A series of laws enacted in 1926 further shaped the armed forces. The most important of these, the Organic Law, gave them a threefold mission: "to defend the integrity and independence of the nation, to maintain the constitution, and to preserve internal order." The basic law subsequently has been modified to keep pace with political, economic, and social changes in the Mexican state.

Three additional laws enacted in 1926 also sought to regularize military practices. The Law of Promotions and Compensation established a pay scale for each rank and competitive examinations for promotion. The Law of Military Discipline further defined the obligations of the armed forces to society, requiring that each soldier, "in fulfillment of his duties, sacri-

Headquarters of Secretariat of National Defense
Courtesy Arturo Salinas

fice all personal interests to the sovereignty of the nation, to loyalty toward its institutions, and to the honor of the National Army." The Law of Pensions and Retirements set a mandatory retirement age and provided pensions for military retirees and allowances for military dependents. Although all of these laws have been modified to meet the needs of changing times, they remain the institutional foundation of the Mexican military.

Organization of National Defense

The organization of the Mexican armed forces at the cabinet level is distinct from that of many other Latin American nations. Instead of a single ministry consolidating the command of the army, navy, and air force, two government ministries are directly responsible for national defense: the Secretariat of National Defense and the Secretariat of the Navy. The head of each of these secretariats is a military officer who holds cabinet rank and has regular, direct access to the president of the republic, who is the supreme commander of the armed forces.

After President Carlos Salinas de Gortari took office in 1988, five cabinet-level councils were created within the offices of the president to oversee principal policy areas. One of these is the National Security Council, which includes representatives of the secretariats of government, foreign relations, national defense, and the navy, as well as the attorney general's office. Narcotics control is one of the topics dealt with in the council.

The secretary of national defense (General Enrique Cervantes Aguirre as of 1996) is selected by the president from the ranks of active army general officers. The secretary normally serves for six years, the same term as the president's. Similarly, the secretary of the navy (Admiral José Ramón Lorenzo Franco in 1996) is chosen from the ranks of active admirals. Operating through the General Staff, the secretary of national defense commands army and air force units, the army zonal commands, and logistics and administrative directorates. Under the secretary of the navy are the chief of naval operations, the chief of naval staff, and the naval zones that control operational forces.

The army is by far the largest service branch. Of some 175,000 active armed forces personnel in 1996, 130,000 were in the army, 8,000 in the air force, and 37,000 in the navy. The army total at any one time included about 60,000 conscripts. No conscripts were assigned to the air force or navy. A "reserve" force of 300,000 is claimed, although this number is a manpower pool rather than an existing trained force.

The size of the armed forces is modest considering Mexico's size and importance. Mexico has the smallest number of military personnel per capita of any country of Latin America. According to the United States Arms Control and Disarmament Agency (ACDA), Latin America as a whole had 3.5 soldiers per 1,000 population in 1991. The corresponding figure for Mexico was 1.9 soldiers per 1,000 population. In spite of the steady increase in the armed forces—they have roughly doubled in size since the mid-1970s—the number of soldiers per capita has remained remarkably steady because of the parallel increase in population.

Army

The principal units of the Mexican army are six brigades and a number of independent regiments and infantry battalions. The brigades, all based in and around the Federal District (encompassing the Mexico City area), are the only real maneuver elements in the army. With their support units, they are believed to account for 40 percent of the country's ground forces. According to *The Military Balance,* published by the International Institute for Strategic Studies in London, the army in 1996 had seven brigades: one armored, two infantry, one motorized infantry, one airborne, one combined military police and engineer brigade, and the Presidential Guard Brigade. The armored brigade is one of two new brigades formed since 1990 as part of a reorganization made possible by an increase in overall strength of about 25,000 troops. The brigade consists of three armored and one mechanized infantry regiment.

Each of the two infantry brigades consists of three infantry battalions and an artillery battalion. The motorized infantry brigade is composed of three motorized infantry regiments. The airborne brigade consists of two army and one air force battalion. The elite Presidential Guard Brigade reports directly to the Office of the President and is responsible for providing military security for the president and for visiting dignitaries. The Presidential Guard consists of three infantry battalions, one special force battalion, and one artillery battalion.

Distinct from the brigade formations are independent regiments and battalions assigned to zonal garrisons. These independent units consist of one armored cavalry regiment, nineteen motorized cavalry regiments, one mechanized infantry regiment, seven artillery regiments, and three artillery and eight infantry battalions. Infantry battalions, each composed of approximately 300 troops, generally are deployed in each zone. Certain zones also are assigned an additional motorized cavalry regiment or one of the seven artillery regiments. Smaller detachments often are detailed to patrol more inaccessible areas of the countryside, helping to maintain order and resolve disputes.

The cavalry historically has been the most prestigious branch of the army; in 1920, there were more cavalry squadrons than infantry companies. By the early 1980s, all mounted cavalry had been transformed into motorized units—except for one squadron retained for ceremonial purposes. The engineers, air defense, and combat support and service units was organized into separate regimental, battalion, and company units, which are distributed among military zone installations.

Mexico in 1996 was divided into twelve military regions with thirty-nine military zones. Zone boundaries usually correspond with those of the country's thirty-one states, with the headquarters of the military zone located in the state capital. Some states, including Veracruz, Guerrero, and Chiapas, which have been the scene of disturbances by peasant and Indian groups, have more than one military zone apiece. The Federal District, where Mexico City is located, is the seat of the First Military Zone and also serves as headquarters of the First Military Region.

Military zone commanders are appointed by the president, usually on the recommendation of the secretary of national defense. The senior zone commander in a given area also acts as the commander of the military region in which the zone falls. Zone commanders hold jurisdiction over all units operating in their territory, including the Rural Defense Force (see Rural Defense Force, this ch.). They occasionally have served the federal authorities as a political counterweight to the power wielded by state governors. Zone commanders provide the secretary of national defense with valuable intelligence regarding social and political conditions in rural areas, and traditionally have acted in close coordination with the Secretariat of National Defense on resource planning and deployment matters.

Under a modernization program initiated in the late 1970s, the army purchased a significant amount of new equipment, in many cases replacing equipment that dated from the World War II period. The army's inventory of armored vehicles was expanded and updated. The Panhard ERC–90 Lynx six-wheeled reconnaissance car and the Panhard VBL M–11 light armored car were acquired from France. Older designs, such as the German HWK–11 tracked armored personnel carrier (APC), remained in the inventory in 1996 (see table 13, Appendix). Several domestic versions, the DN–3 and DN–5 Caballo and the Mex–1, have been added since the mid-1980s. The M4 Sherman medium tank and several models of light tank transferred by the United States after World War II were retired, leaving Mexico without any tanks in its inventory. Plans for a major expansion of the country's own armament industry, which might have included a domestic tank design, were curtailed as a result of the debt crisis of 1982 (see Domestic Defense Production, this ch.).

Except for five self-propelled 75mm howitzers, in 1996 the army's artillery consisted mainly of towed 105mm howitzers. The army's principal antitank weapons are French Milan missiles, some of which are mounted on the VBL M–11s. Antiaircraft weapons systems are limited to 12.7mm air defense guns.

Panhard ERC–90 Lynx tank
Courtesy Panhard

The army has no units equipped with tactical air defense missiles.

Air Force

The Mexican armed forces saw the value of air power early. In 1911 the Madero revolutionaries flew an airplane on a bombing mission using grenades, and a year later, after Madero became president, three military pilots were sent to the United States for training. Shortly thereafter, one of the rebel groups acquired several airplanes, which, flown by foreign mercenary pilots, supported their ground forces during the advance southward in 1914. Unable to obtain additional aircraft because of the war in Europe, the Carranza government successfully developed and produced a biplane trainer and subsequently a series of other models from both local designs and from modifications of foreign planes.

During the 1920s, the army bought various war-surplus bomber, reconnaissance, fighter, and training aircraft at low cost, although the local aircraft industry continued to produce its own models. In 1932 an air regiment was formed, consisting of one squadron each of Vought Corsair, Douglas, and Bristol fighters. After the United States and Mexico entered World War II, the United States transferred a considerable number of primary and advanced trainers to Mexico, followed by light bombers and amphibious reconnaissance planes that were used to conduct antisubmarine patrols in the Gulf of Mexico. The Mexican air force received additional trainers, bombers, and transport aircraft after the signing of the 1947 Rio Treaty. It acquired jet fighters from Canada and armed jet trainers from the United States in the late 1950s.

The air force, organized into two wings and ten air groups, had a personnel complement of 8,000 in 1996, including 1,500 assigned to the airborne brigade. The air force's principal air base, Military Air Base Number 1, is located at Santa Lucía in the state of México. Other major air bases are located at Ixtepec in Oaxaca, Isla Cozumel in Quintana Roo, Zapopán in Veracruz, and Mérida in Yucatán, as well as El Ciprés and La Paz (both in Baja California Sur) and Puebla and Píe de la Cuesta (both in Guerrero).

Delivery, beginning in 1982, of ten F–5E Tiger II fighter aircraft and two F–5F two-seater trainers from the United States enabled Mexico to form a supersonic air defense squadron armed with Sidewinder missiles. As part of a construction agreement with the United States, the runways at the Santa Lucía air base were lengthened and facilities renovated to accommodate the new planes. In 1982 the air force also acquired the first of some seventy Pilatus PC–7 turboprop planes from Switzerland. In 1996 forty of the PC–7s were organized into three counterinsurgency squadrons, and the remainder are available for both training and counterinsurgency operations. Also capable of being armed for counterinsurgency tasks is one squadron of twelve AT–33s (Lockheed Shooting Star), a much older aircraft used mainly as a jet trainer. One squadron of Bell 205, 206, and 212 armed helicopters also is designated for a counterinsurgency role. One squadron of IAI 201s (the Israeli Arava, a short-takeoff-and-landing utility transport) is assigned to search-and-air rescue, and a photo reconnaissance squadron is made up of Rockwell Commander 500Ss. Five transport squadrons are equipped with C–47s, C–118s, C–130s, and some small aircraft. The Presidential Transport Squadron, based at the Benito Juárez International Airport in Mexico City, has seven Boeing 727s and one Boeing 737, together with smaller transport planes and a number of helicopters (see table 14, Appendix).

A Westinghouse mobile radar system purchased in 1988 was activated at the close of 1991 to track suspicious aircraft in Guatemalan air space flying toward the Mexican border. The system was introduced both as a security measure to survey air activity along the Guatemalan border and to track planes smuggling narcotics from South America.

In early 1996, the air force acquired twenty-nine UH–1H "Huey" and eighteen Bell 206 helicopters from the Federal Judicial Police for use in military-assisted counternarcotics operations. In a sign of the growing militarization of Mexico's drug war under the administration of President Ernesto Zedillo Ponce de León, in May 1996, negotiations were underway for the permanent transfer of an additional seventy-three surplus "Hueys" from the United States to the Mexican air force.

Rural Defense Force

The Rural Defense Force (Guardia Rural), composed entirely of volunteers, augments the military presence in the countryside. The corps was formally organized under army jurisdiction according to the Organic Law of 1926. Its origins, however, date back to the period when the revolutionary agrarian reform program was first implemented in 1915. In efforts to protect themselves against the private armies of recalcitrant large landowners, rural peasants organized themselves into small defense units and were provided weapons by the revolutionary government. Until 1955 enlistment in the Rural Defense Force was restricted to peasants working on collective farms or *ejidos* (see Glossary). After 1955 participation in the Rural Defense Force was expanded to include small farmers and laborers. All defense units, however, were attached to *ejidos*, possibly as a means to guarantee control.

The Rural Defense Force numbered some 120,000 in 1970, but was being phased out in the 1990s. *The Military Balance* listed the corps as having only 14,000 members in 1996. The volunteers, aged eighteen to fifty, enlist for a three-year period. Members do not wear uniforms or receive pay for their service but are eligible for limited benefits. They are armed with outmoded rifles, which may be the chief inducement to enlist. Rudimentary training is provided by troops assigned to military zone detachments.

The basic unit is the platoon (*pelotón*) of eleven members under immediate control of the *ejido*. Use of the unit outside the *ejidos* is by order of the military zone commander. One asset of the corps is the capacity of its members to gather intelligence about activities within the *ejidos* and in remote rural areas seldom patrolled by military zone detachments. Corps members also act as guides for military patrols, participate in civic-action projects, and assist in destroying marijuana crops and preventing the transport of narcotics through their areas.

Civic Action

Civic-action programs designed to improve socioeconomic conditions and develop public facilities traditionally have been an important mission of the armed forces. As early as 1921, labor battalions created by order of President Obregón were employed in road construction, irrigation projects, and railroad and telegraph maintenance. The Organic Law of the Armed Forces directs the army and the air force to "aid the civilian population, cooperate with authorities in cases of public necessity, [and] lend assistance in social programs." Programs designed to meet these aims have been given high priority since the 1960s.

By the 1980s, civic-action programs encompassed a wide range of activities carried out by military zone personnel, often in coordination with government agencies. These programs reinforced the army's ties to the country's rural inhabitants and promoted national development. The army was placed in charge of coordinating disaster relief in 1966 under Plan DN III. Military zone personnel assist the rural population in literacy programs, road building, bringing electricity to rural villages, repairing equipment, school restoration, immunization, and dental care, and in some cases provide emergency surgery in military hospitals. Military personnel also serve as escorts on the national railroads, patrol federal highways on national holidays, and participate in campaigns to eliminate livestock disease and crop damage caused by insect infestations.

Secretariat of the Navy

Mexico created a modest navy after gaining independence from Spain in 1821. At the time of the war with the United States in 1846, the fleet was still very small and was forced to remain in port to avoid destruction. Around 1875 several large gunboats were acquired from Britain, and the naval academy was established at the main Gulf of Mexico coast base of Veracruz. Although a number of gunboats and cruiser/transports were added after the turn of the century, the navy played only a limited role in the Mexican Revolution. After World War I and again after World War II, the navy expanded by purchasing surplus gunboats, frigates, and corvettes from the United States and Canada.

To meet its broadened responsibilities, the navy has more than doubled in size since the mid-1970s. According to *Jane's Fighting Ships*, the navy's active-duty personnel numbered 37,000 in 1996. Of these, some 1,100 were assigned to naval aviation, and another 8,600 were marines. Also falling under the command of the navy are members of the coast guard and merchant marine, who support the country's growing maritime fleet.

The navy is entirely a volunteer force. Its personnel are dispersed among various naval zones and port installations. As with the secretary of national defense, being appointed the secretary of the navy requires not only a distinguished service record but also a personal relationship with the president. Although the general headquarters of the Secretariat of the Navy is in Mexico City, naval command is divided between the country's two coasts. The commanding headquarters of the Pacific fleet is at Acapulco; the Gulf of Mexico coast command is at Veracruz. Both commands are organized into three naval regions each. There are seventeen naval zones, one for each coastal state. Some of the naval zones are further subdivided into sectors. Through coordination within each coast command, patrol operations are carried out by the respective naval zones along the country's approximately 9,300 kilometers of coastline and the nearly 3 million square kilometers of ocean that make up Mexico's territorial waters and EEZ.

The navy's primary mission is to protect strategic installations and natural resources. This assignment translates into safeguarding the country's strategic oil installations (both at port facilities and offshore), apprehending foreign vessels that are fishing within Mexico's EEZ without proper permits, and interdicting shipments of drugs, weapons, and other contraband. Although foreign fishing poachers have been a persistent problem for the navy, expanded efforts to conduct maritime surveillance and intercept narcotics traffickers absorb a growing amount of naval resources. Naval personnel also participate in disaster relief efforts and in clean-ups to prevent environmental damage from spills of oil and other toxic substances. The Secretariat of the Navy supervises the dredging of port facilities, the repair and maintenance of vessels assigned to the fleet and to the maritime industry, the conduct of oceanographic research, and the preparation of nautical charts.

During the 1980s, the navy benefited substantially from the acquisition of new vessels and other equipment. Considerable funds also were used for construction of new ports, renovation of existing facilities, and development of shipyards and dry-docks for repairs and maintenance. Many of the navy's combat vessels are World War II ships originally part of the United States Navy, which have been modernized by the addition of new weapons, electronic warfare and communications gear, and the replacement of propulsion systems.

Purchases during the 1980s included two World-War-II vintage Gearing-class destroyers, which joined a Fletcher-class destroyer transferred from the United States Navy in 1970. The Gearing-class vessels are armed with 127mm (5-inch) guns and Bofors 40mm guns for air defense. They also are mounted with antisubmarine rocket (Asroc) homing missiles (see table 15, Appendix). In 1982 and 1983, Mexico acquired from Spain six new Halcón-class large patrol vessels. The new ships are equipped with platforms and hangars for German Bo–105 helicopters and are designed primarily to patrol the EEZ. The navy commissioned four Holzinger-class fisheries-protection vessels constructed at Tampico between 1991 and 1993. Sixteen Auk-class patrol boats built in the United States during World War II are reaching the end of their useful service life. All twelve Admirable-class patrol boats were modernized in 1994. Thirty-one Azteca-class twenty-one-meter inshore patrol boats are used for fishery patrols. The first twenty-one of these were built in Britain and the remainder in Mexico; Mexico modernized the British-built vessels in 1987. The Mexican fleet also includes small patrol craft, a number of river patrol vessels, and survey ships and logistic support vessels. Naval cadets man the Spanish-built sail training ship, the *Cuauhtémoc.*

Despite improvements, the Mexican navy in 1996 was not as well equipped to protect its territorial waters and coasts as were the navies of other large Latin American countries. The navy lacks submarines and missile-armed, fast-attack craft. In addition, Mexico's larger vessels are without modern surface-to-air missiles for air defense.

The naval aviation arm has as its primary missions coastal surveillance and search-and-air rescue operations. Maritime reconnaissance is performed by Bo–105 helicopters armed with machine guns and rockets, most of which operate off ship platforms. In 1994 the naval aviation arm purchased four MD500s, used for training purposes; four Fennée; and eight Russian Mi–8 helicopters. In May 1996, the navy announced it would purchase an additional twelve Mi–8s. Coastal patrols and air rescue are carried out by six HU–16 Grumman Albatross aircraft and nine Spanish-built C–212 Aviocars. A variety of small transport, utility, and liaison planes complete the naval aircraft inventory.

The marine force consists of a paratroop brigade of three battalions, a battalion attached to the Presidential Guard Brigade, three battalions with headquarters in Mexico City, Acapulco, and Veracruz, and thirty-five independent companies distributed among ports, bases, and zonal headquarters. The marines are responsible for port security and protection of the ten-kilometer coastal fringe. In addition to having light arms, the marines are equipped with eight 105mm towed howitzers, 60mm and 81mm mortars, and 106mm recoilless rifles, as well as Pegaso VAP–3550 amphibious vehicles.

Defense Spending

The government sets the overall size of the military budget, but the actual allocation of funds to various activities and purchases is largely determined within the defense ministries. Little information is made available on individual expenditure categories.

Because of exchange-rate variations and scarcity of data, it is difficult to establish budgetary trends and annual expenditures on defense. According to *The Military Balance*, the defense budget for 1996 was 16.6 billion new pesos (NMex$; for value of new peso—see Glossary), equivalent to US$3.0 billion. This figure compared to budget estimates of 1.577 trillion pesos (US$641 million) in 1989 and 1.908 trillion pesos (US$678 million) in 1990. No explanation was offered as to why the defense budget appears to have more than quadrupled between 1990 and 1996.

Data published by the United States Arms Control and Disarmament Agency (ACDA) show higher levels of spending on defense, which, according to ACDA figures, averaged about US$1.5 billion annually during the decade 1983–93. The peak levels of spending were between 1985 and 1987, when levels of about US$2 billion were recorded. As ACDA notes, data on mil-

Various armored vehicles at Independence Day parade
Courtesy Arturo Salinas

itary expenditures are of uneven accuracy and completeness. In addition to accuracy problems caused by sharp variations in exchange rates, capital spending and arms purchases may be omitted in official data.

Based on data from *The Military Balance*, military expenditures were 0.9 percent of gross domestic product (GDP—see Glossary) in 1995. Military expenditures amounted to US$17 per capita in that year, reversing a declining trend that saw per capita expenditures drop from US$20 in 1985 to US$13 in 1991. The economic burden of the Mexican military establishment is comparable to the average expenditure for Central American countries.

Domestic Defense Production

Mexico has had a small defense industry since before the Revolution. In 1996 the defense industry consisted largely of the production of small arms, ammunition, propellants, and uniforms in government factories. As part of the modernization program launched in 1976, the armed forces redirected their efforts toward attaining a degree of self-sufficiency. The General Directorate of Military Industry drew up plans for production of large military systems, in cooperation with foreign arms manufacturers. The major expansion originally envisaged had to be curtailed, however, because of the economic difficulties of the early 1980s, and projects discussed with West German, Israeli, and Brazilian defense industries involving coproduction of armored vehicles were abandoned. The country's military industry has never reached the level of Brazil and Argentina, the other major Latin American producers of defense-related matériel.

Under a coproduction agreement with West Germany, the Mexican defense industry began mass-producing the standard infantry G–3 automatic rifle in the early 1980s. At the same time, the state-owned Diesel Nacional truck factory began manufacturing three-quarter-ton trucks for military use as well as the DN–3 and DN–5 armored car, derived from the United States Cadillac-Gage V–150 Commando. There were periodic reports of negotiations with foreign producers to cooperate in the manufacture of light and medium tanks, but questions of financing and the availability of special steel intervened.

Between 1972 and 1982, the government allocated considerable funds to the industrial sector for scientific and technical development related to military uses. In 1982 a telecommunications network using telex equipment was built to link military zones with the headquarters of the Secretariat of National Defense in Mexico City. The armed forces also began developing short-range, three- to twelve-kilometer, surface-to-surface missiles, but never reached the production stage.

Since the Revolution, Mexico has had an aircraft industry that produced a number of military models—both original designs and licensed manufactures—that formed part of the air force inventory until the 1960s. In an effort to revive the local aircraft industry, Mexico held discussions with both Brazil and Israel to produce trainer and light transport aircraft under license, but plans had to be shelved for financial reasons.

Mexico's major shipyards at Tampico on the Gulf of Mexico and Salina Cruz on the Pacific Ocean have been involved in the construction of patrol craft and auxiliary vessels. The largest program, involving the manufacture of Azteca-class patrol craft, was carried out under a licensed production agreement with a British firm.

Personnel

Recruitment and Conscription

Only volunteers serve in active units of the Mexican armed forces. Most recruits are of a poor or indigent background; for them, induction into the military is often seen as a source of employment and as a means of upward social mobility. Soldiers' pay is slightly higher than established minimum wages, and recruits can hold second jobs. Vocational and literacy training for armed forces personnel improves their chances of employment when their term of enlistment is completed.

The basic requisites for induction into the armed forces are Mexican citizenship by birth, completion of primary schooling, and absence of a criminal record. Initial recruits are between the ages of eighteen and twenty-one. Enlistment is conducted at military zone headquarters and other military installations. Accordingly, most of the recruits tend to originate in the Federal District and central states, where bases are clustered. Vacancies in local units are often filled by youths completing their national military service.

Recruits enlisting for their first three-year term of service receive basic training at the local unit to which they are assigned, which usually is not far from the individual's home. During the first term of enlistment, the emphasis is on developing basic military skills using an on-the-job training approach. There is a high retention rate for first-term recruits, who often elect to enlist for another three years. Recruits usually complete subsequent terms of service away from their districts. Persons completing this second term of service can hope to attain the rank of sergeant. An increasing number of enlisted personnel serve until they are eligible for retirement, which comes after twenty years. The small noncommissioned officer (NCO) corps is concerned primarily with indoctrinating and molding new recruits and serving in specialist functions. With a high ratio of commissioned officers to NCOs, commissioned officers tend to exercise most leadership responsibilities in troop units.

Applicants aspiring to become commissioned officers apply for admission to one of the three service academies. The oldest and most prestigious is the army's Heroic Military College. To be eligible for entrance, an applicant must be a male Mexican citizen by birth, unmarried, and between the ages of sixteen and twenty-one. Most candidates are sixteen to eighteen years of age. Besides paying a processing fee, candidates are required to pass a series of aptitude, psychological, and physical examinations. Screening is rigorous; only top performers are accepted, although those not selected are permitted to retake the examinations the following year. Each year a few senior NCOs who have shown leadership qualities are selected to attend a special one-year course at the Heroic Military College preparatory to commissioning.

The need to travel to Mexico City for the examinations and the required processing fee discourage many potential candidates from applying for admission. Applicants from distant areas must meet their own travel and lodging costs. Along with the fact that the standards of education are relatively higher in the Federal District, these factors tend to ensure that a high percentage of academy entrants are residents of the capital area.

Most officers are drawn from lower-middle-class and middle-class families. Fewer than 5 percent are believed to be from the upper class. Approximately 20 percent of cadets come from military families, and many others have some military affiliation through relatives. Young officers also tend to marry women from military families. In view of the importance of personal relationships within the military, such ties often are relevant factors in the advancement of an officer's career. Because they often come from a lower social stratum than civil-

Cadets of the Heroic Military College
Courtesy Arturo Salinas

ians holding positions of comparable importance, military professionals do not have the same prestige as the officer class in some other Latin American countries.

The practice of women following soldiers on campaigns and sometimes fighting in battles is well established in Mexican history and legend. Until the 1920s, Mexican armies did not provide regular commissary services, and soldiers in effect employed women, known as *soldaderas,* to buy or forage for food and other supplies and to cook their meals. During the Revolution, women sometimes were directly involved in the fighting. By the 1930s, however, the *soldadera* system had been banished from the military as a source of immorality and vice.

Women are permitted to enlist in the modern Mexican military and can enjoy careers in the armed forces, although they are subject to numerous restrictions. The Organic Law states that women have the same rights and duties as men in the armed forces, but in practice women are not permitted to fill combat positions, nor are they eligible for admission to the service academies. Women who enlist receive the same basic training as men, including courses on the handling and knowledge of weapons, followed by training in their assigned specialties.

Women serve almost exclusively in the areas of administration, medical care, communications, and physical education. The highest rank a woman has achieved is that of major general, by a senior military surgeon.

Obligatory military service for males was introduced in 1941 in response to Mexico's possible entry into World War II. During January in the year of their eighteenth birthday, all Mexican men are required to register with the local municipal government for military service. Out of approximately 1.1 million who register each year, some 320,000 are selected by lottery to begin training during January of the following year. The military obligation is for twelve months, which in practice means no more than one morning a week of calisthenics and drilling (although some draftees are now required to fulfill a three-month period of full-time training).

On completing military service, conscripts remain in reserve status until the age of forty. Completion of the service requirement is noted on a Military Identity Card that bears the individual's photograph and must be revalidated every two years. The identity card is required when applying for a passport, driver's license, or employment. This requirement provides the Mexican government with a useful means of keeping track of its adult male population.

Education and Training

One of the key factors in the development of the professional armed forces in Mexico is the military education system. It is designed to underscore the importance of discipline, conformity to law, and obedience to higher authority. The objective is to instill in officers deference to civilian institutions and to discourage any notion of military interference with the functioning of the state. Instruction on political, social, and economic topics is relatively sketchy in school curricula, presumably to avoid heightening the officers' political consciousness. This limited education does not apply, however, to the most senior level, the National Defense College (Colegio de Defensa Nacional).

The military's three service academies form the first tier of the professional education system. The army's Heroic Military College, located in a southern suburb of Mexico City, dates back to the 1830s and is the most prestigious of the three. Air force cadets attend the Heroic Military College for two years, followed by two years at the Air College in Guadalajara. The Heroic Naval Military School for naval cadets is in Veracruz.

In 1991 there were 245 openings at the Heroic Military College for entering cadets although the excellent modern facilities completed in 1976 can accommodate many more. Entrants range from fifteen to nineteen years old, although most are in the sixteen-to-eighteen age-group. The training is physically demanding and rigorous. Students are deliberately left with little free time. Cadets who complete the four years of training are considered to have achieved the equivalent of a preparatory school education.

Graduates of the four-year army curriculum attain the equivalent rank of second lieutenant and usually become platoon or section commanders, spending three years with tactical units. Young officers then may be designated to attend any of the applied schools for advanced training in infantry, artillery, engineering, support services, or cavalry. Graduates of the Air College who select a flight or ground support orientation in their course work receive the rank of second lieutenant as pilots, general specialists, or specialists in maintenance and supply. Cadets completing studies at the Heroic Naval Military School are commissioned as ensigns prior to service with the naval surface fleet or in naval aviation or the marine infantry. The navy also maintains an aviation school at the Benito Juárez International Airport in Mexico City.

If favorably rated, an army officer may be promoted to first lieutenant after two years and remains at that rank for a minimum of three years. The officer can resign his commission after five years or, after passing a competitive examination and being favorably evaluated, may be placed on a promotion list for second captain in order of his test score (see Uniforms, Ranks, and Insignia, this ch.). Similar requirements must be met for advancement through the rank of lieutenant colonel. The minimum service time is eight years to reach first captain, eleven years to reach major, and fourteen years to reach lieutenant colonel. The rate of promotion is fairly predictable. The Senate, which must approve promotions to the rank of colonel and above, generally resists advancing officers who have not served a normal time in grade.

First and second captains who can meet admission standards may be admitted to the Superior War College or, in the case of naval officers, the Center of Superior Naval Studies. The Superior War College offers a three-year program for army officers and a two-year program for the air force. The equivalent naval course is three years. Course work emphasizes preparation for command and staff positions, including the study of administration, strategy and tactics, war gaming, and logistics, as well as more general subjects, such as military history, international law, and foreign languages. On completion of the course, officers are considered to have military training roughly comparable to that of the United States Army Command and General Staff College at Fort Leavenworth, Kansas.

Conditions for acceptance to the Superior War College are strict, as is the course work. Only about half of the entrants complete the full three years, and only 7 percent of the officer corps are graduates of the college. Those completing the course successfully receive the degree of Licenciate in Military Administration and the title of General Staff Graduate, which is used with one's military rank and commands some prestige. Graduates also receive a stipend of between 10 and 25 percent of their salary during the remainder of their active duty.

The National Defense College, created in 1981, is considered the culmination of professional military education. Entrance is offered to a select group of senior army colonels and generals and their counterparts in the air force and navy. The one-year program includes advanced training in national security policy formulation, resource management, international relations, and economics. Each officer is required to write a thesis involving field research on a topic involving national security, politics, or social problems. The majority of the professors at the college are civilians. Although graduation from the college does not bring immediate promotion, most of the generals reaching the highest positions in the military hierarchy are alumni of the college.

A number of other service institutions, separate from the officer training schools and the superior schools, fall under the general categories of applications schools, specialization schools, and schools offering basic NCO training and NCO technical courses. These institutions include the Military School of Medicine, the Military School of Dentistry, a group of schools of nursing and other medical specialties, military schools of engineering and communications, the Military Application School of Infantry and Artillery, the Military Application School of Cavalry, and a one-year school of instruction in leadership for second and first sergeants.

Mexican officers also attend military schools in other countries of Latin America, as well as in France, Britain, Italy, and Germany. Although Mexico sends proportionately fewer officers to military schools in the United States than some Latin American countries, it uses United States training materials, and United States military doctrine is influential.

Pay and Benefits

The Law of Promotions and Compensation and the Law of Pensions and Retirement were promulgated in the 1920s as a means to regularize military practices, bring the armed forces under the control of the central government, and ensure the stability of the electoral system created by the revolutionary government. These laws, which have been adjusted periodically to meet the changing requirements of the government and the armed forces, form the backbone of the military pay and benefits system.

The three branches of the armed forces provide uniform pay and benefits for equivalent rank and years of service. Throughout the 1950s and 1960s, military compensation rose at a faster rate than the cost of living. This situation changed during the 1970s, as pay failed to keep pace either with the rapidly increasing inflation rate or with earning power in the civilian sector. In spite of spiraling inflation during the 1980s, pay raises helped most military personnel keep abreast or slightly ahead of the rising cost of living. Officers of lieutenant rank and above enjoyed comfortable incomes. In the early 1990s, however, pay scales for junior officers were described as so low—about US$300 a month—that moonlighting was accepted as necessary to maintain an adequate standard of living.

Although the government does not disclose the allocation of individual items within the defense budget, it is estimated that approximately 60 percent is dedicated to personnel expenses, including administrative costs, salaries, and benefits. Perquisites, bonuses granted for educational achievements, and supplemental pay for those serving in command positions—from the commander of a company to the secretary of national defense—add considerably to officers' base salaries. Both the amount and the availability of fringe benefits increase as officers ascend in rank. Additional pay is also provided for hazardous duty assignments.

Pensions are extended on a standard basis to all military personnel upon completion of service and to dependents or beneficiaries upon their deaths. This benefit has been increased on numerous occasions to encourage older officers to retire and thus open positions for younger officers. The mandatory retirement age is between forty-five and sixty-five, depending upon rank, but former secretaries of national defense hold active-duty status all their lives. Under a 1983 modification of the Law of Pensions and Retirement, an officer completing thirty years of service can retire at 100 percent of his or her existing salary and receive the same increases granted active-duty personnel. The minimum benefit for those with fewer years of service is 20 percent of base pay.

The Mexican Armed Forces Social Security Institute (Instituto de Seguro Social para las Fuerzas Armadas Mexicanas—ISSFAM) and the National Bank of the Army, Air Force, and Navy (Banco Nacional del Ejército, Fuerza Aérea, y Armada—Banejército) also provide benefits to military personnel and their dependents. Under the ISSFAM, health care is extended through facilities at regional military hospitals in each military zone and the Central Military Hospital in Mexico City. The quality of medical care is reported to be high, and physicians are trained in such sophisticated specialties as microsurgery, organ transplants, and cardiovascular surgery. Banejército offers low-interest credit and life insurance to military personnel and provides financing for the construction of dependent housing at the country's various military installations. Rent for dependent housing is set at 6 percent of an individual's income. Other services and benefits are also available through military zone installations. These services include primary and secondary education for dependents, assistance with moving expenses resulting from service-related transfers, various social services, and access to shops similar to small commissaries. The military also manages a number of farms throughout the country to help produce its own food supply.

Uniforms, Ranks, and Insignia

Mexico originally adopted its system of officer ranks from the Spanish military. With some modifications, it has been retained in the modern armed forces. The highest rank within the Secretariat of National Defense is the rough equivalent of a general in the United States Army. The only officers with the rank of general are current army officers and former secretaries of national defense. Generals are identified by insignia composed of four silver stars and a gold eagle worn on their epaulets (see fig. 12). The next highest rank, open to both army and air force personnel, is the equivalent of lieutenant general. Although there is no difference between the Spanish name for this rank and that held by secretaries of national defense, the officers are separately identified by three stars and an eagle. The rank equivalents of major general and brigadier general are distinguished, in addition to the emblem of the gold eagle on their epaulets, by two silver stars and one silver star, respectively.

Officers holding the rank of colonel command certain brigades and cavalry regiments, serve as chiefs of staff for military zones, or manage staff directorates. Colonels are identified by three gold stars arranged in a triangle on their epaulets. The equivalents of lieutenant colonels, a select few of whom may command a battalion or cavalry squadron but most of whom serve as instructors or administrative aides, wear two gold stars. Majors sometimes serve as second-in-command of battalions or squadrons, but usually are assigned to personnel management and training. They are identified by a single gold star.

Other commissioned ranks include first captain and second captain, both comparable to the United States rank of captain. First captains wear three gold bars on the epaulet; second captains have two-and-one-half gold bars. Captains command companies, squadrons, and batteries. Below these ranks are first lieutenants, with two gold bars, and second lieutenants, identified by a single gold bar.

The rank insignia of commissioned naval officers consist of gold stripes above the sleeve cuff, the uppermost stripe incorporating a braided loop. The rough equivalents of the United States Navy's ranks of admiral, vice admiral, and rear admiral wear insignia consisting of a wide gold stripe plus narrow and looped stripes. The equivalents of admiral and vice admiral are consolidated. The sleeve insignia of other officer ranks are similar to those of the corresponding ranks of the United States Navy, except that the upper stripe is looped. Officers of marine infantry units are distinguished by red piping on their insignia of rank.

The rank titles and rank insignia for enlisted personnel in the army and air force are the same (see fig. 13). The highest rank, sergeant 1st class (or master sergeant), is recognized by green epaulets with three horizontal red bars. The next two lowest ranks, sergeant and private 1st class (or corporal specialist), are distinguished by two and one horizontal red bars,

	SUB-TENIENTE	TENIENTE	CAPITÁN SEGUNDO	CAPITÁN PRIMERO	MAYOR	TENIENTE CORONEL	CORONEL	GENERAL BRIGADIER	GENERAL DE BRIGADA	GENERAL DE DIVISIÓN	GENERAL DE DIVISIÓN*
MEXICAN RANK	SUB-TENIENTE	TENIENTE	CAPITÁN SEGUNDO	CAPITÁN PRIMERO	MAYOR	TENIENTE CORONEL	CORONEL	GENERAL BRIGADIER	GENERAL DE BRIGADA	GENERAL DE DIVISIÓN	GENERAL DE DIVISIÓN*
ARMY											
U.S. RANK TITLE	2D LIEUTENANT	1ST LIEUTENANT	CAPTAIN		MAJOR	LIEUTENANT COLONEL	COLONEL	BRIGADIER GENERAL	MAJOR GENERAL	LIEUTENANT GENERAL	GENERAL
MEXICAN RANK	SUB-TENIENTE	TENIENTE	CAPITÁN SEGUNDO	CAPITÁN PRIMERO	MAYOR	TENIENTE CORONEL	CORONEL	GENERAL DE GRUPO	GENERAL DE ALA	GENERAL DE DIVISIÓN	NO RANK
AIR FORCE											
U.S. RANK TITLE	2D LIEUTENANT	1ST LIEUTENANT	CAPTAIN		MAJOR	LIEUTENANT COLONEL	COLONEL	BRIGADIER GENERAL	MAJOR GENERAL	LIEUTENANT GENERAL	NO RANK
MEXICAN RANK	GUARDA-MARINA	TENIENTE DE CORBETA	TENIENTE DE NAVÍO		CAPITÁN DE CORBETA	CAPITÁN DE FRAGATA	CAPITÁN DE NAVÍO	CONTRAL-MIRANTE	VICE-ALMIRANTE	ALMIRANTE	
NAVY											
U.S. RANK TITLE	ENSIGN	LIEUTENANT JUNIOR GRADE	LIEUTENANT		LIEUTENANT COMMANDER	COMMANDER	CAPTAIN	REAR ADMIRAL LOWER HALF	REAR ADMIRAL UPPER HALF	VICE ADMIRAL	ADMIRAL

*Note— Applies only to present or former secretaries of national defense.

Figure 12. Commissioned Officer Ranks and Insignia, 1996

respectively. The *soldado de primera,* corresponding to the United States rank of private in the army and airman in the air force, has two short vertical red bars. The lowest rank for each service, basic private or airman basic (*soldado*), wears a plain green epaulet.

The rank insignia of enlisted naval personnel are indicated by white stripes above the sleeve cuff. Enlisted personnel in the navy have only three ranks, chief petty officer, petty officer, and seaman. A chief petty officer has three white stripes and a petty officer two. A seaman has a single V-shaped stripe.

The army officer corps has a blue dress uniform and a dark field-green service uniform. A khaki uniform is used for hot weather. The uniforms worn by naval personnel, including marines, are standard dark blue or white. The dress uniforms of army enlisted personnel are dark field-green; their branch of service is designated by a colored bar displayed on the epaulet. Infantry personnel wear a scarlet red bar; cavalry, hussar blue; artillery, crimson; armored, gray; and engineers, cobalt blue. The air force uniform was modified somewhat from that of the army in the early 1980s. Air force personnel are identified by purple bars. Members of the elite airborne brigade are distinguished by their camouflage fatigues and purple berets. Dress uniforms for enlisted army personnel include the use of helmets as headgear. Members of the officer corps wear caps with elaborate visor decorations and rank designations.

Public Order and Internal Security

Criminal activity, much of it engendered by narcotics trafficking and production, has, since the 1970s, constituted the most serious problem facing military and police agencies concerned with internal security. Mexico's leaders are increasingly conscious of the threat that drug cartels, with enormous funds and weapons at their disposal, pose to the nation's political and social stability. The illicit movement of drugs generates huge amounts of money that can be employed to corrupt public officials at both the state and federal levels. Traffickers also can assemble large weapons arsenals, which contribute to the atmosphere of lawlessness in society (see Narcotics Trafficking, this ch.).

Until the uprising in Chiapas in 1994, revolutionary activity amounting to insurrection against the state had not been a major source of concern for several decades. Groups that sprang up to exploit the plight of the downtrodden and the dis-

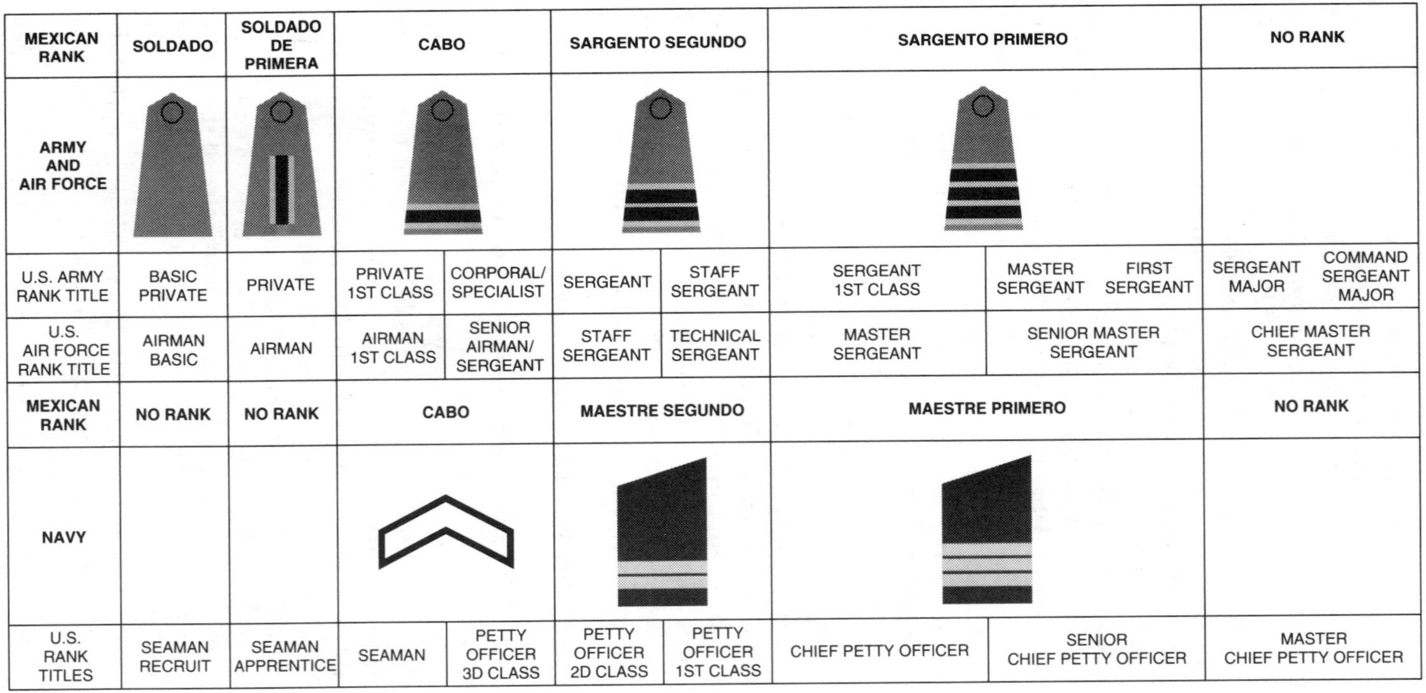

MEXICAN RANK	SOLDADO	SOLDADO DE PRIMERA	CABO		SARGENTO SEGUNDO		SARGENTO PRIMERO		NO RANK	
ARMY AND AIR FORCE (insignia)									NO RANK	
U.S. ARMY RANK TITLE	BASIC PRIVATE	PRIVATE	PRIVATE 1ST CLASS	CORPORAL/SPECIALIST	SERGEANT	STAFF SERGEANT	SERGEANT 1ST CLASS	MASTER SERGEANT · FIRST SERGEANT	SERGEANT MAJOR	COMMAND SERGEANT MAJOR
U.S. AIR FORCE RANK TITLE	AIRMAN BASIC	AIRMAN	AIRMAN 1ST CLASS	SENIOR AIRMAN/SERGEANT	STAFF SERGEANT	TECHNICAL SERGEANT	MASTER SERGEANT	SENIOR MASTER SERGEANT	CHIEF MASTER SERGEANT	
MEXICAN RANK	NO RANK	NO RANK	CABO		MAESTRE SEGUNDO		MAESTRE PRIMERO		NO RANK	
NAVY (insignia)										
U.S. RANK TITLES	SEAMAN RECRUIT	SEAMAN APPRENTICE	SEAMAN	PETTY OFFICER 3D CLASS	PETTY OFFICER 2D CLASS	PETTY OFFICER 1ST CLASS	CHIEF PETTY OFFICER	SENIOR CHIEF PETTY OFFICER	MASTER CHIEF PETTY OFFICER	

Figure 13. Enlisted Personnel Ranks and Insignia, 1996

parities between the rich and poor have failed to coalesce into a single movement powerful enough to threaten the stability of the central government. The fragmentation of the forces of protest has been ascribed to several factors, including the territorial expanse and geographic diversity of the country, the preoccupation with local injustices suffered at the hands of those holding economic power, and the government's determination to deal harshly with any threat to public order.

During the late 1960s and early 1970s, several guerrilla organizations operated in the countryside. The three principal groups were the National Revolutionary Civic Association, the Mexican Proletarian Party, and the Party of the Poor. Each was directed by a charismatic leader, who eventually was tracked down and killed in confrontations with the military or police. None of the groups was able to carry on organized operations after its leader's death.

The police claimed in 1981 that they had destroyed the last cell of the Twenty-Third of September Communist League, the largest and longest-lived of Mexico's urban guerrilla groups. The league reportedly had incorporated members from several other urban guerrilla fronts. Many terrorist acts were committed in the name of the league before its eradication, including the kidnapping of two United States consular officers in 1973 and 1974 (one officer was freed after a ransom was paid, and the other was murdered).

The Chiapas Rebellion

Mexico's rural indigenous peoples periodically have risen in protest against poverty and encroachment by large farmers, ranchers, and commercial interests on contested land. The most recent and serious such uprising occurred on January 1, 1994, when the Zapatista National Liberation Army (Ejército Zapatista de Liberación Nacional—EZLN) rebelled, capturing four municipalities in Chiapas state. Some of the group, believed to number about 1,600, were armed with semiautomatic and assault rifles, whereas others were armed only with sticks and wooden bayonets. Although the group's attacks seemed well planned, army units, supported by air force strikes, were able to regain control after the initial surprise. At least 12,000 troops were transported to the scene. Officials announced that 120 deaths had resulted, although church officials said 400 lives had been lost. Five rebels apparently were executed while bound, and other deaths may have been the result of extrajudicial executions. Many disappearances of peasants were reported, and there was indiscriminate strafing of hamlets. The government declared a unilateral cease-fire after twelve days and announced several goodwill gestures as a prelude to reconciliation talks with the rebels, who were represented by their masked leader, Subcommander Marcos.

According to government sources, the EZLN, commonly known as the Zapatistas, is not a purely indigenous movement, but is instead an alliance of middle-class intellectuals and radicalized indigenous groups dating from the early 1980s. The EZLN began as an offshoot of the National Liberation Forces (Fuerzas de Liberación Nacional—FLN), a Maoist guerrilla group that had been largely dormant since the 1970s. At the start of the Zapatista rebellion, command of the Zapatista army was jointly held by FLN veterans from Mexico City and a "clandestine committee" of Chiapas Indians representing the various ethnic groups residing in the area.

In February 1995, on the eve of a new offensive against rebel strongholds, the government identified Subcommander Marcos as Rafael Sebastián Guillén, a white, middle-class graduate in graphics design from the National Autonomous University of Mexico (Universidad Nacional Autónoma de México—UNAM). In the initial January 1994 Zapatista raids, the charismatic guerrilla leader had become an international media star, quickly assuming the status of a folk hero among many Mexicans. Capitalizing on his newfound fame and his proximity to the rebel army, Marcos is believed to have wrested control of the EZLN from its Mexico City leadership.

Despite a formidable government offensive involving approximately 20,000 army troops venturing into Zapatista-held territory, Subcommander Marcos and his rebel force eluded capture. By late February 1995, a second cease-fire had been declared. Soon thereafter, the government and the rebels embarked on a second major round of peace talks. In early 1996, the Zapatistas declared their willingness in principle to lay down their arms and become a legal political party pending major reforms of the political system. Despite their ability to grab headlines and attract international support, the Zapatistas remain a marginal political force and are not considered a serious military threat outside of Chiapas.

Police and Law Enforcement Organizations

A number of federal, state, and local police and law enforcement organizations exist to provide for internal security. Their responsibilities and jurisdictions frequently overlap, a factor acknowledged in 1984 when the government created a national consulting board designed to "coordinate and advise police forces" throughout the country. The senior law enforcement organization in Mexico is the Federal Judicial Police, which is controlled by the attorney general. The plainclothes force acts as an investigative agency with arrest power for the Office of the Attorney General. The foremost activity of the Federal Judicial Police is carrying out investigations and making apprehensions related to drug trafficking. Espionage, arms trafficking, and bank robberies also fall under its purview. The Federal Judicial Police serves as the government's liaison with the International Criminal Police Organization (Interpol). Its role can be compared to a combination of the United States Federal Bureau of Investigation (FBI) and the United States Drug Enforcement Administration (DEA).

The jurisdiction of the Federal Judicial Police encompasses the entire nation. For control purposes, its jurisdiction is divided into thirteen zones with fifty-two smaller detachment headquarters. Under the coordination of the local federal prosecutor, each zone is headed by a second commandant of the Federal Judicial Police, who in turn directs the group chiefs in the outlying detachments. Individuals arrested by the Federal Judicial Police are placed at the disposition of the local federal prosecutor, who appoints subordinate attorneys to assess each case.

Although it remains one of the smaller law enforcement agencies, the Federal Judicial Police tripled in size between 1982 and 1984, from 500 personnel to an estimated 1,500. In 1988 an assistant attorney general's office for investigating and combating drug trafficking was formed with an additional 1,500 Federal Judicial Police agents. In 1990 the office was expanded and given interagency coordinating functions in the battle against narcotics.

The principal Mexico City police force, the Protection and Transit Directorate, also known as the Traffic Police, consists of some 29,000 officers organized into thirty-three precincts. It is the largest law enforcement organization in Mexico. More than 100 serious crimes are reported each day in Mexico City, and on average in the Federal District in the first quarter of 1997 one police officer was killed and one injured weekly. A sense of insecurity prevails among many citizens because of the lack of confidence in the police and the fear of police misbehavior and crime.

The Federal District police are poorly paid; in 1992 they earned between US$285 and US$400 a month. Double shifts are common, although no extra pay for overtime is provided. Incomes can be supplemented in various ways, including from petty bribes (*mordidas*) from motorists seeking to park in restricted zones. Police are said to be obliged to pay for more desirable assignments where the possibilities of extorting payments from drivers in lieu of fines is greater. However, junior officers are forced to pass along a daily quota of bribes to more senior officers. In one case, a tow truck driver admitted that he had paid more than US$1,000 for his lucrative job and said that he had to contribute US$32 daily to his superior. In 1992 after a number of officers expressed their objections to the system, the mayor of Mexico City set up offices to receive and investigate citizen complaints.

A number of smaller law enforcement bodies exist at the state and local level. Each of the country's thirty-one states and the Federal District has its own judicial police—the State Judicial Police and the Federal District Judicial Police. State police are under the direction of the state's governor; the Federal District Judicial Police fall under the control of the Federal District attorney general. The distinction between crimes investigated by State and Federal Judicial Police is not always clear. Most offenses come under the state authorities. Drug dealing, crimes against the government, and offenses involving several jurisdictions are the responsibility of the federal police.

Cities and municipalities have their own preventive and municipal police forces, which are responsible for handling minor civil disturbances and traffic infractions. The Federal Highway Police patrols federally designated highways and investigates traffic accidents. Highway police are assisted by military personnel on national holidays.

Both state and municipal forces operate from precinct stations, called *delegaciones*. Each *delegación* has an average of 200 police officers attached to it. The ranking officer is known as a *comandante*, equivalent to a first captain in the military. Most of the remaining personnel hold the ranks of first sergeant, second sergeant, and corporal.

Immigration officers, directed by the Mexican Immigration Service under the Secretariat of Government (Secretaría de Gobernación), have the right to detain suspected undocumented aliens and, under certain conditions, to deport them without formal deportation proceedings. Customs officers, controlled by the Secretariat of Finance and Public Credit (Secretaría de Hacienda y Crédito Público), Crédito are deployed at borders and at international airports to interdict contraband entering Mexico. The Bank of Mexico also operates its own security division, which is charged with enforcing banking and monetary laws, including cases of counterfeiting, fraud, and money laundering.

A number of unofficial paramilitary groups incorporating various police officials have existed in the past to deal with rural and urban guerrillas and illegal groups. The most notorious paramilitary group was the White Brigade (Brigada Blanca) whose existence was officially denied, although it was known to be active from 1977 until 1980, when the government dismantled it. The White Brigade consisted of a group of officers from the army and the police forces that used illegal tactics to destroy guerrilla movements. Published reports held that the White Brigade was responsible for the "disappearance" of several hundred leftists, most of whom the government claimed were killed in fights between rival leftist groups. Politically motivated "disappearances" tapered off sharply during the 1980s, but were once again being reported in the mid-1990s in connection with the unrest in Chiapas.

The government has repeatedly denounced abuses and corruption by the Federal Judicial Police and other police forces. Numerous reforms have been announced, personnel shifted, and codes of procedures adopted. Allegations of police brutality have declined, but torture, wrongful arrests, and involvement in drug trafficking have not been eliminated because abuses are so deeply rooted in the police agencies, and violators for the most part have been able to act with impunity (see Human Rights Concerns, this ch.).

In 1991 Attorney General Enrique Álvarez del Castillo, who was reported to have impeded several human rights investigations against the police, was abruptly removed from office and replaced by Ignacio Morales Lechuga. Morales quickly announced a crackdown on corruption, including a reorganization of the Federal Judicial Police, the creation of special anticorruption and internal affairs units, as well as a unit to protect citizens against crimes committed by the police. In addition, all federal police units were placed under the control of a civilian deputy attorney general. New high-level officials supervised police activities in sensitive border areas. These reform measures were announced soon after a jailed drug lord took over a prison in Matamoros, claiming that agents of the Federal Judicial Police aligned with another drug lord were threatening his life.

Despite Morales's reputation as an upright official prepared to dismiss police agents and government prosecutors suspected of ties with drug traffickers, he was replaced in early 1993. Later reports accused some of Morales's subordinates of drug-related corruption. The new attorney general, Jorge Carpizo MacGregor, was a respected human rights activist. Carpizo acknowledged in a detailed report the close relations between criminals and law enforcement agencies and produced his own program to eliminate deficiencies and corruption among the police. His reforms brought some progress; some members of the security forces were charged and sentenced, and human rights violations declined, but the so-called "culture of impunity" still prevailed. Carpizo resigned as attorney general in early 1994 and was replaced by Diego Valádez.

The 1994 assassinations of PRI presidential candidate Luis Donaldo Colosio Murrieta and PRI Secretary General José Francisco Ruiz Massieu shook the highest levels of federal law enforcement. After failing to make significant progress in investigating the Colosio case, Attorney General Valádez was replaced in May 1994 by Humberto Benítez Trevino. Initially declaring that the Colosio assassination was the work of a lone gunman, the Attorney General's office later revised its theory based on videotape evidence that suggested a conspiracy of up to six individuals working in concert to allow the alleged gunman to approach the candidate during a crowded campaign rally. The post of attorney general underwent yet another change in early 1996 when incoming President Zedillo replaced Benítez with an opposition congressman, Fernando Antonio Lozano Gracia. Lozano's tenure was significant because it was the first time a non-PRI official held the post.

Late in 1994, the assassination of José Francisco Ruiz Massieu prompted a special investigation headed by Deputy Attorney General Mario Ruiz Massieu, brother of the slain politician. After calling dozens of PRI officials to testify, Ruiz resigned abruptly in November, accusing high-level PRI functionaries of complicity in the killing and of impeding further progress in the investigation. In early 1996, the investigation still had produced no results.

National Intelligence Agencies

From the 1940s until it was disbanded in 1985, the Federal Directorate of Security, which was under the control of the Secretariat of Government, was the primary agency assigned to preserve internal stability against subversion and terrorist threats. The directorate was responsible for investigating national security matters and performed other special duties as directed by the president. It acted as the equivalent of the United States DEA in the Mexican government. A plainclothes force, the directorate had no legal arrest powers nor formal authority to gather evidence, although it could call upon the assistance of other government agencies and could use other surveillance techniques.

By the final years of its existence, the directorate had more than doubled in size to some 2,000 personnel. The agency's demise came after it became evident that many of its personnel were in league with major drug traffickers. Its successor was the Center for Investigation and National Security (Centro de Investigación y Seguridad Nacional—CISN). Although formally under the Secretariat of Government, CISN is said to operate under direct presidential control. Still primarily concerned with gathering intelligence, CISN also has expanded activities to include opinion polling and analysis of domestic political and social conditions. In 1992 illegal wiretaps were found in a meeting room to be used by the central committee of the opposition National Action Party (Partido de Acción Nacional—PAN). Although the government denied any official involvement, the local representative of CISN was forced to resign.

Human Rights Concerns

Brutality and systematic abuses of human rights by elements of the Mexican internal security forces are pervasive and have largely gone unpunished. Practices cited by human rights groups include the use of torture, extrajudicial killings, disappearances, arbitrary detention, and other cruelties perpetrated against private persons and prisoners. According to several sources, the number and seriousness of such offenses has declined somewhat in the early 1990s. The improvement has been attributed to the greater determination of the national government to prosecute offenders and to the work of national and local human rights agencies in exposing instances of police violations of human rights and in pressing for punishment.

In 1990 the Mexican government established the National Human Rights Commission (Comisión Nacional de Derechos Humanos—CNDH). Initially under the Secretariat of Government, the CNDH was granted constitutional status and full autonomy under a law enacted in 1992. By the following year, similar offices to investigate abuses had been established in all states of Mexico. The CNDH has the power to compel officials to grant access and give evidence. Its recommendations are nonbinding on government agencies, however. As of 1993, 268 of 624 CNDH recommendations had been followed fully. These resulted in eighty-two people being arrested and twenty sentenced to prison terms averaging more than five years for human rights violations.

According to the private human rights organization, Amnesty International, state judicial police and other law enforcement agencies frequently use torture in the form of beatings, near-asphyxiation, electric shock, burning with cigarettes, and psychological torture. Most victims are criminal suspects, but others, such as leaders of indigenous groups or civil rights activists engaged in demonstrations or other peaceful activities, have been targeted as well. According to the CNDH, complaints of torture declined from 446 in its first year of operation to 141 cases in its fourth.

New laws enacted in 1991 permit courts to accept confessions only when made before a judge or court official in the presence of defense counsel. Similar rules were adopted by several states. Formerly, confessions obtained under duress were admitted as evidence in court. Some defendants have claimed that even with the change, they still fear torture if they fail to confess.

Although in the 1990s fewer new cases of human rights violations were reported each year, numerous charges of extrajudicial killings continue to be made against the police. Police linked to drug rings have been accused of narcotics-related executions. In several well publicized instances, civil-rights workers were slain, as were peasant activists involved in disputes over land titles. Police often assist local landowners in evicting peasant and urban squatters in conflicts over land and in employing violence without appropriate judicial orders.

Police officers seldom are prosecuted or dismissed for abuses. In 1992, however, the attorney general removed sixty-seven Federal Judicial Police agents and federal prosecutors and referred 270 cases of alleged corruption or human rights violations for prosecution. Acceptance of the CNDH has grown steadily, and its investigations have resulted in a reduction of reported police misconduct, especially at the federal level.

According to the CNDH, illegal deprivation of liberty is the most common human rights complaint among its human rights cases. Between 1990 and 1992, there were 826 allegations of arbitrary detentions. Torture complaints numbered 446 in the commission's first year but fell to 290 during its second. Nearly 100 nongovernmental human rights monitoring groups also have formed, making it increasingly difficult for law enforcement bodies to remain indifferent to public opinion. Nevertheless, the United States Department of State, in its *Country Reports on Human Rights Practices for 1995*, reported a continuing failure to try, convict, and sentence prison and police officials guilty of abuse.

Criminal Justice System

The judiciary is divided into federal and state systems. Federal courts have jurisdiction over major felonies, including drug trafficking. In the federal system, judicial power is exercised by the Supreme Court of Justice, circuit courts, and district courts (see Judicial, ch. 4). The first chamber of the Supreme Court, composed of a president and four other judges, deals with penal affairs. Twelve collegiate circuit courts, each with three magistrates, deal with the right of *amparo* (constitutional rights of an individual, similar to habeas corpus). Nine unitary circuit courts, of one magistrate each, deal with appeals. There are sixty-eight one-magistrate district courts. State judiciary systems following a similar pattern are composed of state supreme courts, courts of first instance, and justices of the peace or police judges.

In most instances, arrests can be made only on authority of a judicial warrant, with the exception of suspects caught in the act of committing crimes. Suspects often are arrested without warrants, but judges tend to overlook this irregularity. Those arrested are required to be brought before an officer of the court as soon as possible, generally within forty-eight hours (ninety-six hours when organized crime is alleged), whereupon their statements are taken and they are informed of the charges against them. Within seventy-two hours of arraignment, the judge must remand the arrested person to prison or release him or her.

Criminal trials in nearly all cases are tried by a judge without a jury. The judge acting alone bases his or her verdict on written statements, depositions, and expert opinion, although in some instances oral testimony is presented. Defendants have access to counsel, and those unable to afford legal fees can be assigned public defenders. The quality of pro bono counsel is often inferior. The accused and his or her lawyer do not always meet before trial, and the lawyer may not appear at the important sentencing stage. The right to a public trial is guaranteed, as is the right to confront one's accusers and to be provided with a translator if the accused's native language is not Spanish. Under the constitution, the court must hand down a sentence within four months of arrest for crimes carrying a maximum sentence of two years or less, and within one year for crimes with longer sentences.

The entire process—the time for a trial, sentencing, and appeals—often requires a year or more. According to Amnesty International, a large number of persons charged with crimes have been held far beyond the constitutional limits for their detention. The long trial process and the detention of those who cannot qualify for or make bail are major causes of crowded prison conditions.

The penal code stipulates a range of sentences for each offense. Sentences tend to be short, in most cases not longer than seven years. The actual time of incarceration is usually three-fifths of the sentence, assuming good behavior. Those sentenced for less than five years may avoid further time in jail by payment of a bond.

Prison Conditions

The penal system consists of both federal and state correctional institutions. The largest federal prison is the penitentiary for the Federal District. The Federal District also sends prisoners to four detention centers, sixteen smaller jails, and a women's jail. Each state has its own penitentiary. There are, in addition, more than 2,000 municipal jails. As of the end of 1993, nearly 95,000 inmates were in Mexican prisons; almost half were persons still awaiting trial or sentencing.

Overcrowding of prisons is chronic. Mistreatment of prisoners, the lack of trained guards, and inadequate sanitary facilities compound the problem. The United States Department of

State's country reports on human rights practices for 1992 and 1993 state that an entrenched system of corruption undermines prison authority and contributes to abuses. Authority frequently is exercised by prisoners, displacing prison officials. Violent confrontations, often linked to drug trafficking, are common between rival prison groups.

Mexican prisons also exhibit some humane qualities. In 1971 conjugal visiting rights were established for male prisoners and later extended to females. Prisoners held at the penal colony on the Islas Tres Marías off the coast of Nayarit are permitted to bring their entire families to live temporarily. Women are permitted to keep children under five years of age with them.

Based on interviews at a smaller state prison, United States penologist William V. Wilkinson found in 1990 that serious overcrowding, lack of privacy, and poor prison diets were the most common complaints. Wilkinson found no deliberate mistreatment of inmates. The prison fare generally was supplemented by food supplied by prisoners' families or purchased from outside. Prisoners with money could buy items such as television sets and sports equipment. Through bribery, prisoners could be assigned to highly prized individual cells, where even air conditioners were permitted.

A major building program by the CNDH added 800 prison spaces in 1993 and 1994. In 1991 Mexico's only maximum security facility, Almoloya de Juárez, was completed. Major drug traffickers were transferred to it from other prisons. The prison's 408 individual cells are watched by closed-circuit television and the most modern technical and physical security equipment. Violence in prisons is a constant problem as a result of overcrowding, lack of security, and the mixing of male and female prisoners and of accused and sentenced criminals.

Imprisonment of peasants, often for growing marijuana, puts a heavy demand on the system. Through the efforts of CNDH, a program of early release and parole benefited 1,000 people incarcerated on charges of growing marijuana in 1993.

Under the terms of the 1977 Prisoner Transfer Treaty between the United States and Mexico, United States prisoners in Mexican jails and Mexican prisoners in United States jails may choose to serve their sentences in their home countries. An extradition treaty between the United States and Mexico took effect in January 1980. It requires the mutual recognition of a crime as defined by the laws of each nation. Because of the extensive processing required under extradition requests, however, informal cooperation has developed among police on both sides of the border. Suspected criminals who flee to the neighboring country to escape apprehension routinely are turned over without formal proceedings to police in the country where the crime was committed.

Noncompliance with the Prisoner Transfer Treaty has occasionally created friction between the United States and Mexico. The United States strongly criticized Mexico's decision in 1988 to release William Morales, a leader of the Puerto Rican Armed National Liberation Front, who was wanted for a series of bombings in New York in 1978. Mexico rejected a United States extradition request even though a Mexican court had found Morales extraditable. Washington objected particularly to the initial Mexican characterization of Morales as a "political fighter."

The death penalty has not been applied in Mexico since 1929, when the assassin of president-elect Obregón was executed. The federal death penalty was abolished under the Federal Penal Code of 1930, and by 1975 all state codes also had eliminated the death penalty. The military, however, still holds certain offenses as punishable by death, including insubordination with violence causing the death of a superior officer, certain kinds of looting, offenses against military honor, and treason.

Narcotics Trafficking

Mexico is a major source of heroin and marijuana destined for the United States, as well as the principal route of transit for South American cocaine. In 1994 Mexico supplied 60 to 80 percent of marijuana imported into the United States, and Mexican heroin accounted for 20 percent of the United States market. The United States government estimates that 50 to 70 percent of cocaine smuggled into the United States comes by way of Mexico, most of it entering Mexico from Colombia by private aircraft or ship, then transported by land across the United States-Mexican border.

Drug abuse among Mexicans has remained relatively low, although cocaine use is on the rise, particularly along the border area, in major tourist centers, in large universities, and among street children in Mexico City. The Mexican attorney general has said that Mexico is fast becoming a drug-consuming nation. He cited economic hardship, urbanization, and the collapse of traditional family life as primary causes. A national drug control campaign, instituted in 1992, introduced drug education in schools, gave extensive publicity to prevention measures, and created a program to assist hospitalized drug addicts.

Coordination of United States and Mexican efforts to combat drug trafficking increased greatly during the terms of presidents Salinas (1988–94) and Zedillo (1994–). Mexico widened the scope and intensity of its counternarcotics effort, increasing personnel and budgets threefold between 1989 and 1993. As in the past, corruption among the police at both low and higher levels, lax enforcement, and weak legal constraints have continued to hinder the effectiveness of Mexico's interdiction campaign.

Cooperation between the two countries on narcotic crop eradication dates from 1961. For two decades until Mexico assumed all of the costs of the programs in 1993, the United States gave financial support of as much as US$20 million a year to the antidrug campaign. DEA agents continue to serve in Mexico, and the United States supplies leased helicopters to aid Mexico's efforts.

In 1992 the United States estimated that about 6,600 hectares of opium poppies used in the production of heroin had been eradicated, representing 50 percent of the opium poppy crop. The potential amount of heroin that could be produced increased to 6 tons in 1994 from 4.9 tons in 1993. Some 8,500 hectares of marijuana under cultivation, or 44 percent of the crop, were destroyed in 1994. In many areas, marijuana is difficult to detect because it is planted with corn or in small plots concealed by trees or shrubs.

Cocaine shipments generally reach Mexico from Central America by plane or are shipped to Mexican ports on the Pacific. They are then trucked to locations throughout Mexico for later transshipment over land to the Mexican-United States border. In 1990 a joint United States-Mexico air interception program was launched. The Mexican/United States unit responsible is the Northern Border Response Force. It consists of 1,800 members, overwhelmingly Mexican. Their equipment includes UH–1H transport helicopters leased from the United States and Citation II tracker aircraft. The DEA and the United States military supply radar intelligence. The success of the air interdiction operation has forced traffickers to depend more on drugs delivered by sea or hidden in vehicles. In 1994 the

Northern Border Response Force seized 22 tons of cocaine, about half of the amount seized in 1993.

Stiffer drug trafficking penalties have been introduced in the Federal Penal Code, a law covering asset seizures has been passed, and laundering operations through domestic or foreign banks have been made more difficult. Few major traffickers have been arrested, however. Although corruption remains a persistent problem, some limited success has been achieved in prosecuting public officials—who face twenty-five- to forty-year sentences—for drug-related crimes. The murder of Cardinal Juan Jesús Posadas Ocampo in a shoot-out among drug traffickers near the Guadalajara airport in 1993 brought public outrage. Whether Cardinal Posadas was a target of the attack or was shot accidentally was not clear. Many were arrested, including a number of federal and state police. Other gunmen, however, were able to escape aboard a departing scheduled aircraft, and the failure of police to capture the gunmen suggested collusion.

Although laws on money transfers have been tightened, it remains relatively simple to disguise the source of drug money by making cash transactions in currency exchange houses along the United States border. Mexican drug cartels have little difficulty converting their profits into legitimate business operations and real estate. Mexico also plays a critical role in the supply of precursor chemicals needed by South American producers of cocaine and heroin. Most chemicals can be purchased in Mexico and can transit Mexican ports without detection by Mexican customs.

Sensitivities over what Mexico views as United States pressures on its sovereignty have hampered cooperation over drug interdiction. The 1985 kidnapping and murder of DEA agent Enrique Camarena caused lingering tension, in part because of evidence of complicity by Mexican security forces linked with the drug trade. In 1990 bounty hunters hired by the DEA captured a Mexican doctor believed to have participated in the torture of Camarena. He was spirited to the United States for trial, and his conviction in a United States court was upheld by the United States Supreme Court despite Mexican protests over what it viewed as violations of Mexican sovereignty and international law. Mexico's indignation over the United States action resulted in a revision of the rules under which the DEA operates in Mexico.

Security Concerns for the 1990s and Beyond

Since the EZLN uprising in Chiapas began in 1994, the Mexican armed forces have assumed a much higher profile. The reluctance of the armed forces and Zapatistas to engage in full-scale hostilities, the relatively low number of casualties in the uprising, and the idiosyncrasies of Mexico's "revolutionary" political culture suggest, however, that the Chiapas conflict will not necessarily replicate the violent pattern of the Central American guerrilla wars of the 1970s and 1980s.

Analysts predict that the Mexican armed forces will continue a prominent role in narcotics interdiction efforts, as the Mexican drug cartels, bolstered by their links to international organized crime, attempt to consolidate their territorial power and undermine state authority. Observers also expect that the Mexican navy will assume a more prominent role in protecting Mexico's EEZ and combatting illegal immigration and smuggling. For the foreseeable future, Mexico will continue to rely on the United States hemispheric defense umbrella for its external security needs.

*   *   *

A concise history of the Mexican armed forces and an overview of the service branches as of the mid-1980s can be found in the section on Mexico by Adrian J. English in *Armed Forces of Latin America*. Edwin Lieuwen's *Mexican Militarism* is a full study of the modern military during its formative period. *The Modern Mexican Military*, edited by David Ronfeldt, includes contributions by several authorities on the national defense system. Georges Fauriol's article, "Mexico: In a Superpower's Shadow," treats what Mexico considers as its security threats and weighs its military capabilities.

Adolfo Aguilar Zinser appraises the attitude of Mexican military officers toward civilian society and politics as of 1990 in "Civil-Military Relations in Mexico." *Generals in the Palacio* by Roderic A. Camp and an article by William S. Ackroyd, "Military Professionalism, Education, and Political Behavior in Mexico," examine the important role of the military training and education system.

Little up-to-date material has been published on the organizational structure and operational capabilities of the Mexican armed forces. René Luria's brief survey in 1992, "Defense Policy and the Armed Forces of Mexico," summarizes some aspects, although more recent developments are not included. Discussion in this chapter of military units, personnel strengths, and weapons systems is based in part on *The Military Balance*, produced annually by the International Institute for Strategic Studies in London. (For further information and complete citations, see Bibliography.)

Appendix

Table 1. *Metric Conversion Coefficients and Factors*

When you know	Multiply by	To find
Millimeters........................	0.04	inches
Centimeters.......................	0.39	inches
Meters............................	3.3	feet
Kilometers	0.62	miles
Hectares..........................	2.47	acres
Square kilometers	0.39	square miles
Cubic meters	35.3	cubic feet
Liters	0.26	gallons
Kilograms.........................	2.2	pounds
Metric tons.......................	0.98	long tons
....	1.1	short tons
....	2,204	pounds
Degrees Celsius (Centigrade).........	1.8 and add 32	degrees Fahrenheit

Table 2. *Total Population and Population Density by State, 1990[1]*

State	Total Population (in thousands)	Inhabitants per Square Kilometer
Aguascalientes............................	720	131.6
Baja California Norte	1,658	23.7
Baja California Sur	317	4.3
Campeche..............................	529	10.4
Chiapas	3,204	43.2
Chihuahua..............................	2,440	10.0
Coahuila	1,971	13.1
Colima.................................	425	81.9
Durango................................	1,352	11.0
Guanajuato	3,980	130.5
Guerrero...............................	2,622	40.8
Hidalgo	1,881	90.4
Jalisco.................................	5,279	65.3
México.................................	9,816	459.7
Michoacán..............................	3,534	59.0
Morelos	1,195	241.4
Nayarit.................................	816	30.2
Nuevo León.............................	3,086	47.5
Oaxaca.................................	3,922	32.2
Puebla	4,118	121.5
Querétaro	1,044	91.2
Quintana Roo	494	9.8
San Luis Potosí	2,002	31.7
Sinaloa.................................	2,211	37.9
Sonora.................................	1, 822	10.0
Tabasco	1,501	59.4
Tamaulipas	2,244	28.3
Tlaxcala................................	764	190.2
Veracruz................................	6,215	86.7
Yucatán	1,364	42.5
Zacatecas...............................	1,278	17.4
Federal District	8,237	5,569.3
MEXICO	82,041	41.6

[1] These figures differ somewhat from those in the Mexican government's 1990 census.

Source: Based on information from Germany, Statistisches Bundesamt, *Länderbericht Mexiko, 1992*, Wiesbaden, 1992, 31.

Table 3. *Crude Death Rate, Selected Years, 1900–90*

Year	Crude Death Rate[1]
1900–04	34.5
1905–10	33.2
1911–23[2]	n.a.[3]
1930–34	25.6
1940	23.4
1950	16.1
1960	11.5
1970	10.1
1980	7.5
1990	5.2

[1] Number per thousand residents.
[2] Statistics not available for 1911–23 because of Mexican Revolution.
[3] n.a.—not available.

Source: Based on information from Vicente Sánchez, Margarita Castillejos, and Lenora Rojas Bracho, *Población, recursos y medio ambiente en México*, Mexico City, 1989, 36; and Mexico, National Institute of Statistics, Geography, and Informatics, *Mexico Today*, Aguascalientes, 1992, 23.

Table 4. *School Enrollment by Education Level, 1970–71, 1980–81, and 1990–91*
(in thousands)

Education Level	1970–71	1980–81	1990–91
Primary schools	9,248	14,666	14,622
Middle schools and high schools	1,108	4,042	6,034
Vocational high schools	182	492	1,018
Teachers' high schools	53	208	121
Universities and colleges	248	930	1,314[1]

[1] Figure for 1989–90 school year.

Source: Based on information from Germany, Statistisches Bundesamt, *Länderbericht Mexiko, 1992*, Wiesbaden, 1992, 44.

Table 5. Vital Demographic Statistics, Selected Years, 1980–92

	1980	1984	1988	1992
Life expectancy[1]	66	68	69	70
Males[1]	63	65	66	67
Females[1]	69	71	73	74
Births[2]	2,428	2,512	2,622	2,726
Deaths[2]	434	411	413	421

[1] In years.
[2] Registered, in thousands.

Source: Based on information from Germany, Statistisches Bundesamt, *Länderbericht Mexiko, 1992*, Wiesbaden, 1992, 38.

Table 6. Infant Mortality Rate, Selected Years, 1930–90

Year	Infant Mortality Rate[1]
1930	145.6
1940	125.7
1950	96.2
1960	74.2
1970	68.5
1980	38.8
1990	40.0

[1] Number per thousand registered live births.

Source: Based on information from Octavio Mojarro, Juan García, and José García, "Mortality," in Jorge Martínez Manautou, ed., *The Demographic Revolution in Mexico, 1970–1980*, Mexico City, 1982, 378; and *XI Censo General de Población y Vivienda, 1990*, "Mortalidad Infantil en México, 1990. Estimaciones Por Entidad Federativa y Municipio" (http://www.inegi.gob.mx/homepara/estadistica/documentos/censos/censos.html1#OCHO).

Table 7. Selected Economic Indicators, 1988–95

Economic Indicator	1988	1989	1990	1991	1992	1993	1994	1995
GDP[1]	390.5	507.6	868.4	865.2	1,019	1,123	1,248	1,565
GDP growth[2]	1.3	3.3	4.5	3.6	2.8	0.4	3.5	−7.0
GNP per capita[3]	1,990	2,210	2,580	2,970	3,390	3,610	n.a.[4]	n.a.
Inflation[2]	114.1	20.0	26.7	22.7	15.5	10.0	7.0	34.8
External debt[5]	99.2	95.3	104.3	115.4	113.4	118.0	135.5	157.0
Exchange rate[6]	2.27	2.46	2.81	3.02	3.09	3.11	3.37	6.47

[1] GDP—gross domestic product; in billions of current Mexican new pesos (for value of the Mexican new peso—see Glossary).
[2] In percentages.
[3] GNP—gross national product; in current United States dollars.
[4] n.a.—not available.
[5] In billions of current United States dollars
[6] In Mexican new pesos per United States dollar.

Source: Based on information from Economist Intelligence Unit, *Country Report: Mexico* [London], No. 3, 1994, 3; and Economist Intelligence Unit, *Country Report: Mexico* [London], No. 1, 1996, 3.

Table 8. *Production of Selected Crops, 1988–90*

Crop	1988	1989	1990
Beverages			
Cocoa	57	50	36
Coffee	300	343	296
Fruit			
Apples	507	499	310
Avocados	335	320	320
Bananas	1,566	1,185	1,165
Coconuts	1,159	1,057	1,002
Grapefruit	105	100	118
Grapes	563	489	506
Lemons	660	727	463
Mangoes	780	790	800
Melons	826	875	880
Oranges	2,099	1,166	1,558
Papayas	630	640	650
Peaches	265	265	265
Pineapples	248	324	328
Tangerines	151	169	198
Grains			
Barley	350	433	521
Corn	10,600	10,945	14,639
Oats	100	105	105
Rice	456	637	357
Wheat	3,665	4,374	3,880
Legumes			
Beans	857	586	1,247
Chickpeas	150	120	170
Soybeans	226	992	512
Vegetables			
Peppers	654	570	590
Tomatoes	1,980	1,889	1,646

Source: Based on information from Germany, Statistisches Bundesamt, *Länderbericht Mexiko, 1992*, Wiesbaden, 1992, 81.

Table 9. Selected Statistics for Hydrocarbon Production, 1996

	Petroleum[1]	Natural Gas[2]
Proven reserves	49,775,000	68,413
Production (per day)	2,686[3]	1,358
Refining (per day).....................	1,520	3.7

[1] In thousands of barrels.
[2] In billions of cubic feet.
[3] 1995 (estimated).

Source: Based on information from Jim West, ed., *International Petroleum Encyclopedia,*
1996, Tulsa, 1996, 241, 280, 281, 312.

Table 10. Production of Selected Minerals, 1989–91

Mineral	Unit	1989	1990	1991
Metallic minerals				
Aluminum...............	thousands of tons	123	122	96
Antimony...............	tons	1,906	2,627	2,757
Bismuth................	tons	883	733	651
Cadmium	tons	1,439	1,346	1,253
Copper	thousands of tons	249	291	267
Gold...................	tons	6.6	8.2	7.3
Iron ore................	thousands of tons	5,373	6,194	6,391
Lead...................	thousands of tons	163	1,174	153
Manganese	thousands of tons	151	136	79
Silver	tons	2,306	2,324	2,217
Steel..................	thousands of tons	7,392	8,220	5,867
Zinc...................	thousands of tons	110	108	66
Nonmetallic minerals				
Barite.................	thousands of tons	326	310	192
Cement	millions of tons	24	25	18
Fluorite	thousands of tons	780	672	366
Graphite	thousands of tons	40	25	28
Phosphate..............	thousands of tons	624	605	416
Sulfur.................	thousands of tons	2,084	2,137	1,791

Source: Based on information from Germany, Statistisches Bundesamt, *Länderbericht*
Mexiko, 1992, Wiesbaden, 1992, 84.

Table 11. Selected Trade Indicators, 1991–95
(in billions of United States dollars)

Trade Indicator	1991	1992	1993	1994	1995
Exports[1]	42.7	46.2	51.9	60.9	79.9
Imports[1]	50.0	62.1	65.4	79.4	72.5
Current account balance[2]	−15.0	−24.8	−23.4	−28.8	−0.1

[1] Free on board.
[2] Includes transfers of émigré worker remittances and nonmerchandise transfers (services).

Source: Based on information from Economist Intelligence Unit, *Country Report: Mexico* [London], No. 1, 1996, 3.

Table 12. Major Trading Partners, 1993 and 1994
(in millions of United States dollars)

Country	1993	1994
Exports		
Brazil.	291	380
Canada	1,558	1,534
France.	446	519
Germany.	426	406
Japan.	704	997
Spain.	877	858
United States	42,838	52,787
Imports		
Brazil.	1,201	1,207
Canada	1,175	1,627
France.	1,106	1,530
Germany.	2,852	3,210
Japan.	3,929	4,805
Spain.	1,115	1,389
United States	45,317	55,468

Source: Based on information from Economist Intelligence Unit, *Country Report: Mexico*
[London], No. 1, 1996, Appendix 3.

Table 13. Major Army Equipment, 1996

Type and Description	Country of Origin	Number in Inventory
Armored reconnaissance vehicles		
M–8	United States	50
ERC–90 Lynx	France	120
VBL M–11	France	40
DN–3/–5 Caballo	Mexico	70
MOWAG	Germany	30
Mex–1	Mexico	20
Mac–1	n.a.[1]	15
Armored personnel carriers		
HWK–11	Germany	40
M–3 halftrack	United States	30
VCR–TT	France	40
DN–4 Caballo	Mexico	40
AMX–VCI	United States	40
BDX.	n.a.	18
LAV–150 ST	Belgium	26
Towed artillery		
M–116 pack, 75mm	United States	18
M–2A1/M–3, 105mm	United States	16
M–101, 105mm	United States	60
M–56, 105mm	United States	24
Self-propelled artillery		
M–8, 75mm	United States	5
Mortars		
81mm	United States	1,500
Brandt 120mm	France	20
Antitank guided weapons		
Milan (eight mounted on VBL M–11)	France	n.a.
Antitank guns		
M–30, 37mm	United States	30
Air defense guns		
M–55, 12.7mm	United States	40
Surface-to-air missiles		
RBS–70	Sweden	n.a.

[1] n.a.—not available.

Source: Based on information from International Institute for Strategic Studies, *The Military Balance, 1996–1997*, London, 1996, 226.

Table 14. Major Air Force Equipment, 1996

Type and Description	Country of Origin	Number in Inventory
Fighter aircraft		
F–5 (8 F–5E, 2 F–5F)	United States	10
Counterinsurgency		
PC–7 Pilatus	Switzerland	40
AT–33 Lockheed Shooting Star	United States	12
Reconnaissance		
Rockwell Commander 500C	United States	10
SA2–37A	France	1
Search-and-air rescue		
1A1–201 Arava	Israel	12
Armed helicopters		
Bell 205 (5); 206 (5); 212 (15)	United States	25
Utility helicopters		
Bell 205 (4); 206 (12); 212 (15); UH–60 (2); 5–70A (4).........................	United States	37
SA–330 Puma........................	France	3
Transport		
Various, including C–47 (12); C–118 (10); C–130A (9); DC–6 (5); BN–2 (2); C–54 (1); F–27 (2)	various	47

Note: Presidential transport fleet and training aircraft not included.

Source: Based on information from International Institute for Strategic Studies, *The Military Balance, 1996–1997*, London, 1996, 227.

Table 15. *Major Naval Equipment, 1996*

Type and Description	Country of Origin	Commissioned or Transferred	Number in Inventory
Destroyers			
Gearing-class, ASROC launcher, 4 127mm (5in) guns	United States	1982	2
Fletcher-class, 5 127mm guns, Bofors 400mm air defense guns	United States	1970	1
Frigates			
Bronstein-class, ASROC launcher, ASRR, 76mm guns..........	n.a.[1]	n.a.	2
Offshore patrol vessels			
Holzinger-class with Bo–105 helicopters	Mexico	1991–93	4
Uribe-class (Spanish Halcón) with Bo–105 helicopters	Spain	1982–83	6
Guanajuato, 2 102mm guns.....	Spain	1926	1
Auk-class 3in gun, 4 Bofors 40mm air defense guns.	United States	1973	16
Admirable-class, 3in gun, 2 Bofors 40mm air defense guns......	United States	1943–44	12
Inshore patrol boats			
Azteca-class, 1 Bofors 40mm air defense gun	Britain/ Mexico	1974–77; modernized 1987	31
Cape-class	United States	1990–91	3
Point-class.................	United States	1991	2
Polimar-class	Mexico	1962–68	8
Amphibious			
511-class...................	United States	n.a.	2
Naval aircraft			
Bo–105 helicopter	Germany	n.a.	12
Casa C–212 Aviocar (maritime reconnaissance)...........	Spain	n.a.	9
HU–16 helicopter (search-and-air rescue)	United States	n.a.	6

[1] n.a.—not available.

Source: Based on information from Richard Sharpe, ed., *Jane's Fighting Ships, 1993–94*, Alexandria, Virginia, 1993, 415–23, and International Institute for Strategic Studies, *The Military Balance, 1996–97*, London, 1996, 226.

Bibliography

Chapter 1

Aguilar Zinser, A. "Mexico: The Presidential Problem," *Foreign Policy*, 69, Winter 1987–88, 40–60.

Aiton, Arthur S. *Antonio de Mendoza, First Viceroy of New Spain.* Durham: Duke University Press, 1927.

Alba, Victor. *The Mexicans: The Making of a Nation.* New York: Praeger, 1967.

Aldrich, Daniel G., Jr., and Lorenzo Meyer, eds. *Mexico and the United States: Neighbors in Crisis.* San Bernardino, California: Borgo Press, 1993.

Anna, Timothy. "The Last Viceroys of New Spain and Peru: An Appraisal," *American Historical Review*, 81, No. 1, February 1976, 38–65.

Arredondo Muñozledo, Benjamin. *Breve historia de la revolución mexicana.* 8th ed. Mexico City: Porrúa Grupo Editorial, 1970.

Arredondo Muñozledo, Benjamin. *Historia de la revolución mexicana.* Mexico City: Porrúa Grupo Editorial, 1971.

Bailey, John J. *Governing Mexico: The Statecraft of Crisis Management.* New York: St. Martin's Press, 1988.

Baird, Joseph H. *The Churches of Mexico, 1530–1810.* Berkeley: University of California Press, 1962.

Bakewell, Peter J. *Silver Mining and Society in Colonial Mexico: Zacatecas, 1546–1700.* Cambridge: Cambridge University Press, 1971.

Bancroft, Hubert H. *History of Mexico.* 6 vols. San Francisco: Bancroft, 1883.

Barth, Pius J. *Franciscan Education and the Social Order in Spanish North America, 1502–1821.* Chicago: University of Chicago Press, 1945.

Bazant, Jan S. *A Concise History of Mexico: From Hidalgo to Cárdenas, 1805–1940.* Cambridge: Cambridge University Press, 1977.

Beals, Carleton. *Porfirio Díaz.* Philadelphia: Lippincott, 1932.

Benítez, Fernando. *The Century after Cortés.* Trans., Joan McLean. Chicago: University of Chicago Press, 1965.

Benítez, Fernando. *Lázaro Cárdenas y la revolución mexicana: El cardenismo,* 3. Mexico City: Fondo de Cultura Económica, 1978.

Benítez, Fernando. *Lázaro Cárdenas y la revolución mexicana: El caudillismo,* 2. Mexico City: Fondo de Cultura Económica, 1980.

Benítez, Fernando. *Lázaro Cárdenas y la revolución mexicana: El porfirismo,* 1. Mexico City: Fondo de Cultura Económica, 1980.

Bernal, Ignacio. *Mexico Before Cortés: Art, History, and Legend.* Trans., Willis Barnstone. Garden City, New York: Doubleday, 1975.

Bethell, Leslie, ed. *Mexico since Independence.* Cambridge: Cambridge University Press, 1991.

Blanco Moheno, Roberto. *Crónica de la revolución mexicana.* 3 vols. Mexico City: Editorial Diana, 1967.

Borah, Woodrow. *New Spain's Century of Depression.* Berkeley: University of California Press, 1951.

Borah, Woodrow, and Sherburne F. Cook. *The Aboriginal Population of Central Mexico on the Eve of the Spanish Conquest.* Berkeley: University of California Press, 1963.

Braden, Charles. *Religious Aspects of the Conquest of Mexico.* Durham, North Carolina: Duke University Press, 1930.

Bradenburg, Frank R. *The Making of Modern Mexico.* Englewood Cliffs, New Jersey: Prentice-Hall, 1964.

Brenner, Anita. *The Wind That Swept Mexico: The History of the Mexican Revolution, 1910–1942.* Austin: University of Texas Press, 1973.

Calvert, Peter. *Mexico.* New York: Praeger, 1973.

Castañeda, Jorge G. "Mexico's Coming Challenges," *Foreign Policy,* 64, Fall 1986, 120–39.

Castedo, Leopoldo. *History of Latin American Art and Architecture from Precolumbian Times to the Present.* New York: Praeger, 1969.

Castrejón Díaz, Jaime. *La república imperial en los 80s.* Mexico City: Editorial Grijalbo, 1980.

Cerwin, Herbert. *Bernal Díaz, Historian of the Conquest.* Norman: University of Oklahoma Press, 1963.

"The Challenge of Managing Mexico, 1982–88," *Public Administration,* 42, September–October 1982, 405–9.

Chance, John K. *Race and Class in Colonial Oaxaca.* Stanford: Stanford University Press, 1978.

Chevalier, François. *L'Amérique Latine de l'indépendance à nos jours,* 44. Paris: Presses Universitaires de France, 1977.

Chevalier, François. *Land and Society in Colonial Mexico: The Great Hacienda.* Berkeley: University of California Press, 1963.

Chipman, Donald. *Nuño de Guzmán and Pánuco in New Spain, 1518–1533.* Glendale, California: Clark, 1966.

Churruca Peláez, Agustín. *El pensamiento insurgente de Morelos.* Mexico City: Porrúa Grupo Editorial, 1983.

Cline, Howard F. "Mexico: A Matured Latin-American Revolution, 1910–1960," *Annals of the Academy of Political and Social Science,* 5, No. 334, March 1961, 84–94.

Cline, Howard F. *Mexico: Revolution to Evolution, 1940–1960.* New York: Oxford University Press, 1962.

Cline, Howard F. *The United States and Mexico.* New York: Athenaeum Press, 1963.

Cockroft, James D. *Intellectual Precursors of the Mexican Revolution.* Austin: University of Texas Press, 1968.

Coe, Michael D. *The Maya.* New York: Praeger, 1967.

Coe, Michael D. *Mexico.* 2d ed. New York: Praeger, 1977.

Cooper, Donald B. *Epidemic Diseases in Mexico City, 1761–1813.* Austin: University of Texas Press, 1965.

Cortés, Hernán. *Conquest: Dispatches from the New World.* Ed., Harry M. Rosen. New York: Grosset and Dunlap, 1962.

Cortés Conde, Roberto, and Stanley J. Stein, eds. *Latin America: A Guide to Economic History, 1830–1930.* Berkeley: University of California Press, 1977.

Cosío Villegas, Daniel. *The United States Versus Porfirio Díaz.* Lincoln: University of Nebraska Press, 1963.

Cosío Villegas, Daniel, ed. *Historia moderna de México: El porfiriato, la vida económica,* 7. Mexico City: Hermes, 1965.

Cosío Villegas, Daniel, ed. *Historia moderna de México: El porfiriato, la vida política exterior,* 4–6. Mexico City: Hermes, 1960–63.

Cosío Villegas, Daniel, ed. *Historia moderna de México: El porfiriato, la vida política exterior,* 8–9. Mexico City: Hermes, 1970–72.

Cosío Villegas, Daniel, ed. *Historia moderna de México: La república restaurada, la vida política,* 1. Mexico City: Hermes, 1955.

Costiloe, Michael P. *Church Wealth in Mexico: A Study of the "Juzgado de Capellanías" in the Archbishopric of Mexico, 1800–1856.* Cambridge: University Printing House, 1967.

Crosby, Alfred W., Jr. *The Columbian Exchange: Biological and Cultural Consequences of 1492.* Westport, Connecticut: Greenwood Press, 1973.

Cumberland, Charles C. *Mexico: The Struggle for Modernity.* London: Oxford University Press, 1968.

Davies, Nigel. *The Aztecs: A History.* London: Macmillan, 1973.

Delgado Moya, Rubén. *Perfil histórico de la revolución mexicana.* Mexico City: Editorial Diana, 1975.

Díaz del Castillo, Bernal. *The Discovery and Conquest of Mexico, 1517–1521.* Trans., A.P. Maudslay. New York: Farrar, Strauss, and Cudahy, 1956.

Dunne, Peter M. *Pioneer Jesuits in Northern Mexico.* Berkeley: University of California Press, 1944.

Elliott, John H. *Imperial Spain, 1469–1716.* New York: St. Martin's Press, 1962.

Farriss, Nancy. *Crown and Clergy in Colonial Mexico, 1759–1821.* London: University of London Press, 1968.

Fehrenbach, T. *Fire and Blood: A History of Mexico.* New York: Macmillan, 1973.

Fernández, Justino. *Mexican Art.* London: Spring Books, 1965.

Fisher, Lillian Estelle. *The Intendant System in Spanish America.* Berkeley: University of California Press, 1929.

Fisher, Lillian Estelle. *Viceregal Administration in Spanish American Colonies.* Berkeley: University of California Press, 1926.

Florescano, Enrique, et al. *Atlas histórico de México.* Mexico City: Siglo Veintiuno, 1983.

Flynn, Gerard. *Sor Juana Inés de la Cruz.* New York: Twayne, 1971.

Frank, Andre Gunder. *Mexican Agriculture, 1521–1630: Transformation of the Mode of Production.* New York: Cambridge University Press, 1979.

Fuentes Mares, José. *Biografía de una nación.* Mexico City: Editorial Oceano, 1982.

Galarza, Ernesto. *Merchants of Labor: The Mexican Bracero Story.* San José, California: Rosicrucian Press, 1964.

Gamio, Manual. *Forjando patria.* Mexico City: Porrúa Grupo Editorial, 1982.

Gibson, Charles. *The Aztecs under Spanish Rule: A History of the Valley of Mexico, 1519–1810.* Stanford: Stanford University Press, 1964.

Gibson, Charles. *Spain in America.* New York: Harper and Row, 1966.

Gonzalez, Guadalupe, and Marta Tienda. *The Drug Connection in U.S-Mexican Relations.* La Jolla: Center for U.S.-Mexican Studies, University of California, San Diego, 1989.

González Casanova, Pablo. *Democracy in Mexico.* Trans., Danielle Salti. New York: Oxford University Press, 1970.

González Cosío, Arturo. *México: Cincuenta años de revolución.* Mexico City: Fondo de Cultura Económica, 1961.

Greenleaf, Richard E., and Michael C. Meyer, eds. *Research in Mexican History.* Lincoln: University of Nebraska Press, 1973.

Griffin, Charles Carroll, ed. *Latin America: A Guide to the Historical Literature.* Austin: University of Texas Press, 1971.

Griffin, Rodman D. "Mexico's Emergence: Will Economic Reform Work? Can Democracy Wait?" *Congressional Quarterly Researcher,* 1, No. 11, July 19, 1991, 7.

Hamill, Hugh M., Jr. *The Hidalgo Revolt: Prelude to Mexican Independence.* Gainesville: University of Florida Press, 1966.

Hamill, Hugh M., Jr. "The Parish Priest, Miguel Hidalgo." Pages 17–25 in W. Dirk Raat, ed., *Mexico: From Independence to Revolution, 1810–1910.* Lincoln: University of Nebraska Press, 1982.

Hamilton, Earl J. *American Treasure and the Price Revolution in Spain, 1501–1650.* Cambridge: Harvard University Press, 1934.

Hanke, Lewis. *Aristotle and the American Indian: A Study in Race Prejudice in the Modern World.* Bloomington: Indiana University Press, 1970.

Hanke, Lewis. *Bartolomé de las Casas: Bookman, Scholar, and Propagandist.* Philadelphia: University of Pennsylvania Press, 1952.

Hanke, Lewis. *Mexico and the Caribbean.* Princeton, New Jersey: Van Nostrand, 1967.

Haring, Clarence Henry. *The Spanish Empire in America*, New York: Oxford University Press, 1947.

Herring, Hubert. *A History of Latin America from the Beginnings to the Present.* 3d ed. New York: Knopf, 1968.

Hofstadter, Dan. *Mexico, 1946–73.* New York: Facts on File, 1974.

Houtart, François, and Émile Pin. *The Church and the Latin American Revolution.* Trans., Gilbert Barth. New York: Sheed and Ward, 1965.

Howe, Walter. *The Mining Guild of New Spain and Its Tribunal General, 1770–1821.* Cambridge: Harvard University Press, 1949.

"It Hit the Government Worst," *The Economist* [London], 296, No. 28, September 1985, 38.

Iturbide, Augustín de. "Plan de Iguala." Pages 46–48 in W. Dirk Raat, ed., *Mexico: From Independence to Revolution, 1810–1910.* Lincoln: University of Nebraska Press, 1982.

Jacobsen, Jerome V. *Educational Foundation of the Jesuits in Sixteenth Century New Spain.* Berkeley: University of California Press, 1938.

Jennings, Jesse D., and Edward Norbeck, eds. *Prehistoric Man in the New World.* Chicago: University of Chicago Press, 1964.

Johnson, Harold R., ed. *From Reconquest to Empire: The Iberian Background to Latin American History.* New York: Knopf, 1970.

Johnson, Kenneth F. *Mexican Democracy: A Critical View.* Rev. ed. New York: Praeger, 1978.

Johnson, William Weber. *Heroic Mexico: The Violent Emergence of a Modern Nation.* Garden City, New York: Doubleday, 1968.

Katz, Friedrich. *The Ancient American Civilizations.* New York: Praeger, 1974.

Keith, Robert G. "Encomienda, Hacienda, and Corregimiento in Spanish America: A Structural Analysis," *Hispanic American Historical Review,* 41, No. 3, August 1971, 431–46.

Keleman, Pál. *Art of the Americas: Ancient and Hispanic.* New York: Crowell, 1969.

Kubler, George. *Mexican Architecture of the Sixteenth Century,* 1–2. New Haven: Yale University Press, 1948.

Lavrin, Asunción, and Edith Couturier. "Dowries and Wills: A View of Women's Socioeconomic Role in Colonial Guadalajara and Puebla, 1640–1790," *Hispanic American Historical Review*, 59, No. 2, May 1979, 280–304.

Leonard, Irving. *Baroque Times in Old Mexico: Seventeenth Century Persons, Places, and Practices*. Ann Arbor: University of Michigan Press, 1971.

León-Portilla, Miguel. *The Mind of Ancient Mexico*. Norman: University of Oklahoma Press, 1963.

León-Portilla, Miguel, ed. *The Broken Spears: The Aztec Account of the Conquest of Mexico*. Boston: Beacon Press, 1962.

Levy, Daniel C., and Gabriel Székely. *Mexico: Paradoxes of Stability and Change*. Boulder, Colorado: Westview Press, 1983.

Liss, Peggy Korn. *Mexico under Spain, 1521–1556: Society and Origins of Nationality*. Chicago: University of Chicago Press, 1975.

Lockhart, James, "Encomienda and Hacienda: The Evolution of the Great Estate in the Spanish Indies," *Hispanic American Historical Review*, 49, No. 3, August 1969, 411–29.

Lockhart, James, and Stuart B. Schwartz. *Early Latin America: A History of Colonial Spanish America and Brazil*, 46. New York: Cambridge University Press, 1983.

Lombardi, Cathryn L., John V. Lombardi, and K. Lynn Stoner. *Latin American History: A Teaching Atlas*. Madison: University of Wisconsin Press, 1983.

Long, Robert E., ed. *Mexico*. New York: H.W. Wilson, 1986.

López Portillo, José. *Quetzalcoatl: In Myth, Archeology, and Art*. New York: Continuum, 1982.

Lynch, John. *Spain under the Habsburgs*. New York: Oxford University Press, 1964.

MacNutt, F.A. *Fernando Cortés and the Conquest of Mexico, 1485–1547*. New York: Putnam's, 1909.

"Mexico at the Brink," *Foreign Affairs*, 64, Winter 1985–86, 287–303.

"Mexico's Financial Crisis," *Latin American Research Review*, 19, No. 2, 1984, 220–24.

"Mexico's Uneasy Progress," *World Today*, 38, October 1982, 395–401.

Meyer, Jean. *La révolution mexicaine, 1910–1940*. Paris: Calmann-Lévy, 1972.

Meyer, Michael C., and William L. Sherman, eds. *The Course of Mexican History*, New York: Oxford University Press, 1983.

Middlebrook, Kevin J. "Dilemmas of Change in Mexican Politics," *World Politics*, 41, October 1988, 120–41.

Millon, Sylvanus G. *The Ancient Maya*. Rev. ed. Stanford: Stanford University Press, 1965.

Mörner, Magnus. *Race Mixture in the History of Latin America*. Boston: Little, Brown, 1967.

Mörner, Magnus, ed. *The Expulsion of the Jesuits from Latin America*. New York: Knopf, 1965.

Mosk, Sanford A. *Industrial Revolution in Mexico*. Berkeley: University of California Press, 1950.

Mullen, Robert J. *Dominican Architecture in Sixteenth Century Oaxaca*. Tempe: Center for Latin American Studies, Arizona State University, 1975.

Needler, Martin C. *Politics and Society in Mexico*. Albuquerque: University of New Mexico Press, 1971.

North American Congress on Latin America. *Bibliography on Latin America*. New York: 1973.

Nunn, Charles F. *Foreign Immigrants in Early Bourbon Mexico, 1700–1760*. Cambridge: Cambridge University Press, 1979.

"Of Men and Institutions in Mexico," *Journal of Economic Issues*, 17, December 1983, 1142–43.

Padden, Robert C. *The Hummingbird and the Hawk: Conquest and Sovereignty in the Valley of Mexico, 1503–1541*. New York: Harper, 1970.

Palmer, Colin A. *Slaves of the White God: Blacks in Mexico*. Cambridge: Cambridge University Press, 1976.

Parkes, Henry Bamford. *A History of Mexico*. 3d ed. Boston: Houghton Mifflin, 1969.

Parry, John H. *The Age of Reconnaissance*. Cleveland: World, 1963.

Parry, John H. *The Audiencia of New Galicia in the Sixteenth Century: A Study in Spanish Colonial Government*. Cambridge: Cambridge University Press, 1948.

Parry, John H. *The Spanish Seaborne Empire*. New York: Knopf, 1966.

Paz, Octavio. *The Labyrinth of Solitude: Life and Thought in Mexico*. New York: Grove Press, 1961.

Paz, Octavio. *El ogro filantrópico*. Mexico City: Editorial Seis Barral, 1979.

Paz, Octavio. *The Other Mexico: Critique of the Pyramid.* Trans., Lysander Kemp. New York: Grove Press, 1972.

Percy, A. "Revolutionary Potential of Mexico in the 1980s," *Journal of International Affairs*, 40, Winter-Spring 1987, 373–85.

Peterson, Frederick A. *Ancient Mexico: An Introduction to the Pre-Hispanic Cultures.* London: George Allen and Unwin, 1959.

Picón-Salas, Mariano. *A Cultural History of Spanish America from Conquest to Independence.* Berkeley: University of California Press, 1971.

Pike, Frederick B. "The Cabildo and Colonial Loyalty to Hapsburg Rulers," *Journal of Interamerican Studies*, 2, No. 4, October 1960, 405–20.

Prescott, William H. *The Rise and Decline of the Spanish Empire.* New York: Viking Press, 1966.

Priestly, Herbert I. *José de Gálvez, Visitor General of New Spain, 1766–1771.* Berkeley: University of California Press, 1916.

Purcell, Susan Kaufman. "Crisis but No Collapse," *Orbis*, 32, Winter 1988, 57–61.

Purcell, Susan Kaufman. *Debt and the Restructuring of Mexico.* New York: Council on Foreign Relations, 1988.

Purcell, Susan Kaufman. *Mexico in Transition: Implications for U.S. Policy: Essays From Both Sides of the Border.* New York: Council on Foreign Relations, 1988.

Quirk, Robert E. *The Mexican Revolution, 1914–1915: The Convention of Aguascalientes.* Bloomington: University of Indiana Press, 1960.

Raat, W. Dirk. *The Mexican Revolution: An Annotated Guide to Recent Scholarship.* Boston: Hall, 1982.

Raat, W. Dirk, ed. *Mexico: From Independence to Revolution, 1810–1910.* Lincoln: University of Nebraska Press, 1982.

Ramirez, Miguel D. *Mexico's Economic Crisis: Its Origins and Consequences.* New York: Praeger, 1989.

Reed, Nelson. *The Casta War in Yucatan.* Chicago: University of Chicago Press, 1964.

Ricard, Robert. *The Spiritual Conquest of Mexico.* Berkeley: University of California Press, 1966.

Rippy, J. Fred. *Latin America: A Modern History.* Ann Arbor: University of Michigan Press, 1958.

Rodriquez, Jaime E., ed. *The Independence of Mexico and the Creation of the New Nation.* Los Angeles: Latin American Center Publications, University of California, Los Angeles, 1989.

Rojas, Pedro. *The Art and Architecture of Mexico.* Trans., J.M. Cohen. Felthan, Middlesex, United Kingdom: Hamlyn, 1968.

Romero Flores, Jesús. *La revolución mexicana (anales históricos, 1910–1974).* 3d ed. Mexico City: B. Costa-Amic, 1974.

Ross, Stanley R. *Is the Mexican Revolution Dead?* New York: Knopf, 1966.

Sanders, Thomas G. *Mexico in 1975.* American Universities Field Staff, Fieldstaff Reports, North American Series, 3, No. 4, Hanover, New Hampshire: AUFS, September 1975.

Ross, Stanley R., ed. *Views Across the Border: The United States and Mexico.* Albuquerque: University of New Mexico Press, 1978.

Schmitt, Karl M. *Mexico and the United States, 1821–1973.* New York: Wiley and Sons, 1974.

Schurz, William L. *The Manila Galleon.* New York: E.P. Dutton, 1939.

Silva Herzog, Jesús. *Breve historia de la revolución mexicana, 1–2.* Mexico City: Fondo de Cultura Económica, 1960.

Silva Herzog, Jesús. *Comprensión y crítica de la historia.* Mexico City: Editorial Nueva Imagen, 1982.

Silva Herzog, Jesús. *Cuatro juicios sobre la revolución mexicana.* Mexico City: Fondo de Cultura Económica, 1981.

Simpson, Lesley Byrd. *The Encomienda in New Spain.* Berkeley: University of California Press, 1960.

Simpson, Lesley Byrd. *Many Mexicos.* Berkeley: University of California Press, 1969.

Skidmore, Thomas E., and Peter H. Smith. *Modern Latin America.* New York: Oxford University Press, 1984.

Smith, Bradley. *Mexico: A History of Art.* New York: Harper and Row, 1968.

Soustelle, Jacques. *Mexico.* Trans., James Hogarth. Cleveland: World, 1967.

Stein, Stanley J., and Barbara H. Stein. *The Colonial Heritage of Latin America: Essays on Economic Dependence in Perspective.* New York: Oxford University Press, 1970.

Tannenbaum, Frank. *The Mexican Agrarian Revolution.* Hamden, Connecticut: Archon Books, 1968.

Tannenbaum, Frank. *Mexico: The Struggle for Peace and Bread.* New York: Knopf, 1950.

Taylor, William B. *Landlord and Peasant in Colonial Oaxaca.* Stanford: Stanford University Press, 1972.

Thompson, J. Eric. *The Rise and Fall of Maya Civilization.* Norman: University of Oklahoma Press, 1966.

Timmons, Wilbert H. *Morelos: Sacerdote, soldado, estadista.* Mexico City: Fondo de Cultura Económica, 1983.

Toussaint, Manuel. *Colonial Art in Mexico.* Trans. and ed., Elizabeth W. Weismann. Austin: University of Texas Press, 1967.

Turner, Frederick C. *The Dynamics of Mexican Nationalism.* Chapel Hill: University of North Carolina Press, 1968.

Valades, José C. *Historia general de la revolución mexicana.* 5 vols. Mexico City: Editores Mexicanos Unidos, 1976.

Von Hagen, Victor W. *The World of the Maya.* New York: Mentor, 1960.

Wagner, Henry R. *The Rise of Fernando Cortés.* Los Angeles: Cortés Society, 1944.

Wagner, Henry R. *Spanish Voyages to the Northwest Coast of America in the Sixteenth Century.* San Francisco: California Historical Society, 1929.

Wauchopes, Robert. *The Indian Background of Latin American History: The Maya, Inca, and Their Predecessors.* New York: Knopf, 1970.

Webb, Kempton E. *Geography of Latin America: A Regional Analysis.* Englewood Cliffs, New Jersey: Prentice-Hall, 1972.

White, Jon Manchip. *Cortés and the Downfall of the Aztec Empire.* New York: St. Martin's Press, 1971.

Wiarda, Howard J., and C. Guajardo. "Mexico: Unraveling of a Corporatist Regime?" *Journal of Interamerican Studies and World Affairs*, 30, Winter 1998–89, 1–28.

Wilkie, James W. *México visto en el siglo XX.* Mexico City: Instituto de Investigaciones Económicas, 1969.

Wilkie, James W. *La revolución mexicana, 1910–1976: Gasto federal y cambio social.* Mexico City: Fondo de Cultura Económica, 1978.

Willey, Gordon R., ed. *Prehistoric Settlement Patterns in the New World.* Reprint. New York: Wenner-Gren Foundation for Anthropological Research, 1956.

Wolf, Eric R. *Sons of the Shaking Earth.* Chicago: University of Chicago Press, 1959.

Wolfe, Bertrand. *The Fabulous Life of Diego Rivera.* New York: Stein and Day, 1969.

Womack, John, Jr. *Zapata and the Mexican Revolution.* New York: Random House, Vintage Books, 1969.

Zorita, Alonso de. *Life and Labor in Ancient Mexico.* New Brunswick: Rutgers University Press, 1963.

(Various issues of the following publications also were used in the preparation of this chapter: *Mexican Forum, New York Times,* and *Washington Post.*)

Chapter 2

Almada Bay, Ignacio, ed. *Salud y crisis en México.* Cuadernos del CIIM, Serie Seminarios, No. 2. Mexico City: Coordinación de Humanidades, Universidad Nacional Autónoma de México, 1991.

Amatulli Valente, Flaviano. *El protestantismo en México: Hechos, interrogantes, y retos.* Mexico City: Apóstoles de la Palabra, 1987.

Aspe, Pedro, and Paul C. Sigmund, eds. *The Political Economy of Income Distribution in Mexico.* New York: Holmes and Meier, 1984.

Banamex. Estudios Sociales. *México sociales, 1987: Indicadores seleccionados.* Mexico City: 1987.

Banamex. Estudios Sociales. *México sociales, 1988-1989: Indicadores seleccionados.* Mexico City: 1989.

Barbieri, Teresita de. "Sobre géneros, prácticas y valores: Notas acerca de posibles erosiones del machismo en México." Pages 83-105 in Juan Manuel Ramírez Saiz, ed., *Normas y prácticas morales y cívicas en la vida cotidiana.* Colección México: Actualidad y Perspectivas. Mexico City: Porrúa Grupo Editorial, 1990.

"Basic Education: An Unfinished Assignment," *The Mexican Economy: A Monthly Report* [Mexico City], 10, No. 3, May 1992, 23–28.

Bazant, Jan S., et al. *Tipología de vivienda urbana: Análisis físico de contextos urbano habitacionales de la población de bajos ingresos en la Ciudad de México.* Mexico City: Editorial Diana, 1978.

Béjar Navarro, Raúl, and Héctor H. Hernández Bringas, eds. *Población y desigualidad social en México*. Cuernavaca, Mexico: Universidad Nacional Autónoma de México, Centro Regional de Investigaciones Multidisciplinarias, 1993.

Beltrán, Ulises, et al. *Los mexicanos de los noventa*. Mexico City: Instituto de Investigaciones Sociales, Universidad Nacional Autónoma de México, 1996.

Brachet-Marquez, Viviane. *The Dynamics of Domination: State, Class, and Social Reform in Mexico, 1910–1990*. Pittsburgh: University of Pittsburgh Press, 1994.

Campos, Julieta. *¿Qué hacemos con los pobres?: La reiterada querella por la nación*. Mexico City: Aguilar, 1995.

Chinas, Beverly. *The Isthmus Zapotecs: A Matrifocal Culture of Mexico*. Case Studies in Cultural Anthropology. Fort Worth: Harcourt, Brace Jovanovich, 1977.

De la Torre, Rodolfo. "Income Distribution in Mexico During the Second Half of the Eighties," *The Mexican Economy: A Monthly Report* [Mexico City], 10, No, 2, April 1992, 27–33.

Eckstein, Susan. *The Poverty of Revolution: The State and the Urban Poor in Mexico*. Princeton: Princeton University Press, 1988.

Economist Intelligence Unit. *Country Report: Mexico* [London], No. 1, 1993.

Floyd, J. Charlene. "A Theology of Liberation? Religion and Politics in Mexico," *Journal of International Affairs*, 50, No. 1, Summer 1996, 142–65.

Garma Navarro, Carlos. *Protestantismo en una comunidad totonaca de Puebla, México*. Serie de Antropología Social, No. 76. Mexico City: Instituto Nacional Indigenista, 1987.

Gates, Marilyn. *In Default: Peasants, the Debt Crisis, and the Agricultural Challenge in Mexico*. Latin American Perspectives Series No. 12. Boulder, Colorado: Westview Press, 1993.

Germany. Statistisches Bundesamt. *Länderbericht Mexico, 1992*. Wiesbaden, Germany: 1992.

Gilbert, Alan, ed. *Housing and Land in Urban Mexico*. Monograph Series 31. La Jolla: Center for U.S.-Mexican Studies, University of California, San Diego, 1989.

Gilbert, Alan, and Peter M. Ward. *Housing, the State and the Poor: Policy and Practice in Three Latin American Cities*. Cambridge Latin American Studies, 50. Cambridge: Cambridge University Press, 1985.

Gledhill, John. *Casi Nada: A Study of Agrarian Reform in the Homeland of Cardenismo.* Studies in Culture and Society, No. 4. Albany: Institute for Mesoamerican Studies, State University of New York at Albany, 1991.

González de la Rocha, Mercedes. *The Resources of Poverty: Women and Survival in a Mexican City.* Studies in Urban and Social Change. Cambridge, Massachusetts: Blackwell, 1994.

González de la Rocha, Mercedes, and Agustín Escobar Latapí, eds. *Social Responses to Mexico's Economic Crisis of the 1980s.* U.S.-Mexico Contemporary Perspectives Series, No. 1. La Jolla: Center for U.S.-Mexican Studies, University of California, San Diego, 1991.

Grayson, George W. *The Church in Contemporary Mexico.* Significant Issues Series, 14, No. 5. Washington: Center for Strategic and International Studies, 1992.

Grayson, George W., ed., *Prospects for Mexico.* Washington: Foreign Service Institute, United States Department of State, 1988.

Grindle, Merilee S. *Searching for Rural Development: Labor Migration and Employment in Mexico.* Food Systems and Agrarian Change. Ithaca: Cornell University Press, 1988.

Guevara Niebla, Gilberto, ed. *La catástrofe silenciosa.* Sección de Obras de Educación. Mexico City: Fondo de Cultura Económica, 1992.

Hanratty, Dennis M. "The Church." Pages 113–22 in George W. Grayson, ed., *Prospects for Mexico.* Washington: Foreign Service Institute, United States Department of State, 1988.

Hanratty, Dennis M. "Church-State Relations in Mexico in the 1980s," *Thought,* 63, No. 250, September 1988, 207–23.

Hanratty, Dennis M. "The Political Role of the Mexican Catholic Church: Contemporary Issues," *Thought,* 59, No. 233, June 1984, 164–82.

Haro Bélchez, Guillermo. "Gobierno y administración estatal frente a los resultados del censo de 1990," *Revista del IAPEM* [Toluca, Mexico], 15, July–September 1992, 33–86.

Hayashi Martínez, Laureano. *La educación mexicana en cifras.* Mexico City: El Nacional, 1992.

Hernández Medina, Alberto, and Luis Narro Rodríguez, eds. *Como somos los mexicanos.* Mexico City: Centro de Estudios Educativos, 1987.

Iracheta Cenecorta, Alfonso X. "La expansión de la Ciudad de México: De la metrópolis a la megalópolis," *Revista del IAPEM* [Toluca, Mexico], 15, July–September 1992, 91–108.

Krantz, Lasse. *Peasant Differentiation and Development: The Case of a Mexican Ejido.* Stockholm Studies in Social Anthropology, No. 28. Stockholm: Department of Social Anthropology, University of Stockholm, 1991.

Leff, Enrique, ed. *Medio ambiente y desarrollo en México.* Colección México: Actualidad y perspectivas. Mexico City: Porrúa Grupo Editorial, 1990.

Logan, Kathleen. *Haciendo Pueblo: The Development of a Guadalajaran Suburb.* University: University of Alabama Press, 1984.

Lozoya Thalmann, Emilio. "Social Security, Health, and Social Solidarity in Mexico." Pages 397–437 in Pedro Aspe and Paul C. Sigmund, eds., *The Political Economy of Income Distribution in Mexico.* New York: Holmes and Meier, 1984.

Manrique Castañeda, Leonardo, ed. *Atlas cultural de México: Lingüística,* 9. Mexico City: Secretaría de Educación Pública, Instituto Nacional de Antropología e Historia, 1988.

Martínez Manantou, Jorge, ed. *The Demographic Revolution in Mexico, 1970–1980.* Mexico City: Instituto Mexicano del Seguro Social, 1982.

Memorias de la tercera reunión nacional sobre la investigación demografía en México. Mexico City: Universidad Nacional Autónoma de México, 1989.

Mesa-Lago, Carmelo. *Changing Social Security in Latin America: Toward Alleviating the Social Cost of Economic Reform.* Boulder, Colorado: Lynne Rienner, 1994.

Mesa-Lago, Carmelo. *Health Care for the Poor in Latin America and the Caribbean.* PAHO Scientific Publication No. 539. Washington: Pan American Health Organization, 1992.

Mexico. Consejo Nacional de Población. *Sistema de ciudades y distribución espacial de la población en México.* Mexico City: 1991.

Mexico. Instituto Mexicano del Seguro Social. *Planeación familiar y cambio demográfico.* Lecturas en materia de seguridad social. Mexico City: Fondo de Cultura Económica, 1992.

Mexico. Instituto del Seguro Social y Instituto de Seguridad y Servicios Sociales de los Trabajadores del Estado. *La segu-*

ridad social y el estado mexicano. Mexico City: Fondo de Cultura Económica, 1992

Mexico. Instituto Nacional de Estadística, Geografía e Informática. *Area metropolitana de la Ciudad de México (AMCM): Síntesis de resultados. XI censo general de población y vivienda, 1990.* Aguascalientes, Mexico: 1991.

Mexico. Instituto Nacional de Estadística, Geografía e Informática. *Cuaderno de información oportuna.* Aguascalientes, Mexico: 1993.

Mexico. Instituto Nacional de Estadística, Geografía e Informática. *Cuaderno de información oportuna regional (CIOR).* Aguascalientes, Mexico: 1993.

Mexico. Instituto Nacional de Estadística, Geografía e Informática. *Encuesta nacional agropecuaria ejidal, 1988: Resumen general.* Aguascalientes, Mexico: 1990.

Mexico. Instituto Nacional de Estadística, Geografía e Informática. *Estados Unidos Mexicanos. Resultados preliminares. VII censo agropecuario, 1991.* Aguascalientes, Mexico: 1992.

Mexico. Instituto Nacional de Estadística, Geografía e Informática. *Estados Unidos Mexicanos. Resumen general. XI censo general de población y vivienda, 1990.* Aguascalientes, Mexico: 1992.

Mexico. Instituto Nacional de Estadística, Geografía e Informática. *Información estadística: Sector salud y seguridad social.* Aguascalientes, Mexico: 1991.

Mexico. Instituto Nacional de Estadística, Geografía e Informática. "Resultados preliminares del XI censo general de población y vivienda, 1990," *México: Información económica y social* [Aguascalientes, Mexico], 2, No. 2, May–August 1990, 7–13.

Mexico. Instituto Nacional de Estadística, Geografía e Informática. *VI censos agrícola-ganadero y ejidal, 1981. Resumen general. Resultados muestrales a nivel nacional y por entidad federativa.* Aguascalientes, Mexico: 1990.

Mexico. Instituto Nacional de Estadística, Geografía e Informática. *XI censo general de población y vivienda, 1990. Perfil sociodemográfico.* 33 vols. Aguascalientes, Mexico: 1992.

Mexico. Instituto Nacional de Estadística, Geografía e Informática. *XI censo general de población y vivienda, 1990. Resultados definitivos.* 34 vols. Aguascalientes, Mexico: 1992.

Mexico. National Institute of Statistics, Geography, and Informatics. *Mexico Today.* Aguascalientes, Mexico: 1992.

Mexico. Secretaría de Desarrollo Social. Subsecretaría de Desarrollo Regional. Programa Nacional de Solidaridad. *Información básica sobre la ejecución y desarrollo del programa del 1 de diciembre de 1988 al 31 de agosto de 1994.* Mexico City: 1994.

Mexico. Secretaría de Desarrollo Social. Subsecretaría de Desarrollo Regional. Programa Nacional de Solidaridad. *Solidaridad, seis años de trabajo,* Mexico City: 1994.

Mexico. Secretaría de Educación Pública. *Programa para la modernización educativa, 1989–1994.* Modernización educativa, No. 1. Mexico City: 1989.

Mexico. Secretaría de Salud. *Informe de labores, 1991–1992.* Mexico City: 1992.

"México en transición," *Examen de la situación de México* [Mexico City], 67, No. 803, October 1992, 486–517.

Majarro, Octavio, Jean García, and José García. "Mortality." Page 378 in Jorge Martínez Manantou, ed., *The Demographic Revolution in Mexico, 1970–1980.* Mexico City: Instituto Mexicano del Seguro Social, 1982.

Murphy, Arthur D., and Alex Stepick. *Social Inequality in Oaxaca: A History of Resistance and Change.* Philadelphia: Temple University Press, 1991.

"Poverty in Mexico," *Review of the Economic Situation of Mexico* [Mexico City], 69, No. 809, April 1993, 143–51.

Ramírez Saiz, Juan Manuel, ed. *Normas y prácticas morales y cívicas en la vida cotidiana.* Colección México: Actualidad y perspectivas. Mexico City: Porrúa Grupo Editorial, 1990.

Randall, Laura. *The Political Economy of Mexican Oil.* New York: Praeger, 1989.

Randall, Laura, ed. *Changing Structure of Mexico: Political, Social, and Economic Prospects.* Columbia University Seminar Series. Armonk, New York: M.E. Sharpe, 1996.

Randall, Laura, ed. *Reforming Mexico's Agrarian Reform.* Columbia University Seminar Series. Armonk, New York: M.E. Sharpe, 1996.

Riding, Alan. *Distant Neighbors: A Portrait of the Mexicans.* New York: Vintage Books, 1989.

Rubio, Luis, et al. *México en la hora del cambio.* Mexico City: Cal y Arena, 1995.

Sánchez, Vicente, Margarita Castillejos, and Lenora Rojas Bracho. *Población, recursos y medio ambiente en México.* Colección medio ambiente, No. 8. Mexico City: Fundación Universo Veintiuno, 1989.

Sandstrom, Alan R. *Corn Is Our Blood: Culture and Ethnic Identity in a Contemporary Aztec Indian Village.* Civilization of the American Indian Series, No. 206. Norman: University of Oklahoma Press, 1991.

Scheffler, Lilian. *Los indígenas mexicanos: Ubicación, geografía, organización, social y política, economía, religión y costumbres.* Mexico City: Panorama Editorial, 1992.

Scott, Ian. *Urban and Spatial Development in Mexico.* Baltimore: Johns Hopkins University Press, 1982.

Soberán, Guillermo, Jesús Kumate, and José Laguna, eds. *La salud en México: Testimonios, 1988.* 4 vols. Biblioteca de la Salud: Serie testimonios. Mexico City: Secretaría de Salud, Instituto Nacional de Salud Pública, El Colegio Nacional and Fondo de Cultura Económica, 1988.

Sobrino Figueroa, Jaime. *Pobreza, política social y participación ciudadana: Evaluación del programa nacional de solidaridad en el estado de México.* Zinacantepec, Mexico: El Colegio Mexiquense, A.C. and Secretaría de Desarrollo Social, 1995.

"Socio-Political Pulse," *Review of the Economic Situation of Mexico* [Mexico City], 69, Nos. 807–8, February–March 1993, 69–80.

Stephen, Lynn. *Zapotec Women.* Texas Press Sourcebooks in Anthropology, No. 16. Austin: University of Texas Press, 1991.

Tamayo, Jorge I. *Geografía moderna de México.* 8th ed. Mexico City: Editorial Trillas, 1974.

United Nations. *Human Development Report, 1994.* New York: Oxford, 1994.

United Nations. Comisión Económica para América Latina y el Caribe. *Anuario estadístico de América Latina y el Caribe, edición 1993.* New York: 1994.

United Nations. Economic Commission for Latin America and the Caribbean. *Economía campesina y agricultura empresarial: Tipología de productores del agro mexicano.* Mexico City: Veintiuno Editores, 1982.

Vélez, Félix, ed. *La pobreza en México: Causas y políticas para combatirla.* Lecturas, No. 78. Mexico City: Instituto Tecnológico

Autónomo de México and Fondo de Cultura Económica, 1994.

Ward, Peter M. *Welfare Politics in Mexico: Papering over the Cracks.* London Research Series in Geography, No. 9. London: Allen and Unwin, 1986.

Yates, P. Lamartine. *Mexico's Agricultural Dilemma.* Tucson: University of Arizona Press, 1981.

(Various issues of the following publications also were used in the preparation of this chapter: Foreign Broadcast Information Service, *Daily Report: Latin America; Latin American Monitor* [London]; *Latin America Regional Reports: Mexico and Central America Report* [London]; *Latin America Weekly Report* [London]; *Proceso* [Mexico City]; and *Tiempo* [Mexico City].)

Chapter 3

Austin, James, and Gustaro Esteva, eds. *Food Policy in Mexico: The Search for Self-Sufficiency.* Ithaca: Cornell University Press, 1987.

Bailey, John T. *Governing Mexico: The Statecraft of Crisis Management.* New York: St. Martin's Press, 1988.

Barkin, David. *Distorted Development: Mexico in the World Economy.* Boulder, Colorado: Westview Press, 1990.

Camp, Roderic A. *Entrepreneurs and Politics in Twentieth-Century Mexico.* New York: Oxford University Press, 1989.

Clark, W. Reynolds. *The Mexican Economy: Twentieth-Century Structure and Growth.* New Haven: Yale University Press, 1970.

Cypher, James M. *State and Capital in Mexico: Development Policy since 1940.* Boulder, Colorado: Westview Press, 1990.

Dresser, Denise. *Neopopulist Solutions to Neoliberal Problems: Mexico's National Solidarity Program.* La Jolla: Center for U.S.-Mexican Studies, University of California, San Diego, 1991.

Drost, Harry, ed. *The World's News Media: A Comprehensive Reference Guide.* Harrow, Greater London, United Kingdom: Longman Group, 1991.

Economist Intelligence Unit. *Country Report: Mexico* [London], No. 3, 1994.

Economist Intelligence Unit. *Country Report: Mexico* [London], No.1, 1996.

Encyclopedia of the Third World. 4th ed. Ed., George Thomas Kurian. New York: Facts on File, 1992.

The Europa World Year Book, 1993. London: Europa, 1993.

Gentleman, Judith. *Mexican Oil and Dependent Development.* New York: Peter Lang, 1984.

Germany. Statistisches Bundesamt. *Länderbericht Mexico, 1992.* Wiesbaden, Germany: 1992.

Hansen, Roger. *The Politics of Mexican Development.* 2d ed. Baltimore: Johns Hopkins Press, 1973.

Hufbauer, Gary Clyde, and Jeffrey J. Schott. "Prescription for Growth," *Foreign Policy,* 93, Winter 1993–94, 104–14.

Kate, Adriaan Ten. "Trade Liberalization and Economic Stabilization in Mexico," *World Development,* 20, May 1992, 659–72.

Lustig, Nora. *Mexico: The Remaking of an Economy.* Washington: Brookings Institution, 1992.

Maxfield, Sylvia, and Ricardo Anzaldaua, eds. *Government and Private Sector in Contemporary Mexico.* La Jolla: Center for U.S.-Mexican Studies, University of California, San Diego, 1987.

Meyer, Michael C., and William L. Sherman. *The Course of Mexican History.* 3d ed. New York: Oxford University Press, 1987.

Middlebrook, Kevin J. "The Sound of Silence: Organized Labor's Response to Economic Crisis in Mexico," *Journal of Latin American Studies,* 21, No. 1, May 1989.

Nelson, Joan M., ed. *Fragile Coalitions: The Politics of Economic Adjustment.* Overseas Development Council Perspectives, No. 12. New Brunswick, New Jersey: Transaction Books, 1989.

Pardo Maurer, R., and Judith Rodriguez, eds. *Access Mexico: Emerging Market Handbook and Directory.* Arlington, Virginia: Cambridge Data and Development, 1993.

Purcell, Susan Kaufman. "Mexico's New Economic Vitality," *Current History,* 91, No. 562, February 1992, 54–58.

Reynolds, Clark W. *The Mexican Economy: Twentieth-Century Structure and Growth.* New Haven: Yale University Press, 1970.

Sanderson, Steven E. *The Transformation of Mexican Agriculture: International Structure and the Politics of Rural Change.* Princeton: Princeton University Press, 1986.

Sheahan, John. *Conflict and Change in Mexican Economic Strategy: Implications for Mexico and for Latin America.* La Jolla: Center for U.S.-Mexican Studies, University of California, San Diego, 1991.

Sheahan, John. *Patterns of Development in Latin America: Poverty, Repression, and Economic Strategy.* Princeton: Princeton University Press, 1987.

Smith, Geri. "Congratulations, Mexico, You're Due for a Raise," *Business Week*, No. 3338, September 27, 1993, 58.

Smith, Geri. "The Remaking of an Oil Giant, 1993," *Business Week*, No. 3332, August 16, 1993, 84–85.

Stallings, Barbara, and Robert Kaufman, eds. *Debt and Democracy in Latin America.* Boulder, Colorado: Westview Press, 1989.

United Nations. Economic Commission for Latin America and the Caribbean. *Statistical Yearbook for Latin America and the Caribbean, 1992.* Santiago, Chile: 1992.

United States. Department of Energy. *International Energy Annual, 1992.* Washington: GPO, 1994.

United States. Department of the Interior. Bureau of Mines. *The Mineral Industry of Mexico.* Washington: GPO, 1992.

Weintraub, Sidney. "The Economy on the Eve of Free Trade," *Current History*, 92, No. 571, February 1993, 67–72.

West, Jim, ed. *International Petroleum Encyclopedia, 1996.* Tulsa: 1996.

Whiting, Van R. *The Political Economy of Foreign Investment in Mexico: Nationalism, Liberalism, and Constraints on Choice.* Baltimore: Johns Hopkins University Press, 1992.

World Bank. *Trends in Developing Economies, 1990.* Washington: 1990.

(Various issues of the following publications also were used in the preparation of this chapter: *Economist* [London] and *Oil and Gas Journal.*)

Chapter 4

Acosta Romero, Miguel. "Mexican Federalism: Conception and Reality," *Public Administration Review*, 42, No. 5, 1982, 399–404.

Alonso, Jorge, and Silvia Gómez Tagle, eds. *Insurgencia democrática: Las elecciones locales.* Guadalajara, Mexico: Universidad de Guadalajara, 1991.

Ayala, José, and Clemente Ruiz Durán. "Development and Crisis in Mexico: A Structuralist Approach." Pages 243–64 in

Jonathan Hartlyn and Samuel A. Morley, eds., *Latin American Political Economy: Financial Crisis and Political Change.* Boulder, Colorado: Westview Press, 1986.

Bagley, Bruce Michael. "Mexico in the 1980s: A New Regional Power," *Current History,* 80, No. 469, November 1981, 353–56.

Bagley, Bruce Michael. "The Politics of Asymmetrical Interdependence: U.S.-Mexican Relations in the 1980s." Pages 141–59 in H. Michael Erisman, ed., *The Caribbean Challenge: U.S. Policy in a Volatile Region.* Boulder, Colorado: Westview Press, 1984.

Bagley, Bruce Michael, and Sergio Aguayo Quezada, eds. *Mexico: In Search of Lost Security.* New Brunswick, New Jersey: Transaction Books, 1993.

Bailey, John J. *Governing Mexico: The Statecraft of Crisis Management.* New York: St. Martin's Press, 1988.

Bailey, John, and Leopoldo Gómez. "The PRI and Political Liberalization," *Journal of International Affairs,* 43, No. 2, Winter 1990, 291–12.

Barry, Tom. *Mexico: A Country Guide.* Albuquerque: Inter-Hemispheric Education Resource Center, 1992.

Basáñez, Miguel. *El pulso de los sexenios: 20 años de crisis en México.* Mexico City: Siglo Veintiuno, 1990.

Brachet-Márquez, Viviane. "Explaining Sociopolitical Change in Latin America: The Case of Mexico," *Latin American Research Review,* 27, No. 3, 1992, 91–122.

Butler, Edgar W., and Jorge A. Bustamante, eds. *Sucesión Presidencial: The 1988 Mexican Presidential Election.* Boulder, Colorado: Westview Press, 1991.

Camp, Roderic Ai. "The Cross in the Polling Booth: Religion, Politics, and the Laity in Mexico," *Latin American Research Review,* 29, No. 3, 1994, 69–100.

Camp, Roderic Ai. *Entrepreneurs and Politics in Twentieth-Century Mexico.* New York: Oxford University Press, 1989.

Camp, Roderic Ai. *Generals in the Palacio: The Military in Modern Mexico.* New York: Oxford University Press, 1992.

Camp, Roderic Ai. *Intellectuals and the State in Twentieth-Century Mexico.* Austin: University of Texas Press, 1985.

Camp, Roderic Ai. *The Making of a Government: Political Leaders in Modern Mexico.* Tucson: University of Arizona Press, 1984.

Camp, Roderic Ai. *Politics in Mexico.* New York: Oxford University Press, 1993.

Carpizo, Jorge. *La constitución mexicana de 1917.* 8th ed. Mexico City: Porrúa Grupo Editorial, 1990.

Castañeda, Jorge G. "The Clouding Political Horizon," *Current History,* 92, No. 571, February 1993, 59–66.

Centeno, Miguel Angel, and Sylvia Maxfield. "The Marriage of Finance and Order: Changes in the Mexican Political Elite," Pt. 1, *Journal of Latin American Studies,* 24, February 1992, 57–85.

Chabat, Jorge. "Mexico: So Close to the United States, So Far from Latin America," *Current History,* 92, No. 571, February 1993, 55–58.

"Chiapas: Challenging History," *Akwe:kon Journal,* 11, No. 2, Summer 1994.

Conger, Lucy. "Mexico: Zapatista Thunder," *Current History,* 93, No. 581, March 1994, 115–20.

Cornelius, Wayne A., and Ann L. Craig. *The Mexican Political System in Transition.* La Jolla: Center for U.S.-Mexican Studies, University of California, San Diego, 1991.

Cornelius, Wayne A., Judith Gentleman, and Peter Smith, eds. *Mexico's Alternative Political Futures.* La Jolla: Center for U.S.-Mexican Studies, University of California, San Diego, 1989.

Cosío Villegas, Daniel. *El sistema político mexicano.* Mexico City: Planeta, 1991.

Cothran, Dan A. *Political Stability and Democracy in Mexico.* Westport, Connecticut: Praeger, 1994.

Diamond, Larry, Juan J. Linz, and Seymour Martin Lipset. *Democracy in Developing Countries,* 4. Boulder, Colorado: Lynne Rienner, 1980.

Doyle, Kate. "The Militarization of the Drug War in Mexico," *Current History,* 92, No. 571, February 1993, 83–88.

Erisman, Michael H., ed. *The Caribbean Challenge: U.S. Policy in a Volatile Region.* Boulder, Colorado: Westview Press, 1984.

Ferris, Elizabeth G. "Mexico's Foreign Policies: A Study in Contradictions." Pages 213–27 in Jennie K. Lincoln and Elizabeth G. Ferris, eds., *The Dynamics of Latin American Foreign Policies.* Boulder, Colorado: Westview Press, 1984.

Foweraker, Joe, and Ann L. Craig, eds. *Popular Movements and Political Change in Mexico.* Boulder, Colorado: Lynne Rienner, 1990.

Gentleman, Judith. *Mexican Oil and Dependent Development.* New York: Peter Lang, 1984.

Gil, Carlos B., ed. *Hope and Frustration: Interviews with Leaders of Mexico's Political Opposition.* Wilmington, Delaware: SR Books, 1992.

Grayson, George W., ed. *Prospects for Democracy in Mexico.* New Brunswick, New Jersey: Transaction Books, 1990.

Grindle, Marilee S. *Bureaucrats, Politicians, and Peasants in Mexico: A Case Study in Public Policy.* Berkeley: University of California Press, 1977.

Hansen, Roger. *The Politics of Mexican Development.* 2d ed. Baltimore: Johns Hopkins Press, 1973.

Hartlyn, Jonathan, and Samuel A. Morley, eds. *Latin American Political Economy: Financial Crisis and Political Change.* Boulder, Colorado: Westview Press, 1986.

Lenderking, Bill. "The U.S.-Mexican Border and NAFTA: Problem or Paradigm?" *North-South Focus,* 2, No. 3, 1993.

Levy, Daniel C. "The Mexican Government's Loosening Grip?" *Current History,* 86, No. 518, March 1987, 113–16, 132–33.

Levy, Daniel C. "Mexico: Sustained Civilian Rule Without Democracy." Pages 459–97 in Larry Diamond, Juan J. Linz, and Seymour Martin Lipset, *Democracy in Developing Countries,* 4. Boulder, Colorado: Lynne Rienner, 1980.

Levy, Daniel C., and Gabriel Székely. *Mexico: Paradoxes of Stability and Change.* 2d ed. Boulder, Colorado: Westview Press, 1987.

Lieuwen, Edwin. *Mexican Militarism: The Political Rise and Fall of the Revolutionary Army, 1910–1940.* Albuquerque: University of New Mexico Press, 1968.

Lincoln, Jannie K., and Elizabeth G. Ferris, eds. *The Dynamics of Latin American Foreign Policies.* Boulder, Colorado: Westview Press, 1984.

Lutz, Ellen L. "Human Rights in Mexico: Cause for Continuing Concern," *Current History,* 92, No. 571, February 1993, 78–82.

Molinar Horcasitas, Juan. *El tiempo de la legitimidad: Elecciones, autoritarismo y democracia en México.* Mexico City: Cal y Arena, 1991.

Morris, Stephen D. *Corruption and Politics in Contemporary Mexico.* Tuscaloosa: University of Alabama Press, 1991.

Morris, Stephen D. "Political Reformism in Mexico: Past and Present," *Latin American Research Review,* 28, No. 2, 1993, 191–205.

Morris, Stephen D. "Political Reformism in Mexico: Salinas at the Brink," *Journal of Interamerican Studies and World Affairs,* 34, No. 1, 1992, 31–40.

Needler, Martin C. *Mexican Politics: The Containment of Conflict.* 2d ed. New York: Praeger, 1990.

Neil, Harvey, ed. *Mexico: Dilemmas of Transition.* New York: Institute of Latin American Studies, 1993.

Pastor, Robert A., and Jorge G. Castañeda. *Limits to Friendship: The United States and Mexico.* New York: Knopf, 1988.

Payne, Douglas W. "Salinastroika: Less Than Meets the Eye," *National Interest,* 34, Winter 1993–94, 43–51.

Philip, George. *The Presidency in Mexican Politics.* New York: St. Martin's Press, 1992.

Purcell, Susan Kaufman. "Mexico's New Economic Vitality," *Current History,* 91, No. 562, February 1992, 54–58.

Rico F., Carlos. "Mexico and Latin America: The Limits of Cooperation," *Current History,* 86, No. 518, March 1987, 121–24, 133–34.

Riding, Alan. *Distant Neighbors: A Portrait of the Mexicans.* New York: Vintage, 1986.

Rodríguez O., Jaime E. *The Evolution of the Mexican Political System.* Wilmington, Delaware: SR Books, 1993.

Roett, Riordan, ed. *Mexico's External Relations in the 1990s.* Boulder, Colorado: Lynne Rienner, 1991.

Roett, Riordan, ed. *Political and Economic Liberalization in Mexico: At a Critical Juncture?* Boulder, Colorado: Lynne Rienner, 1993.

Ronfeldt, David, ed. *The Modern Mexican Military: A Reassessment.* La Jolla: Center for U.S.-Mexican Studies, University of California, San Diego, 1984.

Ruiz Massieu, José Francisco. *El proceso democrático de México.* Mexico City: Fondo de Cultura Económica, 1993.

Sánchez Susarrey, Jaime. *El debate político e intelectual en México.* Mexico City: Grijaldo, 1993.

Sánchez Susarrey, Jaime. *La transición incierta.* Mexico City: Editorial Vuelta, 1991.

Schmidt, Samuel. *The Deterioration of the Mexican Presidency: The Years of Luis Echeverría.* Tucson: University of Arizona Press, 1991.

Smith, Peter H. *Labyrinths of Power: Political Recruitment in Twentieth-Century Mexico.* Princeton: Princeton University Press, 1979.

Smith, Peter H. "Uneasy Neighbors: Mexico and the United States," *Current History,* 86, No. 518, March 1987, 97-100, 130-32.

Street, James H. "Mexico's Development Crisis," *Current History,* 86, No. 518, March 1987, 101–4, 127–29.

Turner, Frederick C. *The Dynamics of Mexican Nationalism.* Chapel Hill: University of North Carolina Press, 1970.

Vanderwood, Paul J. *Disorder and Progress: Bandits, Police, and Mexican Development.* Wilmington, Delaware: SR Books, 1992.

Vernon, Raymond. *The Dilemma of Mexico's Development: The Roles of the Private and Public Sectors.* Cambridge: Harvard University Press, 1963.

(Various issues of the following publications also were used in the preparation of this chapter: *Current History; Excélsior* [Mexico City]; *Financial Times* [London]; *Latin America and Caribbean Contemporary Record; Latin America Regional Reports: Mexico and Central America Report* [London]; *Latin America Weekly Report* [London]; *Los Angeles Times; New York Times; News* [Mexico City]; *Uno Más Uno* [Mexico City]; *Wall Street Journal;* and *Washington Post.*)

Chapter 5

Ackroyd, William S. "Military Professionalism, Education, and Political Behavior in Mexico," *Armed Forces and Society,* 18, Fall 1991, 81–96.

Aguilar Zinser, A. "Civil-Military Relations in Mexico." Pages 219–36 in Louis W. Goodman, Johanna S.R. Mendelson, and Juan Rial, eds., *The Military and Democracy: The Future of Civil-*

Military Relations in Latin America. Lexington, Massachusetts: Lexington Books, 1990.

Americas Watch. *Human Rights in Mexico: A Policy of Impunity.* New York: Human Rights Watch, 1990.

Americas Watch. *Prison Conditions in Mexico.* New York: Human Rights Watch, 1991.

Americas Watch. *Unceasing Abuses: Human Rights in Mexico One Year after the Introduction of Reforms.* New York: Human Rights Watch, 1991.

Amnesty International. *Amnesty International Report, 1993.* New York: 1993.

Camp, Roderic Ai. *Mexico's Political Stability: The Next Five Years.* Boulder, Colorado: Westview Press, 1986.

Camp, Roderic Ai. "The Military." Pages 85–91 in George W. Grayson, ed., *Prospects for Mexico.* Washington: Foreign Service Institute, United States Department of State, 1988.

Causa International. *Crisis and Response: A Roundtable on Mexico.* New York: 1986.

"Chiapas Rebellion: A Major Embarrassment," *Latin American Regional Reports: Mexico and NAFTA Report* [London], RM–94–01, January 20, 1994, 4–5.

Conger, Lucy. "Mexico: Zapatista Thunder," *Current History,* 93, No. 581, March 1994, 115–20.

Corona del Rosal, Alfonso. *La guerra, el imperialismo, el ejército mexicano.* Mexico City: Grijalbo, 1989.

Cunningham, Alden M. "Mexico's National Security," *Parameters—Journal of the US Army War College,* 24, No. 4, Winter 1984, 56–68.

DMS Market Intelligence Reports. Greenwich, Connecticut: Defense Marketing Services, 1989.

Doyle, Kate. "The Militarization of the Drug War in Mexico," *Current History,* 92, No. 571, February 1993, 83–88.

Encyclopedia of the Third World. 4th ed. Ed., George Thomas Kurian. New York: Facts on File, 1992.

English, Adrian J. *Armed Forces of Latin America: Their Histories, Development, Present Strength, and Military Potential.* London: Jane's, 1984.

Fauriol, Georges. "Mexico: In a Superpower's Shadow." Pages 371–402 in Rodney W. Jones and Steven A. Hildreth, eds.,

Emerging Powers: Defense and Security in the Third World. New York: Praeger, 1986.

Fuentes, Gloria. *El ejército mexicano.* Mexico City: Grijalbo, 1983.

Golden, Tim. "Violently, Drug Trafficking in Mexico Rebounds," *New York Times,* March 8, 1993, A3.

Goodman, Louis W., Johanna S.R. Mendelson, and Juan Rial, eds. *The Military and Democracy: The Future of Civil-Military Relations in Latin America.* Lexington, Massachusetts: Lexington Books, 1990.

Human Rights Watch. "Human Rights and the Chiapas Rebellion," *Current History,* 93, No. 581, March 1994, 121–23.

"Insincere Antidrug Effort Charged," Foreign Broadcast Information Service, *Daily Report: Latin America,* 7, No. 125. FBIS–LAT–93–125. July 1, 1993, 12–13.

Jane's Armour and Artillery, 1992–93. Alexandria, Virginia: Jane's, 1992.

Jane's Fighting Ships, 1993–94. Ed., Richard Sharpe. Alexandria, Virginia: Jane's, 1993.

Jones, Rodney W., and Steven A. Hildreth, eds. *Emerging Powers: Defense and Security in the Third World.* New York: Praeger, 1986.

Keegan, John, ed. *World Armies.* Detroit: Gale Research, 1983.

León Toral, Jesús de. *El ejército y fuerza aérea mexicanos.* Mexico City: Secretaría de Defensa Nacional, 1992.

Lieuwen, Edwin. *Mexican Militarism: The Political Rise and Fall of the Revolutionary Army, 1910–1940.* Albuquerque: University of New Mexico Press, 1968.

Lowenthal, Abraham F., and J. Samuel Fitch, eds. *Armies and Politics in Latin America,* New York: Holmes and Meier, 1986.

Luria, René. "Defense Policy and the Armed Forces of Mexico," *International Defense Review,* 25, No. 9, September 1992, 809–11.

Lutz, Ellen L. "Human Rights in Mexico: Cause of Continuing Concern," *Current History,* 92, No. 571, February 1993, 78–82.

The Military Balance, 1996–1997. London: International Institute for Strategic Studies, 1996.

Milton, T.R. "Our Distant Neighbor," *Air Force Magazine,* 70, No. 8, August 1987, 58–64.

Pastor, Robert A., and Jorge G. Castañeda. *Limits to Friendship: The United States and Mexico.* New York: Vintage Books, 1989.

Reuter, Peter, and David Ronfeldt. "Quest for Integrity: The Mexican-US Drug Issue in the 1980s," *Journal of Interamerican Studies and World Affairs,* 34, No. 3, Fall 1992, 89–154.

Riding, Alan. *Distant Neighbors: A Portrait of the Mexicans.* New York: Vintage Books, 1986.

Robberson, Tod. "Break Police Code of Silence," *Washington Post,* March 6, 1992, A1.

Robberson, Tod. "Mexican Army Short of Funds and Combat Experience," *Washington Post,* January 19, 1994, A21.

Robberson, Tod. "Mexican Drug Dealers Cut Pervasive Path," *Washington Post,* May 31, 1993, A21, A25.

Ronfeldt, David. *The Modern Mexican Military: Implications for Mexico's Stability and Security.* Santa Monica: Rand, 1985.

Ronfeldt, David, ed. "The Modern Mexican Military." Pages 224–50 in Abraham F. Lowenthal and J. Samuel Fitch, eds., *Armies and Politics in Latin America.* New York: Holmes and Meier, 1986.

Ronfeldt, David, ed. *The Modern Mexican Military: A Reassessment.* La Jolla: Center for U.S.-Mexican Studies, University of California, San Diego, 1984.

Salas, Elizabeth. *Soldaderas in the Mexican Military: Myth and History.* Austin: University of Texas Press, 1990.

United States. Arms Control and Disarmament Agency. *World Military Expenditures and Arms Transfers, 1991–1992.* Washington: GPO, 1994.

United States. Department of State. *Country Reports on Human Rights Practices for 1993.* Report submitted to United States Congress, 103d, 2d Session, Senate, Committee on Foreign Relations, and House of Representatives, Committee on Foreign Affairs. Washington: GPO, 1994.

United States. Department of State. *International Narcotics Control Status Report.* Washington: GPO, 1993.

Wesson, Robert, ed. *The Latin American Military Institution.* New York: Praeger, 1986.

Wilkinson, William V. "An Exploration of the Mexican Criminal Justice System: Interviews with Incarcerated Inmates in a Mexican Prison," *International Journal of Comparative and Applied Criminal Justice,* 14, No. 1, Spring 1990, 115–21.

Glossary

amparo—A category of legal actions that guards individual civil rights. Literally, *amparo* signifies protection, assistance, or human refuge.

corporatist, corporatism—A political system in which various groups (for instance, the military, labor, and peasants) are organized into official constituencies. The various constituencies influence government policy and are supported by government patronage.

Contadora—A diplomatic initiative launched by a January 1983 meeting on Contadora Island off the Pacific coast of Panama, by which the "Core Four" mediator countries of Mexico, Venezuela, Colombia, and Panama sought to prevent through negotiations a regional conflagration among the Central American states of Guatemala, El Salvador, Honduras, Nicaragua, and Costa Rica. In September 1984, the negotiating process produced a draft treaty, the Contadora Acta, which was judged acceptable by the government of Nicaragua but rejected by the other four Central American states concerned. The process was suspended unofficially in June 1986 when the Central American governments refused to sign a revised Acta. The Contadora process was effectively superseded by direct negotiations among the Central American states.

ejido—A landholding peasant community or the land owned collectively by the members of such a community. An *ejido*, according to Mexican legislation, is a legal entity of the "social interest sector," and its jurisdiction is in the hands of Mexican-born peasants. Its holdings consist of the *ejidal* plots, i.e., individual farming plots, the school plots, the *ejidal* urban zones, the houses and annexes to each plot, and any water resources and forest areas associated with the community. Two basic kinds of *ejidos* exist: the "individual" *ejido*, in which land tenure and ownership are legally vested in a community but cropland is allocated by plots (*parcelas*) on a semipermanent basis among the individual *ejidatarios* (*ejido* members); and the "collective" *ejido*, in which land resources are pooled for collectively organized production. A majority of *ejidos* are of the individual kind.

fiscal year (FY)—Mexico's fiscal year is the calendar year.

Where reference is made to United States aid appropriations or disbursements, the United States government's fiscal year, which runs from October 1 to September 30, is used with the date of reference drawn from the year in which the period ends. For example, FY 1995 began on October 1, 1994, and ended on September 30, 1995.

gross domestic product (GDP)—A measure of the total value of goods and services produced by the domestic economy during a given period, usually one year. Obtained by adding the value contributed by each sector of the economy in the form of profits, compensation to employees, and depreciation (consumption of capital). Only domestic production is included, not income arising from investments and possessions owned abroad; hence the use of the word *domestic* to distinguish GDP from gross national product (*q.v.*).

gross national product (GNP)—The total market value of all final goods and services produced by an economy during a year. Obtained by adding the gross domestic product (*q.v.*) and the income received from abroad by residents and subtracting payments remitted abroad to nonresidents.

import-substitution industrialization (ISI)—An economic development strategy that emphasizes the growth of domestic industries, often by import protection using tariff and nontariff measures. Proponents favor the export of industrial goods over primary products.

International Monetary Fund (IMF)—Established along with the World Bank (*q.v.*) in 1945, the IMF is a specialized agency affiliated with the United Nations (UN) that takes responsibility for stabilizing international exchange rates and payments. The main business of the IMF is the provision of loans to its members when they experience balance-of-payments difficulties. These loans often carry conditions that require substantial internal economic adjustments by the recipients.

maquiladoras—Assembly plants that are also called "in-bond" industries. Established by Mexico's Border Industrialization Program during the mid-1960s to absorb the unemployed along the border with the United States following the termination of the *bracero* (migrant Mexican worker) program between the United States and Mexico in 1964. Machinery, equipment, and components were initially allowed to be imported duty-free for processing or assembly within a twenty-kilometer strip along the border as long as all the imported products were subsequently reexported. Later legislation permitted the establishment of in-bond industries anywhere in Mexico except Mexico City, Guadalajara, and Monterrey. End-product output from the assembly operations of the in-bond industries cannot be sold within Mexico.

Mesoamerica—literally middle America. Anthropological term for region from central Mexico to northern Honduras that contained advanced civilizations before the arrival of the Europeans.

new peso (NMex$)—Mexican monetary unit divided into 100 centavos. The new peso replaced the peso (*q.v.*) on January 1, 1993, at the rate of 1 new peso = 1,000 pesos. At that time, US$1 = NMex$3.1. In April 1997, US$1 = NMex$7.9.

parastatal—Corporation wholly or partially government-owned and managed. Corporate directors general are appointed by the president of Mexico. Although ostensibly managed semiautonomously, boards of directors are subject to the political guidelines of the government.

peso (Mex$)—Mexican currency prior to 1993. At par with the dollar in the nineteenth century, the Mexican government occasionally devalued the peso in the first half of the twentieth century. From 1954 until 1975, the peso's value was fixed at US$1 = Mex$12.49. In 1976 the peso was allowed to float and depreciated to about US$1 = Mex$100 in 1982. By 1992, however, the peso's value had fallen to US$1 = Mex$3,000, and a new currency, the new peso (NMex$—*q.v.*), was introduced, replacing the peso at the rate of 1 new peso = 1,000 pesos.

Sandinista—Originally a member of the Marxist group in Nicaragua attempting to overthrow the Nicaraguan government in the 1960s and 1970s. The group took its name from Augusto César Sandino, who led a guerrilla struggle against United States occupation of Nicaragua in the 1930s. The political arm of the group, the Sandinista National Liberation Front (Frente Sandinista de Liberación Nacional—FSLN), was the national government of Nicaragua from July 1979 to April 1990. After the late 1970s, the term *Sandinista* is used for a member or supporter of the FSLN or as the adjectival form of the FSLN.

World Bank—The informal name used to designate a group of four affiliated international institutions: the International

Bank for Reconstruction and Development (IBRD), the International Development Association (IDA), the International Finance Corporation (IFC), and the Multilateral Investment Guarantee Agency (MIGA). The IBRD, established in 1945, has the primary purpose of providing loans at market-related rates of interest to developing countries at more advanced stages of development. The IDA, a legally separate loan fund but administered by the staff of the IBRD, was set up in 1960 to furnish credits to the poorest developing countries on much easier terms than those of conventional IBRD loans. The IFC, founded in 1956, supplements the activities of the IBRD through loans and assistance designed specifically to encourage the growth of productive private enterprises in less developed countries. The MIGA, founded in 1988, insures private foreign investment in developing countries against various noncommercial risks. The president and certain officers of the IBRD hold the same positions in the IFC. The four institutions are owned by the governments of the countries that subscribe their capital. To participate in the World Bank, member states must first belong to the International Monetary Fund (*q.v.*).

Index

Acamapichtli: origin of, 8

Acapulco, 210; commanding headquarters of Pacific fleet at, 305; shipping through, 210

ACDA. *See* United States Arms Control and Disarmament Agency

Acir Group (Grupo Acir), 214

acquired immune deficiency syndrome (AIDS), 138

ACS. *See* Association of Caribbean States

Acta Constitutiva de la Federación Mexicana (Constituent Act of the Mexican Federation), 234

Act of Chapultepec (1945), 295

adjustable-rate mortgages, 102

Administrative Affairs Chamber, 243

Aeronaves de México (Aeroméxico), 212

African slaves: in New Spain, 11

Agencia Mexicana de Información, 262

agrarian reform, 43, 112–16, 173, 174

Agrarian Reform Act (1915), 112–16

agriculture: agrarian reforms in, 43, 112–16, 173, 174; barley in, 178, 181; of basic food crops, 148–49; beans in, 177, 178, 181; black market in, 146; *bracero* program in, 49–50; under Calles, 113; under Cárdenas, 46, 113; under Carranza, 173; in Chiapas, 115; in Chihuahua, 115; cocoa in, 184; coffee in, 146, 183; corn in, xxxiv, 177, 178, 180–81; cotton in, 146, 177, 178, 183–84; cottonseed in, 182; under de la Madrid, 114; diversification and expansion of, xxxvii; and drug eradication, 64, 292–93, 335; dysfunctional character of, 116; under Echeverría, 56, 113; *ejidos* in, xxxvi, 34, 102, 112–16, 173, 176, 253; exports of products, 218, 219; fruit production in, 178, 181–82; government agricultural policies, 174–80; grain production in, 180–81; and the Great Depression, 146; in Guanajuato, 113, 115; impact of Mexican Revolution on, 146; irrigation projects in, 50, 172; and land

redistribution, 53; and land tenure, 34, 43, 173–74; level of output in, 146, 176; livestock in, 184–85; under López Portillo, 114; Mexican Food System in, 114, 176–77; in Michoacán, 113; in New Spain, 12; non-*ejido* farmers in, 114–15; under Obregón, 43; practices in, 172–73; and Procampo program, 177–78, 180; public investment in, 151; rice in, 177; and rural to urban migration, xxxvii–xxxviii, 79; under Salinas, 177; in Sinaloa, 113, 115; in Sonora, 113, 115; sorghum in, 177, 178, 181; soybeans in, 177, 178, 182; specialized banks for, 166; sugarcane in, 146, 182; vegetable production in, 178, 181–82; water-control projects in, 172; wheat in, 177

Agua Prieta: and transportation links, 206

Aguascalientes, 40, 102; emigration to United States from, 91; living conditions in, 102

Aguilar Zinser, Adolfo, 290

AIDS. *See* acquired immune deficiency syndrome

Air College: in Guadalajara, 315

aircraft industry, 311

air force, 301–3

air transportation, 211–12, 226

Alamo: siege of, 24–25, 285

Alemán Valdés, Miguel: and corruption, 51; economic policies under, 147; presidency of, 50–51

Alfaro Siqueiros, David, 53

Allende, Hortensia, 56

Allende Gossens, Salvador, 56, 270

Alliance for Economic Recovery (Alianza para la Recuperación Económica—APRE), 158; and minimum wage, 162

Alliance for the Countryside (Alianza para el Campo), 116, 180

Alliance for Well-Being (Alianza para el Bienestar), 107

387

Contributors

Marisabel Brás, formerly a Latin American affairs analyst at the Federal Research Division, Library of Congress, is currently a senior analyst at the Army Intelligence and Threat Analysis Center.

Timothy Goodman is an economist with a specialty in the economies of Latin America.

Richard Haggerty, formerly a Latin American affairs analyst at the Federal Research Division, Library of Congress, is currently a senior analyst at the Defense Intelligence Agency.

Dennis M. Hanratty is a former senior Latin American affairs analyst at the Federal Research Division, Library of Congress, and editor of numerous books for the Country Studies series.

Tim L. Merrill is a former senior Latin American affairs analyst at the Federal Research Division, Library of Congress, and editor of several books for the Country Studies series.

Ramón Miró is a former Latin American affairs analyst at the Federal Research Division, Library of Congress.

Jean R. Tartter is a retired Foreign Service Officer who has written extensively on Latin America for the Country Studies series.

Published Country Studies

(Area Handbook Series)

550–41	Korea, South	550–37	Rwanda and Burundi
550–58	Laos	550–51	Saudi Arabia
550–24	Lebanon	550–70	Senegal
550–38	Liberia	550–180	Sierra Leone
550–85	Libya	550–184	Singapore
550–172	Malawi	550–86	Somalia
550–45	Malaysia	550–93	South Africa
550–161	Mauritania	550–95	Soviet Union
550–79	Mexico	550–179	Spain
550–76	Mongolia	550–96	Sri Lanka
550–49	Morocco	550–27	Sudan
550–64	Mozambique	550–47	Syria
550–35	Nepal and Bhutan	550–62	Tanzania
550–88	Nicaragua	550–53	Thailand
550–157	Nigeria	550–89	Tunisia
550–94	Oceania	550–80	Turkey
550–48	Pakistan	550–74	Uganda
550–46	Panama	550–97	Uruguay
550–156	Paraguay	550–71	Venezuela
550–185	Persian Gulf States	550–32	Vietnam
550–42	Peru	550–183	Yemens, The
550–72	Philippines	550–99	Yugoslavia
550–162	Poland	550–67	Zaire
550–181	Portugal	550–75	Zambia
550–160	Romania	550–171	Zimbabwe